Future Tourism Trends Volume 1

Building the Future of Tourism

Series Editor: Anukrati Sharma

The world is entering the Third Millennium in which great changes are expected in all areas of human interest, life and activity. These changes have been brought on by past and present man-made events, which have had both positive and negative consequences. The coming millennium will be marked by significant social, political, demographic and technological changes, and will definitely differ from the last century. The future will bring more leisure time, a higher standard of living, and a better quality of life for us all. This series examines recent and the most probable changes and gives a wide range of visionary insights, as well as operational takeaways

Forthcoming Volumes

Future Tourism Trends Volume 2: Technology Advancement, Trends and Innovations for the Future in Tourism
Canan Tanrisever, Hüseyin Pamukçu, and Anukrati Sharma

Meaningful Tourism: Strategies and Futuristic Development
Pankaj Kumar Tyagi, Vipin Nadda, and Ajit Kumar Singh

Emerald Handbook of Tourism Economics and Sustainable Development
Ahmed Imran Hunjra and Anukrati Sharma

Value Proposition for Tourism 'Co-opetition': Cases and Tools
Adriana Fumi Chim Miki and Rui Augusto da Costa

Future Tourism Trends Volume 1: Tourism in the Changing World

EDITED BY

CANAN TANRISEVER
Kastamonu University, Türkiye

HÜSEYIN PAMUKÇU
Afyon Kocatepe University, Türkiye

AND

ANUKRATI SHARMA
University of Kota, India

United Kingdom – North America – Japan – India – Malaysia – China

Emerald Publishing Limited
Emerald Publishing, Floor 5, Northspring, 21-23 Wellington Street, Leeds LS1 4DL

First edition 2024

British Library Cataloguing in Publication Data
A catalogue record for this book is available from the British Library

ISBN: 978-1-83753-245-2 (Print)
ISBN: 978-1-83753-244-5 (Online)
ISBN: 978-1-83753-246-9 (Epub)

INVESTOR IN PEOPLE

Contents

List of Figures and Tables

List of Contributors

Albattat Ahmad	Management and Science University, Malaysia
Mehmet Halit Akın	Erciyes University, Türkiye
Manpreet Arora	Central University of Himachal Pradesh, India
Ali Avan	Afyon Kocatepe University, Türkiye
Çağdaş Aydın	Kastamonu University, Türkiye
Ceren Aydın	Independent Researcher, Türkiye
Gonca Aytaş	Afyon Kocatepe University, Türkiye
Engin Aytekin	Afyon Kocatepe University, Türkiye
Erdem Baydeniz	Afyon Kocatepe University, Türkiye
Ahmet Baytok	Afyon Kocatepe University, Türkiye
Mehmet Yavuz Çetinkaya	Pamukkale University, Türkiye
Praveen Choudhry	Vivekananda Global University, India
Hakkı Çılgınoğlu	Kastamonu University, Türkiye
Ahmet Elnur	Ahmet Elnur Suleyman Demirel University, Türkiye
Baghya Erathna	SLTC Research University, Sri Lanka
Fatma Doğanay Ergen	Isparta University of Applied Sciences, Türkiye
Dilara Eylül Koç	Kastamonu University, Türkiye
Krishantha Ganeshan	98 Acres Resort and Spa, Sri Lanka
Puwanendram Gayathri	University of Sri Jayewardenepura, Sri Lanka
Adit Jha	Vivekananda Global University, India
Johney Johnson	Mahatma Gandhi University, Kerala, India
Ayşen Acun Köksalanlar	Bursa Uludag University, Türkiye

Hande Akyurt Kurnaz	Bolu Abant Izzet Baysal University, Türkiye
Halyna Kushniruk	Ivan Franko National University of Lviv, Ukraine
Kottamkunnath Lakshmypriya	CHRIST University, India
Resul Mercan	Afyon Kocatepe University, Türkiye
Azman Norhidayah	Management and Science University, Malaysia
Hüseyin Pamukçu	Afyon Kocatepe University, Türkiye
Zikho Qwatekana	Durban University of Technology, South Africa
Radhika P.C.	Sacred Heart College, Kerala, India
Mustafa Sandıkcı	Afyon Kocatepe University, Türkiye
Himalee de Silva	University of Colombo, Sri Lanka
RHSK de Silva	University of Colombo, Sri Lanka
Suranga Dac Silva	University of Colombo, Sri Lanka
Canan Tanrisever	Kastamonu University, Türkiye
Pinaz Tiwari	GLA University, India
Ndivhuho Tshikovhi	Durban University of Technology, South Africa
Şevki Ulema	Sakarya University of Applied Sciences, Türkiye
Samuel Uwem Umoh	University of Hradec Kralove, Czech Republic
Bindi Varghese	CHRIST University, India
Yurdanur Yumuk	Karabük University, Türkiye
Özcan Zorlu	Afyon Kocatepe University, Türkiye

Preface

In today's world, where the world is becoming a global village, and we are observing this more clearly with the Covid19 epidemic, it is inevitable that tourism trends will differ. As the world entered a rapid digitalisation process with the epidemic, environmental concerns also came to the fore. Today's 'new tourists' are more seasoned travellers looking for untested vacation experiences. One of the main features of the new tourist is the need to get away from the monotony of daily life and achieve self-realisation in different ways. The tendency of 'self-actualisation' coincided with a period when technology was intense, causing a renewal in tourism as in every field. External environmental conditions heavily influence the international tourism market. The rise in the level of welfare in developed countries, the increase in leisure time, the experience of people in travel and the change in their socio-demographic structures have led to the emergence of new tourism trends in the travel market. The socio-demographic structure, in which changes such as the increase in the active youth population, the late marriage age, the increase in the number of families with multiple incomes, the increase in the number of families without children and the number of adults living alone are observed, causes significant changes in the demand for travel and leisure time. The resulting tourist types and needs reveal more specific travel types and activities. The active tourism concept has replaced the passive tourism concept. In this book, we tried to reveal future tourism trends by considering the current trends. In this context, Vol 1 is Tourism in Changing World and Vol 2 is Technology Advancement, Trends and Innovations for the Future in Tourism. We wish you a pleasant school.

Dr Canan Tanrisever
Dr Hüseyin Pamukçu
Dr Anukrati Sharma

Part 1

Bleisure Tourism

Chapter 1

Bleisure Tourism: Business and Leisure Together

Resul Mercan and Mustafa Sandıkcı

Afyon Kocatepe University, Türkiye

Learning Objectives

After reading and studying this chapter, you should be able to:

- understand the definitions and principles of business, leisure and bleisure tourism;
- understand the impacts and contributions of bleisure tourism on the environment;
- understand the bleisure tourist profile and the role of stakeholders.

Abstract

The concept of bleisure is a tourism term that has emerged recently and has become popular. Participation of employees, especially managers and people in business who go on business trips, in leisure activities during their full-time business trips has revealed the bleisure trend. Although bleisure has emerged as a term in recent years, it has been seen that people combine vacations and business trips in previous years.

Considering the research on bleisure tourism, it is thought that bleisure tourism can be helpful to increase employee productivity. The fact that individuals who go on business trips very often are away from their family or friends can create a social deformation. However, people who go on business trips within the scope of bleisure tourism sometimes can take their close friends or family members with them. This provides extra motivation for bleisure tourists and increases work efficiency. However, it is beneficial to plan bleisure tourism. Excessive entertainment or shopping can lead to distraction, being late for work and being over budget on a business trip. For

---

Future Tourism Trends Volume 1, 3–15
Published under exclusive licence by Emerald Publishing Limited
doi:10.1108/978-1-83753-244-520241001

this reason, bleisure should be planned jointly with tourism agencies and companies.

Bleisure tourism will benefit business travellers, travel companies, hotels, restaurants, other tourism businesses and local people. For this reason, it is necessary to focus on studies related to bleisure tourism, a new tourism trend.

Keywords: Bleisure; tourism; business; leisure; new tourism trends; niche

Introduction

Bleisure tourism is a form of tourism that has become increasingly popular in recent years. 'Bleisure' combines business and leisure and refers to doing tourist activities during business trips. This form of tourism allows people to explore local attractions and have a broader tourist experience during their business trips. Bleisure tourism has become popular, especially with the increase in technological developments and more frequent business trips. Business travellers take advantage of bleisure tourism opportunities when they want to explore the tourist attractions in their places, have cultural experiences and relieve stress with activities outside of work. Including touristic activities during business trips, while offering a new market to the tourism industry, also makes it a more attractive option for business travellers. Thanks to bleisure tourism, travel companies, hotels, restaurants and other touristic businesses acquire new customers, while business travellers enjoy discovering different cultures while doing their jobs. Therefore, bleisure tourism has become essential for travellers and the tourism industry (Mercan, 2022).

This chapter will consider the concept of bleisure tourism in more detail and discuss the advantages, disadvantages, trends and future potential of this form of tourism. In addition, suggestions were made by referring to issues such as what should be done in the sectoral and academic sense about bleisure tourism.

Business Tourism

According to the definition of The United Nations World Tourism Organization (UNWTO), business tourism refers to the activities of people travelling to and staying in places outside their environment for commercial purposes. It includes all activities where work is the primary cause of departure, same-day travel and overnight stays. However, it does not include commutes and regular work journeys of business people in their local area (Wootton & Stevens, 1995).

Business tourism has grown enormously since the 1980s. It continues to grow faster than any other form of tourism, despite being shaken by the decline in national and international economic activity in the first half of the 1990s. Business travellers increased at a faster rate than leisure tourists as a whole. At the same time, business tourism is less seasonal than other types of tourism and is less sensitive to demand fluctuations than holiday tourism. As a result, business travellers are a significant source of demand for hotel accommodations, and hotels rely heavily on business travel to stay occupied throughout the week. Business tourism accounts for at least two-thirds of the occupancy rate of leading hotels, 80–90% of the three- and four-star hotel market, and 50% of budget hotels.

Business tourism finds its way into many different fields and sectors. Diplomatic, economic and trade meetings between representatives of different countries, scientific and technical information exchange, meetings to communicate the results of certain research and development projects, cultural and educational meetings, sports competitions, etc. Special events are included in the scope of business tourism. There are many types of business tourism. These include individual trips, group trips and MICE (Meetings, Incentives, Conferences and Exhibitions). According to information from other sources (Davidson & Cope, 2003; Newstrom & Scannell, 1998; Nicula & Elena, 2014):

- Individual business trips, which are common in many professions and therefore travel outside the city where the relevant persons reside.
- Meetings that include a wide variety of events (conferences, seminars, team building, product launches, annual meetings, etc.) of companies or associations to facilitate communication with or between employees, customers, suppliers and shareholders.
- Various trade shows and exhibitions for product presentation in general.
- Incentive trips and trips that employees receive from the employer as a reward for good results in the relevant job.
- Corporate events, which include great entertainment offered by companies to their most valuable customers or potential customers to establish or develop business relations, are considered within the scope of business tourism.

Leisure Tourism

The concept of leisure (leisure) emerges from the word 'licere', which means to be on leave or free. First, licence, which is a Latin word, was transferred to French as 'Loisir', and later, this word, which expresses the time of complete freedom, was transferred to English as leisure and was used as a leisure time concept in the international literature (Kando, 1975).

Leisure is the period individuals have for activities and experiences they voluntarily participate in to have fun freely (Kaplan, 1975). Argan (2007) defined leisure time as time outside of working hours without the purpose of earning money. Metin (2013), on the other hand, defined leisure time as the period in which people use their free time, other than the time they work, to earn money in line with their wishes.

Since the early ages, human beings have started to use the time left over from their compulsory work with better quality to improve themselves and gain various experiences over time. For this reason, the concept of leisure has emerged. The first findings on the distinction between leisure and work time are based on the history of ancient Greece. In the ancient Greek era, leisure was a process in which truth and knowledge were sought, and one thought about eternal truths. Greek nobles and philosophers used their spare time for knowledge, art, recreation and social activities (Barakazı, 2021; Çelik, 2021). In the ancient Roman period, they believed in the good use of free time to have productive work time. Due to this perception, mass recreation activities, sporting events, gladiator fights and other games have emerged. It is known that during this period, Roman emperors built baths, amphitheatres and arenas for the benefit of the public in order to protect their sovereignty (Metin, 2013). The Middle Ages was a period when religious beliefs were more dominant. In this period, with the prohibition of leisure activities by the church in Christian society, people spent their free time performing worship and religious rites in churches. However, despite the churches' bans, people still did not give up on activities such as travel, entertainment and music. In Islamic society, leisure time is based on social or individual benefit. Instead of idleness or wasted time, people have dealt with more beneficial activities such as education (Aytaç, 2002; Chick, 1984). After many years, improvements in business life occurred, thanks to the unions in the 19th century. When social scientists started to work on leisure time, and the effect of the right of leisure on the productivity of production began to be proven, leisure time became a legal right for people. With the development of tourism, industrialisation and urbanisation, the concept of leisure has gained its current meaning (Juniu, 2000).

Leisure activities are activities in which people voluntarily participate in their free time for entertainment. In another definition, leisure activities are all of the passive and active activities a person performs in his spare time (Howe & Carpenter, 1985). In addition to this, Karakucuk (2005) stated that educational activities are also included in leisure time activities. Therefore, many activities that people do for entertainment can be leisure time activities. However, while the activities that an individual participates in for fun are a leisure time activity, the same activity can be a business for different individuals. Therefore, in order for the activity that a person is in to be called a leisure activity, the person must have chosen freely (Karakuş & Gürbüz, 2007).

Hazar (2009) classified leisure time activities in six different ways. These are:

(1) Leisure activities according to how they participate: These are the activities in which active or passive roles are taken.
(2) Leisure time activities by venue: These are activities held indoors or outdoors.
(3) Leisure activities by nationality: These are national or international activities.
(4) Leisure time activities by age: These are activities carried out according to the participation of children, youth, adults and third generation.
(5) Leisure activities according to the number of participants: These are activities with individual or group participation.

Leisure activities according to recreational types in terms of functionality: These activities are attended in the sense of commercial, aesthetic, social, health, physical, artistic, cultural and touristic.

Bleisure Tourism

The fact that individuals combine their travels with purposes such as business, entertainment, education and travel and include friends or family members in these travels makes their travels more enjoyable. Bleisure tourism has emerged as more and more individuals plan their business trips by blending them for different daily purposes. Bleisure seems to have become a popular word in the tourism industry, and it refers to leisure activities with business travel (Çetinsöz & Hazarhun, 2020).

Leisure tourism is defined as a concept derived from the combination of the concepts of work and leisure, which was derived to describe the travel behaviour of business travellers, sometimes their friends, family or colleagues who want to extend a trip to explore the destination visited (Ali & Schmitz, 2018). According to another definition, Sardest and Ivanauskas (2019) defined bleisure tourism as combining individuals' business and leisure intentions, conceptually illustrated in Fig. 1.1.

When the literature on bleisure tourism was examined, it was seen that the definitions made were made with similar expressions, such as combining business and entertainment intentions. Accordingly, the concept of Bleisure tourism can be defined as the use of leisure time by having fun with leisure activities in the destination with family, friends or alone when they go on business trips, or extending the length of stay in business travel depending on the entertainment and activity opportunities of the destination.

Bleisure has already become a way of life for many international business travellers. Business travellers, like leisure travellers, plan to include at least one

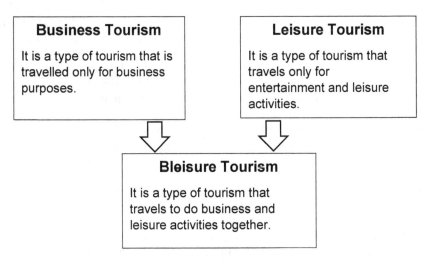

Fig. 1.1.   Bleisure Tourism Concept. *Source:* Sardest and Ivanauskas (2019).

leisure activity. About four out of five respondents say adding leisure time to business trips adds value to their work duties. Thus, the participants agree that bleisure helps them gain cultural experience and knowledge about the cities they travel to. While employees' desire for bleisure is growing daily, most businesses are unaware of it; however, bleisure can benefit the business world by motivating employees to become productive and engaged in their work.

As a result, since only business trips have negative aspects for employees, adding the element of entertainment to the same business trip and transforming it into bleisure travel reduces the negative impact of business travel and motivates employees and makes business trips beneficial for both parties (Chen et al., 2016; Sardest & Ivanauskas, 2019).

Bleisure Tourist

The fact that employees make their business trips more enjoyable by removing the barriers between work and leisure activities during a business trip has made them bleisure tourists. Pinho and Marques (2021) defined bleisure tourists as professionals who avoid work stress by mixing business trips with leisure time (Mercan, 2022).

The majority of Bleisure tourists are millennials born between 1981 and 1996. Mainly, it is seen that participation in bleisure tourism is high in the 25–40 age group, it started to decline in the 40–55 age group and there is less participation in the 55 and older age group. When these limited studies are examined, it is seen that people in business, managers and academicians are the occupational groups that participate most in bleisure tourism activities. Congress, conferences, scientific research and commercial relations are the most significant factors that enable people who feed bleisure tourism to become bleisure tourists (Alp & Yazıcı Ayyıldız, 2020; Çetinsöz & Hazarhun, 2020; Kasalak et al., 2019; Lichy & McLeay, 2018).

In their study, Lichy and McLeay (2018) defined five different bleisure tourist typologies that do not have a standard feature of bleisure tourists and vary according to each tourist's personality traits, wishes and motivations.

- Experiential Learners: Tourists in this category are usually young managers or people just starting. They are single, have no dependents, are hungry for knowledge and learning and want to improve themselves and travel domestically and internationally constantly.
- Escapers: Bleisure tourists who seek travel opportunities to escape from the boredom of the day and routine work and who want to experience the unknown results of travel are called escapers.
- Working Vacationers: They are childless individuals who do not miss the opportunity to combine work and fun, even though they plan to finish their work first during their travels, with professional obligations at the forefront.

- Altruistic Knowledge Sharers: They like to transfer their knowledge units and experiences to younger generations and generally consist of senior academics. They are bleisure tourists near the end of their careers who take less part in their institutions and travel domestically and abroad with the invitations of different institutions and organisations. Meeting new people is their biggest motivation.
- Research-Active Trailblazers: Bleisure tourists in this category are inspired by working abroad to build their reputation and resume by creating an international profile. In the context of this work, they differ from other bleisure travellers in their eagerness to achieve the goals imposed on them for personal or professional gain. In addition, they give importance to professional career development by publishing their works in essential journals.

Bleisure Travel

Bleisure travel combines business and entertainment in a single trip, using the time left from work by people who go on business trips with leisure activities. Ease of transportation is the most critical urban factor in a successful business trip. Other vital considerations include street safety and the quality of workplaces, according to the 2019 Bleisure Barometer survey. While Asian rulers prioritise transportation, Europeans are less concerned about safety than those arriving from elsewhere, revealing regional differences in findings. In the report of the Bleisure Barometer (2019), the urban factor data for a successful business trip are given as follows (Mercan, 2022):

- Ease of transportation: Chosen by Asian travellers as the most critical factor. Europeans are in second place for travellers.
- General safety and order of streets/urban areas: second only to Asian travellers.
- Quality of business facilities (common meeting spaces, conference rooms, etc.): Ranks third for Asians and Europeans.
- Accommodation quality: Ranked first for Europeans and forth for Asians.
- Level of digital connectivity: fifth for Asians and forth for Europeans.
- The prevalence and quality of the English language (in signs, public announcements, etc.): More important to North American travellers, while Asians and Europeans care less.
- Quality of international/regional connections: last for all regions.

Case Study

In 2014, Bridge Street Global Hospitality published a bleisure report based on a survey of 640 international guests. Guests from 56 countries from the Americas, Europe, Africa and Asia participated in the survey. According to the bleisure report; 83% of respondents use their time off from business travel to explore the city they visit. More than half of the respondents extended their business trip by 2 days or more and added personal travel to their business trip. 54% of respondents take family members or friends on their trips. 78% of respondents believe that adding leisure time to business travel increases work efficiency. Almost all business travellers agree that leisure time helps them gain cultural experience and knowledge about the cities where they do business. Notably, most of the respondents are from the United States.

Xiaojian Chen and Junhan Gu (2018), in a study conducted in Xi'an, China, stated that there are many tourist visits in the city due to tourism development and the richness of cultural and natural resources. In addition, due to the city's geographical location and economic development, representatives of many international businesses visit the city and participate in important conferences and exhibitions. At this point, the bleisure tourism potential of the city was emphasised. However, the study stated that the term bleisure is not very well known, and studies have yet to be carried out by hotels and travel agencies on this subject. For this reason, suggestions have been made to increase awareness of bleisure tourism.

Jin Young Chung et al. (2020) examined bleisure marketing practices in Tokyo, the capital of Japan, and showed that various marketing programmes were developed to encourage business travelers to spend extra. Accordingly, a bleisure marketing plan was developed and proposed.

In a research conducted on hotels, agencies and tourist guides in Kuşadası, it was understood that they were not yet aware of the concept of bleisure and that there was no marketing strategy in this field (Alp & Yazıcı Ayyıldız, 2020). Although the concept of bleisure is not known, when the concept of bleisure was explained to the studied audience, they stated that they were not far from this type of tourism. It was understood that the guides extended their travels and made bleisure trips under gastronomy, shopping, entertainment and recreation. It has been revealed that hotels and agencies provide services for business travelers but are unaware of the bleisure tourism market where business and vacation are combined.

Çetinsöz and Hazarhun (2020), in their study, conducted interviews with business people who work in industrial branches in various provinces and go on national or international business trips. As a result of the interviews, it was seen that the driving factors of bleisure travel motivations were determined as the desire to meet new people, to see new places, to relax, to relieve stress and to have fun. Again, cultural heritage, shopping and destination-specific local foods and beverages were identified as the attraction factors of bleisure travel.

Ünal and Özgürel (2021) investigated the destination quality perceptions and revisited intentions of bleisure tourists. The research was conducted in Istanbul, one of the most popular destinations in Turkey for business, congress, meetings, etc. visits. Istanbul is a city that connects the continents of Europe and Asia and attracts everyone's attention regarding its important geographical location, history and culture. Istanbul, which has a strong economy due to its developed industry, is an indispensable destination for business people. Being the centre of entertainment and nightlife also arouses people's interest. All these criteria make Istanbul the most suitable destination for bleisure tourism. As a result of the research, it was concluded that bleisure tourists are satisfied with the destination and intend to visit the destination again.

Mercan (2022) stated in his study that Afyonkarahisar province, which has a high tourism potential, has many visitors coming for business trips. Afyonkarahisar, one of the few thermal regions in Turkey, has advanced thermal hotels with convention centre halls. For this reason, the infrastructure required for bleisure tourism is available. Every business traveller is considered as a potential bleisure tourist. Afyonkarahisar province is a city of commerce in the transportation sector due to its geographical location, mining sector due to its marble reserves and agriculture and livestock sector. For this reason, there are many business trips to Afyonkarahisar. In addition, Afyonkarahisar, which has an important place in thermal tourism and gastronomy tourism, is one of the most visited cities by bleisure tourists.

Research Box

Business travellers do not just do their business in the destination and return. They are curious about the exciting features, history, food and places of the destination. Individuals want to explore the destination and experience the intriguing features of their time off from work. Business travellers have been doing this for years, but this type of tourism has only recently been named. Individuals have become bleisure tourists without realising it. The need for knowledge of destination stakeholders about bleisure tourism persists. Travel agencies or hotels must cooperate with other stakeholders in the destination when organising meetings, congresses and conferences. Marketing strategies should be developed to encourage individuals to spend extra. For example, individuals should be assisted in transportation to other stakeholders, discount agreements or gift vouchers should be made with local shops where they can shop, agreements should be made with restaurants where they can eat and most importantly, all stakeholders should be advertised. Companies should be encouraged to make accommodation deals for their staff and make affordable reservations to motivate their staff to extend the trip and combine vacation and work. Academic studies should be conducted to determine the expectations of individuals visiting the destination from the destination and the occupational groups of these individuals and to support the studies to be carried out.

Conclusion

The development and growth of the tourism sector daily reveal different types of tourism. However, individuals need serious time to evaluate these types of tourism. Especially the intense pace and stress in business life make it even more critical for people to evaluate their free time. For this reason, people want to take a break and discharge by creating free time during their shifts. This is more common in people who go on business trips. Business travellers spend their free time exploring new places, experiencing the region's cuisine and participating in activities in their destination. For this reason, they may even extend their business trips. Combining business travel and these leisure activities has created a new type of tourism, bleisure tourism.

Bleisure tourism is an opportunity for business travellers. Due to a busy schedule during business travel, they often need more time to explore the environment and culture. Bleisure tourism allows you to stay at the place of business travel after business travel and discover places you have never seen before.

Bleisure tourism is also vital for the travel industry. It creates a new market and provides economic benefits due to business travel stays and tourist activities. Moreover, this form of tourism is essential for the tourism industry and sectors that provide accommodation, catering, events and other travel services.

Bleisure tourism is essential for maintaining the balance between work and vacation. By taking some time off during a business trip, a person can meet the needs of his business and personal life. This, in turn, increases job satisfaction and can positively affect job performance. However, bleisure tourism also brings some risks. In particular, people travelling for business purposes are at risk of missing business-critical meetings or tasks. It can also make it difficult for them to concentrate on their work-oriented tasks. In addition, participating in tourism activities during business trips may incur additional costs, which may exceed the travel budget. Therefore, balancing and planning business travel and vacation time is essential.

As a result, bleisure tourism can be an excellent option for business travellers. This form of tourism provides both work and personal satisfaction and economic benefits for the travel industry and other service sectors. However, careful planning and balancing are essential.

Since bleisure tourism is a new trend, it has yet to be well known in the sectoral and academic sense. There need to be more studies on the development and sustainability of bleisure tourism. For this reason, some steps can be taken to make bleisure tourism more known. These are:

- It can organise campaigns to promote bleisure tourism. For example, various events can be organised to inform business travellers about the bleisure tourism opportunity. In addition, vacation packages, discounts and other incentives may be offered.
- In the academic world, researching bleisure tourism and publishing the results will enable the tourism sector and academic circles to have more information about bleisure tourism.
- Collaborating with the business world on bleisure tourism and organising meetings and travels by agencies will inform business travellers about bleisure tourism opportunities.

- The tourism sector can cooperate with relevant organisations on bleisure tourism. For example, tourism ministries, tourism associations and travel agencies should collaborate to promote bleisure tourism and raise awareness.
- Vacation opportunities should be provided during business travel: For business travellers to take advantage of vacation opportunities, the business world and the tourism sector can work together to offer vacation packages and opportunities. This can offer a form of tourism where business travellers can spend more time exploring.

As a result, different steps can be taken to make bleisure tourism more known in the sectoral and academic sense. The tourism sector, academic circles, business world and related organisations can come together to create more awareness about bleisure tourism and make this form of tourism even more popular.

Discussion Questions

- How can businesses in the tourism sector make bleisure tourism more attractive?
- Bleisure tourism may cause additional expenses during business trips. How can businesses reduce or manage these additional costs?
- How could the advancement of technology affect the future of bleisure tourism?

References

Ali, N., & Schmitz, B. (2018). *Bleisure travel report: Worker productivity and well-being*. https://issuu.com/londoncityair/docs/uel_lcy_bleisure_report_full

Alp, B., & Yazıcı Ayyıldız, A. (2020). Turizm pazarında yeni bir fırsat: Bleisure (a new opportunity ın tourism market). *Journal of Tourism and Gastronomy Studies, 8*(1), 336–354.

Argan, M. (2007). *Eğlence Pazarlaması*. Detay Publishing.

Aytaç, Ö. (2002). Boş zaman üzerine kuramsal yaklaşımlar. *Firat University Journal of Social Sciences, 12*(1), 21–34.

Barakazı, E. (2021). *Boş zaman motivasyonu ve yaşam tatmini ilişkisinde boş zaman tatminin aracılık etkisi: üniversite öğrencileri üzerine bir araştırma*. Ankara Hacı Bayram Veli University Graduate Education Institute.

Bridge Street Global Hospitality. (2014). *The bleisure report 2014*. http://skift.com/wp-content/uploads/2014/10/BGH-Bleisure%20Report-2014.pdf

Çelik, Ş. I. (2021). *Türk kültüründe boş zaman değerlendirme faaliyetleri üzerine bir araştırma*. Ankara Hacı Bayram Veli University Graduate Education Institute.

Çetinsöz, B. C., & Hazarhun, E. (2020). Turizm endüstrisinde yeni bir trend: Bleisure seyahatler ve motivasyon unsurları. *Journal of Recreation and Tourism Research/ JRTR, 7*(4), 500–527.

Chen, X., & Gu, J. (2018). *A case study of the sustainable development of bleisure travel in Xi'an China Team.* https://www.gttp.org/wp-content/uploads/2018/01/china-case-study-20171118.pdf

Chen, C. C., Petrick, J. F., & Shahvali, M. (2016). Tourism experiences as a stress reliever: Examining the effects of tourism recovery experiences on life satisfaction. *Journal of Travel Research, 55*(2), 150–160.

Chick, G. E. (1984). Leisure and the development of culture. *Annals of Tourism Research, 11*(4), 623–626.

Chung, J. Y., Choi, Y. K., Yoo, B. K., & Kim, S. H. (2020). Bleisure tourism experience chain: Implications for destination marketing. *Asia Pacific Journal of Tourism Research, 25*(3), 300–310.

Davidson, R., & Cope, B. (2003). *Business travel.* Prentice Hall.

Hazar, A. (2009). *Rekreasyon ve animasyon.* Detay Publishing.

Howe, C. Z., & Carpenter, G. M. (1985). *Programming leisure experiences. A cyclical approach.* Prentice-Hall Inc.

Juniu, S. (2000). Downshifting: Regaining the essence of leisure. *Journal of Leisure Research, 32*(1), 69–73.

Kando, T. M. (1975). *Leisure and popular culture in transition, Saint Louis* (p. 22). The C.V. Mosby Company.

Kaplan, M. (1975). *Leisure: Theory and practice.* John Wil.

Karaküçük, S. (2005). *Rekreasyon boş zaman değerlendirme.* Gazi Bookstore.

Karaküçük, S., & Gürbüz, B. (2007). *Rekreasyon ve kentlileşme.* Gazi Bookstore.

Kasalak, M. A., Bozcave, S., & Bahar, M. (2019). Turist rehberleri için yeni bir turizm türü: Bleisure. *Journal of Travel & Tourism Research, 14*, 27–38.

Lichy, J., & McLeay, F. (2018). Bleisure: Motivations and typologies. *Journal of Travel & Tourism Marketing, 35*(4), 517–530.

Mercan, R. (2022). *Afyonkarahisar'ı ziyaret eden bleisure turistlerin destinasyon imajının ve algılanan hizmet kalitesinin belirlenmesine yönelik bir araştırma.* Afyon Kocatepe University, Institute of Social Sciences.

Metin, T. C. (2013). *Boş zaman literatürünün dünyadaki gelişimi: leisure science dergisinde yayımlanan makaleler üzerine bir inceleme.* Anadolu University Institute of Social Sciences.

Newstrom, J., & Scannell, E. (1998). *The big book of team-building games.* McGraw Hill.

Nicula, V., & Elena, P. R. (2014). Business tourism market developments. *Procedia Economics and Finance, 16*, 703–712.

Pinho, M., & Marques, J. (2021, September). The bleisure tourism trend and the potential for this business-leisure symbiosis in Porto. *Journal of Convention & Event Tourism, 22*(4), 346–362.

Sardest, Z. F., & Ivanauskas, V. O. (2019). *Bleisure tourism' impacts on employees' motivation and quality of life.* Aalborg Universitet. https://projekter.aau.dk/projekter/files/306180061/bleisureTourismImpacts_on_EmployeesMotivation_and_Quality_of_Life.pdf. Access on October 04, 2023.

Ünal, A., & Özgürel, G. (2021). A research on determining the destination quality perceptions and intentions to revisit of bleisure tourists: İstanbul case. *Tourism and Recreation, 3*(1), 1–10.

Wootton, G., & Stevens, T. (1995). Business tourism: A study of the market for hotel-based meetings and its contribution to wales's tourism. *Tourism Management, 16*(4), 305–313.

Part 2

Climate Change

Chapter 2

Tourism Under Siege: Impact of Climate Change on the Global South Tourism Sector

Zikho Qwatekana and Ndivhuho Tshikovhi

Durban University of Technology, South Africa

Learning Objectives

After reading and studying this chapter, you should be able to:

- identify difficulties that the tourism industry in the Global South faces in coping with and reducing the impact of climate change;
- assess the potential strategies and approaches for sustainable tourism development in the context of climate change, and the challenges faced in implementing them in the Global South;
- understand the concept of climate-resilient tourism and its ability to improve the tourism industry's capacity to deal with challenges;
- explain how tourism can play a role in achieving climate justice in the global south and its potential to support fair and sustainable growth in the area.

Abstract

Tourism is a rapidly growing economic sector that contributes significantly to national and local economies globally. Tourism growth in any destination largely depends on the weather and climate, considered prime factors affecting global tourist flows. Global South countries are said to be particularly vulnerable to climate change, owing to their limited adaptation capacity, placing them at greater risk of the impacts of climate change. This adaptive capacity is mainly attributed to a lack of capital intensity and technological flexibility, which is less effective than in developed countries. In addition to a lack of capacity to adjust to the direct hazards of climate

Future Tourism Trends Volume 1, 19–31
Copyright © 2024 Zikho Qwatekana and Ndivhuho Tshikovhi
Published under exclusive licence by Emerald Publishing Limited
doi:10.1108/978-1-83753-244-520241002

change, developing countries are at additional risk due to their heavy reliance on economic sectors and resources sensitive to climate change, such as tourism. An enhanced understanding of climate change's impacts and adaptations to climate change is critical for determining strategic actions for tourism planning and development. This chapter provides a theoretical review of tourism and adaptation strategies, challenges and the dimensions of vulnerability in a tourism context, as well as the implications of climate change on tourism planning in the future. This chapter discusses the impact of climate change on tourism in the Global South, examining case studies and policy frameworks for adaptation and mitigation. It further explores opportunities for sustainable tourism development and partnerships for climate-resilient tourism. Overall, the chapter focuses on the challenges and opportunities for sustainable tourism in the Global South in the face of climate change.

Keywords: Tourism; climate change; global south; economies; adaptation; mitigation

Introduction

Many countries in the Global South rely heavily on tourism. It generates foreign exchange profits and contributes to the general economic development of these countries (Rogerson & Saarinen, 2018; UNWTO, 2021). However, the tourism industry in the Global South is facing enormous problems due to increased concern about climate change (Scott et al., 2019). Climate change is predicted to significantly impact the tourism industry in developing nations due to their high sensitivity to natural disasters, limited resources for adaptation and reliance on tourism for economic growth. Climate change alters the natural environment, including rising sea levels, temperatures, shifting precipitation patterns and extreme weather events. These changes significantly impact the tourism industry, including changes in demand patterns, shifting tourist flows and impacts on tourism infrastructure and attractions (Scott et al., 2019; UNWTO, 2021). Climate change also affects the livelihoods and well-being of local communities, which often depend on tourism for their income.

It is noted that the tourism sector is highly vulnerable to climate change. It also depends on environmental resources, while climate defines and determines the length and quality of tourism seasons. Concurrently, tourism contributes to the emission of greenhouse gases (GHGs), the cause of global warming. Therefore, it is impossible to isolate tourism from the broader systemic processes against which it takes place. Sustainable tourism has become an integral part of the sector in the Global South or developing regions where tourism is more than just a job creation but also a territorial issue. This chapter explores the implications of climate change for the tourism industry in the Global South. It discusses the challenges faced by developing countries in adapting to the impacts of climate change and highlights the need for effective policies and strategies to address the issue. This chapter further examines the role of tourism in contributing to climate change and discusses the potential for sustainable tourism practices to mitigate the impacts of climate change. Lastly, this chapter provides recommendations for tourism stakeholders, including policymakers and tourism operators, to ensure the sustainability of the tourism industry in the face of climate change.

Climate Change Impacts on the Tourism Industry

Developing countries in the Global South are increasingly becoming desirable travel destinations; tourism is one of the largest and fastest-growing industries globally (Ahmed et al., 2021). However, the tourism organisations in these countries are primarily impacted by the effects of climate change, such as rising temperatures, sea level rise and extreme weather conditions. The tourism business in the Global South is affected by climate change in several ways, including altered weather patterns, health concerns, the depletion of natural resources and economic effects (Han et al., 2020). Hurricanes and floods are two examples of extreme weather occurrences that can harm tourism infrastructure, interfere with travel plans and discourage visitors from visiting (Ruhanen, 2019). Furthermore, rising temperatures and changes in weather patterns can spread diseases, such as malaria and dengue fever, which can pose health risks to tourists (Ahmed et al., 2021). In addition, natural resources, such as beaches, wildlife and coral reefs, are degrading due to climate change, negatively impacting tourism (Brouder & Teixeira, 2021). Coral bleaching and the destruction of marine habitats can affect the quality of snorkelling, diving and other tourist experiences.

Climate change impacts can diminish tourism demand, resulting in lost earnings and livelihoods for those who rely on the tourism industry (Han et al., 2020). As a result, adaption techniques are critical for mitigating the detrimental effects of climate change on the global tourism business. Diversifying tourism activities might lessen the industry's reliance on specific natural resources sensitive to climate change's effects (Brouder & Teixeira, 2021). Sustainable tourism practices, such as reducing energy and water consumption, waste management and promoting biodiversity conservation, can help minimise the tourism industry's environmental impact and reduce its contribution to climate change (Ruhanen, 2019). Early warning systems can also aid in mitigating the impacts of extreme weather events by providing timely information to tourists and tourism industry stakeholders to take appropriate actions (Ahmed et al., 2021). Community-based tourism can aid in promoting local livelihoods and creating alternative income sources that are not dependent on tourism alone, thus reducing the vulnerability of communities to the negative impacts of climate change on the tourism industry (Brouder & Teixeira, 2021).

Tourism Industry in the Global South

Climate change has several impacts on the tourism industry in the Global South, including:

(1) *Changing weather patterns*: Climate change affects weather patterns, such as rising temperatures, shifting rainfall patterns and more frequent and severe weather events, all of which can impact the tourism industry. Extreme weather occurrences, such as hurricanes and floods, might, for example, damage tourism infrastructure, interrupt travel plans and discourage tourists from visiting.

(2) *Health risks*: Rising temperatures and shifting weather patterns can promote the development of diseases like malaria and dengue fever, posing health hazards to travellers. This can reduce tourism demand and affect the tourism industry's revenue.

(3) *Natural resource depletion*: Climate change is causing natural resources, such as beaches, wildlife and coral reefs, to degrade, negatively impacting the tourism industry. For example, coral bleaching and destroying marine habitats can reduce the quality of tourist snorkelling and diving experiences.

(4) *Economic impacts*: The tourism industry is a significant contributor to the economy of the Global South. Climate change impacts can lead to reduced tourism demand, resulting in a loss of revenue and livelihoods for people who depend on the tourism industry.

Tourism Industry Adaptation Strategies Adaptation methods are critical for mitigating the detrimental effects of climate change on the global tourism business. Among the strategies that can be adopted are:

(1) *Diversification of tourism activities*: Diversifying tourism activities can reduce the industry's reliance on specific natural resources that are particularly vulnerable to the effects of climate change.

(2) *Sustainable tourist practices*: Sustainable tourism practices such as waste management, reduced energy and water consumption and biodiversity conservation can help to lessen the tourism industry's environmental effect and contribution to climate change.

(3) *Early warning systems*: By providing timely information to travellers and tourism industry stakeholders, early warning systems can help mitigate the effects of extreme weather occurrences and conditions.

(4) *Community-based tourism*: Community-based tourism is essential for boosting local livelihoods and providing alternative income sources that are not just dependent on tourism. This can make communities less vulnerable to the detrimental effects of climate change on the tourism industry (Buckley, 2012; Dodds & Joppe, 2017; Gössling & Scott, 2018; Hall & Williams, 2018).

The tourism industry in the Global South has also embraced technology as an adaptation strategy, which enhances the tourist experience and improves the industry's efficiency (Xiang et al., 2015). For instance, some destinations have adopted virtual reality and augmented reality technologies to enhance the tourist experience (Buhalis & Neuhofer, 2018). Resilience is the ability of the tourism industry to bounce back from shocks and recover quickly. The tourism industry's ability to adapt to changing circumstances is closely linked to its resilience (Hall et al., 2018). The tourism industry in the Global South has demonstrated resilience in the face of various shocks (Kousaridas et al., 2020). For example, after the Ebola outbreak in West Africa in 2014, the tourism industry in the region rebounded quickly due to its ability to adapt and implement effective measures to prevent the spread of the disease (Hall, 2017). However, the tourism industry is vulnerable to all the shocks mentioned above. It has, however, demonstrated an ability to adapt and implement effective strategies to mitigate the negative impacts. Therefore, there is a great need for governments, tourism industry stakeholders and communities to collaborate to implement effective adaptation strategies and enhance the resilience of the tourism industry in the Global South.

Case Studies

Climate Change in the Global South

Numerous studies have investigated climate change's impact on various tourism industry sectors. Three such studies are highlighted in this section: (i) the effects of climate change on coral reefs in Belize, (ii) extreme weather events in the Caribbean and (iii) wine tourism in South Africa. The findings of these studies provide important insights into the complex relationship between climate change and tourism, emphasising the need for more sustainable and resilient tourism practices.

The Impacts of Climate Change on Coral Reefs in Belize by Mora et al. (2016)

Coral reefs are vital ecosystems that provide habitat for a wide range of marine species and income for many coastal communities through fishing and tourism. Rising sea temperatures, ocean acidification and sea-level rise have all caused severe damage to coral reefs worldwide, including in Belize. Mora et al. (2016) investigated the vulnerability of coral reefs in Belize to the effects of climate change. Rising sea temperatures have been linked to increased coral bleaching and mortality, while ocean acidification and sea-level rise pose additional threats to these fragile ecosystems. Belize's coral reefs are a significant revenue source for the tourism industry and local communities. It was determined that policies and management interventions were necessary to mitigate the impacts of climate change on coral reefs in Belize and protect the ecological and economic benefits they provide to local communities. Protecting ecological and economic benefits that coral reefs provide also ensures the continued sustainability of marine life and local communities in Belize for generations to come.

The Effects of Extreme Weather Events on the Tourism Industry in the Caribbean by Dodds and Ali (2019)

The Caribbean region is highly vulnerable to extreme weather events, such as hurricanes, floods and droughts, which can devastate tourism infrastructure and visitor numbers. Extreme weather occurrences have resulted in significant economic losses for the Caribbean tourism industry, owing to damage to hotels, airports, and other infrastructure, cancellations and decreased visitor numbers. Due to their limited resources and capacity to respond, small and medium-sized enterprises (SMEs) in the tourist industry are particularly exposed to the effects of extreme weather events. Therefore, it was determined that disaster risks reduction and management techniques, such as infrastructure upgrades, insurance coverage and crisis communication plans, should be prioritised by tourist stakeholders throughout the Caribbean. The need to plan for extreme weather occurrences in the Caribbean tourism business is emphasised. Furthermore, pre-emptive actions to limit the dangers connected with extreme weather are urgently needed.

The Impacts of Climate Change on Wine Tourism in South Africa by Hölscher et al. (2021)

The wine industry contributes significantly to the South African economy, and wine tourism is an essential component of the tourism industry. On the other hand, climate change has substantially impacted wine tourism in South Africa in various ways. One of the immediate impacts is the changing weather patterns, which have led to changes in grape harvest times and quality. The rising temperatures and decreasing precipitation levels have also led to earlier grape harvests and a decline in grape quality. This contributed to a shift in wine production from high-quality to lower-quality wines, negatively affecting the wine tourism industry. Climate change has also affected the scenic landscapes that attract wine tourists to South Africa. Changes in rainfall patterns and the increasing occurrence of extreme weather events such as droughts and wildfires have further led to landscape degradation and a decline in biodiversity, thus negatively affecting the attractiveness of wine tourism destinations and, consequently, tourist numbers. These challenges necessitate adaptations to irrigation systems, water conservation measures and the implementation of sustainable farming practices, which increases operational costs for businesses in the industry. It was concluded that sustainable farming practices, improved water conservation measures and promotion of low-carbon tourism activities could significantly build resilience and protect the wine tourism industry in South Africa.

Climate Change Adaptation and Mitigation in Tourism

Policy and governance frameworks can be critical in supporting climate change adaptation and mitigation in the tourism sector. This section provides an overview of current policy and governance frameworks for climate change adaptation and mitigation in the tourism sector in the Global South.

Frameworks for Governance and Policies for Adaptation

Tourism businesses and destinations in the Global South can adapt to the effects of climate change with the help of adaptation strategies and governance frameworks. Measures that can be included in these frameworks include risk assessments, emergency planning and infrastructure upgrades. To reduce the vulnerability of the tourism infrastructure to the effects of climate change, the Indian Ministry of Tourism, for instance, has developed Sustainable Tourism Criteria for India (Cater & Gossling, 2019). Similarly, Brazil's Sustainable Tourist Destination Management Program promotes long-term tourist development, including climate change adaptation strategies (Afonso & Jardim, 2021).

Mitigation Policies and Governance Frameworks

The Global South's tourism industry's GHG emissions are being reduced through mitigation policies and governance frameworks. These frameworks include adopting renewable energy sources, increases in energy efficiency and carbon offsetting plans. For example, the Kenya Sustainable Tourism Alliance (KSTA), which promotes sustainable tourism practices such as using renewable energy and energy-saving techniques, illustrates a successful mitigation strategy (WTTC, 2019). Equally, the South African Tourism Sustainability Framework aims to reduce GHG emissions by adopting sustainable tourism practices (Cater & Gossling, 2019).

Challenges and Future Directions

Despite the existence of adaptation and mitigation regulations and governance structures, implementing these actions in the Global South tourist industry faces substantial hurdles. A significant concern is a need for improved information and understanding of the consequences of climate change, along with the need for action by tourist operators and destinations (Afonso & Jardim, 2021). Furthermore, more political will and financial resources must be needed to execute climate change adaptation and mitigation measures (Cater & Gossling, 2019). Finally, there is a strong need for enhanced collaboration and communication among tourist stakeholders in the Global South and increased public awareness and education (Afonso & Jardim, 2021).

Sustainable Tourism Development in Climate Change

Sustainable tourism development plays a crucial role in addressing challenges posed by climate change in the Global South countries. It encompasses the balance of economic growth with environmental and social considerations and can aid in plummeting the vulnerability of the tourism industry to climate change impacts. Sustainable tourism development entails increased energy efficiency, waste management and preserving natural and cultural resources (UNWTO, 2021). These actions can assist in reducing GHG emissions and enhance resource efficiency, increasing the resilience of tourism infrastructure and destinations to climate change. There are various instances of sustainable tourist development initiatives in the Global South that are addressing climate change challenges. The Masungi Georeserve in the Philippines is one example of a sustainable tourism destination that promotes conservation and eco-tourism while providing economic benefits to local communities (Cochrane et al., 2019).

Similarly, the Mountain Partnership, a global alliance of mountain stakeholders, promotes sustainable tourism development in mountain regions of the Global South by offering technical assistance and finance for sustainable tourism initiatives (FAO, 2021). However, despite programmes for sustainable tourism development, there are significant hurdles in implementing these measures in the tourism business. One significant difficulty remains a need for more awareness and understanding among tourism operators and destinations about the effects of climate change and the urgent need for action (UNWTO, 2021).

Climate-Resilient Tourism and the Global South

Climate change poses substantial risks to the tourist industry, impacting the environment and the local communities that rely on tourism for revenue. As a result, sustainable tourism development has developed as an essential strategy for harmonising economic expansion with environmental and social concerns. Partnerships and partnerships can be crucial in adopting climate-resilient tourism development policies. Partnerships and collaborations give chances for technical expertise, finance and information sharing for sustainable tourist development efforts. For example, the International Centre for Integrated Mountain Development (ICIMOD) collaborates with local people in Nepal to create community-based eco-tourism initiatives that promote sustainable lifestyles while conserving natural resources (ICIMOD, 2021). However, partnerships and collaborations have several challenges, such as:

(1) Lack of trust and cooperation: Trust and cooperation are essential to successful partnerships and collaborations. Partnerships and collaborations are only possible with trust and cooperation (Jafari et al., 2019).
(2) Limited resources: Partnerships and collaborations necessitate allocating time, money and workforce resources. However, organisations' limited resources make it harder for them to participate in partnerships and collaborations. 2015 report by the United Nations Environment Programme (UNEP) highlights the need for adequate financial resources to support partnerships and collaborations in the tourism sector (Olhoff et al., 2015).
(3) Lack of common goals and objectives: Partnerships and collaborations require shared goals and objectives to be effective. However, in some circumstances, tourism organisations may have competing interests and purposes, hindering partnerships and cooperation (Rasoolimanesh et al., 2020).
(4) Communication barriers: Partnerships and collaborations require effective communication. Communication hurdles such as language issues, cultural

differences and a lack of clear communication channels impede productive partnerships and collaborations (Hall et al., 2018).

(5) Resistance to change: Changes in organisational structures, processes and cultures are frequently required for partnerships and collaborations. Resistance to change challenges organisations to fully participate in partnerships and collaborations (Intergovernmental Panel on Climate Change – IPCC; Allen et al., 2018).

Tourism and Climate Justice for the Global South

Climate justice is the equitable distribution of the costs and rewards associated with climate change mitigation and adaptation. The subject has garnered more attention in recent years, particularly in the context of tourism in the Global South. This section reviews the current knowledge regarding the relationship between tourism and climate justice in the Global South countries. Climate justice is based on the notion that climate change mitigation and adaptation costs and benefits should be distributed evenly, considering historical responsibility, capacity and susceptibility. Therefore, climate justice in the context of tourism in the Global South implies ensuring that all stakeholders equally allocate the costs and benefits of climate change adaptation and mitigation (Scott et al., 2019). There are numerous examples of tourism and climate justice initiatives aimed at promoting more equitable and sustainable tourism practices. For example, the Global Sustainable Tourism Council (GSTC) developed a set of criteria for sustainable tourism, which outlines specific guidelines for destinations and tourism businesses to implement energy efficiency measures, use renewable energy sources and reduce waste and water consumption (GSTC, 2021). Similarly, the International Tourism Partnership (ITP) also set goals for the hotel industry to reduce carbon emissions by 66% by 2030 and implement sustainable supply chain practices (ITP, 2021).

In addition, several community-based tourism initiatives prioritise the participation and empowerment of local communities in decision-making processes related to tourism development. For example, the Community-Based Tourism Network in the Mekong Region (CBT-MR), a regional network of community-based tourism initiatives in Cambodia, Laos, Thailand and Vietnam, empowers local communities through training, skills development initiatives and capacity building, thus ensuring they take an active role in tourism development. This also ensures that tourism benefits are shared equitably and that the industry holistically contributes to sustainable development in the region (CBT-MR, 2021). However, despite numerous tourism and climate justice initiatives in the Global South, significant challenges still need to be solved in promoting more equitable and sustainable tourism practices. One major challenge is the propensity of tourism businesses to prioritise short-term economic gains over long-term sustainability goals, particularly in developing countries where tourism is a significant source of income. In some cases, tourism development projects may even exacerbate social and economic inequalities, leading to social injustice and the exclusion of local communities.

Research Box

In this chapter, we have discussed the challenges and opportunities for sustainable tourism development in the face of climate change in the Global South. While our review provides valuable insights, there are still many areas that require further research. Here are some suggestions for future research in this field:

(1) An examination of the role of technology, such as renewable energy and digital platforms, in promoting sustainable tourism practices and enhancing climate resilience in the tourism sector.
(2) Analysing the effectiveness of policy and governance frameworks for addressing the challenges of climate change in the tourism industry in the Global South, and identify best practices that could be replicated in other regions.
(3) A comparative analysis of the policy and governance frameworks for sustainable tourism in the Global South and the Global North, including an examination of their effectiveness in addressing the challenges of climate change.

Conclusion

In this review of various topics related to tourism and climate change in the Global South, it is evident that the tourism industry is vulnerable to the impacts of climate change, and that adaptation and resilience measures are necessary to maintain sustainable tourism practices. The case studies provided demonstrate that climate change, including changes in weather patterns, sea level rise and natural disasters, could significantly impact tourism, resulting in a decline in tourism profits and affecting the livelihoods of those who rely on the industry. In the face of climate change, however, there are opportunities for sustainable tourism development, such as eco-tourism, responsible travel and green infrastructure. Additionally, effective policy and governance frameworks are essential for addressing the challenges of climate change in the tourism sector, including setting emissions reduction targets, implementing sustainable tourism practices and promoting climate-resilient infrastructure. Collaboration and partnerships between the tourism industry, governments and communities are also crucial for ensuring that tourism development is sustainable and equitable and that disadvantaged groups are not left behind. Finally, tourism and climate justice are essential considerations in the face of climate change, as tourism development has both positive and negative impacts on local communities and the natural environment. Therefore, it is critical to ensure that tourist development is sustainable and equitable to reconcile the rights and well-being of local populations with the support for environmental sustainability.

Discussion Questions

- How has climate change affected the tourism industry in the Global South?
- What are some of the challenges faced by the tourism industry in the Global South in adapting to and building resilience against the impacts of climate change?
- How can policy and governance frameworks support climate change adaptation and mitigation in the tourism sector in the Global South?
- What are some examples of successful sustainable tourism development in the face of climate change in the Global South?

Acknowledgements

I want to acknowledge the National Institute for Humanities and Social Sciences (NIHSS) through the DUT BRICS Research Institute Grant Ref: BRI22/1215 for supporting me as part of their Capacity Development Fellows.

References

Afonso, R., & Jardim, S. (2021). A critical review of climate change, tourism and governance in the global south. *Journal of Sustainable Tourism, 29*(5), 677–696. https://doi.org/10.1080/09669582.2020.1835034

Ahmed, U., Umrani, W. A., Yousaf, A., Siddiqui, M. A., & Pahi, M. H. (2021). Developing faithful stewardship for the environment through green HRM. *International Journal of Contemporary Hospitality Management, 33*(10), 3115–3133. https://doi.org/10.1108/IJCHM-09-2020-1066

Allen, M., Dube, O. P., Solecki, W., Aragón-Durand, F., Cramer, W., Humphreys, S., & Kainuma, M. (2018). Special report: Global warming of 1.5 C. In *Intergovernmental Panel on Climate Change (IPCC)*.

Brouder, P., & Teixeira, R. (2021). Climate change and tourism in the global south: What does the future hold? *Current Issues in Tourism*, 1–5. https://doi.org/10.1080/13683500.2021.1929633

Buckley, R. (2012). Sustainable tourism: Research and reality. *Annals of Tourism Research, 39*(2), 528–546. https://doi.org/10.1016/j.annals.2011.11.008

Buhalis, D., & Neuhofer, B. (2018). Augmented reality in tourism. *Journal of Travel Research, 57*(8), 1093–1108. https://doi.org/10.1177/0047287518755806

Cater, E., & Gossling, S. (2019). *Tourism and water: Interactions, impacts and challenges*. Channel View Publications.

Cochrane, J., Larrinaga, C., & Sardinha, B. (2019). Tourism sustainability in protected areas: A Masungi Georeserve, Philippines case study. *Journal of Ecotourism, 18*(3), 255–271.

Community-Based Tourism Network in the Mekong Region (CBT-MR). (2021). https://www.cbtmr.org/about-us/

Dodds, R., & Ali, F. (2019). The effects of climate change on Caribbean tourism. *Current Issues in Tourism, 22*(8), 936–946.

Dodds, R., & Joppe, M. (2017). Sustainable tourism and the dilemma of growth: How can we achieve sustainable tourism in a world that wants more tourism? *Journal of Sustainable Tourism, 25*(1), 1–17. https://doi.org/10.1080/09669582.2016.1240138

FAO. (2021). *Sustainable tourism in mountain regions of the global south: A joint initiative by the mountain partnership secretariat and Swisscontact.* http://www.fao.org/mountain-partnership/resources/publications/detail/en/c/1387126/

Global Sustainable Tourism Council (GSTC). (2021). Criteria for hotels and tour operators. https://www.gstcouncil.org/gstc-criteria/gstc-criteria-for-hotels-and-tour-operators/

Gössling, S., & Scott, D. (2018). The decarbonisation impasse: Global tourism leaders' views on climate change mitigation. *Journal of Sustainable Tourism, 26*(12), 2071–2086. https://doi.org/10.1080/09669582.2018.1529771

Hall, C. M. (2017). Ebola, tourism and fear: Lessons from the past. *Journal of Tourism and Resilience, 1*(1), 20–33.

Hall, C. M., Scott, D., Gössling, S., & Amelung, B. (2018). *Tourism and water: Interactions, impacts and challenges.* Channel View Publications.

Hall, C. M., & Williams, A. M. (2018). *Tourism and innovation.* Channel View Publications.

Han, J., Chen, B., & Yang, L. (2020). Climate change impacts on global tourism: A comprehensive review. *Journal of Sustainable Tourism, 28*(8), 1098–1120. https://doi.org/10.1080/09669582.2020.1713207

Hölscher, J., Kleynhans, E. P., De Villiers, J., & Stander, M. W. (2021). The effects of climate change on wine tourism in the Western Cape of South Africa: A case study. *Climate Risk Management, 31*, 100281.

ICIMOD. (2021). *Sustainable tourism development in Nepal.* https://www.icimod.org/sustainable-tourism-development-nepal

International Tourism Partnership (ITP). (2021). Goals. https://www.greenhotelier.org/our-news/2018/01/31/international-tourism-partnership-announces-new-goals-for-2030/

Jafari, J., Scott, N., & Cooper, C. (2019). *Tourism and hospitality partnerships: An international perspective.* Routledge.

Kousaridas, A., Koniordos, M. A., & Tsionas, M. G. (2020). Tourism resilience to economic crises and terrorism attacks: Evidence from Greece. *Journal of Destination Marketing & Management, 15*, 100409. https://doi.org/10.1016/j.jdmm.2019.100409

Mora, C., Wei, C. L., Rollo, A., Amaro, T., Baco, A. R., Billett, D., & Weil, E. (2016). Coral bleaching causes widespread loss of reef building corals in the tropical western Atlantic. *Science Advances, 2*(4), e1500409.

Olhoff, A., Christensen, J. M., Burgon, P., Bakkegaard, R. K., Larsen, C., & Schletz, M. C. (2015). *The emissions gap report 2015: A UNEP synthesis report.*

Rasoolimanesh, S. M., Jaafar, M., Hashim, N. H., & Rahmati, M. (2020). An exploratory study of partnership success in tourism: The Malaysian context. *Current Issues in Tourism, 23*(5), 549–566.

Rogerson, C. M., & Saarinen, J. (2018). Tourism for poverty alleviation: Issues and debates in the global South. In *The SAGE handbook of tourism management: Applications of theories and concepts to tourism* (pp. 22–37). SAGE Publications.

Ruhanen, L. (2019). Climate change and tourism. In M. Stone, R. L. Dowling, S. J. Page, & E. K. Smith (Eds.), *The Routledge handbook of tourism impacts: Theoretical and applied perspectives* (pp. 73–84). Routledge.

Scott, D., Hall, C. M., & Gössling, S. (2019). *Tourism and water: Interactions, impacts, and challenges.* Channel View Publications.

UNWTO. (2021). *Tourism and the SDGs: A practical guide for addressing the Sustainable Development Goals through tourism.* World Tourism Organization. https://www.e-unwto.org/doi/pdf/10.18111/9789284422195

WTTC. (2019). *Kenya Sustainable Tourism Alliance (KSTA).* https://www.wttc.org/policy/policy-frameworks/sustainable-tourism-alliance/kenya-sustainable-tourism-alliance-ksta/

Xiang, Z., Du, Q., Ma, Y., & Fan, W. (2015). A comparative analysis of major online review platforms: Implications for social media analytics in hospitality and tourism. *Tourism Management, 46*, 202–212. https://doi.org/10.1016/j.tourman.2014.06.001

Chapter 3

Climate Change in Tourism: Understanding the Impacts and Opportunities for Sustainability

Canan Tanrisever[a], Hüseyin Pamukçu[b] and Erdem Baydeniz[b]

[a]Kastamonu University, Türkiye
[b]Afyon Kocatepe University, Türkiye

Learning Objectives

- identify the potential impacts of climate change on the tourism industry, including changes in weather patterns and risks to tourism infrastructure and destinations;
- analyse the role of diversifying tourism products and developing climate-resilient infrastructure in reducing vulnerability to climate change;
- assess the benefits of engaging local communities in sustainable tourism practices and implementing conservation and restoration measures to protect ecosystems and biodiversity.

Abstract

Climate change places significant pressure on the tourism sector by altering environmental and socio-economic conditions that influence tourist behaviour and the attractiveness of destinations. Rising temperatures, changing precipitation patterns and the increasing frequency and severity of extreme weather events affect tourism supply and demand. On the supply side, climate change threatens tourism infrastructure, natural attractions, recreational opportunities and accessibility of destinations. Coastal destinations are particularly vulnerable to sea-level rise and coastal flooding, which can damage tourism assets. On the demand side, changing climatic conditions alter visitor comfort levels, health risks and the seasonality of destinations, influencing tourists' choice of destinations. In addition, small island destinations face unnecessary

---

Future Tourism Trends Volume 1, 33–45
Copyright © 2024 Canan Tanrisever, Hüseyin Pamukçu and Erdem Baydeniz
Published under exclusive licence by Emerald Publishing Limited
doi:10.1108/978-1-83753-244-520241003

risks due to their economic dependence on climate-sensitive activities such as beach and nature tourism. Adapting the tourism sector to climate change requires reducing vulnerability through diversification, green infrastructure, ecosystem conservation, community-based adaptation and policy support. Mitigating tourism's contribution to climate change requires minimising energy use, switching to renewable energy, improving efficiency, reducing long-haul flights and promoting sustainable consumption and production. Collective and concerted efforts by all stakeholders are needed to transition to a climate-resilient and low-carbon tourism sector that continues to provide socio-economic benefits while minimising its environmental footprint.

Keywords: Climate change; climate; impacts of climate changes; tourism; future; carbon footprint

Introduction

Tourism is an important and rapidly growing sector of the global economy, generating around 10% of global Gross Domestic Product (GDP) and supporting over 300 million jobs. However, tourism also contributes to greenhouse gas (GHG) emissions, accounting for about 8% of global emissions (SHT, 2020). Transport, accommodation and activities are the primary sources of GHG emissions in tourism. Transport alone accounts for about 75% of tourism emissions, with aviation being the most significant contributor. Accommodation accounts for about 20% of tourism emissions, mainly from energy use for heating, cooling, lighting and appliances (Zachariadis & Zachariadis, 2016). In addition, activities such as skiing, golfing, diving and wildlife watching can also generate emissions from energy use, land-use change, waste generation and disturbance of natural habitats.

Climate change is one of our most pressing issues; its effects are felt worldwide. The tourism industry is no exception and will likely be one of the most affected by climate change in the coming years. Climate change already affects tourism in several ways (Schmidhuber & Tubiello, 2007). Rising sea levels threaten coastal resorts and other tourist destinations. Extreme weather events such as floods, droughts and heat waves are becoming more frequent and disrupting tourism activities. Climate change is also expected to have a significant impact on tourism demand. As the world's population grows and incomes rise, more people can afford to travel. However, climate change will make some destinations less attractive to tourists (Proebstl-Haider et al., 2021). Destinations already hot and dry are likely to become hotter and drier, making them less attractive to sun-seekers. Developing countries, which are often more dependent on tourism for economic growth, are likely to be hardest hit by the effects of climate change.

Several strategies can be used to mitigate the impact of climate change on tourism. First, reducing GHG emissions is critical and can be achieved by investing in renewable energy sources, improving energy efficiency and changing transport patterns. Another critical step is to adapt to the impacts of climate change that are already occurring (Dillimono & Dickinson, 2015). This can be achieved by building sea walls to protect coastal resorts, developing drought-resistant crops and improving early warning systems for extreme weather events. By taking steps to reduce GHG emissions and adapt to the impacts of climate change, the tourism industry can help mitigate the environmental and economic impacts of climate change (Hanger et al., 2013).

Climate change affects tourism directly and indirectly by altering environmental and socio-economic conditions that influence tourist behaviour and destination attractiveness (Seetanah & Fauzel, 2018). Changes in temperature and precipitation patterns can affect the length and quality of the tourism season, the availability and cost of water and energy, the comfort and health of tourists and workers and the suitability of destinations for specific activities (Hein et al., 2009; Proebstl-Haider et al., 2021). Extreme weather events can damage tourism infrastructure and assets, disrupt transport and communication networks, increase operating costs and insurance premiums, reduce tourist demand and satisfaction and threaten the safety and well-being of tourists and workers (Hamilton & Tol, 2007). Sea-level rise can erode beaches and coastal areas, inundate low-lying islands and coastal cities, increase the risk of coastal erosion and flooding, damage coastal infrastructure and cultural heritage sites, degrade coastal ecosystems such as coral reefs and mangroves and reduce the availability of land for tourism development. Biodiversity loss can reduce the aesthetic value and ecological functions of natural attractions such as forests, wetlands, mountains and wildlife, which can affect tourist demand and satisfaction, as well as the provision of ecosystem services such as water purification, erosion control and pollination (Saroinsong, 2020; Schirpke et al., 2016). To better understand the impacts of climate change on tourism, a conceptual framework or theoretical model could be developed to guide the analysis. In addition, a more comprehensive and up-to-date literature review could be undertaken to support the article's arguments. Furthermore, the article would benefit from a more rigorous editing process to improve the clarity and coherence of the writing, particularly in terms of sentence structure. Finally, proper citation of all claims made in the article would enhance its credibility and reliability.

Case Study

The Impacts of Climate Change on Tourism Destinations

Climate change is already having a significant impact on the tourism industry, and this impact is likely to increase in the future. One of the most apparent impacts of climate change on the tourism industry is changes in weather patterns, including an increased frequency of extreme events such as heatwaves, droughts, floods and storms. For example, scientists predict that Europe could experience 10 times more heatwaves, making summer holidays hotter than ever (Hamilton et al., 2005). Correspondingly, the safety of visitors during their travels could be compromised; high tides would regularly flood historic destinations such as Venice, while some mountainous areas may no longer have snow – a harsh reality for winter sports destinations such as Davos (Trincardi et al., 2016). In addition, tourism infrastructures, such as buildings, roads, airports, etc., are at risk of a future escalation of extreme conditions (Suppasri et al., 2021).

Rising sea levels are another major threat to coastal destinations and islands worldwide, endangering both property and lives. In addition, saltwater intrusion threatens freshwater sources, further complicating livelihoods along these different stages of the tourism supply chain, driven by individual decisions and systemic failures within the sector (Stylos et al., 2021). To address these issues, an ecosystem approach is needed in which all aspects of the tourism value chain operate coherently under sound governance principles, not only relying on compliance systems but actively promoting transparency, integrity and account-ability through internal procedures and external reporting (Langle-Flores et al., 2022). Companies can evade environmental responsibilities by manipulating inspectors and skipping best practice measurements. However, customers can ask questions about new disruptive technologies that automatically provide verifiable analysis. Detecting mismanagement by omitting questionable actions and allowing lousy behaviour is more straightforward with big data, accessible across platforms, if companies want to take advantage of themselves. Therefore, it is essential to carefully consider whether they should operate in other competitive environments without scrutiny (Song, 2012).

Tourism mitigation refers to reducing GHG emissions from tourism activities and enhancing the removal of GHGs from the atmosphere by tourism systems. Various stakeholders, such as tourists, businesses, governments, communities and non-governmental organisations, can undertake tourism mitigation (Scott et al., 2010). Tourism mitigation can be voluntary or mandatory, market-based or regulatory, technological or behavioural. Some of the possible strategies for tourism mitigation are:

Improving Efficiency: This involves enhancing the performance and produc-tivity of tourism systems to reduce the energy and resources needed to produce a unit of tourism service or product. For example, improving efficiency can include adopting renewable energy sources, upgrading equipment and appliances, opti-mising building design and insulation and implementing energy management systems (Wang et al., 2022).

Reducing Consumption: This involves decreasing the demand and use of energy and resources by tourism systems to lower the GHG emissions associated with tourism activities. For example, reducing consumption can include promoting low-carbon modes of transport, encouraging shorter and less frequent trips, offering low-impact tourism products and services, and raising awareness and education on sustainable tourism practices (Alfredsson et al., 2018; Kelly & Williams, 2007).

Enhancing Sequestration: This involves increasing the capacity and potential of tourism systems to remove and store GHGs from the atmosphere by enhancing natural or artificial sinks. For example, enhancing sequestration can include restoring and conserving natural habitats such as forests, wetlands and grasslands, supporting afforestation and reforestation projects and developing carbon capture and storage technologies (Neogi et al., 2022; Seddon et al., 2021).

The Impact of Climate Change on Tourism

Tourism is a sector that makes up a large part of the global economy and is an essential source of income for many countries. However, climate change poses a significant threat to the attractiveness and activities of tourism. Climate change increases the severity and frequency of weather events, alters the climatic characteristics of tourist destinations, threatens natural attractions and increases water stress. All this reduces the attractiveness of places as tourist destinations and negatively impacts tourism facilities, infrastructure and activities. Therefore, adaptation and mitigation efforts are needed for the tourism sector to cope with this changing climate.

Changing Destinations: Climate change affects natural landscapes and ecosystems, altering the appeal and viability of traditional tourist destinations. Rising temperatures can result in the loss of snow-covered landscapes, impacting winter tourism. Coastal regions are at risk due to rising sea levels and increased storm intensity, threatening beach tourism and infrastructure (Prideaux et al., 2010).

Extreme Weather Events: More frequent and severe weather events, such as hurricanes, heatwaves and wildfires, disrupt travel plans and infrastructure. These events pose risks to visitor safety and can result in economic losses for tourism-dependent communities (Wilbanks & Fernandez, 2014).

Threats to Biodiversity: Climate change accelerates habitat loss, causing a decline in biodiversity. This loss impacts ecotourism, which relies on intact ecosystems and wildlife. In addition, the disappearance of iconic species and natural wonders diminishes the tourism appeal of affected regions (Hanski, 2011).

Water Scarcity and Quality: Changing precipitation patterns and increased water demands lead to water scarcity in many areas. Tourism, particularly in water-dependent activities like swimming, boating and fishing, suffers when water resources are compromised by pollution or scarcity (Rocha et al., 2020).

Challenges Faced by the Tourism Industry

Climate change threatens the tourism sector in many ways. Small island developing states are particularly vulnerable to climate impacts because they depend on tourism revenues. Tourism infrastructure is damaged by climate events such as storms and floods, travel seasons change, making planning brutal, economic revenues decline and natural attractions are damaged. All these problems require adaptation to climate change and emission reductions. However, climate action in the tourism sector must be improved or completed. Tourism stakeholders must change their strategies, develop more sustainable and resilient travel models and significantly reduce emissions to limit global warming.

Vulnerability of Small Island Developing States: Small island nations, heavily reliant on tourism, are particularly vulnerable to climate change impacts.

Rising sea levels, coral bleaching and extreme weather events threaten their tourism-dependent economies and livelihoods (Hay, 2013).

Infrastructure Vulnerability: Hotels, resorts, airports and other tourism-related infrastructure are exposed to the risks of extreme weather events and sea-level rise. Inadequate adaptation measures can increase maintenance costs, property damage and operational disruptions (Ruiz-Ramírez et al., 2019).

Seasonal Variability: Climate change alters weather patterns and can disrupt tourism seasonality. Unpredictable weather conditions affect visitor flow and impact businesses that depend on specific seasons for their revenue (Amelung et al., 2007).

Economic Implications: Tourism contributes significantly to global GDP, and climate change impacts can lead to economic losses. Reduction in tourist arrivals, cancellations, and diminished visitor spending affect local economies and employment opportunities (Mackay & Spencer, 2017).

Opportunities for Adaptation and Sustainable Practices

Climate change threatens the tourism sector in many ways. The climatic characteristics of tourist destinations are changing, natural attractions are at risk and infrastructure is being damaged. These harm tourism revenues and employment and pose serious problems, particularly for small island developing states. At the same time, however, the tourism sector can seize opportunities to meet the challenges by adapting to climate change and adopting sustainable practices. Investing in sustainable green infrastructure, conserving natural resources, diversifying tourism into different seasons and involving local communities can increase the sector's resilience. However, all this requires rapid and comprehensive action. The policy supports from governments and cooperation between sector stakeholders can accelerate the fight against climate change and prepare the tourism sector for the future. Otherwise, the climate crisis will continue to impact tourism profoundly.

Diversification of Tourism Offerings: As traditional tourist destinations face challenges, diversifying tourism offerings can help mitigate climate change impacts. Developing new experiences, such as cultural and heritage or adventure tourism, can attract visitors to alternative locations (Garanti, 2022).

Sustainable Infrastructure Development: Investing in climate-resilient infrastructure and incorporating green building practices can reduce vulnerability to climate risks. Renewable energy adoption and energy-efficient practices can minimise the carbon footprint of tourism operations (Corfee-Morlot et al., 2012).

Community Engagement and Resilience: Building local capacity and engaging communities in sustainable tourism practices enhance resilience. Training programmes, community-based tourism initiatives and responsible tourism practices can create economic opportunities while preserving natural and cultural assets (Cerveny et al., 2022; Qu & Cheer, 2021).

Conservation and Restoration: Protecting and restoring ecosystems and biodiversity can enhance the resilience and attractiveness of tourism destinations. Sustainable management of protected areas, reforestation projects and wildlife conservation efforts contribute to the long-term sustainability of tourism (Zari et al., 2019).

Policy Support and Collaboration: Governments, international organisations and stakeholders in the tourism industry must collaborate to develop and implement climate change adaptation and mitigation policies. Supporting sustainable practices, providing incentives and fostering public–private partnerships can drive positive change (Tonmoy et al., 2020).

Furthermore, addressing climate change in tourism requires a collective effort from all stakeholders. Therefore, here are some additional considerations and recommendations for the industry (Amore et al., 2018; Carswell et al., 2023; Melián-Alzola et al., 2020; Pan et al., 2018):

Education and Awareness: Increasing public awareness about the impacts of climate change on tourism is crucial. Educational campaigns targeting tourists can encourage responsible travel behaviours, such as reducing carbon emissions, conserving water and respecting local cultures and environments. The industry can contribute to a more sustainable tourism future by fostering a sense of responsibility among travellers.

Technological Innovations: Embracing technological advancements can help the tourism industry mitigate and adapt to climate change. For example, data analytics and artificial intelligence can improve resource management, optimise energy consumption and enhance the overall efficiency of tourism operations. In addition, innovation in transportation, such as using electric vehicles and sustainable aviation fuels, can reduce the carbon footprint of travel.

Collaboration with Local Communities: Engaging and involving local communities in decision-making is vital for sustainable tourism development. Their knowledge and insights can contribute to identifying climate change risks and formulating effective adaptation strategies. In addition, inclusive approaches prioritising residents' well-being can ensure that tourism benefits are shared equitably, and that communities are actively involved in shaping their sustainable futures.

Sustainable Transportation: The transportation sector significantly contributes to GHG emissions in tourism. Encouraging the use of public transportation, promoting cycling and walking tours and supporting the development of efficient and low-emission transportation systems can reduce the carbon footprint of tourism. In addition, collaboration with transportation providers, such as airlines and cruise lines, is essential to foster sustainable practices within these sectors.

Destination Resilience Planning: Tourism destinations must integrate climate change considerations into long-term planning and management strategies. This includes conducting vulnerability assessments, developing adaptation plans and implementing measures to enhance resilience. In addition, building partnerships between tourism authorities, environmental agencies and local communities can facilitate the exchange of knowledge and resources to support destination resilience.

Carbon Offsetting and Compensation: To address the unavoidable carbon emissions associated with travel, the tourism industry can support and invest in credible carbon offsetting projects. This involves calculating the carbon footprint of tourism activities and offsetting it by investing in initiatives that reduce GHG emissions or promote sustainable development. Transparent and verified offsetting mechanisms can ensure the integrity of such efforts.

Responsible Tourism Certifications and Standards: Adopting responsible tourism certifications and standards can help guide tourists in making sustainable choices. These certifications can include criteria related to climate change mitigation, environmental conservation, community involvement and cultural preservation. In addition, governments and industry associations can also incentivise adopting such certifications and promote responsible tourism practices.

Research Box

In the example given for 'Climate Change in Tourism: Understanding the Impacts and Opportunities for Sustainability', the research box discusses the importance of ensuring a representative sample when conducting a study of customers of an ecotourism club. The aim is to understand their perspectives on various issues related to the club. To ensure that the sample is representative of the larger population of clients, it is essential to consider the composition of the population. In this case, the researcher has information about the customers' country of origin but lacks other demographic details such as gender, age, income and education. As country of origin is considered necessary in this scenario, the researcher may use quota or stratified random sampling to obtain information. The researcher has a client base of 12,000, with approximately 7,500 clients from the United States, 2,000 from the United Kingdom, 1,500 from Australia and 1,000 from Turkey. Suppose the researcher wants to draw a sample of 800 customers. Using the proportions shown in the available sample, the researcher would include in the sample 62.5% (or 500) US customers, 16.6% (or 134) British customers, 12.5% (or 100) Australian customers and 12% (or 96) Turkish customers. By using quota sampling to match the proportions of countries of origin in the population, the researcher can ensure that the sample reflects the diversity of customer perspectives. This approach increases the likelihood of obtaining a representative sample for the survey of the ecotourism club's customers.

Research Box 2

Question: How does climate change affect tourism demand and destination choice?

Hypothesis: Climate change has a negative impact on tourism demand and destination choice, especially for destinations that are vulnerable to extreme weather events, sea level rise, biodiversity loss and water scarcity.

Null hypothesis: Climate change does not affect tourism demand and destination choice.

Predictions: Based on the hypothesis, we predict that

• Tourists will reduce the frequency and duration of their trips due to increased costs and risks associated with climate change.
• Tourists will shift their preferences from destinations exposed to climate change impacts to more resilient or adaptive destinations.
• Tourists will seek alternative forms of tourism that are less dependent on natural resources and more compatible with low-carbon lifestyles.

Experimental set-up: We survey potential tourists from different countries and regions to test the predictions. We ask them about their travel intentions, preferences, motivations and perceptions of climate change and its impact on tourism. We also collect data on their socio-demographic characteristics, travel behaviour and environmental attitudes. Finally, we use a discrete choice experiment to elicit their willingness to pay for different tourism attributes under different climate change scenarios.

Results and conclusions: The results show that climate change significantly and negatively impacts tourism demand and destination choice. Tourists are less likely to travel to destinations affected by climate change, such as coastal areas, mountainous regions and tropical islands. They are likelier to choose destinations that offer climate change mitigation or adaptation measures, such as renewable energy sources, water conservation practices and biodiversity protection. They also more interested in alternative forms of tourism with a lower environmental impact, such as ecotourism, cultural tourism and volunteer tourism. The results support the hypothesis and reject the null hypothesis.

Conclusion

Climate change poses significant challenges to the tourism industry, affecting destinations, infrastructure and livelihoods. However, amidst these challenges, there are opportunities to adapt and adopt sustainable practices that can help mitigate the impacts of climate change. Diversifying tourism offers is one way to reduce pressure on highly vulnerable areas and support the development of more resilient destinations. This can include promoting cultural and heritage tourism, adventure tourism or exploring emerging destinations not traditionally associated with tourism. By spreading tourism demand across different regions, the industry can reduce pressure on highly vulnerable areas and support the development of more resilient destinations (Ghosh et al., 2022). Investing in climate-resilient infrastructure is essential to protect tourism assets and ensure the safety of visitors. Incorporating green building practices, such as energy-efficient design and renewable energy sources, can reduce carbon emissions and operating costs. In addition, considering the potential risks of climate change in planning and developing tourism infrastructure can help minimise vulnerability (Pörtner et al., 2022).

Involving local communities in sustainable tourism practices is essential for building resilience. Training programmes and capacity-building initiatives can empower communities to actively participate in tourism activities while preserving their natural and cultural heritage (UNWTO, 2021). Community-based tourism initiatives can also create economic opportunities for residents, reducing their dependence on traditional tourism models and increasing their adaptive capacity (Holladay & Powell, 2013). Conservation and restoration efforts play an essential role in protecting ecosystems and biodiversity, which are fundamental to the appeal of many tourism destinations. Sustainable management of protected areas, reforestation projects and wildlife conservation initiatives can contribute to climate change mitigation and enhance tourism destinations' long-term sustainability and attractiveness (Wang et al., 2019). Policy support and cooperation are critical to addressing the challenges of climate change in the tourism sector. Governments must develop and implement robust climate change adaptation and mitigation policies that guide and support the tourism sector. International organisations can facilitate knowledge sharing and provide financial support to vulnerable destinations. Public–private partnerships can drive innovation and encourage adopting sustainable practices across the industry (UNWTO, 2021).

In conclusion, climate change poses significant challenges to the tourism industry and offers opportunities to adapt and adopt sustainable practices. By diversifying tourism products, developing climate-resilient infrastructure, engaging local communities, conserving ecosystems and promoting cooperation, the tourism sector can mitigate the effects of climate change and contribute to a more sustainable and resilient future. The collective efforts of governments, organisations and stakeholders are needed to ensure the long-term viability and sustainability of the tourism industry in the face of climate change.

Discussion Questions

- What are some of the critical impacts of climate change on the tourism industry discussed in this chapter? Which impacts are most worrying and why?
- How does this chapter suggest that vulnerable tourism destinations may be disproportionately affected by climate change? What types of destinations would fall into this category?
- Describe some strategies the tourism industry could adopt to mitigate and adapt to climate change. Which strategies seem most promising and feasible, and why? Which might face implementation challenges?

References

Alfredsson, E., Bengtsson, M., Brown, H. S., Isenhour, C., Lorek, S., Stevis, D., & Vergragt, P. (2018). Why achieving the Paris Agreement requires reduced overall consumption and production. *Sustainability: Science, Practice and Policy, 14*(1), 1–5.

Amelung, B., Nicholls, S., & Viner, D. (2007). Implications of global climate change for tourism flows and seasonality. *Journal of Travel Research, 45*(3), 285–296.

Amore, A., Prayag, G., & Hall, C. M. (2018). Conceptualising destination resilience from a multilevel perspective. *Tourism Review International, 22*(3–4), 235–250.

Carswell, J., Jamal, T., Lee, S., Sullins, D. L., & Wellman, K. (2023). Post-pandemic lessons for destination resilience and sustainable event management: The complex learning destination. *Tourism and Hospitality, 4*(1), 91–140.

Cerveny, L. K., Derrien, M. M., Miller, A. B., & Meyer, C. (2022). Partnership and community engagement models for stewarding national scenic trails: A social-ecological systems perspective. *Tourism Planning & Development, 19*(3), 204–226.

Corfee-Morlot, J., Marchal, V., Kauffmann, C., Kennedy, C., Stewart, F., Kaminker, C., & Ang, G. (2012). *Towards a green investment policy framework: The case of low-carbon, climate-resilient infrastructure.* https://doi.org/10.1787/19970900

Dillimono, H. D., & Dickinson, J. E. (2015). Travel, tourism, climate change, and behavioural change: Travellers' perspectives from a developing country, Nigeria. *Journal of Sustainable Tourism, 23*(3), 437–454.

Garanti, Z. (2022). Alternative and special interest tourism to mitigate the effects of tourism seasonality: The debate from Cyprus. *Worldwide Hospitality and Tourism Themes, 14*(5), 451–460.

Ghosh, S., Dinda, S., Chatterjee, N. D., Dutta, S., & Bera, D. (2022). Spatial-explicit carbon emission-sequestration balance estimation and evaluation of emission susceptible zones in an Eastern Himalayan city using Pressure-Sensitivity-Resilience framework: An approach towards achieving low carbon cities. *Journal of Cleaner Production, 336*, 130417.

Hamilton, J. M., Maddison, D. J., & Tol, R. S. (2005). Climate change and international tourism: A simulation study. *Global Environmental Change, 15*(3), 253–266.

Hamilton, J. M., & Tol, R. S. (2007). The impact of climate change on tourism in Germany, the UK and Ireland: A simulation study. *Regional Environmental Change, 7*, 161–172.

Hanger, S., Pfenninger, S., Dreyfus, M., & Patt, A. (2013). Knowledge and information needs of adaptation policy-makers: A European study. *Regional Environmental Change, 13*, 91–101.

Hanski, I. (2011). Habitat loss, the dynamics of biodiversity, and a perspective on conservation. *Ambio, 40*(3), 248–255.

Hay, J. E. (2013). Small island developing states: Coastal systems, global change and sustainability. *Sustainability Science, 8*, 309–326.

Hein, L., Metzger, M. J., & Moreno, A. (2009). Potential impacts of climate change on tourism; A case study for Spain. *Current Opinion in Environmental Sustainability, 1*(2), 170–178.

Holladay, P. J., & Powell, R. B. (2013). Resident perceptions of social – Ecological resilience and the sustainability of community-based tourism development in the Commonwealth of Dominica. *Journal of Sustainable Tourism, 21*(8), 1188–1211.

Kelly, J., & Williams, P. W. (2007). Modelling tourism destination energy consumption and greenhouse gas emissions: Whistler, British Columbia, Canada. *Journal of Sustainable Tourism, 15*(1), 67–90.

Langle-Flores, A., López-Vázquez, Z., Chávez-Dagostino, R. M., & Aguilar-Rodríguez, A. (2022). COVID-19 impacts on whale-watching collaboration networks. *Sustainability, 14*(21), 13846.

Mackay, E. A., & Spencer, A. (2017). The future of Caribbean tourism: Competition and climate change implications. *Worldwide Hospitality and Tourism Themes, 9*(1), 44–59.

Melián-Alzola, L., Fernández-Monroy, M., & Hidalgo-Peñate, M. (2020). Hotels in contexts of uncertainty: Measuring organisational resilience. *Tourism Management Perspectives, 36*, 100747.

Neogi, S., Sharma, V., Khan, N., Chaurasia, D., Ahmad, A., Chauhan, S., Singh, A., You, S., Pandey, A., & Bhargava, P. C. (2022). Sustainable biochar: A facile strategy for soil and environmental restoration, energy generation, global climate change mitigation and circular economy. *Chemosphere, 293*, 133474.

Pan, S. Y., Gao, M., Kim, H., Shah, K. J., Pei, S. L., & Chiang, P. C. (2018). Advances and challenges in sustainable tourism toward a green economy. *Science of the Total Environment, 635*, 452–469.

Pörtner, H. O., Roberts, D. C., Adams, H., Adler, C., Aldunce, P., Ali, E., Begum, R. A., Betts, R., Kerr, R. B., Biesbroek, R., Birkmann, J., Bowen, K., Castellanos, E., Cissé, G., Constable, A., Cramer, W., Dodman, D., Eriksen, S. H., Fischlin, A., . . . Ibrahim, Z. Z. (2022). *Climate change 2022: Impacts, adaptation and vulnerability* (p. 3056). IPCC.

Prideaux, B., Coghlan, A., & Mcnamara, K. (2010). Assessing tourists' perceptions of climate change on mountain landscapes. *Tourism Recreation Research, 35*(2), 187–200.

Proebstl-Haider, U., Wanner, A., Feilhammer, M., & Damm, A. (2021). Tourism and climate change – An integrated look at the Austrian case. *Journal of Outdoor Recreation and Tourism, 34*, 100361.

Qu, M., & Cheer, J. M. (2021). Community art festivals and sustainable rural revitalisation. *Journal of Sustainable Tourism, 29*(11–12), 1756–1775.

Rocha, J., Carvalho-Santos, C., Diogo, P., Beça, P., Keizer, J. J., & Nunes, J. P. (2020). Impacts of climate change on reservoir water availability, quality and irrigation needs in a water-scarce Mediterranean region (southern Portugal). *Science of the Total Environment, 736*, 139477.

Ruiz-Ramírez, J. D., Euán-Ávila, J. I., & Rivera-Monroy, V. H. (2019). Vulnerability of coastal resort cities to mean sea level rise in the Mexican Caribbean. *Coastal Management, 47*(1), 23–43.

Saroinsong, F. B. (2020). Supporting plant diversity and conservation through landscape planning: A case study in an agro-tourism landscape in Tampusu, North Sulawesi, Indonesia. *Biodiversitas Journal of Biological Diversity, 21*(4).

Schirpke, U., Timmermann, F., Tappeiner, U., & Tasser, E. (2016). Cultural ecosystem services of mountain regions: Modelling the aesthetic value. *Ecological Indicators, 69*, 78–90.

Schmidhuber, J., & Tubiello, F. N. (2007). Global food security under climate change. *Proceedings of the National Academy of Sciences, 104*(50), 19703–19708.

Scott, D., Peeters, P., & Gössling, S. (2010). Can tourism deliver its "aspirational" greenhouse gas emission reduction targets? *Journal of Sustainable Tourism, 18*(3), 393–408.

Seddon, N., Smith, A., Smith, P., Key, I., Chausson, A., Girardin, C., House, J., Srivastava, S., & Turner, B. (2021). Getting the message right on nature-based solutions to climate change. *Global Change Biology, 27*(8), 1518–1546.

Seetanah, B., & Fauzel, S. (2018). Investigating the impact of climate change on the tourism sector: Evidence from a sample of island economies. *Tourism Review, 74*(2), 194–203.

SHT, K. (2020). *Impact of COVID-19 on tourism industry: A review.* https://mpra.ub.uni-muenchen.de/102834/

Song, H. (2012). *Tourism supply chain management.* Routledge.

Stylos, N., Zwiegelaar, J., & Buhalis, D. (2021). Big data empowered agility for dynamic, volatile, and time-sensitive service industries: The case of tourism sector. *International Journal of Contemporary Hospitality Management, 33*(3), 1015–1036.

Suppasri, A., Maly, E., Kitamura, M., Pescaroli, G., Alexander, D., & Imamura, F. (2021). Cascading disasters triggered by tsunami hazards: A perspective for critical infrastructure resilience and disaster risk reduction. *International Journal of Disaster Risk Reduction, 66*, 102597.

Tonmoy, F. N., Cooke, S. M., Armstrong, F., & Rissik, D. (2020). From science to policy: Development of a climate change adaptation plan for the health and well-being sector in Queensland, Australia. *Environmental Science & Policy, 108*, 1–13.

Trincardi, F., Barbanti, A., Bastianini, M., Benetazzo, A., Cavaleri, L., Chiggiato, J., & Umgiesser, G. (2016). The 1966 flooding of Venice: What time taught us for the future. *Oceanography, 29*(4), 178–186.

UNWTO. (2021). *Climate action in tourism: Responding to the climate challenge.* World Tourism Organization.

Wang, W. C., Lin, C. H., Lu, W. B., & Lee, S. H. (2019). When destination attractiveness shifts in response to climate change: Tourists' adaptation intention in Taiwan's Kenting National Park. *Current Issues in Tourism, 22*(5), 522–543.

Wang, Q., Yang, L., & Yue, Z. (2022). Research on the development of digital finance in improving the efficiency of tourism resource allocation. *Resources, Environment and Sustainability, 8*, 100054.

Wilbanks, T. J., & Fernandez, S. (2014). *Climate change and infrastructure, urban systems, and vulnerabilities: Technical report for the US Department of Energy in support of the national climate assessment.* Island Press.

Zachariadis, T., & Zachariadis, T. (2016). Climate change impacts. *Climate Change in Cyprus: Review of the Impacts and Outline of an Adaptation Strategy*, 25–49.

Zari, M. P., Kiddle, G. L., Blaschke, P., Gawler, S., & Loubser, D. (2019). Utilising nature-based solutions to increase resilience in Pacific Ocean Cities. *Ecosystem Services, 38*, 100968.

Part 3

Community-Based Tourism

Chapter 4

Community-Based Tourism (CBT) in Changing Economy in the Case of Sri Lanka

Puwanendram Gayathri[a], Baghya Erathna[b], Krishantha Ganeshan[c], Suranga DAC Silva[d] and Himalee de Silva[d]

[a]University of Sri Jayewardenepura, Sri Lanka
[b]SLTC Research University, Sri Lanka
[c]98 Acres Resort and Spa, Sri Lanka
[d]University of Colombo, Sri Lanka

Learning Objectives

At the end of this chapter reading, you will be able:

- to identify community-based tourism in a changing economy. It carried as a case study based on the tourism industry in Sri Lanka;
- the reason is that Sri Lanka is facing considerable challenges during this ongoing economic crisis. Due to that, the study discussed community-based tourism as an economic generating tool in Sri Lanka tourism.

Abstract

This chapter considers the current situation of community-based tourism (CBT) in Sri Lanka, available potentials to promote this for the future tourism industry in Sri Lanka and demand and global trends of CBT. This chapter consists of an introduction examining CBT in the global scenario. This chapter's second title discusses the potential of CBT in Sri Lanka. The third topic concerns the demand and trends of CBT in a changing economy.

Future Tourism Trends Volume 1, 49–60
Published under exclusive licence by Emerald Publishing Limited
doi:10.1108/978-1-83753-244-520241004

The fourth topic is discussing global best practices and policies for CBT development. Finally, it concludes with recommendations and suggestions for CBT development in Sri Lanka.

This case study was conducted through qualitative analysis, and data will be collected with primary and secondary data. Primary data will be collected through interviews with industry stakeholders, tourists and other relevant interviewees. In addition, it will be carried out observation on selected community-based destinations. Furthermore, the secondary data will be gathered through books, articles, research papers, websites and other materials. This chapter conducted an empirical study on CBT in Sri Lanka. It brings the values of CBT to a changing economy. Furthermore, this study identified problems, potentials, demands and trends for future tourism development by evaluating global best practices and policies.

Keywords: Wellness tourism; demand and trends; global best practices; future values; authentic wellness experience; new parameters

Introduction

Tourism has become an important economic activity in many countries worldwide, contributing significantly to the Gross Domestic Product (GDP) and providing employment opportunities for local communities. Furthermore, tourism contributes to generating foreign exchange earnings and the development of infrastructure and services. According to the World Travel and Tourism Council (WTTC), the tourism sector created 319 million jobs worldwide in 2018, accounting for 1 in 10 jobs globally (WTTC, 2019). Also, according to the United Nations World Tourism Organization (UNWTO), international tourism receipts reached US$1.7 trillion in 2018, representing a 4% increase from the previous year (UNWTO, 2019).

Tourism can create opportunities for small and medium-sized enterprises (SMEs) to provide goods and services to tourists. Furthermore, constructing new infrastructure can also create job opportunities in the construction sector. This would stimulate entrepreneurship and innovation by providing opportunities for new business ventures and encouraging the development of new products and services. This can lead to the diversification of the local economy and the creation of new job opportunities. Furthermore, the tourism industry has a multiplier effect, meaning that the impact of tourism spending is multiplied through the economy as income generated from tourism is spent on other goods and services. This can contribute to developing local economies, particularly in rural and remote areas. Therefore, it is visible that tourism significantly impacts the host community, and there is a positive relationship between tourism and the lives of the community where if one thrives, the other thrives as well.

Community-Based Tourism (CBT)

CBT is a type of tourism that is organised and managed by local communities to promote sustainable development and empower local people. CBT involves the participation of local communities in the planning, development and operation of tourism activities to preserve local culture and protect the environment. Different international bodies have defined CBT differently, and a few are as follows:

- According to The International Ecotourism Society (TIES), CBT 'is a form of sustainable tourism that allows travellers to connect closely with local people by participating in activities and experiences that are authentic, culturally sensitive and environmentally responsible' (TIES, 2019).
- The United Nations Development Programme (UNDP) defines CBT as 'a type of tourism that involves the participation of local communities in the planning, development and management of tourism activities, to empower local people and promote sustainable development' (UNDP, 2018).

According to both definitions of CBT, it can be identified that it talks about local people's participation and sustainability as critical points. CBT is a growing trend in the tourism industry, with many destinations recognising the importance of involving local communities in tourism development. The International Labour Organization (ILO) reports that 'community-based tourism has been recognised as a promising approach to promoting local economic development, reducing poverty and promoting sustainable development' (ILO, 2015).

Promoting CBT

CBT can have several benefits for local communities, including generating income and employment opportunities, preserving cultural traditions and protecting natural resources. It can also provide visitors with an authentic and unique travel experience while promoting sustainable and responsible tourism practices.

Additionally, the traditional model of tourism development, which is focused on maximising profits and attracting mass tourism, has led to several negative impacts, such as the depletion of natural resources, degradation of local culture and social inequality. In response, CBT has emerged as a sustainable alternative that prioritises the participation and empowerment of local communities in tourism development.

Throughout the study, the researchers wish to bring attention to a discussion of the positive economic impacts of tourism and how it helps uplift the community in the country, especially the stakeholders in the field of tourism.

Purpose of the Study

CBT is an approach to tourism that involves the active participation of the local community in all aspects of tourism development, from decision-making to management and marketing. TIES defines CBT as 'tourism that is owned and managed by local communities that share in the benefits and demonstrate respect for their natural and cultural environment' (TIES, 2019). CBT aims to empower local communities by involving them in the tourism development process, promoting sustainable practices, and providing authentic cultural experiences for tourists.

CBT has gained popularity in recent years, particularly in developing countries where tourism can significantly impact local communities and the environment. The UNWTO recognises the importance of CBT in achieving sustainable tourism development goals, stating that 'tourism can only be sustainable if it is based on the principles of social, economic, and environmental sustainability, with the involvement of local communities' (UNWTO, 2019).

The changing global economy has also contributed to the rise of CBT. For example, the COVID-19 pandemic has brought significant challenges to the tourism industry, with many countries experiencing a sharp decline in tourism revenue due to travel restrictions and safety concerns. This has highlighted the need for more sustainable and resilient tourism models to adapt to changing circumstances and promote local economic development.

CBT can support the recovery of the tourism industry in the post-COVID-19 era by providing a more sustainable and community-centred approach. By involving the local community in tourism development, CBT can create a sense of ownership and responsibility for tourism activities, leading to greater participation and engagement from residents. This can contribute to the preservation of natural and cultural resources and promote the development of SMEs that can provide alternative sources of income for local communities.

Therefore, this study is an effort to identify CBT in a changing economy. It carried as a case study based on the tourism industry in Sri Lanka. The reason is that Sri Lanka is facing considerable challenges during this ongoing economic crisis. Due to that, CBT is identified as an economic generating tool in Sri Lanka tourism.

CBT in the Global

CBT is a form of sustainable tourism that emphasises the participation of local communities in tourism activities. It seeks to empower communities by allowing them to manage tourism resources, develop tourism products and services and benefit from tourism's economic, social and cultural impacts. CBT is gaining popularity globally to support sustainable development, preserve cultural heritage and promote social equity. This study discusses the concept of CBT, its benefits and challenges, and some examples of CBT initiatives worldwide.

Benefits of CBT

CBT can bring numerous benefits to host communities, such as:

CBT can create significant economic benefits such as employment opportunities. This would generate income for local communities and diversify local economies. For example, in Nepal, the Community Homestay Network has created over 200 jobs and generated more than US$ 100,000 in income for local families (SNV, 2020). At the same time, CBT can promote social equity by empowering marginalised communities, such as women, indigenous people and rural communities. By participating in tourism activities, they can access education, health and other services and have a voice in decision-making processes. For example, in Peru, the Awamaki organisation has created a weaving cooperative that empowers women in rural communities and provides them with income and skills (Awamaki, 2022).

CBT can be recognised as a tool for sustainable development in a country. Under sustainability, the people and the planet are vital areas apart from the economic benefits. Keeping cultural authenticity is one of the critical challenges in tourism. However, it is identified that CBT can help to preserve and promote local cultures, traditions and heritage. By sharing their culture with visitors, local communities can raise awareness and appreciation of their customs, beliefs and values. For example, in the Ecuadorian Amazon, the Kichwa community of Sani Isla has developed a tourism programme that showcases their traditional practices, such as hunting, fishing and medicinal plant use (TIES, 2019).

Furthermore, CBT can contribute to protecting and conserving natural resources and biodiversity. By involving local communities in tourism activities, they become stewards of their environment and have a vested interest in its conservation. For example, in Tanzania, the Mpingo Conservation and Development Initiative has promoted community-based forest management and sustainable harvesting of mpingo, a hardwood used in musical instruments (UNEP, 2019).

Challenges of CBT

Despite its potential benefits, CBT faces several challenges, such as: a lack of resources, market competition and mainly sociocultural issues. Local communities often need more resources, skills and knowledge to develop and manage tourism activities effectively. Therefore, they may require technical assistance, training and capacity-building to overcome these barriers. At the same time, CBT may face competition from mainstream tourism products that offer more amenities, services and marketing. Therefore, local communities must differentiate their products, improve quality and market them effectively to attract visitors.

Moreover, CBT may encounter sociocultural issues, such as conflicts over resource use, power relations and cultural appropriation. Local communities may need to address these issues through dialogue, negotiation and mutual understanding. Therefore, it is essential to manage the negatives in CBT and promote CBT more positively through proper strategic planning as it bears many optimistic benefits to its stakeholders.

CBT to Address Changing Economy

CBT has emerged as an alternative form of tourism that aims to empower local communities by involving them in developing and managing tourism activities. CBT is seen as a way to promote sustainable tourism development while also preserving local cultures and environments. This study explores the concept of CBT and its possibility of addressing the challenges in the changing economy.

CBT is 'tourism owned and operated by local communities, which leads to direct benefits for those communities and a better understanding and appreciation of the local culture, environment, and economy' (Ashley & Roe, 2002). CBT focuses on community involvement in tourism planning, development and management, as well as on creating economic opportunities for local people. CBT's main objective is to benefit the local communities and make tourism a tool for poverty reduction, cultural preservation and environmental conservation.

The Potential of CBT in Sri Lanka

Sri Lanka has a rich cultural heritage and diverse natural attractions, making it a popular destination for international tourists. However, there has been a growing interest in CBT to promote sustainable tourism development and empower local communities in recent years. In this section, the researcher will explore the potential of CBT in Sri Lanka.

Case Study: CBT in Ella Sri Lanka

Ella City is one of the major attractions in Sri Lanka. There are community-centred businesses in Ella City which can be identified as homestays, restaurants and activities. Even though the city consists of CBT, there are considerable problems and challenges during changing economy in Sri Lanka. However, the economic crisis brought more difficulties for the industry in Ella City. Significant challenges were identified as fuel issues, gas shortages, inflations, weak tourism marketing and limited training facilities. The community that only survives on the tourism industry encountered high job risk, unemployment and low income. Tourist arrivals for the destination and limited transportation facilities became a considerable problem in this area.

For example, community-based activities in this area faced considerable problems and challenges due to the economic crisis. With the increasing prices of goods and services, getting raw materials for the activity took work during this period. Even though the cost is high, it could not increase the price reasonably. Regarding the accommodation sector, the prices were increased due to the high cost of homestays and other community-based services. This made low service sales and needed to meet the expected income. Due to low sales opportunities, these services were at considerable risk. CBT can be identified as one of the sustainable trends in the tourism industry. It may consider both host and guest sustainability. However, the crisis caused high travel costs in the country. It causes to discourage high tourist involvement in the community.

Considering the entire CBT sector in Ella City, tourism infrastructure and products could be better developed and maintained. For example, handmade products such as souvenirs, pottery, Sri Lankan textiles and the Bathik industry were severely affected.

Research Box: Case Study Analysis of CBT

The study considered community-based businesses in Ella City, especially the homestays, restaurants and activities. These are the main community-oriented phenomena that can be identified in Ella City and according to that two of each category of tourism businesses are interviewed and observed. The interviews were conducted with employees, entrepreneurs tourists and the community in the area. The research conducted focused group interviews and gathered the following results based on 25 participants. The result highlighted the need for community-based development during the crisis in Sri Lanka. The responses from stakeholders in public and private sectors highlighted:

(1) Need for sustainability CBT development.
(2) The economic impact of CBT in Sri Lanka.
(3) Demand and trends for CBT in the global market.

Based on these factors, this study discusses the development and management of CBT and global best practices to enhance the sector. Furthermore, these practices provide a framework for CBT development in Sri Lanka. According to the result identified in this study, the trends and future can be enhanced based on sustainable development. Furthermore, the partnership between the public–private sector and other sectors is also much important. It is important to develop a policy framework for sustainable CBT for the changing economic environment.

Suitability of CBT in Sri Lanka

Sri Lanka has a rich cultural heritage reflected in its architecture, arts and traditions. CBT can provide opportunities for visitors to experience this cultural heritage by engaging with local communities and participating in cultural activities. This can generate income for local communities and contribute to preserving cultural traditions. At the same time, Sri Lanka is known for its diverse natural attractions, including national parks, beaches and wildlife reserves. CBT can provide opportunities for visitors to explore these natural attractions sustainably and responsibly while providing income for local communities that can be used to support conservation efforts (Samarathunga et al., 2015).

Another reason for promoting CBT in Sri Lanka is that it can empower local communities by involving them in the planning, development and management of tourism activities. This can allow local people to generate income and develop skills while promoting a sense of ownership and pride in their communities. Through this, CBT can support rural development by providing income and employment opportunities for people living in rural areas (UNDP, 2018). This can reduce poverty and promote sustainable economic growth in rural communities.

One of the most significant advantages of CBT is that it can be used to increasing cultural understanding. Sri Lanka is a country with a history that goes back 2,500 years. However, due to the 30 years of civil unrest and incidences like the Easter Attack in 2019, it has developed a negative understanding of the mindset of foreigners. Therefore, CBT can promote cultural understanding by providing opportunities for visitors to engage with local communities and learn about their customs and traditions. This promotes cross-cultural understanding and contributes to a more peaceful and tolerant society.

CBT has great potential in Sri Lanka to promote sustainable tourism development and empower local communities. By providing opportunities for visitors to engage with local communities, experience Sri Lanka's rich cultural heritage and diverse natural attractions and support rural development, CBT can contribute to poverty reduction, cultural preservation and sustainable economic growth. First, however, it is important to ensure that CBT is developed responsibly and sustainably, with the involvement and consent of local communities.

The Economic Impact of CBT in Sri Lanka

CBT has the potential to help the Sri Lankan economy by generating income and employment opportunities for local communities, promoting sustainable tourism development and supporting rural development.

One of the most significant advantages of CBT is that it can generate income for local communities by providing opportunities for visitors to engage in activities such as homestays, handicraft making and cultural performances. According to a study by Alwis (2016), CBT has the potential to provide an additional source of income for rural communities in Sri Lanka. Through this, indirectly, it can create employment opportunities for local people by involving them in the planning, developing and managing of tourism activities. According to CBT Sri Lanka (n.d.), CBT can employ local people in areas such as tour guides, transport and hospitality. This could support rural development by providing income and employment opportunities for people living in rural areas. This can reduce poverty and promote sustainable economic growth in rural communities. According to Jenkins (2019), CBT has the potential to promote rural development by providing income and employment opportunities for people living in remote areas.

Furthermore, another prime advantage of CBT is that it can promote sustainable tourism development by involving local communities in the planning and managing of tourism activities. This can ensure that tourism development is compatible with local needs and resources, and that the benefits of tourism are distributed more evenly. According to the UNDP (2018), CBT can contribute to conserving natural and cultural resources and support local ownership and control of tourism development.

In conclusion, CBT has the potential to help the Sri Lankan economy by generating income and employment opportunities for local communities, promoting sustainable tourism development and supporting rural development.

However, it is important to ensure that CBT is developed responsibly and sustainably, with the involvement and consent of local communities.

Demand and Trends of CBT in a Changing Economy

The World Tourism Organization (UNWTO) has recognised 32 locations as 'Best Tourism Villages 2022', ranging from Austria to Vietnam. The honour is given to rural areas embracing tourism as a source of growth, new employment possibilities and money while conserving and promoting community-based values and goods. The project also honours villages for their dedication to innovation and sustainability in all facets, including economic, social and environmental sustainability, as well as a focus on advancing tourism through the Sustainable Development Goals (SDGs). In total, 32 communities from 22 nations and five different world regions received the designation in 2022 (UNWTO, 2023).

The UNWTO's list of the Best Tourism Villages (Table 4.1) demonstrates how the industry can promote economic diversification and open doors for everyone outside major cities. An impartial Advisory Board evaluated the settlements using a set of standards covering nine different categories:

Table 4.1. List of Best Tourism Villages by the United Nations World Tourism Organization (UNWTO) 2022.

Austria	*Chile*	*China*	*Colombia*
Zell am See	Puqueldón	Dazhai	Choachí
Wagrain		Jingzhu	
Ecuador	*Ethiopia*	*Georgia*	*Israel*
Aguarico	Choke Mountains	Mestia	Kfar Kama
Angochagua	Ecovillage		
Italy	*Jordan*	*Mexico*	*Morocco*
Sauris-	Umm Qais	Creel	Ksar Elkhorbat Moulay
Zahre		El Fuerte	Bouzerktoune
Isola del			
Giglio			
Peru	*Portugal*	*Republic of*	*Romania*
Lamas	Castelo Novo	*Korea*	Rasinari
Raqchi		Pyeongsa-ri	
Saudi	*Slovenia*	*Spain*	*Switzerland*
Arabia	Bohinj	Rupit	Murten
AlUla Old		Alquézar	Andermatt
Town		Guadalupe	
Türkiye	*Vietnam*		
Birgi	Thái Hải		

(1) Cultural and Natural Resources.
(2) Promotion and Conservation of Cultural Resources.
(3) Economic Sustainability.
(4) Social Sustainability.
(5) Environmental Sustainability.
(6) Tourism Development and Value Chain Integration.
(7) Governance and Prioritisation of Tourism.
(8) Infrastructure and Connectivity.
(9) Health, Safety and Security.

European tourists increasingly strive to travel ethically and look for unique experiences. The biggest markets are Germany, the Netherlands and the United Kingdom. CBT has a wealth of potential for you as a business owner in the tourism industry in a developing nation by allowing visitors to observe daily life in your town. Nevertheless, despite the promising future, the CBT market is only one of the simplest to enter because it calls for various abilities, including those related to administration and organisation as well as tourism (Union, 2020).

Global Best Practices and Policies for CBT Development

Through education and training, investments, innovation and technology, UNWTO and its member states have worked together to put inclusive community development at the centre of tourism policies. This can transform the livelihoods of millions of people while preserving the environment and culture and promoting a more inclusive and sustainable recovery of tourism (World Tourism Organization & Republic of Maldives, 2020).

Under the direction of the Saudi Presidency, UNWTO and the G20 Tourism Working Group produced the AlUla Framework for Inclusive Community Development via Tourism in 2020 to advance this crucial objective. The framework encourages a holistic and integrated approach to inclusive community development through tourism, which offers direction and inspiration to all governments and other significant players in the tourism industry.

The 2022 UNWTO Global Summit on CBT, organised jointly by UNWTO and the Ministry of Tourism of the Maldives, takes place at a crucial time as the primary source markets are beginning to open up following the COVID pandemic and an increasing number of destinations are easing or lifting travel restrictions, which helps to unleash stifled demand for international tourism.

Thailand is a popular tourist destination worldwide. By offering creative ideas for redefining the nation's tourist industry, particularly from the perspective of CBT, UNDP Accelerator Lab Thailand grasped this chance to set out on a journey to assist the growing momentum for sustainable tourism. In Thailand in the 1990s, 'community-based tourism' proposes the idea of 'tourism by the local people for the local people'. Environmental conservation and waste management and tap into opportunities from the rise of corporate social responsibility (CSR) and Thailand's Bio-Circular-Green (BCG) Economy Model of the government, stakeholder collaboration, digital transformation, academia on CBT-related curriculum for young leaders and setting up CBT development funds are few actions taken by Thailand Policy Lab. Sharing experiences and learning with locals are other practices identified in Thailand's CBT (Rungchavalnont, 2022).

Conclusion

When it concludes the study of CBT in changing economy, this is a case study about Ella, Sri Lanka. The case study highlights the potential to promote and develop CBT in Ella City. It may be caused prevent the causes that arise due to nature tourism and sustainable development of the city. However, the problem of the study highlighted that the city is affected recent economic crisis in Sri Lanka. CBT provides numerous solutions to overcome the issues in changing economy. According to that, it will provide global best practices and policies based on UNWTO, European Union Commission and other best destination practices in CBT.

The considerable solution highlighted that policy framework and destination, community development plan for Community Based Tourism. Furthermore, funding is considered to enhance services and products in CBT. Fundings, policy framework and stakeholder interconnection are other keys to this niche market enhancement. Education and learning from the community are also the primary way to CBT development in changing economy with low cost and much more effective and efficient manner. Digital transformation is also trending in the industry, and the destination should also develop these facilities. Sustainable economic model development will bring a fundamental guideline to avoid upcoming issues during this kind of situation.

Discussion Questions

- What are the challenges encountered during changing economy in your CBT business?
- What kind of possibilities and potentials can you bring from the community to the tourism industry?
- What is your opinion on stakeholder participation in CBT development in this area during an economic crisis?

References

Alwis, A. C. (2016). The potential of community-based tourism in Sri Lanka: An analysis of constraints and opportunities. *Journal of Tourism and Hospitality Management*, 127–138.

Ashley, C., & Roe, D. (2002). Making tourism work for the poor: Strategies and challenges in Southern Africa. *Development Southern Africa*, 61–82.

Awamaki. (2022). *Woven in community*. https://www.awamaki.org/

Community-Based Tourism Sri Lanka. (n.d.). https://www.CBT.lk/

ILO. (2015). *Community-based tourism: A pathway to development?* International Labour Organization. https://www.ilo.org/wcmsp5/groups/public/—ed_emp/documents/publication/wcms_364234.pdf

Jenkins, C. L. (2019). Community-based tourism in Sri Lanka: A case study. *Journal of Travel Research*, 422–436.

Rungchavalnont, P. (2022, November 6). *Community-based tourism: Empowering local champions for sustainable tourism in Thailand.* United Nations Development Programme, UNDP. https://www.undp.org/thailand/blog/community-based-tourism-empowering-local-champions-sustainable-tourism-thailand

Samarathunga, W., Wimalarathana, W., & Silva, D. (2015). Community-based tourism management experience. In *International Research Symposium – The Rajarata University of Sri Lanka* (pp. 3–5).

SNV. (2020, June). *SNV Annual Report 2019.* https://snv.org/update/snv-annual-report-2019

TIES. (2019). *What is community-based tourism?* The International Ecotourism Society. https://www.ecotourism.org/what-is-ecotourism/what-is-community-based-tourism

UNDP. (2018). *Community-based tourism.* United Nations Development Programme. https://www.greengrowthknowledge.org/

UNEP. (2019). *UNEP Annual Report.* United Nations Environment Programme.

Union, E. (2020, August 4). *The European market potential for community-based tourism.* CBI. https://www.cbi.eu/market-information/tourism/community-based-tourism/market-potential

UNWTO. (2019). *International tourism highlights.* World Tourism Organization.

UNWTO. (2023, January 19). *'Best tourism villages' of 2022 named by UNWTO.* Best Tourism Villages. https://www.unwto.org/tourism-villages/en/news/best-tourism-villages-of-2022-named-by-unwto/

World Tourism Organization, U. N., & the Republic of Maldives, M. of T. (2020, May 20). *UNWTO global summit on community-based tourism.* UNWTO.

WTTC. (2019). *Economic impact reports.* World Travel and Tourism Council. https://wttc.org/research/economic-impact#:~:text=In%202019%2C%20the%20Travel%20%26%20Tourism,the%20share%20increasing%20to%206.1%25

Chapter 5

Conceptual Evaluation of Community-Based Tourism

Özcan Zorlu, Ali Avan and Ahmet Baytok

Afyon Kocatepe University, Türkiye

Learning Objectives

After reading and studying this chapter, you should be able to:

- understand the concept, definition, characteristics and principles of community-based tourism (CBT);
- understand the role of local communities and stakeholders in CBT and their participation in planning and decision-making processes;
- understand the theoretical weaknesses of CBT as a tourism type.

Abstract

The objective of this study is to make a conceptual analysis of Community-based tourism (CBT). CBT, one of the tourism activities that internalised sustainability, has several common threads with nature-based tourism activities. However, these similarities/common elements must be more understandable between those relevant tourism activities. From this fact, this research aims to assign a theoretical framework for CBT and reveal the differences between CBT activities from other tourism types.

Tourism, unavoidably, is one of the critical sectors that require sustainable usage of resources. Because visiting natural, historical and cultural values/attractions constitute the primary reason for tourists' travel motivations, making those values/attractions sustainable for the future is essential. However, the sustainable usage of those values/attractions can be enabled with protection and maintenance balance. On the other hand, this philosophy will only come true if obtaining the locals support it. Therefore, CBT propounds that local people should make the most of tourism at all levels,

---

Future Tourism Trends Volume 1, 61–73
Published under exclusive licence by Emerald Publishing Limited
doi:10.1108/978-1-83753-244-520241005

especially the economic contribution. Within this context, the importance and necessity of these issues will be manifested in this chapter, presenting a conceptual framework. Additionally, this chapter will support other researchers in constituting the conceptual framework and will guide policymakers and other stakeholders to understand the importance of CBT.

Keywords: Community-based tourism; sustainability; socio-economic and environmental development; stakeholders; local communities; Ayazini

Introduction

Using environmental resources, tourism, directly and indirectly, affects the natural and human-made sociocultural environment and converts these environmental resources into sales in the consumer market (Garrod & Fyall, 1998, p. 199). In this frame, the conservation and development of natural areas and local culture are essential to pursue the existence of tourism and its economic benefits (Mathieson & Wall, 1982, p. 97). At this point, the concept of sustainability, based on environmentalism in the 1970s, was formed to reduce and prevent human activities' adverse effects on natural resources. Sustainable development is 'an equilibrium among human activities and their natural, social, and cultural environment' (Middleton & Hawkins, 1998, p. 247). Hence, ensuring sustainability is only possible with sustainable development. Unlike the classic protectionism notion in resource use, sustainable development, which is generated as a result of the combination of economic development theory and environmentalism approaches (Hardy et al., 2002, p. 475; Sharpley, 2000, p. 2), proposes the socio-economic transformation without degradation of social and ecological systems on which societies and peoples depend (Gunn, 1994, p. 85). It also refers that there is a complex and convergent relationship among the environment, economy and communities. The studies carried out from the first period to the present day considering sustainable development emphasise that although the development criteria and plans are well-defined, there are constant problems in implementing economic development, social equality and environmental protection issues (Drexhage & Murphy, 2010, p. 6).

The reflection of sustainability and sustainable development in the tourism sector is the formation of alternative tourism as an idea or philosophy and the enhancement of alternative tourism types. Within the context of the different approaches to the sustainability of various researchers in tourism literature (Clarke, 1997; Jafari, 1989, 2001; Sharpley, 2000; Weaver, 2006), it can be assigned the time and reasons for forming the alternative tourism phenomenon. Clarke's (1997) movement and convergence approach to the realisation of the goals of reducing the negative impacts of the tourism sector in positioning sustainable tourism; Sharpley's (2000) alternative development theory referring the participation of locals in tourism development; Weaver's (2006) comprehensive sustainable tourism type (to surveillance the equality among environmental, sociocultural and economic impacts) encompassing a holistic approach; and the adapting platform of Jafari (1989, 2021) who categorised the transformation of tourism industry beginning from the 1950s in four platforms (advocacy, cautionary, adapting and knowledge-based), explain the formation period and the formation reasons of alternative tourism.

On the other hand, Cohen (1987) asserts that alternative tourism developed as a reaction, as a counterculture to modern consumption concepts and exploitation of third-world countries. The response to the exploitation of third-world countries is also the adoption of small-scale and locally-owned alternative tourism development approaches rather than the approaches referring to using local resources through new colonisation and transferring benefits to developed countries. These two under-standings have supported the development of alternative tourism types. Responsible tourism, pro-poor tourism, cultural tourism, ecotourism and community-based tourism (CBT) can be counted among the types of tourism that have developed within the scope of alternative tourism and have many common points with each other. CBT is one of the alternative tourism types developing in this context.

CBT is usually considered ecotourism or a concept closely related to the sustain-able tourism approach and making different senses for different people a critical concept (Ishihara, 2020). CBT is a form of tourism that proposes to put local people at the centre of tourism development planning and management in a destination to create a sustainable industry. Locally-owned operation of tourism enterprises, increasing local employment and positive approach and attitude of locals to tourists could also be considered as other primary and essential determinants of CBT (Blackstock, 2005). CBT, defined as 'managed and owned by the community for the community', is developing with joint efforts of different stakeholders such as gov-ernments, tourism enterprises, non-governmental organisations (NGOs), interna-tional organisations, local communities and the environment. Extensive literature reveals that researchers have searched for and discussed the CBT concept for about 60–70 years. Among the main focal points of the related studies, relations between stakeholders, the reasons and conditions for the success and failure of CBT projects, and models for creating CBT processes come to the fore. This chapter shares the basic conceptual information about sustainability and the emergence of alternative tourism, which encompasses the CBT notion. In the central part, firstly, the con-ceptual evaluation of CBT (CBT idea, CBT definitions, features, benefits and stakeholders) and its criticism will be made with the support of the literature.

CBT Concept

Tourism is a distant and extraneous concept for many developing countries that need more experience, depend on foreign expertise and help distinguish long-term and short-term community effects (Tolkach & King, 2015, p. 396). Within this context, CBT is a means that creates opportunities for the development of communities that do not have sufficient economic resources, knowledge and experience in planning, management, marketing and other processes in the field of tourism and improves the livelihoods of people with low incomes (Mtapuri & Giampiccoli, 2013). Mayaka et al. (2019, p. 177) claim that CBT could be discussed from four perspectives: needs, process, participatory approach and participatory outcomes. Based on this emphasis on CBT, the authors clarify two main strategies for CBT: 'facilitating tourism development in communities' and 'developing communities through tourism'.

CBT, generally considered a means of socio-economic and environmental development by offering tourism products (Goodwin & ve Santilli, 2009, p. 4), is an effective way of enabling sustainability in tourism (Blackstock, 2005, p. 39). CBT has emerged as a possible solution to the adverse effects of mass tourism (López-Guzmán et al., 2013, p. 131). The emergence of CBT can be placed in the context of two developments: one, recent worldwide activities that promote sustainable and responsible forms of tourism, and two, the emergence of alternative approaches to protected area management and conservation efforts that link biodiversity conservation with local community development (Hiwasaki, 2006, p. 677). CBT activities aim for tourism development, considering the needs and benefits of the local community. Thus, CBT requires steady institutions to enhance local participation and promote locals' economic, social and cultural well-being. Within this period, the CBT development strategy should be compatible with other tourism activities and other components of the local economy (Brohman, 1996, p. 60). Despite this, it is noteworthy that CBT cannot solve all development problems in poor communities but provides an additional strategy through which communities can diversify their livelihoods (Mtapuri & Giampiccoli, 2013, p. 4). Four dimensions are critical to CBT activities to achieve sustainability:

(1) CBT incomes should exceed costs.
(2) CBT activities should be ecologically sustainable.
(3) Cost and benefits should be equally distributed among all participants in the activity.
(4) An appropriate organisation should be ensured.

Additionally, the CBT organisation should be established to represent all community members' interests and reflect actual ownership (Rozemeijer, 2001, p. 13; Salazar, 2012, p. 11). Considering four dimensions, a well-structured small-scale CBT empowers local communities. First, local communities recognise the importance of natural resources and control over their development and share costs and benefits equally. Furthermore, such CBT initiatives could complement and counterbalance mass tourism (Kibicho, 2008, p. 227).

CBT primarily promotes community participation and seeks to deliver more comprehensive community benefits (Mgonja et al., 2015, p. 378). The community should be well-informed and educated about its trust to ensure maximum community participation. The CBT management should be transparent and accountable in its dealings. Moreover, stakeholder dialogue should be encouraged and facilitated (Stone & Stone, 2011, p. 112).

Moreover, local, regional and national networks should be established to enhance the efficiency of local community participation. Those networks reinforce the bonding relations inside the community, facilitate the development process and enable them to gain essential ties and connections with the outside world (Iorio & Corsale, 2014, pp. 48–49). Considering community participation and networks, successful CBT development requires coordinated joint ventures consisting of governmental, non-governmental and private entities. Different CBT development strategies are possible within this context. Those entities (particularly private ones) could be a single community-owned, or they could be micro-small enterprises under a joint organisation leading CBT initiative for the sake of them. No matter which strategy is implemented, different CBT actors are linked with others regarding community benefits. The participation of community members in the various activities should all be related to the CBT for coordination and cooperation in the CBT ventures (Mtapuri & Giampiccoli, 2013, pp. 7–9). As a result, CBT is a tourism type that is insigne of the proposition 'small is beautiful'. CBT could be characterised by small-scale enterprises that have strong ties with local industries and are human-centred. Further, as a part of the social economy, CBT could be implied as a counterweight to neocolonialism, neoliberalism and conventional mass tourism (Tolkach & King, 2015).

CBT Definition

In the literature, there are various CBT definitions. For instance, World Wildlife Fund (WWF) considers CBT as a form of ecotourism and defines it as 'where the local community has substantial control over, and involvement in, its development and management, and a major proportion of the benefits remain within the community' (Denman, 2001, p. 2). UNWTO (2009) defined CBT as tourism development that places the community at the centre of tourism planning, development and management. CBT aims to improve the residents' quality of life by optimising local economic benefits, protecting the natural and cultural environments, and providing high-quality visitor experiences. Meanwhile, Hiwasaki (2006, p. 677) proposes a comprehensive definition with four targets based on the project of Asia-Pacific Environmental Innovation Project/Research on Innovation and Strategic Policy Options, as follows: '(1) empowerment and ownership: increasing local community empowerment and ownership through participation in the planning and management of tourism in protected areas; (2) conservation of resources: having a positive impact on the conservation of natural and cultural resources in and around protected areas through tourism; (3) social and economic development: enhancing or maintaining economic and social activities in and around a protected area, with substantial benefits – economic and social – to the local community; and (4) quality visitor experience: ensuring that visitor experience is of high quality and is socially and environmentally responsible'. On the other hand, Goodwin and ve Santilli (2009, p. 129) define CBT as 'tourism owned and managed by communities and intended to deliver wider community benefit'. Haywood (1988, p. 106) defines community participation as a 'process of involving all [stakeholders] (local government officials, local citizens, architects, developers, business people, and planners) in such a way that decision-making is shared'. The CBT definitions of different institutions and researchers show that the scope of the tourism type and the necessity of its execution as a process is emphasised. The most highlighted issues in definitions are particularly the central role of locals as decision-makers in the process making and the necessity of ownership of local resources at an economic level. This fact also stems from the fact that CBT is the key to protecting local culture and environmental resources; namely, it is the key to sustainability. Ultimately, environmental resources are the assets that locals use to create economic value both for tourism-oriented usage and different purposes. Within this scope, as emphasised in other parts of this chapter, when the financial contribution and the welfare level of the environmental resources to the local people through tourism is higher than the other alternatives, it will be easier to protect relevant environmental resources.

CBT Characteristics and Benefits

A well-structured and successful CBT initiative should have specific characteristics that provide multidimensional benefits regardless of implementation scale and place. Initially, CBT initiatives must protect and enhance the quality of natural resources and cultural heritage (Denman, 2001, p. 14). A successful and sustainable CBT depends on effectively managing scarce resources and maximising the return from distributing and managing commercial activities, including service management and tourism. In this context, tourism should transform existing and planned resources into more economic and social returns than alternatives or substitutes (Robinson & Wiltshire, 2011). When properly implemented and managed, CBT supports promoting community benefits and the development of a sustainable, long-term local tourism industry (Ellis & Sheridan, 2015, p. 254).

A well-planned and managed CBT initiative also means to have some positive outcomes, as given below (ASEAN, 2016; Asker et al., 2010, p. 3):

- CBT supports local economic development through the diversification of employment.
- CBT involves and empowers the community to ensure ownership and transparent management.
- Improves social well-being and maintenance of human dignity.
- CBT is financially viable and self-sufficient.
- CBT respects and encourages equitable participation of the local community and establishes partnerships with relevant stakeholders.
- Include a fair and transparent benefit-sharing mechanism.
- CBT is ecologically sustainable and minimises impact on the environment, and contributes to natural resource conservation.
- CBT conserves and promotes living cultural heritage, tradition and welfare.
- CBT educates visitors about culture and nature.
- CBT demonstrates good management practices and gains recognised standing with relevant authorities.
- Improves the quality of visitor experiences by strengthening meaningful host and guest interaction.

Goodwin and ve Santilli (2009), who discuss the established criteria of a successful CBT from the perspectives of different stakeholders, show in which areas the benefits are manifested. These are social capital and empowerment, local economic development, livelihoods, conservation/environment and commercial viability.

Social capital and empowerment: Informing the local people to build trust and ensure their participation in CBT activities will make them feel empowered; in other words, it will strengthen their sense of having a say (Ellis & Sheridan, 2015). The high level of control and economic benefits of CBT are dominated by residents, one of the generally accepted aspects from the theoretical point of view (Iorio & Corsale, 2014, p. 234). However, as emphasised by Stone and Stone (2011, p. 112), ensuring the participation of local people at the highest level is possible if they are well-informed, educated and trustworthy. Furthermore, to achieve full empowerment, management must be transparent and accountable and enable local people to access all resources.

Local economic development: Rapid tourism development provides economic benefits in the short term. However, the social and economic costs very quickly exceed the benefits. Therefore, CBT locally-owned tourism businesses, especially in developing countries, both for the continuation of the financial benefit and the successful existence of the long-term industry, support and develop the local economy with its contributions such as increasing employment, meeting the needs of local sectors and reducing economic leakages (Ellis & Sheridan, 2015).

Livelihoods: As Iorio and Corsale (2014, p. 251) emphasise, 'Tourism is enhancing the livelihood strategies of the community members. It has become a complementary activity to agriculture, crafting, and territory activities and assures cash income that the families use to meet their needs'.

Conservation/environment: As a natural consequence of the increase in economic income with tourism, local people will become more sensitive to the use and protection of cultural and natural resources within the scope of ensuring the continuity of their income through tourism. At this point, the necessity of raising awareness of the local people about tourism will create added value in ensuring sustainability.

Commercial viability: Defined as 'the ability of a business, product, or service to compete effectively and to make a profit' (Cambridge Dictionary, 2023), commercial viability requires the consideration of supply and demand conditions and good planning of management and marketing activities within the scope of CBT. In a sense, this will benefit the continuation of the existence of the enterprises and improve competitiveness by increasing the knowledge and skills of the local people in service delivery, quality, supply chain and other issues.

Discussions on CBT

CBT is a type of tourism in which local people and local public authority, central public authority, international official and non-governmental organisations and especially private sector enterprises for tourism purposes are stakeholders

(Ishihara, 2020). Considering the roles of stakeholders in CBT, in particular, central and local public authorities come to the fore as the decision-maker regarding legal regulations and infrastructure in all studies. International officials and non-governmental organisations ensure that local people are informed about tourism, especially with the projects they create and their financial support, sustainable development and educational activities. Private sector enterprises ensure the arrival of tourists to the destination by their intermediary roles, promoting and marketing the destination (especially the superstructure) and increasing the touristic appeal of the destination. On the other hand, local people play an active role in developing the sector in the destination and are considered decision-makers (Ishihara, 2020, p. 29). Theoretically, CBT comes to the forefront with its features of reducing poverty and increasing the welfare of the local people as a type of tourism in which the local people have a say and control in all stages of tourism in a destination. The irony in CBT starts at this point. First of all, although the tourism superstructure owned by the local people is the main target in CBT, the emphasis in many studies that the local people's economic opportunities are insufficient creates a contrast.

The other contrast is that the constant participation of locals is an indispensable criterion at all stages of planning, establishing, developing and executing CBT in a destination. Because locals need to gain sufficient knowledge about tourism, tourism businesses, tourism marketing, tourism planning, etc. Simons and de Groot (2015, p. 73) explain developing CBT, empowering communities and realising the power transition (from other stakeholders to local people) within the metaphor of 'to open a Pandora's Box' and draws attention to the fact that it is difficult to measure power and empowerment. At this point, the actual situation is that the locals are the resource utilisation stakeholders in using economic resources within the tourism scope. They are taken into account due to their role as they are decisive in tourist satisfaction and touristic consumption in the destination. Blackstock (2005) supports all these evaluations, expresses CBT as naive and unrealistic, and criticises that society is considered a homogeneous structure in the evaluations within the scope of CBT because many societies are complex, heterogeneous and stratified. Therefore, subgroups and individuals focus on their interests before collective well-being and joint action remain theoretically grounded.

A Case Study on Ayazini Village

Türkiye, one of the leading tourism destinations on the Mediterranean Coast, presents more and more examples of the CBT concept due to increased awareness about the protection of the environment and alternative tourism activities. However, CBT initiatives become more feasible if the initiative has government assistance and bonus. Within this context, Ayazini village, which belongs to the İhsaniye district of Afyonkarahisar, constitutes a good example of CBT development through a joint venture of the government and public enterprises. Ayazini has recently gained popularity with its Phrygian monuments, village life and micro-scale locally-owned tourism enterprises. Ayazini, home to many civilisations, such as the Roman and Byzantine Empires, Seljuks and Ottoman Empire, has one natural protected area and three archaeological protected areas. The village has many rock graves and tombs (Aslanlı mezar, Tanrıçalı mezar, Soylu mezarı), rock settlements, churches (Meryem, Nazlı, Metropolis and Genç İsa) and chapels. For more than 10 years, this small village has hosted a major transformation from a traditional farm village to a tourism destination due to vigorous efforts of government and private stakeholders under the leadership of the Afyonkarahisar governorate. Within this context, the Afyonkarahisar governorate put the Ayazini project into practice.

Regarding the project, a meeting centre and exhibition hall opened at the village entrance, street rehabilitation works, landscaping, in-village infrastructure works (parquet, cleaning, etc.), cleaning works of archaeological sites, tourist promenade and lighting works were carried out. Some of these works are still in progress. In addition to these, cafes, restaurants and tea houses serving the local delicacies of Afyonkarahisar were opened, as well as handicraft sales points. Most of these micro-scale enterprises are owned by local people who live in the village. Today, tourism activities in the village are majorly carried out by the locals as proposed in CBT philosophy, and the sustainability of the area is supported by both locals and the government.

Research Box

Avan and Zorlu (2017), also the authors of this chapter, in their paper exploring CBT activities within the context of sustainability of tourism, render Gelemiş Village's current position regarding CBT initiatives as given below.

Purpose: The study aims to determine the current position of Gelemiş Village in the context of CBT initiatives and then present a CBT development model considering different actors representing the local community.

Design/methodology/approach: The interview technique was used together with secondary data analysis. Secondary data analysis mainly consists of literature on CBT and general information about Gelemis (location, geography, population, number of tourism establishments, etc.). To obtain in-depth information, face-to-face interviews were conducted with the participants determined by the judgemental sampling technique. During the interviews, data were obtained on topics such as CBT potential, ownership of enterprises, employment strategies, local entrepreneurship rate, etc. The data obtained by the interview technique were analysed by content analysis.

Findings: The research results show that Gelemis village, known as Patara, has some advantages in terms of CBT, such as the protected nature of the region, small-scale tourism businesses serving traditional food, high level of local ownership and employment. However, CBT also has disadvantages, such as the lack of a tourism master plan that needs to be prepared specifically for Patara, insufficient government support and incentives, lack of tourism associations and non-governmental organisations managed by local people and partially ineffective marketing efforts.

Conclusion

Tourism is one of the sectors in which sustainability and sustainable development are most interesting. Because the primary resources are natural and sociocultural, tourism shapes the society and environment where it develops (Murphy, 1983). However, the private sector's creation of a superstructure and resource use, taking into account pure economic concerns, ironically destroys the objects that are the source of its existence (Briassoulis, 2002, p. 1076). Butler (1999) states that the most fundamental problem in tourism is ensuring all stakeholders' satisfaction. The expectation of the tourist in a destination is satisfaction, while the expectation of the locals is benefiting from the infrastructure and economic benefits provided by tourism, and at the same time, the protection of cultural and natural values and the absence of problems such as water, energy, crowding and pollution. The expectation of the sector enterprises is the preservation of their economic profitability and the continuity of the demand.

On the other hand, central and local policymakers expect their policies and plan to yield results as soon as possible to ensure their continuity in administration. However, implementation of plans for sustainability takes time (Dodds & Butler, 2009, p. 48). Therefore, according to Weaver (2006, p. 22), if the external factors that have an impact on sustainability are not taken into account, especially in the management and planning of the destination and businesses, sustainable tourism becomes a meaningless structure. Alternative tourism, which became fashionable in the 1980s with cultural heritage and sustainable development, and which is the umbrella concept of tourism types that are sensitive to nature or need to be developed according to sustainable principles, is a phenomenon that is criticised as something that can happen or as a 'Trojan Horse' metaphor and is still discussed today (Butler, 1990).

As emphasised in the previous sections, CBT is a type of tourism central to the local people's economic, social, cultural, psychological and political dimensions in the development of tourism in a destination or region. CBT is one of the best alternative development models for economically depressed rural areas. In addition, CBT is integrated with sustainable tourism and environmental protection (Lee et al., 2013, p. 456). One of the reasons for the development of CBT in different parts of the world is that tourists seek different places from traditional destinations. According to the researchers, this enables the creation of new products through tourism as a complementary sector that is not a substitute for traditional industries that create jobs and increase welfare for local communities.

However, it is stated in the literature that many CBT projects fail for different reasons. For example, Goodwin (2006) points out that CBT projects fail for the following reasons (Cited by Stone & Stone, 2011):

• There needs to be more understanding of the need for commercial activities. For example, local people must sell crafts, food, accommodation and wildlife or cultural experiences to tourists. This is the only way to ensure sustainable local income or conservation funds.

- There needs to be more engagement with the private sector, including travel agents, tour operators and hoteliers. The earlier this engagement takes place and the closer the partnership is, the more likely the project will succeed.
- Location is critical. For poor people to benefit, tourists must stay near these communities. Very few communities have tourism assets that are sufficiently strong to attract tourists. They rely on selling complementary goods and services. Tourists need to be close by for this to happen. CBT projects, only sometimes, provide appropriate tourism facilities for generating income. Too many CBT initiatives rely on building lodges, which are capital intensive and need considerable maintenance, or walking trails from which it can be challenging to secure revenue.
- Protected areas increasingly rely on money from tourists to pay for conservation initiatives. As a result, local communities often have to compete with conservation projects for revenues.

CBT, a type of tourism developed primarily in developing countries to improve the welfare of the local people and protect the resources, functions like a double-edged sword, while providing opportunities to local communities and people to increase income or welfare also results in a large portion of the benefit flowing out (Mitchell & Reid, 2001, p. 114). As a result, as Simons and de Groot (2015, p. 78) stated, although CBT will not bring what was initially intended and emphasised in its theoretical structure within the scope of hope remaining in Pandora's Box, it will continue to be a type of tourism and increase its benefits, especially with the optimistic approaches of the stakeholders in their areas of responsibility and volunteering practices. Moreover, it will significantly contribute to protecting natural resources and culture.

Discussion Questions

- How does CBT differ from traditional forms of tourism in terms of its impact on the environment and local communities?
- What are the main challenges in ensuring the sustainability of CBT activities?
- How can CBT be effectively controlled to minimise negative impacts on nature to maximise local people's participation and the local communities' welfare?

References

ASEAN. (2016). *ASEAN community based tourism standard.* https://www.asean.org/wp-content/uploads/2012/05/ASEAN-Community-Based-Tourism-Standard.pdf

Asker, S., Boronyak, L., Carrard, N., & Paddon, M. (2010). *Practical community based tourism: A best practice manual.* Sustainable Tourism Cooperative Research Centre, Griffith University.

Avan, A., & Zorlu, Ö. (2017). Community-based tourism activities within the context of sustainability of tourism: A case of Gelemiş Village. In *Proceeding Book of 1st*

International Sustainable Tourism Congress, Kastamonu, Türkiye, November 23–25.

Blackstock, K. (2005). A critical look at community-based tourism. *Community Development Journal, 40*(1), 39–49.

Briassoulis, H. (2002). Sustainable tourism and the question of the commons. *Annals of Tourism Research, 29*(4), 1065–1085.

Brohman, J. (1996). New directions in tourism for third world development. *Annals of Tourism Research, 23*(1), 48–70.

Butler, R. W. (1990, Winter). Alternative tourism: Pious hope or trojan horse. *Journal of Travel Research*, 40–45.

Butler, R. W. (1999). Sustainable tourism: A state of the art review. *Tourism Geographies, 1*(1), 7–25.

Cambridge Dictionary. (2023). Commercial viability. https://dictionary.cambridge. org/dictionary/english/commercial-viability,2023

Clarke, J. (1997). A framework of approaches to sustainable tourism. *Journal of Sustainable Tourism, 5*(1), 224–233.

Cohen, E. (1987). Alternative tourism-a critique. *Tourism Recreation Research, 12*(2), 13–18.

Denman, R. (2001). *Guidelines for community-based ecotourism development.* WWF International Publications.

Dodds, R., & Butler, R. W. (2009). Inaction more than action. In S. Gössling, C. M. Hall, & D. B. Weaver (Eds.), *Sustainable tourism perspectives on systems, restructuring and innovations* (pp. 43–57). Routledge, Taylor & Francis Group.

Drexhage, J., & Murphy, D. (2010, September). *Sustainable development: From Bruntland to Rio 2012.* Background Paper. International Institute for Sustainable Development, United Nations Headquarters.

Ellis, S., & Sheridan, L. (2015). The role of perceptions in achieving effective community-based tourism for least developed countries. *Anatolia, 26*(2), 244–257.

Garrod, B., & Fyall, A. (1998). Beyond the rhetoric of sustainable tourism? *Tourism Management, 19*(3), 199–212.

Goodwin, H., & ve Santilli, R. (2009). Community-based tourism: A Success. *ICRT Occasional Paper, 11*(1), 1–37.

Gunn, C. A. (1994). *Tourism planning: Basics, concepts, cases* (3rd ed.). Taylor & Francis.

Hardy, A., Beeton, R. J. S., & Pearson, L. (2002). Sustainable tourism: An overview of the concept and its position in relation to conceptualisation of tourism. *Journal of Sustainable Tourism, 10*(6), 475–496.

Haywood, K. M. (1988). Responsible and responsive tourism planning in the community. *Tourism Management, 9*(2), 105–118.

Hiwasaki, L. (2006). Community-based tourism: A pathway to sustainability for Japan's protected areas. *Society & Natural Resources, 19,* 675–692.

Iorio, M., & Corsale, A. (2014). Community-based tourism and networking: Viscri, Romania. *Journal of Sustainable Tourism, 22*(2), 234–255.

Ishihara, Y. (2020). Overview of community-based tourism. In S. K. Walia (Ed.), *The Routledge handbook of community-based tourism management: Concepts, issues & implications* (pp. 26–38). Routledge. http://www.routledgehandbooks.com/doi/10. 4324/9780429274664-4. Accessed on January 25, 2023.

Kibicho, W. (2008). Community-based tourism: A factor-cluster segmentation approach. *Journal of Sustainable Tourism, 16*(2), 211–231.

Lee, T. H., Jan, F. H., & Yang, C. C. (2013). Conceptualizing and measuring environmentally responsible behaviors from the perspective of community-based tourists. *Tourism Management, 36,* 454–468.

López-Guzmán, T., Borges, O., & Hernandez-Merino, M. (2013). Analysis of community-based tourism in Cape Verde. A study on the Island of São Vicente. *Anatolia, 24*(2), 129–143.

Mathieson, A., & Wall, G. (1982). *Tourism: Economic, physical and social impacts.* Longman.

Mayaka, M., Croy, W. G., & Cox, J. W. (2019). A dimensional approach to community-based tourism: Recognising and differentiating form and context. *Annals of Tourism Research, 74,* 177–190.

Mgonja, J. T., Sirima, A., Backman, K. F., & Backman, S. J. (2015). Cultural community-based tourism in tanzania: Lessons learned and way forward. *Development Southern Africa, 32*(3), 377–391.

Middleton, V. T. C., & Hawkins, R. (1998). *Sustainable tourism: A marketing perspective.* Butterworth-Heinemann.

Mitchell, R. E., & Reid, D. G. (2001). Community integration island tourism in Peru. *Annals of Tourism Research, 28*(1), 113–139.

Mtapuri, O., & Giampiccoli, A. (2013). Interrogating the role of the state and nonstate actors in community-based tourism ventures: Toward a model for spreading the benefits to the wider community. *South African Geographical Journal, 95*(1), 1–15.

Murphy, P. (1983). Tourism as a community industry. *Tourism Management, 4*(3), 180–193.

Robinson, P., & Wiltshire, P. (2011). Community tourism. In P. Robinson, S. Heitmann, & P. Dieke (Eds.), *Research themes for tourism* (pp. 87–99). CAB International.

Rozemeijer, N. (2001). *Community-based tourism in Botswana: The SNV experience in three community-tourism projects.* SNV Botswana.

Salazar, N. B. (2012). Community-based cultural tourism: Issues, threats and opportunities. *Journal of Sustainable Tourism, 20*(1), 9–22.

Sharpley, R. (2000). Tourism and sustainable development: Exploring the theoretical divide. *Journal of Sustainable Tourism, 8*(1), 1–19.

Simons, I., & de Groot, E. (2015). Power and empowerment in community-based tourism: Opening pandora's box? *Tourism Review, 70*(1), 72–84.

Stone, S. L., & Stone, T. M. (2011). Community-based tourism enterprises: Challenges and prospects for community participation; Khama Rhino Sanctuary Trust, Botswana. *Journal of Sustainable Tourism, 19*(1), 97–114.

Tolkach, D., & King, B. (2015). Strengthening community-based tourism in a new resource-based island nation: Why and how? *Tourism Management, 48,* 386–398.

Weaver, D. (2006). *Sustainable tourism: Theory and practice.* Elsevier, Butterworth-Heinemann.

World Tourism Organization. (2009). *Tourism and community development – Asian practices.* UNWTO. https://doi.org/10.18111/9789284411948

Part 4

Ecotourism

Chapter 6

Ecotourism: For a Sustainable Future

Erdem Baydeniz[a], Hakkı Çılgınoğlu[b] and Mustafa Sandıkcı[a]

[a]Afyon Kocatepe University, Türkiye
[b]Kastamonu University, Türkiye

Learning Objectives

After reading and studying this chapter, you should be able to:

- understand the definition and principles of ecotourism and sustainability;
- identify tourism's positive and negative impacts on natural and cultural environments;
- understand the role of local communities in ecotourism, their participation in planning and decision-making and the importance of responsible tourism practices.

Abstract

Ecotourism is a sustainability approach that has emerged as an alternative to the negative environmental impacts of tourism, where natural, cultural and historical values are used as sources. Ecotourism is a nature-based tourism activity that ensures the sustainability of natural resources and promotes the economic development of local populations. It also preserves sociocultural values and protects the ecological system for future generations. However, if ecotourism is well-controlled, it can positively affect nature, natural life, local people and the local and national economy. This study highlights the importance of ecotourism for sustainability in the tourism industry. It examines ways to deal with the ecotourism phenomenon. In this direction, the study defines the concepts of ecological tourism and sustainability. It describes the general characteristics of ecotourism and sustainable tourism and the developing and potential environmental impacts associated with them. The study highlights that any tourist activity that does not have a sustainable quality cannot be long-term and will increase awareness on this topic.

Future Tourism Trends Volume 1, 77–89
Copyright © 2024 Erdem Baydeniz, Hakkı Çılgınoğlu and Mustafa Sandıkcı
Published under exclusive licence by Emerald Publishing Limited
doi:10.1108/978-1-83753-244-520241006

Keywords: Ecotourism; sustainable tourism; sustainable development; environmental interaction; environmental management

Introduction

Ecotourism, also known as sustainable tourism, is a form of travel that minimises the negative impact on the natural environment and local communities while promoting conservation and sustainability (Mbaiwa & Stronza, 2009). As the world becomes increasingly aware of the need to protect the planet for future generations, ecotourism has gained popularity to achieve these goals (Powell & Ham, 2008). This chapter will discuss the concept of ecotourism and its role in promoting sustainable development. Ecotourism can take many forms, but at its core, it is a form of responsible travel that priorities the protection of natural and cultural heritage (Siswanto, 2015). Additionally, ecotourism often includes education and awareness-raising activities, such as guided tours and workshops, to educate visitors about the importance of conservation and sustainable development (Mirsanjari, 2012). One of the critical benefits of ecotourism is its potential to promote conservation and sustainability (Butcher, 2007). By generating income for local communities and providing an alternative to more destructive forms of development, ecotourism can help to protect vulnerable ecosystems and preserve traditional cultures (Reimer & Walter, 2013). Additionally, ecotourism can promote a greater understanding and appreciation of the natural world, leading to more informed and responsible environmental decision-making.

However, it is essential to note that ecotourism is not without its challenges. Ensuring sustainable ecotourism practices requires careful planning and management (Cater, 1993). There are instances where poor planning can lead to negative impacts, such as overcrowding and degradation of natural resources. Furthermore, the benefits of ecotourism are only sometimes equitably distributed. There have been instances where local communities have yet to benefit from ecotourism activities as much as they should (Scheyvens, 2000).

In conclusion, ecotourism has the potential to promote sustainable development and conservation by generating income for local communities and raising awareness about the importance of protecting natural and cultural heritage. However, to truly achieve this potential, it is essential to ensure that ecotourism practices are well-planned and managed and that the benefits are shared equitably. Therefore, this chapter draws attention to the importance of ecotourism and how it can be a sustainable solution for the future of the travel industry while preserving our planet and culture.

Case Study

Looking at the etymological origin of the word 'sustainable', it comes from the Latin 'subgenre', which is used in the sense of 'protecting' or 'supporting from below' (Ozmehmet, 2008). The concept of sustainable tourism is based on the idea of 'sustainable development'. Despite the diversity in the definition of sustainability, the

United Nations Commission on Environment and Development has accepted the idea of sustainability. Scientific circles widely accept the definition made in the Brundtland report in 1987. According to the Brundtland report, sustainable development is 'the ability of humanity to meet the needs of the present without compromising the ability of future generations to meet their own needs' (Wackernagel, 1994, p. 32). According to this, sustainable development is based on three main elements: the unsustainability of current growth, meeting today's needs and ensuring future generations' quality of life and welfare (Keiner, 2005).

Busch (2011) defines sustainability as the ability of a society, ecosystem or any system with continuity to maintain its operations uninterrupted without being damaged by not overusing or overloading the primary resources vital to the system. According to Gilman (1992), in the broadest sense, sustainability is defined as the ability of a society, ecosystem or any continuing system to maintain its function without consuming its essential resources for an uncertain future. Neumayer (1999) states that sustainability is 'economy within society and society within the economy and environment'. It emphasises that the economy, environment and society create sustainability. The United Nations World Tourism Organization (UNWTO) has also adopted three main elements in evaluating sustainable tourism. Environmental, social and economic elements make up these. The main factor of the sustainability concept is humans and the environment. Since meeting human needs depends on the environment, all fields that study human–environment relations must act according to the principle of sustainability. Kurter and Ünal (2009) observed increased studies following sustainability principles in many fields, including history, geography, sociology, political science, philosophy, archaeology, anthropology, biology, medicine, economy, finance and tourism.

Sustainable Tourism

Sustainable tourism began to develop in the 1970s as a solution to the adverse effects of over-tourism, which exceeded the region's carrying capacity and damaged environmental and cultural values (Bramwell & Lane, 2012). Gössling et al. (2009) note that sustainable tourism development is achieved through the cooperation of the local population, the tourism industry and the interdependent environmental supporters of sustainable tourism. The main difference between sustainable and traditional tourism is that in sustainable tourism, the local population not only benefits from the tourism industry but also plays a role at certain stages (Okazaki, 2008).

Sustainable tourism is a holistic approach to tourism development that balances economic, social and environmental concerns. Hunter (1995) notes that sustainable tourism involves protecting and preserving the natural, cultural and heritage resources being visited and the active participation of local communities. This allows tourism development to be a positive experience for tourists and host communities and for the resources to be managed sustainably for the future (Byrd, 2007). Sustainable tourism is a tourism approach that recognises the importance of the local community and aims to maximise its economic benefits. This concept has been widely used since the early 1990s (Edgell & Swanson, 2013). Villanueva-Cuevas (2011) notes that the European Union recognised this concept in the 'Green Book' published on tourism in 1995. In addition to all the developments mentioned, the following approaches have been described in explaining the development of the concept of sustainable tourism (Demir & Çevirgen, 2006, p. 101):

- *Polarised Approach*: Sustainable and mass tourism are seen as opposite poles. Here, if sustainable tourism is to be developed, it is stated that it is necessary to give up mass tourism.
- *Integrative Approach*: Sustainable and mass tourism are no longer opposite poles. However, it is accepted that there are differences between them while also having some common points.
- *Actionable Approach*: A positive approach in which activities that make mass tourism more sustainable are proposed.
- *Compromise Approach*: An approach that fights for all types of tourism to be sustainable.

These approaches provide different perspectives on how sustainable tourism can be developed and implemented. Byrd (2007) notes that while mass tourism has some criticisms, it is not always necessary to abandon it but to find ways to make it more sustainable. These can include regulating the number of visitors, preserving natural and cultural resources, promoting local cultures and economies and incorporating the needs and perspectives of local communities (Hassan, 2000). Sustainable tourism is often used in the same sense as nature tourism or ecotourism. However, sustainable tourism carries a different meaning from these two concepts (Butler, 1999). The 2001 Mountainous Areas Ecotourism Conference in Salzburg, Austria, determined that ecotourism is not synonymous with sustainable tourism and that the sustainability of all types of tourism can be discussed. However, ecotourism should be considered one of the tourism types (Gunes & Hens, 2007).

In the concept of sustainable tourism, not only the sustainability of the physical environment but also the social, cultural and economic systems must be considered as well (Lane & Kastenholz, 2015). Sustainable tourism is an integrated approach to responsible and ethical travel that minimises the negative impacts on the environment, local communities and cultures while maximising the benefits for all stakeholders (Chiu et al., 2014). This approach is closely related to other concepts such as responsible tourism, green tourism, community-based tourism and ethical tourism (Giampiccoli et al., 2020; Okazaki, 2008).

Responsible tourism is planned and executed in a way that considers the activities' social, economic and environmental impacts. It aims to balance economic growth, social development and environmental protection (Fernandes et al., 2021). On the other hand, green tourism focuses on environmentally friendly travel. It seeks to minimise the impact on the natural environment. It often concentrates on ecotourism, travel to natural areas and sustainable practices such as energy conservation and waste reduction (Kiper, 2013). Community-based tourism is a concept that emphasises developing tourism opportunities that are owned, managed and benefit the local communities (Prakoso et al., 2020). Ethical tourism refers to travel guided by ethical principles such as respect for human rights, fairness and justice. It may include activities such as voluntourism and responsible and sustainable tourism practices (Jamal & Camargo, 2014). All these terms share the same goal: to minimise the negative impact of tourism while maximising the positive impact on local communities, cultures and the environment. Therefore, we can consider different aspects of the same comprehensive approach to responsible and ethical travel.

Ecotourism

Ecotourism, or nature-based tourism, is a form of travel that focuses on appreciating and conserving natural and cultural resources (Blamey, 2001). Sustainable tourism minimises the negative impacts on the environment and local communities while maximising the benefits for all stakeholders (Wan & Li, 2013). The concept of ecotourism has recently gained popularity as global awareness of the need to protect the environment for future generations has grown (Lane & Kastenholz, 2015). Ecotourism involves visiting natural areas such as national parks, wildlife reserves and UNESCO World Heritage sites and participating in hiking, bird watching and wildlife safaris (Hvenegaard & Dearden, 1998).

Ecotourism is a form of tourism that involves observing and appreciating nature and local cultures in natural areas while minimising negative impacts and supporting conservation efforts. Ecotourism can generate economic, social and environmental benefits for host communities, tourists and natural areas. However, it also poses challenges and risks if not well-managed. Understanding ecotourists perceptions, preferences, satisfaction and loyalty is essential.

Case scenario: You are a tourism researcher who wants to study the interlinkage of perceived ecotourism design affordance, the perceived value of destination experience, destination reputation and loyalty among the tourists visiting Frig Valley, Afyon, Turkey. Frig Valley is an emerging ecotourism destination that offers diverse natural attractions, such as rock formations, caves, wetlands and wildlife. It also has a rich cultural heritage from the ancient Phrygian civilisation that carved houses, temples, monuments and roads on the rocks. You can access a database of 400 tourists who visited Frig Valley in the past year and completed a questionnaire about their ecotourism experience. The questionnaire includes items that measure the four constructs of interest and demographic and trip-related information.

Question: How can you ensure that the sample represents the ecotourist population it represents? If you had information about the composition of the population, you could design a process by which to draw tourists that resemble the composition of the target population. For example, you could use stratified random or cluster sampling to ensure that the sample reflects the distribution of ecotourists by age, gender, nationality, travel mode, length of stay or other relevant variables. Other sampling methods may work better for your research if you do not have this information. For example, you could use purposive sampling to select tourists who meet specific criteria or characteristics relevant to your research question. Alternatively, you could use snowball sampling to recruit tourists referred by other tourists who have already participated in your study. What are the advantages and disadvantages of these sampling methods for your research? How would you justify your choice of sampling method?

Ecotourism and Environmental Interaction

Ecotourism is a form of tourism that focuses on appreciating and conserving natural environments while minimising negative impacts on the environment and local communities (Björk, 2007). It is often associated with hiking, bird watching and wildlife viewing. Therefore, it is considered a sustainable form of tourism. However, as ecotourism continues to grow, it is crucial to consider this type of tourism's potential environmental interactions and impacts (Wood, 2002).

One potential impact of ecotourism is the disturbance of wildlife and their habitats (Shannon et al., 2017). This can occur through hiking and wildlife viewing activities and developing tourism infrastructure such as roads, trails and lodges (Rahman et al., 2022). This disturbance can change the behaviour and distribution of wildlife and impact their breeding and feeding patterns. Additionally, the construction of tourism infrastructure can lead to the fragmentation of habitats and the displacement of wildlife (Lane & Kastenholz, 2015).

Another potential impact of ecotourism is the degradation of ecosystems and natural resources (Ogutu, 2002). This can occur through activities such as off-road driving and removing natural resources such as firewood and water (Fernandes et al., 2021). Additionally, ecotourism can lead to the introduction of invasive species and disease spread, which can negatively impact native species and ecosystems. Finally, ecotourism also potentially impacts local communities' socioeconomic well-being (Mbaiwa, 2012). In developing countries, people often see ecotourism as generating income and promoting sustainable development. However, suppose ecotourism needs to be managed correctly (Dorobantu & Nistoreanu, 2012). In that case, it can negatively impact local communities, such as the displacement of people and the erosion of traditional cultures and livelihoods.

To minimise negative impacts and maximise ecotourism benefits, Wan and Li (2013) suggest adopting a holistic and participatory approach to ecotourism planning and management. This approach should involve the active participation of local communities and incorporating best practices in environmental management and sustainable development. Furthermore, we should continuously evaluate and monitor sustainable ecotourism to ensure it preserves the environment and benefits the local communities (Barrow, 2006). Overall, ecotourism has the potential to provide significant environmental, social and economic benefits. However, it is essential to understand the potential environmental interactions and impacts of ecotourism. We must manage ecotourism to minimise negative impacts and maximise benefits.

The Natural, Social and Economic Impacts of Ecotourism

Ecotourism is a form of tourism that emphasises the conservation of natural environments and the well-being of local communities (Amalu et al., 2018). However, as ecotourism grows in popularity, it is vital to consider the potential impacts that it may have on the natural, social and economic systems in which it operates (Stronza, 2007).

From a biological perspective, ecotourism can positively and negatively impact the environment (Hultman et al., 2015). On the positive side, ecotourism can increase awareness and support for conservation efforts, which can protect natural resources and biodiversity. Boley and Green (2016) found that ecotourism can encourage local communities to conserve natural resources and protect wildlife habitats. However, ecotourism can also lead to negative impacts, such as the disturbance of wildlife and the degradation of ecosystems. In order to minimise these negative impacts, it is essential to adopt best practices in environmental management and conservation and continuously monitor and evaluate ecotourism operations (Gaymans & Hikes, 1996).

From a social perspective, ecotourism can positively and negatively impact local communities. On the positive side, ecotourism can provide economic benefits, such as employment and income opportunities (Stronza & Gordillo, 2008). Additionally, ecotourism can promote cultural preservation by highlighting local people's customs, traditions and stories. However, ecotourism can also lead to negative impacts, such as the displacement of local communities and the erosion of traditional cultures and livelihoods (Amalu et al., 2018). Eshun and Tichaawa (2019) suggest involving local communities in ecotourism planning and management to minimise adverse impacts. This ensures that ecotourism benefits are distributed equitably among residents.

From an economic perspective, ecotourism can benefit local communities and the country. Ecotourism can generate income, create jobs and promote sustainable development. However, to realise these benefits, it is essential to ensure that ecotourism operations are well-managed and financially sustainable (Zacarias & Loyola, 2017). This may involve promoting investment in local businesses, encouraging fair trade and ecotourism-friendly policies and ensuring that a fair share of the revenue generated by ecotourism is reinvested in local communities and conservation efforts (Gurung & Seeland, 2011).

Consumer Profile in Ecotourism

Ecotourism is a growing market segment. Many consumers seek experiences that allow them to connect with nature and learn about the environment (Carvache-Franco et al., 2022; Ruhanen, 2019). Therefore, understanding the consumer profile for ecotourism is vital for tourism operators and marketers (Beaumont, 2011). Cheng et al. (2022) found that ecotourism consumers are well-educated individuals with middle to high incomes. They are often from urban areas and likely intensely interested in the environment, conservation and sustainable development (Kwan et al., 2008; Perera et al., 2012). They also tend to be older, with many retiring or nearing retirement age. This demographic is often associated with having more disposable income, which they can spend on travel and experiences.

Regarding travel behaviour, ecotourism consumers tend to be more adventurous and independent than traditional tourists. They are often interested in outdoor activities such as hiking, wildlife and bird watching (Arnegger et al., 2010). They also tend to seek more authentic experiences, such as staying in local homestays or camping, rather than traditional hotels. Additionally, they are more likely to engage in voluntourism, or volunteer-based travel, which can involve working on conservation projects or assisting with community development (Ellis, 2003).

Ecotourism consumers also tend to be more environmentally conscious and socially responsible than traditional tourists (Suhariyanto, 2022). As a result, they often prioritise travel companies and operators that have a solid commitment to sustainable practices and are willing to pay a premium for eco-friendly products and services. They are also interested in learning about local communities' culture and way of life. They are often willing to engage in activities that promote cultural exchange (Scheyvens, 2000).

Research Box

Translating research themes into research questions.

Ecotourism proliferates worldwide as more tourists seek environmentally friendly and authentic travel experiences. While ecotourism aims to promote conservation and benefit local communities, too much tourism activity can threaten the natural environments and cultures on which ecotourism depends. As an environmentalist and an avid ecotourist, you may have noticed some worrying changes in popular ecotourism destinations. There are more tourists, infrastructure and commercialisation in these places. If left unregulated, you are concerned that ecotourism could threaten environmental integrity and cultural authenticity.

Their concerns could form an important research topic. Some key questions emerge:

- At what point does ecotourism move from sustainable to unsustainable? How can this tipping point be identified?
- What are the impacts (environmental, social and economic) of uncontrolled ecotourism growth? How can these impacts be measured and evaluated?
- What management strategies can effectively curb tourism and ensure a sustainable future for eco-tourism? How can these strategies be implemented ethically and equitably?

These questions explore the complex relationship between eco-tourism, sustainability and impacts. Systematically exploring them could provide insights into maximising ecotourism's benefits while mitigating costs. Policies and practices could then be updated to support a sustainable future for this important global industry. In conclusion, unregulated ecotourism poses risks to the very values on which it relies. Research is urgently needed to identify limits, measure trade-offs and guide the responsible management of ecotourism for future generations. With a view to a sustainable future, the research questions here aim to transform ecotourism from a threat to an opportunity.

Conclusion

Ecotourism is a vital tool for promoting sustainable development and preserving natural environments. Ecotourism can create sustainable livelihoods and preserve biodiversity by providing economic incentives for local communities to conserve and protect their natural resources. Additionally, ecotourism allows individuals to learn about and experience different cultures and ecosystems, promoting a greater understanding and appreciation of the natural world. However, it is essential to note that we must manage and regulate ecotourism adequately to achieve its potential benefits. Ecotourism operators and local governments should collaborate to develop sustainable management plans prioritising natural resource conservation and community well-being. Additionally, ecotourism must be inclusive, ensuring that the benefits of tourism are shared among all members of local communities, including women and marginalised groups (Nyaupane & Poudel, 2011). Overall, ecotourism has the potential to play a critical role in creating a sustainable future for both people and the environment.

It is a powerful tool for promoting conservation, sustainable development and fostering a deeper connection with nature (Robinson, 2004). Moreover, with proper management and planning, it can be used to create a more sustainable future for all. In addition to the benefits already mentioned, ecotourism can also contribute to developing local infrastructure and services. This can include constructing lodges, visitor centres and trails and providing transportation, guides and souvenirs. These investments can improve the overall ecotourism experience, create jobs and stimulate economic growth in local communities.

Moreover, ecotourism can also provide financial resources for conservation and environmental protection. By charging visitors, a fee to access protected areas or participate in ecotourism activities, local communities and governments can generate revenue for conservation and management efforts. This funding can be used for habitat restoration, wildlife monitoring and invasive species control initiatives. Finally, ecotourism has the potential to foster a sense of environmental stewardship among both locals and visitors.

By providing opportunities for people to learn about and appreciate the natural world, ecotourism can inspire individuals to take action to protect the environment and conserve natural resources. Additionally, by providing economic incentives for local communities to conserve their natural resources, ecotourism can foster a sense of pride and ownership over the environment, encouraging people to take an active role in its protection. In conclusion, ecotourism can significantly benefit both local communities and the environment. Furthermore, ecotourism can be crucial in building a more sustainable future by creating sustainable livelihoods, preserving biodiversity and fostering environmental stewardship. Therefore, promoting and supporting ecotourism as a critical sustainable development and conservation tool is essential.

Discussion Questions

- How does ecotourism differ from traditional forms of tourism regarding its impact on the environment and local communities?
- What are the main challenges in ensuring the sustainability of ecotourism activities?
- How can ecotourism be effectively controlled to minimise negative impacts on nature, local people and the economy?
- What are some examples of successful ecotourism initiatives, and what elements have contributed to their success?

References

Amalu, T. E., Otop, O. O., Duluora, E. I., Omeje, V. U., & Emeana, S. K. (2018). Socio-economic impacts of ecotourism attractions in Enugu state, Nigeria. *Geojournal, 83*(6), 1257–1269.

Arnegger, J., Woltering, M., & Job, H. (2010). Toward a product-based typology for nature-based tourism: A conceptual framework. *Journal of Sustainable Tourism, 18*(7), 915–928.

Barrow, C. (2006). *Environmental management for sustainable development.* Routledge.

Beaumont, N. (2011). The third criterion of ecotourism: Are ecotourists more concerned about sustainability than other tourists? *Journal of Ecotourism, 10*(2), 135–148.

Björk, P. (2007). Definition paradoxes: From concept to definition. In *Critical issues in ecotourism* (pp. 41–63). Routledge.

Blamey, R. K. (2001). Principles of ecotourism. In *The encyclopedia of ecotourism* (pp. 5–22). Cabi Publishing.

Boley, B. B., & Green, G. T. (2016). Ecotourism and natural resource conservation: The 'potential' for a sustainable symbiotic relationship. *Journal of Ecotourism, 15*(1), 36–50.

Bramwell, B., & Lane, B. (2012). Towards innovation in sustainable tourism research? *Journal of Sustainable Tourism, 20*(1), 1–7.

Busch, T. (2011). Organisational adaptation to disruptions in the natural environment: The case of climate change. *Scandinavian Journal of Management, 27*(4), 389–404.

Butcher, J. (2007). *Ecotourism, NGOs and development: A critical analysis.* Routledge.

Butler, R. W. (1999). Sustainable tourism: A state-of-the-art review. *Tourism Geographies, 1*(1), 7–25.

Byrd, E. T. (2007). Stakeholders in sustainable tourism development and their roles: Applying stakeholder theory to sustainable tourism development. *Tourism Review, 62*(2), 6–13.

Carvache-Franco, M., Carrascosa-López, C., & Carvache-Franco, W. (2022). Market segmentation by motivations in ecotourism: Application in the Posets-Maladeta Natural Park, Spain. *Sustainability, 14*(9), 4892.

Cater, E. (1993). Ecotourism in the third world: Problems for sustainable tourism development. *Tourism Management, 14*(2), 85–90.

Cheng, Y., Hu, F., Wang, J., Wang, G., Innes, J. L., Xie, Y., & Wang, G. (2022). Visitor satisfaction and behavioural intentions in nature-based tourism during the COVID-19 pandemic: A case study from Zhangjiajie National Forest Park, China. *International Journal of Geoheritage and Parks, 10*(1), 143–159.

Chiu, Y. T. H., Lee, W. I., & Chen, T. H. (2014). Environmentally responsible behaviour in ecotourism: Antecedents and implications. *Tourism Management, 40*, 321–329.

Demir, C., & Çevirgen, A. (2006). *Ekoturizm yönetimi* (ISBN 975-591-844-2, p. 222). Nobel yayın dağıtım.

Dorobantu, M. R., & Nistoreanu, P. (2012). *Rural tourism and ecotourism – The main priorities in sustainable development orientations of rural local communities in Romania.* Economy Transdisciplinarity Cognition.

Edgell, D. L., Sr., & Swanson, J. R. (2013). *Tourism policy and planning: Yesterday, today, and tomorrow.* Routledge.

Ellis, C. (2003). Participatory environmental research in tourism: A global view. *Tourism Recreation Research, 28*(3), 45–55.

Eshun, G., & Tichaawa, T. M. (2019). Reconsidering participation for local community well-being in ecotourism in Ghana. *Geo Journal of Tourism and Geosites, 27*(4), 1184–1200.

Fernandes, S., Ferreira, D., Alves, T., & de Sousa, B. M. B. (2021). Glamping and the development of sustainable tourism: A Portuguese case study. In *Handbook of sustainable development and leisure services* (pp. 201–222). Springer.

Gaymans, H., & Hikes, V. (1996). Five parameters of ecotourism. *The Ecotourism Equation: Measuring the Impacts. Bulletin, 99.*

Giampiccoli, A., Mtapuri, O., & Dłużewska, A. (2020). Investigating the intersection between sustainable tourism and community-based tourism. *Tourism: An International Interdisciplinary Journal, 68*(4), 415–433.

Gilman, R. (1992). "Sustainability", from the 1992 UIA/AIA Call for Sustainable Community.

Gössling, S., Hall, C. M., & Weaver, D. B. (2009). Sustainable tourism futures: Perspectives on systems, restructuring and innovations. In *Sustainable tourism futures* (pp. 21–36). Routledge.

Gunes, G., & Hens, L. (2007). Ecotourism in old-growth forests in Turkey: The Kure mountains experience. *Mountain Research and Development, 27*(3), 281–283.

Gurung, D. B., & Seeland, K. (2011). Ecotourism benefits and livelihood improvement for sustainable development in the nature conservation areas of Bhutan. *Sustainable Development, 19*(5), 348–358.

Hassan, S. S. (2000). Determinants of market competitiveness in an environmentally sustainable tourism industry. *Journal of Travel Research, 38*(3), 239–245.

Hultman, M., Kazeminia, A., & Ghasemi, V. (2015). Intention to visit and willingness to pay a premium for ecotourism: The impact of attitude, materialism, and motivation. *Journal of Business Research, 68*(9), 1854–1861.

Hunter, C. J. (1995). On the need to re-conceptualise sustainable tourism development. *Journal of Sustainable Tourism, 3*(3), 155–165.

Hvenegaard, G. T., & Dearden, P. (1998). Ecotourism versus tourism in a Thai National Park. *Annals of Tourism Research, 25*(3), 700–720.

Jamal, T., & Camargo, B. A. (2014). Sustainable tourism, justice and an ethic of care: Toward the just destination. *Journal of Sustainable Tourism, 22*(1), 11–30.

Keiner, M. (2005). Re-emphasising sustainable development—The concept of 'Evolutionability'. *Environment, Development and Sustainability, 6*(4), 379–392.

Kiper, T. (2013). *Role of ecotourism in sustainable development.* InTech.

Kurter, N., & Ünal, E. H. (2009). Sürdürülebilirlik Kapsamında Ekoturizmin Çevresel. *Ekonomik ve Sosyo-Kültürel Etkileri, Kastamonu Üniversitesi, Orman Fakültesi Dergisi, 9*(2), 146–156.

Kwan, P., Eagles, P. F., & Gebhardt, A. (2008). A comparison of ecolodge patrons' characteristics and motivations based on price levels: A case study of Belize. *Journal of Sustainable Tourism, 16*(6), 698–718.

Lane, B., & Kastenholz, E. (2015). Rural tourism: The evolution of practice and research approaches – Towards a new generation concept? *Journal of Sustainable Tourism, 23*(8–9), 1133–1156.

Mbaiwa, J. E. (2012). The realities of ecotourism development in Botswana. In *Responsible tourism* (pp. 233–252). Routledge.

Mbaiwa, J. E., & Stronza, A. L. (2009). The challenges and prospects for sustainable tourism and ecotourism in developing countries. In *The Sage handbook of tourism studies* (pp. 333–351). SAGE Publications.

Mirsanjari, M. M. (2012). Importance of environmental ecotourism planning for sustainable development. *OIDA International Journal of Sustainable Development, 4*(2), 85–92.

Neumayer, E. (1999). The ISEW: Not an index of sustainable economic welfare. *Social Indicators Research,* 77–101.

Nyaupane, G. P., & Poudel, S. (2011). Linkages among biodiversity, livelihood, and tourism. *Annals of Tourism Research, 38*(4), 1344–1366.

Ogutu, Z. A. (2002). The impact of ecotourism on livelihood and natural resource management in Eselenkei, Amboseli ecosystem, Kenya. *Land Degradation & Development, 13*(3), 251–256.

Okazaki, E. (2008). A community-based tourism model: Its conception and use. *Journal of Sustainable Tourism, 16*(5), 511–529.

Ozmehmet, E. (2008). Dünyada ve Türkiye Sürdürülebilir Kalkınma Yaklaşımları. *Yaşar Üniversitesi E-Dergisi, 3*(12), 1853–1876.

Perera, P., Vlosky, R. P., & Wahala, S. B. (2012). Motivational and behavioural profiling of visitors to forest-based recreational destinations in Sri Lanka. *Asia Pacific Journal of Tourism Research, 17*(4), 451–467.

Powell, R. B., & Ham, S. H. (2008). Can ecotourism interpretation lead to pro-conservation knowledge, attitudes and behaviour? Evidence from the Galapagos Islands. *Journal of Sustainable Tourism, 16*(4), 467–489.

Prakoso, A. A., Pradipto, E., Roychansyah, M. S., & Nugraha, B. S. (2020). Community-based tourism: Concepts, opportunities and challenges. *Journal of Sustainable Tourism and Entrepreneurship, 2*(2), 95–107.

Rahman, M. K., Masud, M. M., Akhtar, R., & Hossain, M. M. (2022). Impact of community participation on sustainable development of marine protected areas: Assessment of ecotourism development. *International Journal of Tourism Research, 24*(1), 33–43.

Reimer, J. K., & Walter, P. (2013). How do you know it when you see it? Community-based ecotourism in the Cardamom mountains of southwestern Cambodia. *Tourism Management, 34*, 122–132.

Robinson, J. (2004). Squaring the circle? Some thoughts on the idea of sustainable development. *Ecological Economics, 48*(4), 369–384.

Ruhanen, L. (2019). The prominence of eco in ecotourism experiences: An analysis of post-purchase online reviews. *Journal of Hospitality and Tourism Management, 39*, 110–116.

Scheyvens, R. (2000). Promoting women's empowerment through involvement in ecotourism: Experiences from the Third World. *Journal of Sustainable Tourism, 8*(3), 232–249.

Shannon, G., Larson, C. L., Reed, S. E., Crooks, K. R., & Angeloni, L. M. (2017). Ecological consequences of ecotourism for wildlife populations and communities. In *Ecotourism's promise and peril* (pp. 29–46). Springer.

Siswanto, A. (2015). Ecotourism development strategy Baluran national park in the regency of Situbondo, East Java, Indonesia. *International Journal of Evaluation and Research in Education, 4*(4), 185–195.

Stronza, A. (2007). The economic promise of ecotourism for conservation. *Journal of Ecotourism, 6*(3), 210–230.

Stronza, A., & Gordillo, J. (2008). Community views of ecotourism. *Annals of Tourism Research, 35*(2), 448–468.

Suhariyanto, J. (2022). Green marketing and ecotourism model development concept. *Journal Mantic, 6*(2), 1823–1828.

Villanueva-Cuevas, A. (2011). New perspectives for tourism in European Union law. *International Business & Economics Research Journal, 10*(7), 13–20.

Wackernagel, M. (1994). *Ecological footprint and appropriated carrying capacity: A tool for planning toward sustainability*. School of Community and Regional Planning. University of British Columbia.

Wan, Y. K. P., & Li, X. (2013). Sustainability of tourism development in Macao, China. *International Journal of Tourism Research, 15*(1), 52–65.

Wood, M. (2002). *Ecotourism: Principles, practices and policies for sustainability*. United Nations Environment Programme.

Zacarias, D., & Loyola, R. (2017). How ecotourism affects human communities. In *Ecotourism's promise and peril* (pp. 133–151). Springer.

Chapter 7

Green Hotels and Green Practices in South Africa

Samuel Uwem Umoh

University of Hradec Kralove, Czech Republic

> **Learning Objectives**
>
> After reading this chapter, you should be able to:
>
> - understand the definition and principles of green hotels and green practices;
> - highlight the need for green hotels and practices;
> - identify the case study on green hotels and practices in South African hotels.

Abstract

The hotel sector in South Africa is also aware of the detrimental impact of its activities on the environment. As a result, it has taken steps to mitigate such effects, evidenced by implementing green hotel practices. 'Green hotels' refers to lodging establishments that try to consume less energy, water and materials while still offering high-quality services. Unfortunately, although the hotel sector contributes significantly to employment and economic growth globally, its activities harm the environment through pollution, overuse of natural resources and solid and liquid waste.

This chapter discusses the concepts of green hotels and green practices. This chapter also highlights the need for green practices and identifies a case study on green hotels and practices in a South African context. This chapter found that the green hotel sector implements green practices, such as water-saving practices due to the risk of water insecurity, the growing demand for sustainability and the necessity to boost revenues. Green hotels and practices are a step to actualise the objectives of Sustainable Development Goals (SDGs) 12 and 13, which focus on clean water and sanitation

Future Tourism Trends Volume 1, 91–98

Copyright © 2024 Samuel Uwem Umoh

Published under exclusive licence by Emerald Publishing Limited

doi:10.1108/978-1-83753-244-520241007

and climate change, respectively. The study underscores the importance of green practices and how South Africa responds to the challenge. It is believed that hotels contribute significantly to environmental degradation, but they can also help to preserve the environment through their activities through green practices. Strategies like adopting green practices would be a remedy to mitigate pollution and its effects on environmental sustainability.

Keywords: Tourism; eco-tourism; green practices; green tourism; green hotels; sustainability

Introduction

The hospitality industry, specifically hotels, is increasing its engagement with climate change mitigation and adaptation issues by becoming green hotels and adopting green practices. This alludes to hotel activities significantly causing environmental deterioration in key areas such as energy, water and waste. The hotel industry is not left behind due to environmental awareness of the impact of its activities on the environment (Dwivedi et al., 2022; Mihaela et al., 2021). Hence, to preserve the environment and meet the demands of environmentally conscious customers, the hospitality industry is rapidly expanding globally in its acceptance and implementation of such green practices (Acampora et al., 2022; Robertson & Barling, 2017). Many hotels are adopting green practices and becoming 'eco-hotels' to target eco-aware customers, boost financial performance and lessen hotel activities' impact on the environment by making environmental considerations a core component of their business activities (Acampora et al., 2022; Hou & Wu, 2021). The Green Hotels Association (2019) describes green hotels as environmentally friendly properties where owners implement measures that conserve energy and water and reduce solid waste while saving money to help protect the earth. Green hotel is a lodge that adheres to green living principles and is committed to protecting the environment (Abdou et al., 2020; Acampora et al., 2022). Green practices are ethical business decisions and eco-friendly initiatives promoted in the hotel industry to decrease solid waste, preserve water and energy, save operational expenses and safeguard the environment (Dwivedi et al., 2022; Mihaela et al., 2021).

Green building designs are an important aspect of the green characteristic of green hotels (Hou & Wu, 2021). Green Hotel practices are environmentally friendly initiatives that aim to reduce the negative impact on the environment by reducing water consumption (e.g. by installing water-efficient devices and equipment and implementing the reuse of a linen and towel programme) saving energy (e.g. by installing energy-efficient appliances and implementing renewable energy programmes) (Abdou et al., 2020; Acampora et al., 2022; Green Hotels Association, 2019). Hotels can use a variety of green practices as preventative steps to cut costs where possible. This includes recycling old beds, linen reuse programmes in guest rooms, green dining and green procurement (Dwivedi et al., 2022; Green Hotels Association, 2019; Mihaela et al., 2021). In recognition of the benefits of green practices, institutions such as the World Travel and Tourism Council (WTTC) monitor and provide green policies and green accreditation to certify hotels as sustainable based on green building rating systems, criteria and hotel sustainability practices (Christina et al., 2022; Leadership in Energy and Environmental Design-LEED, 2020; United Nations Environment Programme's-UNEP, 2021).

Hence, green hotels have environmentally friendly policies evident in management declaration on their commitment to the environment and protecting it from the depletion of natural resources (Ismail & Rogerson, 2016). The term 'green hotels' refers to energy-efficient buildings and environmentally responsible ones aimed at sustainability (Green Building Council South Africa (GBCSA), 2014). Furthermore, green hotels seek to address environmental issues, such as global climate change, ozone depletion and pollution (Dwivedi et al., 2022; Mihaela et al., 2021). This also includes minimising carbon footprint and solid waste (Imran & Reynolds, 2016). The motive behind green hotels and practices is also echoed in the Paris Accord 2017, which seeks to reverse the increasingly negative effects of carbon omission on climate change, also referred to as global warming, which is increasingly becoming an issue of great concern.

Consequently, green hotels diligently practice environmental management, such as procedures, practices and initiatives, reducing detrimental environmental impacts from their operations (Green Hotels Association, 2019). In addition, a set of best practices distinguishes green hotels. These best practices include implementing in-room recycling, selling organic food in restaurants and reusing linens when visitors stay for more than one night (Enz, 1999). Given this context, this chapter discusses the concepts of green hotels and green practices. This chapter also highlights the need for green practices and identifies a case study on green hotels and practices in a South African context.

Need for and Benefits of Implementing Green Practices in Green Hotel

Hotel sectors significantly contribute to environmental deterioration because of the industry's extensive usage of energy, water and garbage due to continuous hotel operations (Dwivedi et al., 2022; Mihaela et al., 2021). Environmental issues, including global warming, pollution, biodiversity loss, depletion of natural resources, ozone layer depletion, deforestation and waste management, are recognised as significant issues on a global scale which necessitates hotels to review the impact of their activities on the environment (Acampora et al., 2022; Robertson & Barling, 2017). Although the hotel sector contributes significantly to employment and economic growth globally, its activities harm the environment through pollution, overuse of natural resources and solid and liquid waste (Christina et al., 2022; De Freitas, 2018; Giessen, 2018). Consequently, there is a growing concern for sustainable and eco-friendly practices in the hotel sector because the effects of global warming are being witnessed in tourist destinations (Imran & Reynolds, 2016). Furthermore, the Emissions Gap Report 2021 from the United Nations Environment Programme (UNEP) cautioned that despite renewed climate commitments from nations, the globe may still experience a 2.7°C increase in average global temperature by the end of the century (UNEP, 2021).

The motive behind green hotels alludes to the need for hotels to increase their engagement with issues around climate change mitigation and adaptation (Acampora et al., 2022; Ismail & Rogerson, 2016). Green practices are adopted in hotels because their activities significantly impact global resources due to hotel operations. These include high consumption of water, high demand for energy used to make the guests comfortable and the production of large quantities of waste (Mbasera et al., 2018). In recognition, the hotel industry has started several initiatives demonstrating its commitment to sustainability, including adopting environmental management systems, placing eco-labels and adopting sustainable behaviour norms (Abdou et al., 2020; Dwivedi et al., 2022; Mihaela et al., 2021; Robertson & Barling, 2017). Green practices are also echoed in the United Nations' Sustainable Development Goals (SDGs) 12, highlighting the importance of sustainable consumption and production. Adopting green practices in hotels has many advantages, such as increasing profitability, revenue and profits while saving money (Abdou et al., 2020; Acampora et al., 2022). Green hotel practices are crucial in actualising SDGs (Abdou et al., 2020; Ismail & Rogerson, 2016). Thus, green hotels play a vital role in actualising SDGs (Abdou et al., 2020). Many countries are developing strategies to increase sustainability, as evidenced by 81% of tourists being concerned about the environment and inclined to stay in 'green' hotels (Diana, 2021). South Africa hotels are not an exception.

The South Africa National Development Plan reiterates that South Africa is committed to reducing its carbon emissions below a set baseline of 34% by 2020 and 42% by 2025 based on the Intended National Determined Contribution (INDC). This is evident in implementing the 'Responsible Tourism Guidelines of 2002', which echoes that the tourism sector minimises negative economic, environmental and social impacts. Despite the benefit of green practices, the challenges of implementing green hotels and green practices are rife and highlighted in the literature (De Freitas, 2018; Ismail & Rogerson, 2016; Leonard & Dlamini, 2015; Mbasera et al., 2018). Ismail and Rogerson (2016) argue that environmental sustainability is not a priority for most hotels despite the importance of green hotel practices. Other challenges include limited hotel procurement, government support, measures, initiatives and commitment to encourage environmental sustainability (De Freitas, 2018; Giessen, 2018).

Mbasera et al. (2018) examine the link between green management policies and hotel performance in two Sub-Saharan developing countries from the manager's perspective. They argue that green hotel responds to stakeholders' environmental concerns, including (internal stakeholders) customers, employees, shareholders, owners, suppliers and (external stakeholders) academics, government agencies and competitors. They argue that only a few hotel managers have green management policies. Mail & Guardian (2019) notes that the biggest hurdle in adopting green hotel practices is convincing suppliers to walk the green path; if they did exist, they were expensive. Mail & Guardian (2019) reported that the average cost of utilities per room, night in 2015, in a green hotel was recorded at R27.39 versus a standard Cape Town hotel of R90.30. This suggests some barriers and obstacles to effectively implementing sustainable, environmentally friendly hotel initiatives. Rahman et al. (2015) argue that there is a conflict between green hotel practices and hotel guests' satisfaction because the conservation of resources could detract from the quality of a guest's visitor experience. Hence, effective green practices also require both the customer and the hotel to actively reduce adverse environmental impacts and commit to mitigating environmental damage (Mbasera & Mutana, 2014). Ismail and Rogerson (2016) argue that many hotels use 'greenwashing' only for marketing purposes and that greening is a marketing ploy without being green. Hotels equate simple practices such as changing bed linen less frequently or eliminating disposable toiletry in guest rooms as green hotel practices (Ismail & Rogerson, 2016; Rahman et al., 2015).

Case Study: Protea Hotel South Africa

In the context of South Africa, Chapter 5 of the National Development Plan (NDP) reiterates the need for a transition to a low-carbon and resource-efficient economy for South Africa. South Africa's vision for 2030 is underpinned by the country's path towards a low-carbon, resilient economy and society is expected to be marked by a decreased reliance on low-carbon energy sources and natural resources while also skilfully balancing the twin developmental imperatives of increasing employment and reducing poverty and inequality (Adila et al., 2021, p. 14).

This also necessitates South African hotels implementing green practices to minimise their negative environmental impact. Although there are no direct green policies in the hotel sector in South Africa, the environmental management policy and the 2002 responsible tourism are measured by the South African government put in place to ensure the environment.

Green initiatives like energy and water saving, proper solid waste disposal, recycling, reusing and conservation activities (Protea Hotels, 2022). The research conducted through the internet and observation enabled the creation of a list of retrofitted Protea Hospitality Group (PHG) of hotels, out of which green practice was retrofitted practices.

One of the largest hotel chains in South Africa, the PHG of Hotels, green practice is reflected in retrofitting its portfolio of hotels by installing energy, water-saving measures and recycling efforts. As a South African hotel brand, the PHG of hotels was established in 1984 (Marriott International Inc., 2014). In addition to Nigeria, Zimbabwe, Uganda, Namibia, Malawi, Zambia and Tanzania, Protea has expanded its corporate footprint over the whole African continent from its South African base (Marriott International Inc., 2014; Protea Hotels, 2022). Protea, comprised of the Protea brand, the Fire&Ice brand and the African Pride brand (Marriott), manages, rents and franchises hotels throughout the group (Marriott International Inc., 2014; Protea Hotels, 2022).

Protea adheres to the policies of the green practice documented in its Hotel Environmental Management Plan, created and released in 2012. The Protea head office also created an Environmental Management Minimum Requirements and Operational Standards Policy (EMMREOP). The EMMREOP mandates that management staff members commit to the green plan, and everyday staff members receive training on the green plan. In addition, to green plan should be included in the hotel induction guides. It also comprises sections on procurement, electricity, environmental management, energy consumption, water use and wastewater management (Protea Intranet, 2022). Following the environmental strategy, each hotel operated by Protea must identify three of the five result objectives and put them into practice. Then, hotels must develop measurement techniques and reasonable goals in their checklist. The checklist covers procurement, housekeeping, dining and maintenance (Protea Intranet, 2022).

Protea retrofitted practices include LED lighting; in the heat pump system; double glazed windows; insulated water tanks; the half-flush/full-flush system; a waterless urinary system; in-house washing machines; a central air-conditioning system that operates based on a timer; recycling items like card boxes, paper, plastic, batteries, glass and light bulbs.

Research Box

This chapter suggests that further research should examine the challenges hotels in South Africa face when adopting and implementing greening practices. As this chapter has demonstrated, despite the volume and variety of environmental impacts that hotels exert on the environment there remain significant opportunities for more studies on green hotels in South Africa.

Conclusion

This chapter examines the green practices in South Africa. Hotels can significantly reduce their environmental impact by being green. However, studies have indicated that many South African hotels still need to embrace greening measures due to weak administration and supervision from the South African government.

This chapter indicates that green hotels have green practices that mitigate adverse environmental effects. Green practices align with the UN SDGs. Undoubtedly, the hotel industry will only be able to move into the future if sustainability and resource conservation are included in its business culture. Promoting green practices in hotels results in a decrease in energy and water usage, increasing hotel competitiveness and hotel reputation. Due to sustainability and a strong emphasis on environmental conservation, the hotel sector has been pursuing green practices. Green practices and green hotels are essential elements for advancing sustainable practices. The hotel sector's use of resources like energy and water strains the environment. Through their operations and strategies, the sector can, however, also improve environmental preservation. This study examined the relationship between green competitive advantage and environmental orientation (internal and external). The hotel sector in South Africa is also aware of the detrimental impact of its activities on the environment and has taken steps to mitigate such effects.

Discussion Questions

- How can hotels promote green practices?
- What are the primary green practices in the tourism industry?
- How can green practices be implemented in the hospitality industry?

References

Abdou, A., Hassan, T., & Moustafa, M. (2020). A description of green hotel practices and their role in achieving sustainable development. *Sustainability*, *12*(22). https://doi.org/10.3390/su12229624

Acampora, A., Lucchetti, M. C., Merli, R., & Ali, F. (2022). The theoretical development and research methodology in green hotels research: A systematic literature review. *Journal of Hospitality and Tourism Management*, *51*, 512–528. https://doi.org/10.1016/j.jhtm.2022.05.007

Adila, C., Jack-Vincent, R., Natasha, D., & Steven, M. (2021). *African climate finance landscape*. https://www.green-cape.co.za/assets/South-African-Climate-Finance-Landscape-2020-January-2021.pdf

Christina, C., Oscar, H. C., Ian, K., & Xun, X. (2022). Narrowing the intention-behaviour gap: The impact of green hotel certification. *International Journal of Hospitality Management*, *107*, 103305. ISSN 0278-4319. https://doi.org/10.1016/j.ijhm.2022.103305

De Freitas, D. (2018). *Exploring and predicting South African consumers' intended behaviour towards selecting green hotels: Extending the theory of planned behaviour*. https://uir.unisa.ac.za/bitstream/handle/10500/25304/dissertation_de%20freitas_d.pdf?isAllowed=y&sequence=1

Diana, H. (2021, August 23). 6 ways that more hotels are embracing sustainability in South Africa. https://blueandgreentomorrow.com/sustainability/ways-that-more-hotels-are-embracing-sustainability-in south africa/

Dwivedi, R. K., Pandey, M., Vashisht, A., Pandey, D. K., & Kumar, D. (2022). Assessing behavioural intention toward green hotels during COVID-19 pandemic: The moderating role of environmental concern. *Journal of Tourism Futures*. https://doi.org/10.1108/JTF-05-2021-0116

Enz, C. (1999). Best hotel environmental practices. *Cornell Hotel and Restaurant Administration Quarterly*, 1–8.

Giessen, V. (2018). *Progress with the implementation of green procurement practises (GPP) in the hotel industry – The South African experience. Environmental Management*. North-West University.

Green Building Council South Africa (GBCSA). (2014). What is a Green Building? http://old.gbcsa.org.za/about/about.php

Green Hotels Association. (2019). What are green hotels? www.greenhotels.com/

Hou, H. C., & Wu, H. (2021). Tourists' perceptions of green building design and their intention of staying in green hotels. *Tourism and Hospitality Research, 21*(1), 115–128. https://doi.org/10.1177/1467358420963379

Imran, I., & Reynolds, D. (2016). Predicting green hotel behavioral intentions using a theory of environmental commitment and sacrifice for the environment. *International Journal of Hospitality Management, 52,* 107–116. https://doi.org/10.1016/j.ijhm.2015.09.007

Ismail, S., & Rogerson, J. M. (2016). Retrofitting hotels: Evidence from the Protea Hospitality Group of hotels within Gauteng, South Africa. *African Journal of Hospitality, Tourism and Leisure Special Edition, 5*(3). ISSN 2223-814X. http://www.ajhtl.com

LEED. (2020). LEED rating system. www.usgbc.org/leed

Leonard, L., & Dlamini, T. (2015). Greening within the tourism and hospitality sectors: The case of Protea Hotel, Wanderers, Johannesburg. *African Journal of Hospitality, Tourism and Leisure, 4*(1), 2–8.

Mail & Guardian. (2019). *The Mail & Guardian Newspaper, South Africa.* The Mail & Guardian. https://mg.co.za/about/

Marriott International Inc. (2014). Marriott International completes acquisition of Protea Hospitality Group; becomes the largest hotel company in Africa. https://www.prnewswire.com/news-releases/marriott-international-completes-acquisition-of-protea-hospitality-group-becomes-the-largest-hotel-company-in-africa-253338521.html

Mbasera, M., du Plessis, E., Saayman, M., & Kruger, M. (2018). Determining the impact of green management policies on hotel performance: A manager's perspective. *African Journal of Hospitality, Tourism and Leisure, 7*(3), 1–13. ISSN 2223. http://www.ajhtl.com

Mbasera, M., & Mutana, S. (2014). An analysis of environmentally friendly waste management initiatives in hotels in Zimbabwe. *International Journal of Advanced Research in Management and Social Sciences, 3*(8), 36–48.

Mihaela, S. M., Irene, G., & María, E. R. M. (2021). The importance of green practices for hotel guests: Does gender matter? *Economic Research-Ekonomska Istraživanja, 34*(1), 3508–3529. https://doi.org/10.1080/1331677X.2021.1875863

Protea Hotels. (2022). http://www.proteahotels.com

Protea Intranet. (2022). Protea News. https://www.protea.ltd.uk/news

Rahman, I., Park, J., & Chi, C. G. (2015). Consequences of greenwashing: Consumers' reactions to hotels' green initiatives. *International Journal of Contemporary Hospitality Management, 27*(6), 1054–1081. https://doi.org/10.1108/IJCHM-04-2014-0202

Robertson, J., & Barling, J. (2017). Toward a new measure of organizational environmental citizenship behaviour. *Journal of Business Research, 75,* 57–66. https://doi.org/10.1016/j.jbusres.2017.02.007

UNEP. (2021, November 10). Travel and tourism industry chart a new, greener course at COP 26. https://www.unep.org/news-and-stories/story/travel-and-tourism-industry-chart-new-greener-course-cop-26

Chapter 8

Indigenous Tribes and Inclusive Engagement: An Integrated Approach for Sustainable Livelihood Into the Future

Kottamkunnath Lakshmypriya and Bindi Varghese

Christ University, India

Learning Objectives

After reading and studying this chapter, you should be able to:

- appreciate ethnicity of indigenous tribes and their cultural intricacies;
- understand their capabilities and skills and the adversities they face in their habitat;
- appraise the interventions for sustainable livelihood for the tribal community through tourism.

Abstract

Tourism acts as a stimulant in rural poverty reduction and inclusive socioeco-nomic development. Sustainable tourism can significantly contribute to the economic diversification and local economic development of rural areas with its ability to create jobs and encourage infrastructural development focusing on preserving the environment, culture and indigenous groups. The detrimental effects of tourism on the economy, society and culture have shifted attention to sustainable travel. As a result, terms like 'tribal tourism', 'ecotourism' and 'sustainable tourism' have become popular. Inclusive engagement is a crucial agenda item in future tourism development and a major concern of many international organisations, including the United Nations. This chapter focuses on exploring the tribal communities and their involvement in sustainable tourism initiatives with an overarching focus on the role of the indigenous community and their skill sets in creating sustainable livelihoods through tribal tourism. Apart from creating direct and indirect employment opportunities,

Future Tourism Trends Volume 1, 99–114

Copyright © 2024 Kottamkunnath Lakshmypriya and Bindi Varghese

Published under exclusive licence by Emerald Publishing Limited

doi:10.1108/978-1-83753-244-520241008

tribal tourism will support the growth of locally produced goods and have significant multiplier effects as capability-building initiatives will give impetus to the community's socioeconomic development.

Additionally, the sector offers notable advancements in the development of the tribal region. Tribal tourism will help people comprehend the significance of the ecosystem, local biodiversity and emission control activities on a deeper level (Thanikkad & Saleem, 2021). This chapter explores the indigenous tribes of Kerala and their ethnic skill sets, capabilities and means of livelihood. Further, the discussion on how the tourism domain promotes inclusive engagement of these tribes and aids in mapping skill sets, livelihood and inclusive engagement through tourism initiatives is explored.

Keywords: Indigenous tribes; indigenous values; sustainable livelihoods; social vulnerabilities; social inclusion; capability building; economic inclusion; cultural identity; tribal culture; inclusive engagement

Introduction

Indigenous communities inherit a symbiotic relationship connecting nature and traditional knowledge systems, differentiating them in sustainably handling environmental resources and the skills to connect generations. Tribal and native groups have long been kept from discussions on society, culture and civilisation in India, except for anthropological studies. However, these communities have faced various issues and challenges, such as displacement, deforestation and loss of traditional knowledge, threatening their livelihoods and way of life. Poverty and poor means of livelihood have been the overarching discourse in tribal development initiatives. However, poor living conditions are only one aspect of social exclusion, as the situation of these tribes demonstrates. The socioeconomic conditions of the tribals are depleting; it is noted that the average landholding of the tribes has reduced, indicating that they are pushed out of their land for infrastructural projects and other development activities, triggering intense levels of exclusion (Panda, 2016).

The tribal communities also face social vulnerabilities and exclusions regarding access to educational and health facilities and are subject to atrocities (Rajasenan et al., 2019). In his study notes that several problems, including huge debts, deforestation, land alienation, and migration, have a negative impact on tribes' living standards in modern India, irrespective of various tribal support schemes of the central and state government. Kerala has made significant progress in literacy, health, education, etc. However, some groups continue to be marginalised and deny the advantages of growth (Haseena, 2014). Though Kerala is ranked as one of the top states in India in socioeconomic development, the situation of the tribal community remains the same. Inclusive engagement is essential to address these challenges and ensure the sustainability of their livelihoods in the future.

Kerala, the southernmost state of the Indian subcontinent, is flanked by the mountain ranges of the Western Ghats on the east and the Arabian Sea on the west.

The ethnic tribals inhabit the western slopes of the Ghats. As per the Census, 2011, total scheduled tribal population is 484,839, which is 1.43% of the state's total population. The two tribal districts in Kerala with the highest populations are Wayanad and Attappady. Tribal population density is highest in Wayanad (31.2%), then Idukki (11.5%) and then Palakkad (10%). In Kerala, the tribes have a far lower rate of literacy (75.81%) than the overall population. In 1976, 75 tribal groups, sections and villages were classified as Primitive Tribal Groups (PTGs) by the Indian government based on pre-agricultural technologies, less than 5% literacy rates, and growth rates that were either marginal or stagnant, among other factors. In India, there are 15 states and union territories where PTGs are present. There are five PTGs in Kerala, namely the Koraga community of Kasaragode district; the Cholanaickan of Nilambur Valley, Malappuram district; the Kurumbar of Attappady, Palakkad district; the Kattunayakan of Wayanad, Malappuram and Kozhikode Districts and the Kadar of erstwhile Cochin area; this study is specific to the four tribes in the northern part of the state, hence the Kadar community is not part of the study.

Indigenous Communities and Ethnicity

The Koraga Tribe – Culture and Ethnic Skill

Indigenous communities are very competitive, and the settlements are considerably evolving with large opportunities with economic opportunities, and the future directives indicate mechanisms to achieve sustainability. The tribes require an overall holistic approach to develop sustainable indigenous tourism businesses.

The Koraga community is one of the ancient tribes who have predominantly inhabited Tulu Nadu, which comprises the districts of Karnataka's Dakshina Kannada, Udupi, Uttara Kannada, Shimoga and Kodagu, as well as Kerala's Kasaragod district (Jayarajan, 1990) noted that there are several exogamous clans or sects among the Koragas. The clan is referred to as the Bali. Koragas are one of the ancient tribes in India and an oppressed community by the practice of 'Ajalu', an evil social system which is part of the caste system that existed in India. According to the Dakshina Kannada District Gazetteer, Koragas were considered slave labourers until the turn of the 20th century. The population of the Koraga community was 14,294 in Karnataka and 1,582 in Kerala, as per the 2011 Census.

The Koragas are primarily farmers who make a meagre living off forest products like bamboo, cane and creepers to create baskets (Aravinda, 2008). To please their god for abundant crops and to end epidemics, the Koragas undertake folk dances, rituals and sorcery. Koragas are skilled at splitting and weaving bamboo, canes and creepers into attractive baskets. The primary source of income for the Koraga tribal people is basketry because the government has already outlawed the scavenging and orderly professions. The ability to weave baskets is passed down from generation to generation. Children used to weave baskets as well. Even though plastic baskets have become more popular, around 70% of the community still relies on basketry for their daily needs. The remaining 30% engaged in wage employment, laterite stone cutting, beedi rolling and agricultural labour. The majority of income is used to purchase alcoholic beverages. Both sexes depend on alcohol and other vices like smoking and chewing betel. The Koraga tribe has its own traditional medicine, primitive literature, culture and rituals. For thousands of years, they relied on plant and animal products to learn which plant parts to employ for specific illnesses.

Using their ancient techniques and materials from the forest, they created rope, curve, saran, added saran, mora, avalakki mora, tottilu, but, kale, milk strainer curve, simbi, markers, etc. Koragas is inextricably linked to music, literature and the arts. They perform using traditional instruments such as the doll, change, flute and talas, which produce unique and captivating music. The government sanitation division hires the Koragas as sanitation workers. They also trade in hides, horns and bones of dead cattle primarily to Moppilla traders. Some are skilled in making cradles, baskets, paddy cylinders, winnowing and sowing baskets, scale pans, boxes, rice-water strainers, ring stands for supporting pots, coir (coconut fibre) rope, brushes for washing livestock, etc. Additionally, they produce numerous household items out of soapstone, which they sell to market vendors for a very low price (Basha, 2022).

The Cave Dwellers – The Cholanaickan Tribe

Cholanaickans are a diminishing tribe in India, with a population of fewer than 200 members (Vahia et al., 2017). They are primarily isolated from society and live a semi-nomadic lifestyle in the forests of Nilambur, Malappuram district. The tribe's existence was unknown until 1974. They had yet to be listed on India's voter or census survey. Few traders interacted with them. These traders travelled the last 20 km on foot after setting up camp, where the roads ended in the wilderness. They have been heavily exploited and are deteriorating or on the verge of extinction (India Today, October 14, 2013). The reason for their deteriorating state – malnutrition, drunkenness and spreading venereal disease – is their remoteness due to outsiders intruding into their space and exploiting them. Till the mid-1980, the tribal people did not wear any clothing, nor did they cover their bodies by any means; later, government agencies and other non-profit organisations engaged in the welfare activities of the tribes provided them with clothing. The lifestyle involves no ownership of wealth or weapons; though now government agencies provide them with iron weapons, there is no evidence that they had used wooden weapons in the past. They need to be more skilled; occasionally, they come with bamboo baskets and other forest produce, which they sell to the government agency for food supplies and other essentials. They approach government agencies for their weekly supply of food. Their development as a community to mainstream education and health facilities is grim due to the unreachable colonies in which they reside in the forests and their reluctance and fear to engage with modern civilised humans.

Kurumbar – The Fierce Race

Kurumbar is a tribe that inhabits the thick forests of Attappadi Valley in the Palakkad District. They are also known as Kurumba Pulayans, Mala Pulayans, Hill Pulayans and Pamba Pulayans. Kurumba Basha is the name of the Kurumba's native dialect. There is 18 hamlets total, 12 of which are located in Reserve Forests and the remaining six in Vested Forests of the Attapady region of Wayanad District (Government of Kerala, 2017). They are distributed in the taluks of Vythiri, Manathavady and Sulthanbathery in the Wayanad district.

The Kurumbar depend on non-wood forest produce and shifting cultivation for their food. Kurumbar Girijan Service Cooperative Society handles the sale of the gathered non-wood forest products. They grow seeds such as foxtail millet, chickpeas, red gram and vegetables (Kakkoth, 2005). Uraali Kurumas are an artisan tribe, and their versatile skill in art and handicrafts are well known. They play the flute and drum during festivals. The only tribal group that pursued a variety of artisanal activities, such as pottery, basketry and blacksmithing, and is exceptional in their artisanal abilities (Vineeth, 2009) through skilling and upskilling efforts is the Uralikurumar tribe which is a subgroup of the Kurumbar tribe in the Wayanad District of Kerala State, India. However, The Kurumbar tribal community is a disadvantaged population in education. Tribal education is still a major issue as noted by Syam, S. K. (2021). They have yet to enter the mainstream education system despite several efforts. Nearly all students admitted into schools drop out of formal schooling, which is a severe concern regarding skill development and government efforts to develop their livelihoods.

Kattunayakan – Livelihood and Indigenous Skillset

Kattunayakan tribes are seen in the deep forests of Kidaganad, Purakadi, Pulpalli, Noolpuzha, Maruthenkara, Tharuvana of the Western Ghats and Nallornad Amsoms of the Vythiri Taluk; Kattikulam Vemom, Chempara Peak and Nathapuram which are part of Kozhikode and Kannur districts. They speak Malayalam and Tamil, and some are fluent in Kannada.

The Kattunayakan's economy has historically been based on the forest. They survive on the forest resources for food, drink, shelter and non-consumable produce to earn a livelihood. Hunting and collecting forest produce for trade and personal use is the community's main occupation. Forest produce such as honey, wild pepper, cinnamon, tubers, berries, medicinal leaves, mushrooms, seeds and nutmeg are also traded. They harvest and gather food using essential technologies like bamboo collecting baskets and digging sticks. They employ a strategy of high-value, low-volume collection ('Indegenious people's plan, Kattunayakans', 2017). However, these products do not find a sophisticated market even in a period of green and organic enthusiasts.

Role of Inclusive Engagement in Preserving Ethnicity and Cultural Erosion to Development

Indigenous tribes have been living in intense harmony with nature for centuries. However, their approach to life and life skills are differentiators in the current times. The tribes depend on their traditional knowledge and practices to sustain their livelihoods. However, with the flavour of development and modernisation, many indigenous communities have been marginalised, and their approach to leading life has been disturbed or instead threatened (Fernandaz et al., 2020). In recent years, there has been a growing recognition of the importance of inclusive engagement of indigenous tribes for sustainable livelihoods in the future (Chambers, 2021).

Inclusivity in practice is an integrated effort of inclusive engagement with a collaborative approach that involves indigenous communities and recognises their skills, knowledge, practices and rights (Scheyvens & Biddulph, 2002). Inclusivity is best engaged with the engagement of the indigenous communities, and considerations are laid to build their perspectives in planning and implementing developmental projects. The Forest Stewardship Council (FSC) engages the tribal communities with innovative, inclusive engagement practices to promote responsible forest management, thereby working closely with the communities to protect their interests (Ebuenyi et al., 2021). This pattern of inclusive engagement also empowers and enables them while to involve the indigenous communities in decision-making processes (Pingeot, 2014). These mutually beneficial pedagogies also sufficiently recognise the tribal communities on their traditional knowledge and practices in forest management. This practice has resulted in improved forest conservation and increased livelihood opportunities for indigenous communities.

The indigenous and community conserved areas can be best maintained by proactive communities engaged in inclusive practices in conserving biodiversity and ecosystems. These local communities can be most significant in conserving natural resources and biodiversity through their traditional skills, knowledge and practices (Kannaiyan, 2007). These approaches are good initiatives addressing the structural inequalities by instilling support systems in building a sustainable livelihood for indigenous communities while preserving their cultural heritage and protecting the environment. Inclusive engagement can primarily measure the structural inequalities impacting marginalised and unempowered indigenous communities (Goodwin, 2009). The crucial concerns affecting these marginalised communities are the educational level, sanitisation and basic healthcare services (Chouhan, 2022). Therefore, an inclusive engagement of indigenous tribes is crucial for sustainable livelihoods in the future. This approach recognises the importance of traditional knowledge and practices in preserving the environment and promoting sustainable development. It also addresses the structural inequalities impacting the marginalised indigenous communities, and an inclusive approach can protect their rights on land and other utilitarian resources. Through inclusive engagement, indigenous communities can thrive while preserving their cultural heritage and protecting the environment in future.

Research Box 1. Research Question

An avid online influencer, my friend, had received permission to scale the Western Ghats in the Attapady region of Wayanad district in Kerala, India to interact and showcase the life, culture, traditions, artefacts and art forms of the forest dwellers. The tribes have grown in their choice of attire, while their hamlets remained the same as read in many documented narratives, nevertheless their livelihoods primarily come from Government initiated programmes alongside trade of forest produce. Opening out these dwellings to the general public through the means of tourism has not been a viable proposition in enhancing their livelihood. A day of interaction with different sect of the tribals is ended with the misty evening followed by the cold night which was lit by the warmth of the bonfire and their iconic dances and showcase of cultural expressions. A memorable experience, as the beats of the music resonated throughout the camp, amidst the vibrant crimson of the flames we couldn't stop grooving to the tempo of the beats. The next morning, as the rays of shining gold seek through the dense, humid cover of the canopies, we began scaling down the hills.

My Friend Had This Big Question

How do we preserve the culture and ethnic tribal knowhow and integrate it to the global community at large, leveraging the power of tourism ecosystem?

Preserving and Showcasing Indigenous Tribal Life Through Tourism

Indigenous tribal tourism is an experiential engagement with indigenous communities, while exploring their values, cultures and traditions. The tribal life paves the way towards indigenous perspectives and indigenous knowledge systems to experience authentic and immersive cultural experiences, which are getting eroded. The socioeconomic dimension to this unique community-based touristic experience engages the indigenous communities to preserve their culture and heritage as they inherit rich history and unique values passed down from generation to generation. However, tourism can be a mechanism to reduce the risk of these traditions disappearing due to the pressures of the commodification of tribal life influenced by modernisation (Mansury & Damanik, 2020). A conscious effort to preserve the culture and heritage of indigenous communities is essential for a broader reach to generate awareness and appreciation for their way of life. Perhaps, a proactive indigenous community can capitalise on tribal tourism as an additional source of income, which can help preserve the cultural heritage.

Tribal tourism can be a means to reap economic benefits by showcasing disappearing lifestyles, knowledge systems and unique cultural heritage. Indigenous communities can be benefitted from tourism-related activities such as guided tours, handicraft and souvenir sales, and prototypes of accommodation. (World Bank Report, 2003) The Mekong region of Southeast Asia practised an inclusive mechanism of engagement through ecotourism, where the indigenous communities witnessed an average increase of 20% in household income which enhanced the local economy with larger opportunities for socioeconomic mobility. The multiplier effects of tourism attract improved infrastructure and services with the development of new services and businesses. This can contribute to community well-being and destination well-being through socioeconomic development for improved quality of life.

While tribal tourism attracts socioeconomic benefits, there are risks as outliers, which are exposed to the commodification of the historicity of the vulnerable tribal communities (Mitra, 2018). The possibilities of cultural exploitation can also drive the marginalised communities with a negative toll, keeping the overall morale down. Perhaps, the tourists may see the socially vulnerable indigenous groups as primitive and exotic, which can lead to a lack of respect for the cultural determinants, value propositions and traditional knowledge systems, which is their way of life (Gunapal, 2017). These challenges can lead to negative impacts like; loss of social disruption due to cultural erosion and inferior approach towards traditional values. Tourism also can be a reason for poor environmental quality resulting in environmental degradation due to tourism activities. The indigenous communities are largely close to nature and are rooted in regions rich in biodiversity; thereby, the endangered species and habitats are to be conserved (McKercher & Du Cros, 2012). The vulnerable areas of natural beauty, such as forests, mountains and rivers where indigenous communities are settled, must be environmentally conscious to preserve the natural resources to ensure that these areas remain protected and sustainable for future generations.

Case Study 1– A Prototype for Integrating Tribal Culture – *En Ooru, Wayanad, Kerala, India*

En Ooru was planned in 2012 and launched as a prototype in June 2022 to promote tribal lifestyle and sustainable tourism in Wayanad, a district in the Indian state of Kerala. En Ooru is envisaged as an entity to offer experiential tourism opportunities to facilitate the tourist to embrace and engage with the lifestyle of tribal communities and to experience the local region's culture, ethnicity, history and environment. En Ooru is a semi-government entity, under the scheduled tribe's development department, which collaborates with the state authorities, local communities and allied tourism stakeholders to foster and generate economic benefits and fosters community and destination well-being. The term 'en oooru' in Malayalam language translates to 'My Land'.

The active pedagogy of this innovative establishment is governed by sub-collector Wayanad, who is also the permanent president, and the district collector is the chairman of the advisory body. This entity offers touristic activities, including village walks, treks into the wilderness and nature and enriching cultural experiences. En Ooru personifies an immersive and engaging exercise, connecting the visitors and the host to interact with local ethnic groups. This inclusive engagement unravels traditional skills, knowledge and experience. The appeal of the destination reveals the natural beauty of the region. This prototype exhibiting the lifestyle of the ethnic group showcases the huts occupied by the indigenous communities in the past, depicting the lifestyle, archetype and other aspects depicting the culture of the groups. A village walk engages the visitors by giving a perspective on the traditional farming practices and the local cuisine and engages intrinsically with the local community members giving employable options like selling wild honey, oil-producing units, etc.

Inclusive Mechanism

En Ooru is a socially responsible business entity, and is a very successful enterprise with inclusive business practices that support the local community and the environment. The entity is networked with government and local communities providing employment opportunities while enabling them with sustainable livelihood engagement through tourism. Social engagement also has supported community projects with improved access to education and healthcare facilities for the unempowered local people. As a successful social business enterprise, it has demonstrated sustainable livelihood and inclusive engagement through tourism. This integrated effort has offered economic development and community well-being. In addition, En Ooru has successfully depicted the local lifestyle and inherited culture and offers authentic and engaging tourism experiences with local initiatives and facilitates environmental sustainability.

Case 2 – A Model Tourist Village of Karbi Anglong and the Orchid and Biodiversity Park

This ethnic village is a model architype which serve to present the unique social life of close to a dozen aborigine tribes who use to reside in this district. The Karbi Anglong district is unique and is referred as the heart of Assam, India. The mesmerising hill destination is rich in flora and fauna and is very diverse. The elegant Karbi Anglong is perceived as a museum due to being a home of aboriginal ethnic tribes which comprises of races like the Karbi, Dimasa, Bodo, Tiwa, Garo, Kuki, Hmar, Mantai, Khasi, Adivasi, Rengma and Nepali. As an inclusive engagement initiated by the Karbi Anglong Autonomous Council (KAAC), to capitalize on tourism prospects – KAAC extends a luxurious ethnic village established at Kohora, Karbi Anglong near the Kaziranga National Park (KNP). This initiative is a result of the vision to showcase the ethnic groups of Karbi Anglong. There are 12 luxury huts on particular ethnic patterns of the indigenous communities set up with an objective to represent and position the Tribal lifestyle and promote sustainable tourism.

These establishments (Model Tourist Village and Orchid and Biodiversity Park) are pro tourism establishments with an interest to offer experiential tourism opportunities to enrich and embrace the lifestyle of tribal communities. With this the local region's culture, ethnicity, history and environment can be well demonstrated. These entities extend large touristic activities, including a walk through well maintained nurseries and explanations given by the authorities, to understand the wilderness and nature, to enrich the cultural experiences. These establishments personify an immersive engagement exercise, blending the local culture and destination image to enrich the visitors experience about the local ethnic groups. This inclusive mechanism unravels the traditional skills, knowledge and experience. The prototype exhibits the lifestyle of the ethnic group and thereby, showcases the huts occupied by the indigenous communities which depict the lifestyle, and other aspects of cultural dimensions. Establishments give employable engagement with the local community members giving options like; selling local cuisines, and other produce of the region. The experiential aspect is demonstrated by the local dances and music shows.

Methodology

This case let was developed through a combination of observations, document analysis and interviews. The objective was a stakeholder assessment through interviews conducted with key stakeholders, including the CEO of En Ooru, tour operators and tourists.

Respondent 1: Mr Syam Prasad P. S, CEO of En Ooru, who governs the overall operations and functional aspects, was interviewed about his vision behind En Ooru and its initiatives. Mr Syam Prasad explained how his team worked behind to engage the tribal population in building livelihoods. . ...

> I have been working with the En Ooru since 2012, and it has been a positive experience for me. . .En Ooru is an exclusive and permanent platform for tribal indigenous skills.

> We are giving awareness and facilities for starting a livelihood based on indigenous skills.

> En Ooru never engages tribes as workers. Instead, we provide support for achieving self-reliance with their traditional skills. They engage themselves and become entrepreneurs via En Ooru without help and exploitation, e.g. people sell honey, and indigenous medicinal practitioners sell medicines. They decide their price n service terms. En Ooru is not taking any revenue share.

Mr Syam explained how En Ooru has helped him connect with indigenous groups and other local tribals and access new markets for his produce. He also discussed the importance of building sustainable livelihood that benefits indigenous groups and tourists.

> En Ooru started selling tribal products in 2020 in a model organised setup very recently. Currently, the availability of tribal products is minimal, and most of them are not doing their indigenous jobs/ not dealing with their indigenous skills. Hence most of their products need to be standardised.
>
> We are trying to standardise their products with specific training and value addition.
>
> Due to forest norms and *climate* changes, the collection of natural resources and agricultural resources is limited. However, we started an initiative to build a new ecosystem to collect and supply the tribal traditional resources.

Mr Syam also explained the capacity-building initiatives to meet the market requirements for tribal produce. 'We are starting Colony based units for the production/collection of indigenous items. The major objective of the upcoming projects is to safeguard tribes from the exploitation of middleman and provide government assistance for their skills to market tribal goods and connect them to various agencies or market. We look at providing trainings & technical support. Standardisation of their products and thereby, establishing more units in all colonies is what we are looking at in future conducting various national and international events/exhibitions where we look to create more future livelihood opportunities'.

Respondent 2: Ms Sini K Mathew, Director-Operations, Travelfins, who governs the overall operations and Marketing, was interviewed to know, being in the travel business for two decades. . .how she sees En Ooru and its initiatives. Ms Sini explained how En Ooru and its team imbibed the idea of the first model tribal village in Kerala and how it enables a sustainable outlook for livelihood *opportunities* for the tribal/Adivasi community. . . ..

> "**Happy** to see such an appreciated infrastructure depicting the tribal life, their way of life, their skill-sets like Archery etc. are exhibited in En Ooru. One would see how Adivasi led their life in Wayanad; their jewellery. . .Thoda etc.. took me to my childhood days when we witnessed how they led their life, ethnicity, culture and knowledge system . . . especially their medical system. It is a great initiative to conserve and preserve the indigenous community and their evidence of existence.

Ms Sini explained how En Ooru could incorporate her suggestions to have the indigenous groups at En Ooru *connect* with visitors coming to this attraction. . .. 'The local tribals can directly witness the significance of preserving and conserving the tribal culture and exhibit the evidence of their skill, art, cuisine etc. . .'

Respondent 3: A Tourist From Mumbai, India

> "We are overwhelmed by the outpouring depiction of Tribal Model Village. . ."It kept us going during the walk we had here. . . great to see the structure of the huts, and I was surprised to see the primitiveness restored well. Great experience and the first of a kind I visited. The restaurant, too, looks great here. I want to experience the local cuisines of the indigenous community to experience. We bought honey and some oil as their produce.
>
> The En Ooru community showcased their support through social media and word of mouth. They started offering online bookings. I suggest the team here widen the presentation of handicrafts or develop sales of indigenous products that could be sold here.

The case highlights the importance of indigenous community-led initiatives in building a sustainable livelihood. The *En Ooru* group has demonstrated how local indigenous communities can work together to create new opportunities for sustainable livelihood options. The insights gained from interviews with key stakeholders have helped to provide a more nuanced understanding of the challenges and opportunities associated with building a sustainable livelihood for the indigenous community. Inclusive practices can imbibe social entrepreneurship facilities with training and capacity-building programmes.

Sustainable Livelihood Strategies in Tribal Communities

Inclusive Business mechanisms benefit the unempowered and marginalised communities and enhance their confidence levels through community engagements, thereby empowering the communities to participate in business processes (Scheyvens & Biddulph, 2002). The impact of inclusion builds the community and leads towards the building of social enterprises for value creation. In the long run, the significance of inclusive mechanisms will lead to the inclusion of the economically backward local population (Goodwin, 2009). The ideology of inclusive business practices in a larger context includes the participation of the marginalised communities at the destination in the tourism decision-making process (Pingeot, 2014). Another case explains a transformative process of how an educational institution imbibes the inclusive mechanism in enabling the community, thereby leading to financial empowerment.

Undoubtedly inclusive growth is a buzzword resonating across the state's development agenda. This would require bringing the tribal population from the outlier strata to the mainstream of socioeconomic activity (Kerala Development Report-Initiative, Achievements and Challenges, 2021). The tribal people of Kerala are isolated from modern culture because they live primarily in the thick woods of the Western Ghats. The three basic categories of employment of the tribal population in Kerala are forestry, agriculture and allied non-agricultural and allied sectors. The forestry industry encompasses activities related to forestry, such as gathering natural produce from the forest, medicinal herbs and customary forest-based vocations (Sujathan, 2019). Agriculture and animal husbandry are also part of their livelihood. They also work in the non-agriculture sectors, including employment under various government initiatives and cooperatives, petty trade, non-agricultural work, plantation labour and employment in the private sector (Vijaykumar & Ushadevi, 2022). However, most of the PTGs make a living either through primitive agricultural systems or by having free access to forest resources, which they exploit using traditional skills. Non-wood forest goods, often known as minor forest produce, are a significant source of income for tribal people. This covers all non-timber forest products with plant origins, such as bamboo, bamboo rice, canes, medicinal herbs, fodder, leaves, gums, waxes, dyes, resins and various foods like nuts, wild fruits, honey, lac, etc. For those who live in or close to woods, the minor forest produces provide both a means of subsistence and a source of income. These commodities contribute significantly to their food, fruits, medications and other consumables and generate sales revenue (Kalavathy, 2023). They are familiar with the forest, its biodiversity and the value of its resources for a sustainable way of life. Nevertheless, tribes frequently face the threats of constructing new infrastructure, encountering dangerous wildlife and the severe forest climate.

An Integrated Approach With Future Directions

Currently, the community themselves are not able to create a livelihood with the skills and jobs they are involved in; hence, community empowerment would require identifying their ethnic skills and identifying the market requirement; this is a crucial step to assess the skill gap and implement inclusive capacity building interventions. Inclusiveness encourages the long-term sustainable growth of the tribal group as a whole. The Ministry of Tribal Affairs, through the Tribal Cooperative Marketing Development Federation of India Ltd. (Trifed, 2023), initiated schemes to support tribal with the entire range of product development and production. Reservation of tribal traditional heritage, better infrastructure, development of latest designs for their products, transparency in pricing and agencies buying the products of the tribal were initiated to establish sustainable marketing of tribal produce at a reasonable price. Sustainable tourism and tribal circuit will improve not only the tourism landscape of the state but also the livelihood and inclusive engagement of the tribals in these regions. The tribal circuits in Manali, Nagaland, Chhattisgarh and Telangana have been planned and prioritised based on the ideals of preserving ecological diversity, high tourist value, competitiveness, sustainability and generating local employment prospects for the tribal community.

Conclusion

Cultural tourism has also been vouched for its potential to promote inclusive engagement of tribal; tribal tourism is a form of cultural tourism. It can also include rural tourism that showcases indigenous cultural communities' traditions, values and way of life (such as festivals and rituals), and it is also reported that cultural tourists spend substantially more than other tourists (Barman et al., 2010). In addition to spending money on food and housing, cultural tourists also purchase souvenirs that are more expensive than regular tourists, such as cultural artefacts. This requires capacity building among tribal to meet the requirements of global tourists. Building one's capacity is obtaining and developing the skills, information, tools and resources necessary for organisations and communities to survive, adapt and thrive in an environment of rapid change. The process enables fluidity and flexibility to sustain ventures in a globally competitive environment, while it also requires a clear demarcation from the traditional misconception that training is capacity building. Non-profit organisations and government agencies must go beyond skill training to build tribal communities with enhanced capability and capacity to improve their livelihood. Collaboration and participative processes through innovative methods can go a long way in this initiative.

Discussion Questions

- Analyse the relevance of preserving and showcasing indigenous tribal culture, artefacts through tourism.
- Develop a roadmap to skill enhancement and capacity building among tribal community as an intervention to engage tourist.
- Brainstorm on mapping innovative interventions through tourism as a method to promote sustainable livelihood for tribals.

References

Aravinda, M. (2008). *Koraga jananga vshleshanatmaka adhyayana*. Dakshina Kannada Zilla parishad, Mangalore Budakattu Vruthi Mattu Paramparika Gnana. Karnataka Sahitya Academy.

Barman, A., Singh, R., & Rao, Y. V. (2010). *Empowering tribes through cultural tourism in India – A dream project on ICT integration*. https://doi.org/10.2139/ssrn.1718126

Basha, K. (2022). Practice and preservation of material culture among the Koraga Tribe of South Canara. *International Journal of Advanced Research in Science, Communication and Technology*, 2(2).

Chambers, D. (2021). Are we all in this together? Gender Intersectionality and sustainable tourism. https://sure.sunderland.ac.uk/ id/eprint/13348/1/13348.pdf

Cholanaickans, one of the most primitive tribesmen of India, face exploitation threat. (2013, November 20). *India Today*. https://www.indiatoday.in/magazine/living/story/19810615-cholanaickans-one-of-the-most-primitive-tribes men-of-india-face-exploitation-threat-772977-2013-11-20

Chouhan, V. (2022). Developing a sustainable tribal tourism model vis-a-vis the tribal region of Rajasthan. *Journal of Tourism, Heritage & Services Marketing, 8*(1), 58–63.

Ebuenyi, I. D., Smith, E. M., Munthali, A., Msowoya, S. W., Kafumba, J., Jamali, M. Z., & MacLachlan, M. (2021). Exploring equity and inclusion in Malawi's National Disability Mainstreaming Strategy and Implementation Plan. *International Journal for Equity in Health, 20*(1). https://doi.org/10.1186/s12939-020-01378-y

Fernandaz, C. C., Parthiban, K. T., Sudhagar, R. J., & Sekar, I. (2020). Perception of Tribal Communities on Indigenous Technical Knowledge (ITKs). *International Journal of Pure and Applied Bioscience, 8*(2), 429–437.

Goodwin, H. (2009). Reflections on ten years of pro-poor tourism. *Journal of Policy Research in Tourism, Leisure and Events, 1*(1), 90–94. https://doi.org/10.1080/19407960802703565

Government of Kerala. (2017). *Kurumbar*. https://kirtads.kerala.gov.in/2017/10/11/kurumbar/

Gunapal, S. (2017). *Koraga Samudaya Olanotagalu*. Samagra Grameena Ashrama.

Haseena, V. A. (2014). Land alienation and livelihood problems of scheduled tribes in Kerala. *Research on Humanities and Social Sciences, 4*(10), 76–81.

Jayarajan, V. (1990). *Ethnic identity and intangible cultural heritage: A study of the Koraga Community of South India.* https://www.seameo.org/LanguageMDGConference2010/doc/presentations/day1/V.Jayarajan-ppt.pdf

Kakkoth, S. (2005). The Primitive Tribal Groups of Kerala: A situational appraisal. *Studies of Tribes and Tribals*, 47–55.

Kalavathy (2023). Skill and Koragas. *Journal of emerging technologies and innovative research, 10*(4).

Kannaiyan, S. (2007, July 16). *Biological Diversity and Traditional Knowledge.* National Biodiversity Authority. https://nbaindia.org/uploaded/docs/traditionalknowledge190707.pdf

Kerala Development Report-Initiative, achievements and challenges. (2021). Kerala State Planning Board, Government of Kerala. https://spb.kerala.gov.in/sites/default/files/inline-files/Kerala-Development-Report2021.pdf

Mansury, Y., & Damanik, J. (2020). Tourist experiences of tribal tourism in North Sumatra. *Indonesia. Journal of Tourism and Cultural Change, 18*(2), 135–148.

Mckercher, B., & Cros, H. D. (2012). *Cultural tourism: The partnership between tourism and cultural heritage management* Routledge.

Mitra, A. (2018). Eco-tourism revenue in Sunderban Tiger Reserve. *Techno International Journal of Health, Engineering, Management and Science, 2*(1).

Panda, R. K. (2016). *Social exclusion and inequality: Opportunities in Agenda 2030.* New Delhi: Socially Excluded Task Force & Center for Equity Studies.

Pingeot, L. (2014). *Corporate Influence in the post-2015 Process* (Working Paper). Misereor, Brot fur die Welt, Global Policy Forum. http://www19.iadb.org/intal/intalcdi/PE/2014/13575.pdf

Rajasenan, D., Venanzi, A. D., & Rajeev, B. (2019). Tribal populations in Kerala's development process: An impact evaluation of policies and schemes. *Revista Venezolana de Análisis de Coyuntura, XXV*(2), 85–110.

Scheyvens, R., & Biddulph (2002). Backpacker tourism and third world development. *Annals of Tourism Research, 29*(1), 144–164.

Sujathan, P. K. (2019). *Impact and implications of institutional interventions among tribes in Kerala*. IUCAE,University of Kerala.

Syam, S. K. (2021). *Literacy and demographic aspects of Kurumbar of Palakkad District of Kerala*. http://www.languageinindia.com/nov2021/drsyam kurumbarli teracydemographykerala1.pdf

Thanikkad, J., & Saleem, S. (2021). *Cultural tourism centers – A geographical presentation of cultural tourism product in Kerala*. https://doi.org/10.2139/ssrn.3934176

Trifed. (2023). *Tribes India | PMVDY*. https://trifed.tribal.gov.in/artisan

Vahia, M. N., Ramachandran, V. S., Gangopadhyay, J., & Justin, J. (2017). Understanding rationality, culture and scientific temperament of Cholanaikkan Tribe of Kerala Heritage. *Journal of Multidisciplinary Studies in Archaeology*, 862–882.

Vijaykumar, N., & Ushadevi, K. N. (2022). Problems faced by Tribals in collection and marketing of non-timber forest products (NTFPs) in Kerala, India. *Asian Journal of Agricultural Extension, Economics & Sociology*, 251–258. https://doi.org/ 10.9734/ajaees/2022/v40i111708

Vineeth, S. (2009). Interaction pattern and livelihood strategies of an Artisan Tribe. *Studies of Tribes and Tribals*, *7*(1). https://doi.org/10.1080/0972639X.2009. 11886591

World Bank Report. (2003). *Mekong integrated water resources management project*. https://projects.worldbank.org/en/projects-o perations/project-detail/P124942

Part 5

Co-Creating Event Experience

Chapter 9

A Strategy Towards Destination Promotion

Pinaz Tiwari

GLA University, India

Learning Objectives

After reading and studying this chapter, you should be able to:

- understand the concept of co-creation and its application in events;
- identify the strategic role of co-creation in events as a destination promotion tool;
- understand the multi-stakeholders approach towards co-creation at events.

Abstract

As the consumer-centric approach is evolving in the 21st century, especially in the post-COVID-19 era, people seek unique experiences. Adopting co-creation in promoting a destination implies involving tourists, stakeholders and organisers in creating value for a product or service. The innovative strategy of co-creating experiences encourages tourists' engagement, leading to destination promotion. Some notable examples of co-creation in tourism are gastronomic tours, virtual tours and travel guides. This chapter aims at the significance of co-creating experiences at events that lead to destination promotion. Co-creation of experiences at events brings the spotlight from the stage to the audience and is considered the future of the experience economy. The study presents a case study of Jal Mahotsav in Madhya Pradesh, India. The study highlights the multi-stakeholder approach adopted by the authorities to co-create the event experience.

Keywords: Tourism; consumer-centric approach; event tourism; experience tourism; co-creation; marketing

Future Tourism Trends Volume 1, 117–131
Copyright © 2024 Pinaz Tiwari
Published under exclusive licence by Emerald Publishing Limited
doi:10.1108/978-1-83753-244-520241009

Introduction

The global tourism and hospitality industry is highly competitive owing to the various services offered at destinations and the ever-changing requirements of travellers. Moreover, the existence of different stakeholders makes the industry fragmented, thereby increasing the need to focus on the quality of tourists' experiences. Subsequently, visitors' engagement in the consumption process could be considered a way to enhance their experiences. Thus, one way to offer travellers personalised experiences is by involving them in the process through co-creation (Neuhofer, 2016).

Ramaswamy and Gouillart (2010) define co-creation as creating products and services involving different organisation beneficiaries. In contemporary times, various companies have used co-creation strategies to engage their customers and offer personalised products or services. For example, McDonald's, a popular fast-food restaurant chain, encouraged customer co-creation by organising a competition that allowed the re-invention of their iconic hamburgers or Lays. In addition, this potato chip manufacturing firm asked customers about new chip flavours (Innovators, 2019). Likewise, the concept is widely discoursed and researched in the tourism and hospitality domain. The emergence of an experiential economy predominates the need for innovation to survive the fierce competition in the market. Service experience lies at the core of tourism and hospitality-related services. A tourist's perception of exchange value creation is directly proportional to the levels of authenticity and engagement while consuming the services (Choo & Petrick, 2014).

Even though the tourism sector is known to produce and consume experiences simultaneously (Tussyadiah & Zach, 2013), not all sub-sectors have gained much importance in research (Mohammadi et al., 2021). One of those sectors is events. Although some authors have studied co-creation in events such as green sports events and branding through co-creation (Bjerke & Naess, 2021), experience co-creation in food and wine tourism (Rachão et al., 2021) and intelligent event experience (Bustard, 2019). As per the author's knowledge, the existing literature fails to acknowledge the scope of co-creation in event settings, especially in a country like India which is well known for its plethora of events and cultural resources. Consequently, this chapter aims to bridge the gap by determining stakeholders' role in co-creating unique events and experiences.

Events are a part of tourism attractions and are attended to and organised by people from diverse backgrounds. In contemporary times, events and festivals have become crucial in demonstrating the uniqueness of a destination (Zhang et al., 2019). Events represent any destination's socio-culture values and physical attributes, attracting tourists and encouraging re-visitations (Getz, 2010). As tourism events aim at increasing the experiential value for visitors, Suntikul and Jachna (2016) mentioned that this value is co-created with the unique physical features of a destination.

Co-creation is a service-related concept introduced in 2004 (Prahalad & Ramaswamy, 2004). Several studies have been conducted in tourism and hospitality (Pandey & Kumar, 2021). Additionally, Campos et al. (2015) emphasized the existence of co-creation in tourism experiences. In the same vein, Mohammadi et al. (2021) underpinned the theoretical emergence of co-creation in the tourism research. However, based on the existing literature reviews on co-creation in tourism and hospitality, co-creation's scope in the events sector still needs to be acknowledged.

Accordingly, this study would fill the underlying gap by highlighting the scope of implementation of co-creation in the events sector. Consequently, with greater levels of engagement, co-creation can further be used to promote events at several destinations. Moreover, the study would also discuss the advent of the virtual dimension in co-creating events experiences at destinations. Therefore, this chapter aims to signify the scope of the co-creation strategy in improving the event experience that would further lead to destination branding and promotion. Co-creation of event experiences brings the spotlight from the stage to the audience and other stakeholders involved in making the event experiential. The study is conceptual and presents the case of Jal Mahotsav in Madhya Pradesh (India). The event followed a multi-stakeholder approach to co-creating the event experience and has now become a popular tourism product in the Madhya Pradesh tourism promotional campaigns.

This chapter is divided into three broad sections. Firstly, a literature review on co-creation in the tourism, hospitality and events sectors is summarised, indicating the development across different countries. Secondly, the case study of Jal Mahotsav is presented that underlines the significance of co-creation in events with the help of diverse stakeholders at a destination. The case also emphasises co-creating events experiences as a tool for destination promotion. The last section of this chapter will discuss the future directions to encourage co-creation as a branding tool in events through virtual experiences and building a co-creating community.

Co-creation

Experience is the primary element while consuming a product or a service. The notion of 'co-creation of experiences' was coined by Prahalad and Ramaswamy in 2004. The term implies co-creating unique customer experiences and adding value through a co-creation process facilitated by the service providers (Rachão et al., 2020). It is defined as 'creating services and products through collaboration among company managers, employees, consumers and other beneficiaries of an organisation' (Ramaswamy & Gouillart, 2010). Collaboration between the stakeholders benefits them in the co-creation process (Sthapit & Björk, 2019).

Co-creation is one of the prolific strategies that help companies drive innovation in highly competitive markets. The by-products of implementing co-creation in businesses include innovative product ideas, overcoming supply chain problems and offering technical solutions to intricate product design

(Innovators, 2019). Some examples of co-creation are asking people for feedback about a new product and involving them in product design.

Organisations benefit from the co-creation process since it allows them to understand the customers' likes, dislikes and preferences and offer customised products or services. As a result, co-creation process creates a win-win situation for both the tourism organisations (in terms of increased customers' loyalty, market share and service innovation) as well as for customers (in terms of fulfilled demand and better experience). Indeed, the effectiveness of the value co-creation process depends on the intensity of customer engagement.

Jaakkola and Alexander (2014) conceptualised the role of customer engagement behaviour in value co-creation as:

> The customer provision of resources during non-transactional, joint value processes that interact with the focal firm and other stakeholders, thereby affecting their respective value processes and outcomes.

Similarly, Ostrom et al. (2010) reported that engaged customers are likelier to share information and seek opportunities to co-create their experiences. Several authors have examined the role of customer engagement in value co-creation in different contexts (Buhalis & Sinarta, 2019; Lei et al., 2020; Pandey & Kumar, 2021). The existing studies on co-creation have given rise to novel concepts such as co-destruction, co-production and presumption in marketing and management studies. The value co-creation process has been examined from several view-points; however, its application in tourism, hospitality and events is of greater significance owing to its distinctive characteristic of being an active service pro-vider (Chathoth et al., 2016).

Co-creation in Tourism, Hospitality and Events

Despite being introduced as a concept in marketing studies, the subject of tourism and hospitality has largely preponderated the literature on value co-creation (Pandey & Kumar, 2021). To reason, Mohammadi et al. (2021) mentioned that the innate characteristic of the tourism and hospitality sector, i.e. the insepara-bility of consumption and delivery of services, makes the scope of examining co-creation larger. Considering the criticality of co-creation in-service experience in tourism-related services, numerous researchers have analysed different dimensions of value co-creation in this subject, such as Kamboj and Gupta (2020), Kim et al. (2018) and Tjandra et al. (2021).

Concerning tourism and hospitality management, Prebensen et al. (2016) defined co-creation as the interest of tourists in physical and psychological participation in any activity and its subsequent role in tourists' quality of expe-rience (p. 1). Moreover, adopting a value co-creation process would help com-panies grow sustainably (Tuana et al., 2019). Since sustainability in tourism and hospitality is a stakeholder concern, several authors have examined the significance of value co-creation in creating sustainability (Font et al., 2021; Plichta, 2019; Wanga et al., 2014).

The proliferation of information and communication technology helped in the development of tourism and related sector. The emerging concept of Industry 4.0 identifies the need for innovation, customer engagement and sustainability in the business process. To face the market challenges, the tourism sector seeks a co-creation process that would help innovatively create positive experiences. Rihova et al. (2015) emphasised that the predisposition of tourism market forces is slowly shifting from 'creating value for tourists' to 'co-creating value with tourists'. It indicates the direct relationship between the involvement of tourists in product co-creation and their satisfaction with the destination experience (Buonincontri et al., 2017). Moreover, several studies have indicated tourists' satisfaction with the co-creation process as they could express their needs and wants clearly, and customise the products and services in collaboration with tourism organisations (Kamboj & Gupta, 2020). Indeed, the active engagement of travellers in events helps create positive trip experiences and helps destinations create brand value and promote themselves globally.

Co-creation and Destination Marketing: Multi-Stakeholders' Perspective

Collaboration is the key to the co-creation process of adding value to the products and services. In the majority of cases, organisations co-create with consumers by inviting them to become part of product designing, such as Lays and BMW. However, the process of co-creation could spread its roots to other stakeholders. Collaborating with other stakeholders, for instance, co-creating in supply chain management, helps organisations to create a shared value hierarchy.

According to Deloitte Insights (2020), an effective co-creation process allows a broad range of stakeholders to support organisational innovation. As demonstrated in Fig. 9.1, stakeholders include suppliers, consumers, government, competitors, non-profit organisations and academic institutions. An effective co-creation process includes stakeholders working together to deliver value in the marketplace.

In tourism and destination marketing, implementing the multi-stakeholder approach in the co-creation process would lead to developing the tourism sector, especially events. Notably, diverse stakeholders organise an event and make it successful by delivering a unique event experience to the attendees. Therefore, it would be helpful to gain better insights into co-creating value with the help of stakeholders. Accordingly, the role of different stakeholders involved in the co-creation process in destination marketing is discussed below:

Travellers/Visitors/Tourists

Tourists are the epicenter of every tourism-related activity. The unprecedented use of the internet, technologies and social media platforms has empowered travellers

Fig. 9.1.   Co-creation With Different Stakeholders. *Source:* Adapted from Deloitte Insights (2020).

to get the required information to search for an explored place or an accommodation and share their experiences as global citizens. Furthermore, the user-generated content shared by travellers, such as photos, blogs, tweets, reviews, etc., impacts the perception and image of a destination in the minds of other travellers (Kim & Stepchenkova, 2015). This further increases the travellers' influence as destination marketing agents (Kim et al., 2018).

Government

While travellers play a dominant role in co-creation and promoting a destination, the role of government must be supported. National, state and local government bodies should be included in promoting and branding a destination (Sahin & Baloglu, 2014). Several events have witnessed that engaging government bodies helps create value. For instance, in the Gamcheon Cultural Village Project study, Hong and Lee (2015) reported that the financial assistance provided by the central government and Busan city government encouraged the locals' participation in the project. Likewise, the Indian government's initiative of the Swadesh Darshan Scheme in 2014 is another example of the government's role in promoting and branding destinations (Roy & Gretzel, 2020) through co-creation.

Academic/Higher Educational Institutions

Several studies have emphasised the imperative role of tourists in the co-creation process. However, promoting and branding a destination with the help of academia has yet to be acknowledged. Higher Educational Institutes (HEIs) around a tourist destination could engage and become an essential part of the co-creation process. Chowdhary et al. (2020) discussed the potential of HEIs, tourism graduates and researchers to promote destinations by following the Principles of Responsible Management Education (PRME). Encouraging students to organise, participate and promote the local events would lead to their active engagement in delivering value through co-creation. For instance, Hong and Lee (2015) suggested continuous promotion and education would help preserve the Gamcheon Culture Village Regeneration Project.

Competitors

Committing to innovation is the new norm in Industrial era 4.0. Subsequently, companies look for opportunities that would help them create value – both for customers and other stakeholders. Amidst the race to offer unique experiences and deliver quality, organisations understand the significance of cooperative business environments and gradually collaborate with competitors (Proximus, 2018). It has led to a concept termed 'coopetition', and several destinations and tour organisations co-create value through competition. Miki and Canino (2018) developed a tourism coopetition model and reported seven factors. These are – co-production, co-entrepreneurship, strategic management, associationism, co-location, competition and cooperation. Therefore, tourism organisations can co-create with competitors by delivering services to tourists through these paradigms.

Ecosystem Partners

Co-creation in tourism and events can also occur with the help of ecosystem partners such as non-governmental organisations (NGOs), local tourism bodies, tourist police, tourist facilitation offices, independent researchers, volunteers and the local community. Since tourism is a fragmented sector, ecosystem partners contribute significantly to co-creating value at the destination. However, the impact of ecosystem partners in co-creating value in tourism-related activities must be explored in research.

The Case of Jal Mahotsav, Madhya Pradesh section would discuss the case of Jal Mahotsav in Madhya Pradesh, which implemented the multi-stakeholder approach. The event is a successful case of using co-creation to offer a unique event experience to the visitors.

Case of Jal Mahotsav, Madhya Pradesh

Situated at the Heart of India, Madhya Pradesh is one of the largest states in the country. The state has everything that would appeal to people of every age group. Madhya Pradesh offers exquisite attractions ranging from the lush green forests of Panna to intricately carved stone temples. The mighty rivers, unique physical features, rich cultural and tribal heritage, diverse wildlife, glorious forts and palaces, age-old temples and pre-historic caves have provided a competitive edge to state tourism. The state is a fascinating example of history uniting with colonialism and modernism in the 21st century. Owing to the grandeur of tourism resources, three famous sites are listed in UNESCO's World Heritage Sites. These are – the Khajuraho Group of Monuments, the Buddhist Monuments at Sanchi and the Rock Shelters of Bhimbetka (UNESCO, 2021).

Indeed, the state utilises its physical features to deliver unique tourist experiences at the destination. The state tourism board promotes different types of products, attracting tourists from all over the world. Furthermore, each tourism product taps the tourists' requirements and encourages engagement. One such tourism product Madhya Pradesh Tourism offers is Jal Mahotsav, which means water carnival in English. The event is held from October to January at the Hanuwantiya Island near the Khandwa district. The island must be explored, promising a serene visiting experience for tourists. Located near the Indira Sagar Dam, built on the Narmada River, India's most significant water carnival offers adventure activities to visitors. Moreover, to provide a thrilling oceanic experience, an artificial water body has been created (Patel, 2017).

The Jal Mahotsav is well-equipped with a temporary tent city that caters to more than 100 Swiss tents. The tents provide a hassle-free accommodation unit for visitors. The temporary city also houses a multi-cuisine dining hall and conference facilities. Moreover, the events at the Hanuwantiya Island also organised several water, land and air-based adventure activities along with cultural evening, craft display and island trekking (MP Tourism, 2020). Some of the activities organised are – cycle tours, treasure hunts, water zorbing, parasailing, tug of war, bird watching, glamping, hot air ballooning, water-skiing, kite flying, banana boat riding and paramotoring (MP Tourism, 2020).

The Jal Mahotsav is organised and promoted by the Madhya Pradesh Tourism Board (MPTB) and offers tenders for the development and management of the event. The event is a successful example of co-creation at a tourist destination because of the following two main reasons:

Common Online Platform for Suggestions

In coordination with the central government, the state government has launched a common online platform. The platform invites stakeholders and tourists to share their suggestions, opinions and areas of improvement for the Hanuwantiya Jal Mahotsav in comments. Introducing a common online platform, encouraging people or potential attendees and other stakeholders to discussions, and putting forward their suggestions, is a crucial step towards co-creating events experience at the water carnival. In addition, the MPTB's initiative to co-create event experience through a technological medium has made this event popular among domestic travellers.

Co-creating Experience at the Event Through Activities

One of the biggest reasons for the popularity of the Jal Mahotsav is the level of tourist engagement. The event offers a wide array of activities for people belonging to different age groups. The activities deliver a unique experience to the visitors' minds, bodies and soul. Moreover, the event ensures value co-creation by engaging tourists with thrilling adventurous activities to spiritual exercises like yoga and meditation (Fig. 9.2).

Future Directions

Co-creating Through Online Platforms

The essence of co-creation lies in collaboration. One such platform that offers shared experiences is Nibana. The platform encourages people to interact, communicate and co-create experiences at the Nibana Festival. The platform adheres to seven founding principles – Collaborative community, Live and Let

Fig. 9.2.   Jal Mahotsav, Hanuwantiya Island, Madhya Pradesh (India). *Source:* Belongs to the Author.

live, Try, No intoxication, Loving communication, Enthusiastic consent and Care for Earth (Nibana, 2019). The development of similar platforms would be the future of co-creating experiences in events and festivals. Common online platforms like Nibana Festival encourage people to collaborate and co-create experiences and become a part of a global community.

Virtual Approach to Co-create Experience

The post-pandemic era has gradually signified technological deployments in the tourism sector. These include augmented reality, virtual reality (VR), chatbots, wearable technology and enhanced use of artificial intelligence. These tools have increasingly become crucial in the events spectrum globally (Buhalis & Leung, 2018; Tiwari & Chowdhary, 2022). The developing incorporation of VR in events would bring technology-driven co-creation of experiences for the visitors. However, only some events have retorted to VR to co-create, such as Anheuser-Busch giving a virtual tour of St Louis brewery at the 2016 SXSW fest (Maskeroni, 2016). The immersive experience allowed attendees to see, smell and taste their Budweiser.

Nevertheless, involving diverse stakeholders would increase engagement and co-create experiences and value; Bustard (2019) stressed the challenge of mapping stakeholders. Accordingly, the authors suggested following the conventional classification given by Freeman in 1984, which includes – competitors, media, government, customers, local community, environmentalists, suppliers and so on (Freeman, 1984).

Research Box

The case study method of research. The case study is a qualitative enquiry or a retrospective exploration into a research area (Flick, 2009). It analyses the state/process in-depth, and includes well-structured narratives that reflect the challenges and paradoxes of a real-life scenario (Flyvbjerg, 2006). As case study method of research aims to unveil the hidden and unexplored connotations of a phenomena related to a destination (Hollinshead, 2004), it is widely used in the field tourism and hospitality. Accordingly, this chapter has adopted the case study method approach to understand the significance of co-creation in promoting an event, and destination as a whole.

Conclusion

The emergence of co-creation in strategic management and marketing decisions must be noticed. In the current industrial era, delivering value holds the utmost importance. Consequently, business processes, product designing, supply chain management systems, service and product marketing and service delivery aim to co-create. Co-creation has become a key element in the tourism, hospitality and events industry, where services' production and consumption co-occur. Long-term survival will be questionable if tourism products and services eliminate value co-creation.

The study proposed the significance of co-creating value with the help of multiple stakeholders, namely academia, tourists, government, competitors and ecosystem partners. Co-creating value for every stakeholder would lead to inclusive development of the tourism sector. The process of co-creation experiences should be sought in a manner that brings both innovation and sustainability while delivering value. Further, this chapter presented a case study of Jal Mahotsav, India's largest water carnival, held annually in the Madhya Pradesh State from October to January. The event has gained massive popularity among domestic visitors and assistance from the local government bodies. The event is branded and promoted under the Madhya Pradesh Tourism Campaign as a unique product.

Furthermore, the water carnival has become a hallmark tourism product in the state and a successful example of co-creating experiences at the destination. However, there is a scope for further improvement to make this event an international brand. For instance, event organisers can influence the co-creation experience by using VR tools. It would arbitrate the impact of co-creation on visitors' satisfaction.

Learning and implementing the strategic actions adopted by similar events worldwide would lead to better promotion of the event. For instance, to increase the co-creation experience, the Macao International Parade organisers aimed to encourage interaction between the performers and attendees (Zhang et al., 2019). Consequently, they invited local schools, artists and organisations to perform in the parade, attracting their families and friends who had come to cheer for the performers (Zhang et al., 2019).

Future studies are suggested to explore the nuances of co-creation experience in events, and their impact on event loyalty, word-of-mouth publicity and overall satisfaction among event attendees. As this chapter has undertaken a single case to understand the relationship between co-creation and destination promotion, future studies can compare and contrast two or more cases to identify the differences.

Discussion Questions

- How does co-creation through the multi-stakeholders approach contribute to sustainable tourism development goals?
- What could be the significant issues of adopting a multi-stakeholders approach in co-creation?
- What are the challenges and benefits of co-creating event experiences through virtual mode?
- How does co-creation help promote a destination or event?

References

Bjerke, R., & Naess, H. E. (2021). Toward a co-creation framework for developing a green sports event brand: The case of the 2018 Zürich E Prix. *Journal of Sport & Tourism, 25*(2), 129–154. https://doi.org/10.1080/14775085.2021.1895872

Buhalis, D., & Leung, R. (2018). Smart hospitality—Interconnectivity and interoperability towards an ecosystem. *International Journal of Hospitality Management, 71*, 41–50. https://doi.org/10.1016/j.ijhm.2017.11.011

Buhalis, D., & Sinarta, Y. (2019). Real-time co-creation and nowness service: Lessons from tourism and hospitality. *Journal of Travel & Tourism Marketing, 36*(5), 563–582. https://doi.org/10.1080/10548408.2019.1592059

Buonincontri, P., Morvilloa, A., Okumus, F., & Niekerk, M. V. (2017). Managing the experience co-creation process in tourism destinations: Empirical findings from Naples. *Tourism Management, 62*(October), 264–277. https://doi.org/10.1016/j.tourman.2017.04.014

Bustard, J. (2019). *The smart event experience: A many-to-many co-creation* (Doctoral dissertation). Ulster University.

Campos, A. C., Mendesl, J., Valle, P. O., & Scott, N. (2015). Co-creation of tourist experiences: A literature review. *Current Issues in Tourism, 21*(4), 369–400.

Chathoth, P. K., Ungson, G. R., Harrington, R. J., & Chan, E. S. (2016). Co-creation and higher order customer engagement in hospitality and tourism services: A critical review. *International Journal of Contemporary Hospitality Management, 28*(2), 222–245. https://doi.org/10.1108/IJCHM-10-2014-0526

Choo, H., & Petrick, J. F. (2014). Social interactions and intentions to revisit agritourism service encounters. *Tourism Management, 40*(February), 372–381. https://doi.org/10.1016/j.tourman.2013.07.011

Chowdhary, N., Tiwari, P., & Kainthola, S. (2020). PRME: The way forward to deal with overtourism and related perverse impacts. In H. Séraphin, T. Gladkikh, & T. V. Thanh (Eds.), *Overtourism: Causes, implications and solutions* (pp. 319–339). Springer International. https://doi.org/10.1007/978-3-030-42458-9_17

Deloitte Insights. (2020, April 20). *How cocreation is helping accelerate product and service innovation.* https://www2.deloitte.com/uk/en/insights/focus/industry-4-0/cocreation-accelerating-product-innovation.html. Accessed on November 7, 2021.

Flick, U. (2009). *An introduction to qualitative research* (4th ed.). SAGE.

Flyvbjerg, B. (2006). Five misunderstandings about case-study research. *Qualitative Inquiry, 12*(2), 219–245.

Font, X., English, R., Gkritzali, A., & Tian, W. S. (2021). Value co-creation in sustainable tourism: A service-dominant logic approach. *Tourism Management, 82*, 104200. https://doi.org/10.1016/j.tourman.2020.104200

Freeman, R. E. (1984). *Strategic management: A stakeholder approach.* Pitman.

Getz, D. (2010). The nature and scope of festival studies. *International Journal of Event Management Research, 5*(1), 1–47. https://www.ijemr.org/wp-content/uploads/2014/10/Getz.pdf

Hollinshead, K. (2004). Ontological craft in tourism studies. In J. Phillimore & L. Goodson (Eds.), *Qualitative research in tourism: Ontologies, epistemologies and methodologies* (pp. 83–101). Routledge.

Hong, S. G., & Lee, H. M. (2015). Developing Gamcheon Cultural Village as a tourist destination through co-creation. *Service Business, 9*, 749–769. https://doi.org/10. 1007/s11628-014-0252-z

Innovators. (2019, October 15). Some examples of co-creation that bring brand and consumer together. Ideas4all Innovators. https://www.ideas4allinnovation.com/ innovators/examples-cocreation-consumers/

Jaakkola, E., & Alexander, M. (2014). The role of customer engagement behavior in value co-creation: A service system perspective. *Journal of Service Research, 17*, 247–261.

Kamboj, S., & Gupta, S. (2020). Use of smartphone apps in co-creative hotel service innovation: Evidence from India. *Current Issues in Tourism, 23*(3), 323–344. https:// doi.org/10.1080/13683500.2018.1513459

Kim, H., & Stepchenkova, S. (2015). Effect of tourist photographs on attitudes towards destination: Manifest and latent content. *Tourism Management, 49*(August), 29–41.

Kim, H., Stepchenkova, S., & Babalou, V. (2018). Branding destination co-creatively: A case study of tourists' involvement in naming a local attraction. *Tourism Management Perspectives, 28*, 189–200. https://doi.org/10.1016/j.tmp.2018.09.003

Lei, S. I., Ye, S., Wang, D., & Law, R. (2020). Engaging customers in value co-creation through instant mobile messaging in the tourism and hospitality industry. *Journal of Hospitality & Tourism Research, 44*(2), 229–251. https://doi.org/10.1177/ 1096348019893066

Maskeroni, A. (2016, March 5). How the Budweiser Garage Brewed up an immersive experience for SXSW attendees. [Video]. Adweek.com. https://www.adweek.com/ brand-marketing/how-budweiser-garage-brewed-immersive-experience-sxsw-attendees-video-170177/

Miki, A. F., & Canino, R. M. (2018). Development of a tourism coopetition model: A preliminary Delphi study. *Journal of Hospitality and Tourism Management, 37*, 78–88. https://doi.org/10.1016/j.jhtm.2018.10.004

Mohammadi, F., Yazdani, H. R., Jami Pour, M., & Soltani, M. (2021). Co-creation in tourism: A systematic mapping study. *Tourism Review, 76*(2), 305–343. https://doi. org/10.1108/TR-10-2019-0425

MP Tourism. (2020, April 1). *Enjoy the Tent City in – Jal Mahotsav 2020.* https:// www.mptourism.com/tentcity-in-jalmahotsav-2020.html

Neuhofer, B. (2016). Value co-creation and co-destruction in connected tourist experiences. In A. Inversini & R. Schegg (Eds.), *Information and communication technologies in tourism* (pp. 779–792). Springer International Publishing. https:// doi.org/10.1007/978-3-319-28231-2_56

Nibana. (2019). The concept. https://nibanafestival.com/en/concept

Ostrom, A., Bitner, M. J., Brown, S. W., Burkhard, K. A., Goul, K., Smith-Daniels, V., & Rabinovich, E. (2010). Moving forward and making a difference: Research priorities for the science of service. *Journal of Service Research, 13*, 4–36. https:// doi.org/10.1177/1094670509357611

Pandey, S., & Kumar, D. (2021). From a literature review to a conceptual framework for customer-to-customer value co-creation. *Contemporary Management Research, 17*(3), 189–221. https://doi.org/10.7903/CMR.20663

Patel, C. (2017, October 11). Dive into the heart of India at Jal Mahotsav. Natgeo Traveller. https://natgeotraveller.in/dive-into-the-heart-of-india-at-the-jal-mahotsav/

Plichta, J. (2019). The co-management and stakeholders theory is a useful approach to managing the problem of overtourism in historical cities–illustrated with an example of Krakow. *International Journal of Tourism Cities, 5*(4), 685–699. https://doi.org/10.1108/IJTC-12-2018-0107

Prahalad, C., & Ramaswamy, V. (2004). Co-creation experiences: The next practice in value creation. *Journal of Interactive Marketing, 18*(3), 5–14.

Prebensen, N. K., Kim, H., & Uysal, M. (2016). Cocreation as a moderator between the experience value and satisfaction relationship. *Journal of Travel Research, 55*(7), 934–945. https://doi.org/10.1177/0047287515583359

Proximus. (2018, May 1). Co-creation: Innovating together with your competitors? Proximus – Inspire. https://www.proximus.be/en/id_b_cl_co_creation/companies-and-public-sector/blog/news-blog/inspire/co-creation.html

Rachão, S., Breda, Z., Fernandes, C., & Joukes, V. (2020). Cocreation of tourism experiences: Are food-related activities being explored? *British Food Journal, 122*(3), 910–928. https://doi.org/10.1108/BFJ-10-2019-0769

Rachão, S. A. S., de Jesus Breda, Z., de Oliveira Fernandes, C., & Joukes, V. N. P. M. (2021). Drivers of experience co-creation in food-and-wine tourism: An exploratory quantitative analysis. *Tourism Management Perspectives, 37*, 100783. https://doi.org/10.1016/j.tmp.2020.100783

Ramaswamy, V., & Gouillart, F. (2010). *The power of co-creation: Build it with them to boost growth, productivity, and profits.* Simon and Schuster.

Rihova, I., Buhalis, D., Moital, M., & Gouthro, M.-B. (2015). Conceptualising customer-to-customer value co-creation in tourism. *International Journal of Tourism Research, 17*(4), 356–363. https://doi.org/10.1002/jtr.1993

Roy, N., & Gretzel, U. (2020). Themed route marketing in India. *Anatolia, 31*(2), 304–315. https://doi.org/10.1080/13032917.2020.1747222

Sahin, S., & Baloglu, S. (2014). City branding: Investigating a brand advocacy model for distinct segments. *Journal of Hospitality Marketing & Management, 23*(3), 239–265. https://doi.org/10.1080/19368623.2013.779562

Sthapit, E., & Björk, P. (2019). Sources of value co-destruction: Uber customer perspectives. *Tourism Review, 74*(4), 78–794. https://doi.org/10.1108/TR-12-2018-0176

Suntikul, W., & Jachna, T. (2016). The co-creation/place attachment nexus. *Tourism Management, 52*, 276–286. https://doi.org/10.1016/j.tourman.2015.06.026

Tiwari, P., & Chowdhary, N. (2022). Technology and crowd management at events: A case study of Kumbh Festival in India. In *Festival and event tourism: Building resilience and promoting sustainability* (pp. 151–158). CABI.

Tjandra, N. C., Rihova, I., Snell, S., Den Hertog, C. S., & Theodoraki, E. (2021). Mega-events brand meaning co-creation: The Olympic case. *Journal of Product & Brand Management, 30*(1), 58–73.

Tuana, L. T., Rajendrana, D., Rowley, C., & Khaic, D. C. (2019). Customer value co-creation in the business-to-business tourism context: The roles of corporate social responsibility and customer empowering behaviours. *Journal of Hospitality and Tourism Management, 39*, 137–149. https://doi.org/10.1016/j.jhtm.2019.04.002

Tussyadiah, I., & Zach, F. (2013). Social media strategy and capacity for consumer co-creation among destination marketing organisations. In L. Cantoni & Z. Xiang (Eds.), *Information and communication technologies in tourism* (pp. 242–253). Springer. https://doi.org/10.1007/978-3-642-36309-2_21

UNESCO. (2021). *World Heritage List.* https://whc.unesco.org/en/list/

Wanga, J. O., Hayombe, P. O., Onyango, M., & Agong, S. G. (2014). Co-creating value in ecotourism experiences (tour guides, craft makers, and tourists in Dunga beach, Kisumu city). http://ir.jooust.ac.ke/handle/123456789/9168

Zhang, C. X., Fong, L. H. N., & Li, S. (2019). Co-creation experience and place attachment: Festival evaluation. *International Journal of Hospitality Management*, *81*, 193–204.

Chapter 10

In the Quest of Deeper Meaning of Life: Perspectivising the Bliss of Mystic Experiences by Following Spiritual Gurus

Manpreet Arora

Central University of Himachal Pradesh, India

Learning Objectives

After reading and studying this chapter, you should be able to:

- understand why spiritual gurus and their teachings becoming very famous worldwide;
- explore how spiritual gurus and the spiritual tourism in general are creating opportunities for the tourism sector;
- explore how spiritual, wellness and religious tourism trends are diverted towards mystic experiences bringing bliss by knowing deeper meanings of life by these spiritual gurus.

Abstract

The COVID-19 pandemic forced us not only to think but also to pause and objectively reflect on how to deal with the situation that has arisen and how to develop well-being and resilience strategies for the welfare of humanity at large. We long to be in those vicinities where we want to calm our minds in the quest for a deeper meaning of one existence. It can be a nature-based destination, a pilgrim destination or a part of a religious tour depending on one's faith, belief and orientation towards spirituality and bliss. The abundance of natural resources available in nature is the prime source of overall wellness in all parts of the world, as are the traditional Indian practices of *Yoga*, *Ayurveda* and the practices suggested by traditional holy scriptures. This chapter attempts to see the wave of spiritual gurus boosting the wellness

---

Future Tourism Trends Volume 1, 133–144
Copyright © 2024 Manpreet Arora
Published under exclusive licence by Emerald Publishing Limited
doi:10.1108/978-1-83753-244-520241010

sector associated with travelling. Gurus like Sri Sri Ravi Shankar, Sadguru Vasudev Jaggi and HH Dalai Lama are some of the international gurus who have influenced spiritual and wellness tourism to a large extent. The discourse analysis revealed that people long for spirituality for peace and wellness. It also reveals being spiritual has no fixed dimension; it varies from person to person.

Keywords: Religion; spirituality; wellness; mysticism; spiritual gurus; spiritual tourism; tourism experiences; qualitative research; consumption of religion

Introduction

Religion has been the most critical force since time immemorial. It affects not only the personal life of people but their public or professional life affected by their faith orientations. Even a business's organisational culture is affected by a leader's faith. Many countries have provided safeguards for religious freedom through their constitutions and provisions in various laws and constitutions. They have guided established principles of protecting free religious practices or the freedom to opt for religion or no religion. It has also been seen that in many countries, conversion of religion is again mushrooming like a good business. Religious freedom has fostered the development of a dynamic religious marketplace in inducing the entrepreneurial and service sector. Opting for religious beliefs or spirituality has also been considered a resilience strategy during and after COVID-19. Religious congregations have been contributing to people's social life in many ways. They not only foster the people's economic and other life needs but are regarded as emotional, social psychological support for many.

The COVID-19 pandemic forced us not only to think but also to pause and objectively reflect on how to deal with the situation that has arisen and how to develop well-being and resilience strategies for the welfare of humanity at large (Arora & Sharma, 2022a). Wellness and nature go hand in hand, and now everybody has realised that the ultimate peace and bliss can be found within us, especially by controlling our thoughts, mind and energy (Simone & Vasudev, 2008). The superpower designs our body to heal when it is close to nature automatically, and one has controlled their ways of living. Saints, *Sadhus*, *gurus* and people who had some mystical experiences have always shared that whatever peace and bliss comes to their soul has been achieved by them by staying for a long time in nature and following practices like *yoga, dhyana, meditation*, being part of religious gatherings, congregations, charities, *etc.* The inner state of happiness and a healed body and mind is the prime motivation of most of the world after experiencing the pandemic. We long to be in those vicinities where we want to calm our minds in the quest for a deeper meaning of one existence. It can be a nature-based destination, a pilgrim destination or a part of a religious tour depending on one's faith, belief and orientation towards spirituality and bliss. The abundance of natural resources available in nature is the prime source of overall wellness in all parts of the world, as are the traditional Indian practices of *Yoga, Ayurveda* and the practices suggested by traditional holy scriptures (Arora & Sharma, 2022b). Every destination in India and around the World has its unique set of natural treats in the form of beauty, food, culture and much more. The experiences of these destinations lead us to have spiritual and mystical experiences which gadgets, materialistic lifestyles, luxuries and any highest form of technology can never give. Nature is simply irreplaceable. It is the basis of our existence. Nature has its way of healing. It knows how to make balance.

Moreover, a shift towards seeing these practices very close to nature can be seen following the spiritual gurus, famous worldwide. In order to learn these practices, people worldwide are watching their YouTube channels and seeking to visit their centres in India or the international centres in various countries. Therefore, in this post COVID era, a newer dimension of travelling, not only for spirituality, can be seen. It has a deeper dimension of mysticism, inner bliss and wellness (Arora & Sharma, 2021; Teasdale, 2001). Masses worldwide acknowledge that spending time in spiritual centres, *ashrams* and places attached to divinity and divine gurus is the leading source of rejuvenation, peace, joy and happiness. It is, therefore, attracting the interest of researchers and academicians to ponder their thoughts towards how spiritual gurus, their teachings and living practices can be a source to the various issues and challenges of the modern-day World and how to save it and preserve it for future generations. Overall, well-being comprises not just physical wellness but focuses on a healthy and peaceful mind. This chapter attempts to see the wave of spiritual gurus boosting the wellness sector associated with travelling. Gurus like Sri Sri Ravi Shankar, Sadguru Vasudev Jaggi and HH Dalai Lama are some of the international gurus who have influenced spiritual and wellness tourism to a large extent. Centres of Osho, Isha Centre and Vipashana are famous worldwide, and people schedule their visits every year to be in these centres. They are a significant boost not only to the economy and related entrepreneurial ventures but also to the digitalisation of the tourism sector in a vast sense. The following research questions will be answered conceptually, along with the proposed methodology.

Methodology

This chapter will be opinion-based, and primary qualitative data will be used to support the argument. In addition, a qualitative piece of paper will illuminate the emerging trends in the tourism sector, which can be helpful to academicians and researchers in shaping their empirical research for the future. For content analysis based on literature and data visualisation techniques by using VosViewer has been used.

A perspective or opinion will be formulated further by identifying the effect of the growing followership of spiritual gurus across the World on the tourism sector by addressing the research questions stated below.

RQ 1 Why are the spiritual gurus and their teachings becoming very famous worldwide?

In various religions, following certain spiritual gurus has been a practice to enlighten oneself. The path towards divinity and achieving the higher goals of life, which can be understood only by the human brain, were taught and practised by many in various religions. The ultimate goal of any religion is to achieve the higher dimensions of energy called spirituality. In modern times also, it has been seen that people are following the path of spirituality to a great extent. There is a thin line between religion and spirituality. Many believe that a certain kind of faith or following a religion can help them gain the path of spirituality and higher life goals. While others are of the opinion that religion binds them and it is not a right approach for achieving the spiritual goals of life. Whatever it is, spirituality has always been kept above religion. During and after COVID-19, there has been a continuous increase in the followers of various spiritual gurus across the world. We can attribute various reasons to the rise in these spiritual gurus and their followership. However, something needs to be more decisive, measurable and accurate. It is subjective, but spiritual and wellness tourism growth can also be attributed to such spiritual gurus. The following are the listed reasons behind the increase in the followership of spiritual gurus worldwide:

- The reasons behind the popularity of spiritual gurus and their teachings can be attributed to various factors in which they have a universal appeal towards seeking truth and the meaning of life.
- Most of them make a broader appeal to the need to cope up with stress and anxiety by following a spiritual path with the help of social media. So, they reach a larger audience and can appeal to many simultaneously.
- Most spiritual gurus do not tie themselves to a particular religion or culture. Their teachings are universal and appeal to the broader masses from all walks of life. They promote the wellness and well-being of the whole of humanity.
- With the growing materialism and chaos in life, many people in the world are still seeking more profound meaning and truth in their lives. Spiritual gurus provide teachings, ways or means to individuals through various yogic practices, meditation, exercises, etc., to connect them with their inner selves and help them find answers to more important questions of life.
- Today, the world is so fast-paced that stress and anxiety have become common issues at every age. Practices like yoga, breathing techniques, mindful meditation and joining religious congregations are helpful in coping up with stress and anxiety. Most spiritual gurus follow the path of enlightenment and peace towards achieving the bliss of life through such techniques. That is why these techniques are continuously gaining the attention of the worldwide audience.
- The world's barriers have become minimal with the internet and digitalised social media networks. World has become more connected, and people are exposed to diverse cultures with spiritual practices worldwide. This has increased interest in various spiritual and mystic practices followed by spiritual gurus worldwide. Their teachings are readily available on social media

networks and YouTube channels. They have websites which propagate various kinds of products relating to their teachings. They carry online sessions and reach a larger audience. They spend months on tours, and people follow them in congregations and visit various kinds of gatherings, shows and healing therapy activities from different nations. People learn from various traditions when exposed to such kinds of activities. That is why an increased spiritual inclination towards the practices followed by the spiritual gurus is becoming very famous.

• A rising trend in most of the population can be seen where many people search for spiritual practices that do not require them to follow any particular religion or dogma. Spiritual gurus often offer teachings not tied to any particular religion, and they can be practised by any faith or not at all. They do not follow any particular dimension of any religion which binds any soul or mind. They allow freedom of mind and try to explore the most profound dimensions of life. The experiences of various people who follow such dimensions and certain yogic practices to achieve a better life by following the wellness practices of life achieve a state of bliss and happiness. It leads them to different life levels with specific mystic dimensions or fulfiling experiences. They can be soul-satisfying life, and may lead one person to a state of bliss and happiness. Such experiences can hardly be found in religion. That is why people want to be more spiritual than religious.

In order to understand why people try to be spiritual and what reasons can be attributed for being them spiritual. A random discourse analysis was conducted with 50 tourists in the Dharamshala region of Himachal Pradesh, India, a famous spiritual destination. The researcher kept in mind 12 basis points to be asked in an unstructured manner from the discourse of these respondents. These were the following:

(1) Spirituality is the search for meaning and purpose in life.
(2) It helps in relieving stress and anxiety.
(3) Spirituality can be found without religion.
(4) They follow spirituality for cultural curiosity and learning.
(5) Social media exposure leads to growing spirituality or an inclination towards spirituality.
(6) High followership on Instagram of spiritual gurus is due to advertisements and faith-based propaganda.
(7) Interviews/talks of spiritual gurus on YouTube videos stimulating their faith or leading them towards spirituality or religion.
(8) Spirituality is a mode of coping with stress.
(9) Faith helps them feel positive.
(10) Spirituality promotes peace.
(11) Being spiritual leads to a better lifestyle.
(12) Spirituality helps them achieve wellness goals and leads to experiences of mysticism.

The significant findings of this discourse analysis were following:

The majority of them attributed the reason behind being their most spiritual is the social media impact. The second main reason was to adopt a better lifestyle or achieve their wellness goals. Seventy-five percent of the respondents believed it helps relieve stress and anxiety. Only 15% agreed that spiritual goals are for the search of meaning and purpose of life. Eighty-five percent of the respondents believed that faith helps them to feel positive. Ninety percent of them believed that being spiritual and not religious promotes peace. All of them agreed that spirituality is a way to cope with stress.

RQ 2 How are they creating opportunities for the tourism sector?

Religion has been a significant as well as potent source of economic as well as social strength in many economies around the world. Let us take for example, the most developed nation in the world, the United States. As per, World Economic Forum, the contribution through religion is more than 1.2 trillion dollars in the United States. It is higher than the revenue earned by top tech companies annually. The concept of religion here is not confined only to faith in a particular religion, but it also has broader and deeper connotations of spirituality and wellness. The various components which contribute towards religion in the United States, as per World Economic Forum, are through 'institutions', 'congregations', 'healthcare activities', 'faith inspired businesses', etc. The central source of strength in the economy is 'charities and congregations'. There are enormous contributions through religious congregations, like churches, mosques, temples and chapels. They are not only the source of income for the economy but also attract many tourists annually, fostering employment for thousands of people. The consumption through these religious congregations of services is worth billions, further providing opportunities for the local masses to help them earn their livelihoods (Arora & Sharma, 2023).

Such congregations are found around the world. They are not just only the places to worship. They have attracted millions of people with some belief or faith and a higher sense of spirituality, promoting wellness and peace. The significant businesses which are induced by such congregations are related to the utilities of diverse kinds like; sound and music camps, retreats and gatherings, food, hospitality, tourism related ventures, sound systems, maintenance facilities, transport, water, flower decorations, singers, preachers, *dharama gurus and much more.* Another aspect of the faith is a 'community orientation' or 'community focus'. These community-related orientations are not just lectures or congresses. They affect spiritual pilgrimage and religious tourism primarily. This is experience-based travel, and a need to experience religious aspirations through visiting various destinations plays an important role in promoting spirituality.

The social and volunteering effects of the communities' congregations are many. The congregations of many have promoted not only education, but, has many other social impacts also. Moreover, civic engagements have also led to a decrease in crime and promoted mental health, decreased illness and spirituality.

In countries like America, many studies have shown that religious congregations and other faith-based activities have positively affected the health and welfare of millions of Americans.

RQ 3 How are spiritual, wellness and religious tourism trends diverted towards mystic experiences bringing bliss by knowing deeper meanings of life by these spiritual gurus?

Overall, spiritual tourism is a growing trend around the world as more people seek out meaningful travel experiences that allow them to connect with their spiritual self and explore different cultures and traditions. In various dimensions, tourism and spirituality are deeply connected. People around the world travel to different destinations to explore spiritual destinations to have magical experiences.

Mysticism is a term used to describe a range of spiritual practices and beliefs that focus on the direct experience of the divine or ultimate reality. It is often associated with religious traditions such as Christianity, Islam, Judaism, Buddhism and Hinduism but can also be found in non-religious or secular contexts. Spirituality has no boundaries or confinements. Mystics seek a deeper understanding of the universe and their place in it and strive for direct communion with the divine or ultimate reality. They often use meditation, prayer, fasting and asceticism to achieve spiritual experiences and insights. Mystical experiences can be described as a sense of unity with all things, a feeling of transcendence or ecstasy, or a direct encounter with the divine. Mysticism has a long history and can be found in many different cultural and religious traditions. Some well-known mystics include the Christian mystics Saint Teresa of Avila and Saint John of the Cross, the Sufi poet Rumi, the Hindu saint Ramakrishna and the Buddhist monk Thich Nhat Hanh. The modern mystic gurus from India especially are Sadhguru and Sri Sri Ravi Shankar. Whereas some are the internationally famous spiritual leaders like HH Dalai Lama and Pope Francis, who are being followed and admired by millions. They achieve their spiritual goals by travelling to various destinations and places of spiritual importance. Mystical practices and beliefs can be controversial and are often difficult to define or measure (Arora et al., 2021). Some people believe that mystical experiences help access spiritual truths and insights, while others view them as subjective experiences that cannot be verified or tested. Despite these debates, mysticism remains an essential aspect of many religious and spiritual traditions and continues to inspire and influence people around the world.

Further, in order to understand what literature highlights about spirituality and tourism, a Scopus search with the following string was made.

Title – ABS – Key

('Spiritualgurus' OR 'Spirituality' OR 'Mystic' OR 'mysticism' OR 'bliss' OR 'Spiritual') AND (LIMIT-TO (DOCTYPE, 'ar')) AND (LIMIT-TO (SUB-JAREA, 'BUSI')) AND (LIMIT-TO (LANGUAGE, 'English')) AND (LIMIT-TO (SRCTYPE, 'j'))

Initially, more than 97,000 documents were received for all the fields of study as per the search mentioned above keywords, which was further refined to the articles published in English only in business accounting and management. It refined the documents up to 2,758 documents.

In order to understand the key thrust areas of research and implications, the content analysis of all the abstracts of these documents was performed. With that help, a cloud chart (Fig. 10.1) has been prepared to understand the significant dimensions of research. If we go by the major highlights of the major thrust areas of researchers, it is on 'spirituality and leadership'. Most of them talk about spiritual leadership in an organisational set-up. Another dimension is 'spirituality and tourism', which is undoubtedly a growing area. It also highlights certain important aspects of spirituality like 'human values', 'ethics', 'religion', 'education' 'health', 'well-being', 'quality of life experiences', 'cultural aspects', 'marketing of spiritual products', 'behavioural dimensions of spirituality', 'commitment', 'psychology', etc. The content analysis highlights that only a few studies discuss mysticism and magical experiences. It highlights the area of future research and the scope for further explorations.

The concept of spirituality is closely associated with following a spiritual guru, mentor or a teacher. Various religions propagate following a specific mechanism to achieve the higher stage of spirituality. In common parlance, any person who is the master in a particular branch of knowledge and can impart that knowledge to

Fig. 10.1.   Cloud Chart of the Most Frequent Keywords. *Source:* Created by author by using Scopus data.

others is considered a guru, preacher, teacher or master. Various religions like Christianity, Hinduism, Sikhism and Muslims consider their spiritual texts, rituals, processes and spiritual gurus essential for reaching the higher dimensions of mind and body beyond what one could express in its mystic form. It promotes wellness and peace in humanity. It can be community-based or an individual effort and orientation. When we talk about spirituality and mystic experiences, they are typically individual experiences (Coleman III et al., 2019). These are sometimes inexpressible in words.

The concept of following a spiritual leader for spiritual enlightenment is a concept that has been introduced previously. The ancient wisdom of India, China and many other nations propagate and provide activities, practices, processes, prayers, mantras, etc. A spiritual leader is a person who helps to remove mental blocks and leads the way from spiritual darkness to enlightenment for walking on the road of spirituality. Further, anyone adept in certain branches of knowledge is known as a spiritual guru or has a path of wisdom to follow to lead the way for others who accept to follow him. If we talk about Hinduism specifically, spiritual gurus are the pillars of the social system or religions propagated in the country. Almost all of them were self-appointed and self-made and propagated their own selves through various modes. They have been emerging as one of the significant drivers of spiritual tourism. Most of the modern spiritual gurus are on social media platforms and have a huge fan following. They propagate themselves as self-appointed savers, angels, reincarnations, pillars, stewards and guardians of *dharma*. Many religions call themselves messengers of gods and preach values and ethics, which are the best behaviours for humankind to follow. They have engaged in tour visits, conferences and religious gatherings on average, with thousands of people joining their gatherings to hear and follow them. In many religions, like those following Muslims, Jainism, Christianity and Hinduism sector, the spiritual gurus or the messengers are primarily responsible for spreading the religious teachings to the whole world. Many spiritual or religious gurus play different, diverse and exciting societal roles. They not only control the moral conduct of the followers but also regulate the ways of life in many ways. They provide counselling, one-to-one session, healing sessions, act as exorcists and protectors of humankind.

When we mainly talk about the travel associated with spiritual gurus or spiritual destinations, they can also be related to the wellness sector, which has seen a sharp increase after COVID. Many tourists travel to nature-based areas, *ashrams, meditation centres* or religious camps to seek 'wellness and peace'. Travelling to a particular destination or *Ashrama* or visiting some spiritual gurus, congregation or gathering increases the entrepreneurial opportunities for the localities and boosts the related service sector. It not only generates employment opportunities for the local people but also helps them to become self-sufficient. Various allied industries like souvenir making, local products, art, cuisine, food items, etc., come into demand and contribute to national economic growth. The consumption of religion has become an essential aspect of every economy these days. Whether any nation is a Christian nation, an Islamic nation or any other nation, some religious destinations are spiritual places which attract thousands of tourists every year, boosting not only the travel and tourism sector but also the related sectors.

The keyword analysis of the data highlights the niche area of the research topics on various dimensions of spirituality and mysticism. Further, it also

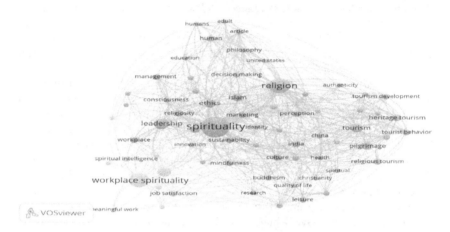

Fig. 10.2.   Keyword Analysis. *Source:* Created by the author using the SCOPUS database.

highlights the areas that need to be researched more and can have a better scope for research in the future. Fig. 10.2 shows the visual depiction of keywords.

If we look at the keyword analysis in Fig. 5.4., the central cluster is spirituality, which is related to the keywords 'leadership', 'sustainability', and 'religiosity'. On the other hand, one cluster talks about the tourism sector, which is quite broad and is emerging, and talks about 'tourism development', 'authenticity', 'perception', 'Pilgrimage' or 'religious tourism' and 'tourist behaviour'. Countries like India and China, along with Buddhism and Christianity, figure in that cluster. It also indicates the keywords related to 'quality of life', 'leisure' and 'mindfulness and culture'. It directly indicates that the researchers are exploring the areas of 'religious tourism' about the 'quality of life' and 'overall well-being' of humankind. People are now talking about mindful eating and mindful travelling, which ultimately bring them bliss and a higher state of spirituality. At the same time, another cluster talks about 'religion', where the 'philosophical, human and educational perspectives' are being researched. Another niche area which is developing at this stage is 'workplace spirituality', which leads to 'job satisfaction', 'meaningful life' and 'spiritual intelligence'.

Research Box

Suggestions for Future Research

There are many motivations and experiences of the tourists who visit destinations associated with various spiritual gurus. Very less research is available on the perception of the impact of these gurus on their travel experiences. Researchers can explore this area in the future. Further, the economic impact of spiritual tourism is very high. Undoubtedly, these spiritual gurus and their various organisations earn great revenue by the tourists who visit them. But on the same hand, the economic benefits for the local communities, entrepreneurial opportunities and the other employment opportunities associated with such arrivals increase. Empirical studies can be conducted on investigating the impact of spiritual tourism related with economic benefits of the local communities in the near future to contribute towards the literature on the spiritual tourism. Further, the spiritual gurus also offer certain cultural and social practices of different communities. It can have a great and deeper impact on the sustainable tourism development. Future research can also focus on examining the impacts of spiritual gurus on the sustainable tourism development. Spiritual gurus have also the potential in promoting interfaith dialogue and bringing social cohesion and peace building. This area is hardly explored in relation to tourism. Excessive use of social media is also used by spiritual gurus in order to promote tourism, and it also influences their credibility, authenticity and influence. Researchers can also ponder about investigating the use of social media by spiritual gurus and their impact on the credibility, authenticity and influence in future. Tourism in relation to spiritual gurus can have negative impacts on the tourism also. It has commodified the cultural heritage, and the risk of cultural distortions is also there in the name of spirituality. The religion has also been commercialised and commodified. Very few studies in the world talk about the commodification of religion and spirituality and its negative impacts on society as a whole, particularly in relation to tourism. This can be a wonderful area of research for the future generations in order to contribute towards the literature on spirituality in tourism.

Conclusion

There is a thin line between spirituality and religiosity. It is tough to explain spiritual or mystic experiences in words. Very few empirical experiences are available about the mystic and spiritual dimensions. There is a greater possibility to explore this sector, especially tourism. Tourism is a great driver of spiritual experiences, and all over the world, various spiritual leaders are playing a pivotal role in this relation to boosting spiritual tourism and religious consumption of the products. This field of mystic experiences driven by spirituality needs to be explored more and provide researchers opportunities to pursue research in this direction.

Discussion Questions

Based upon the opinions put forward in this chapter by the author, the following discussion questions are open for the academicians/research community to explore further:

- What role do spiritual gurus play in promoting tourism to destinations that are significant to their teachings and practices?
- How can spiritual gurus contribute to the development of spiritual tourism and what impact can this have on local economies?
- In what ways do spiritual gurus act as cultural ambassadors for their communities and how can they leverage their influence to attract more tourists?
- What can be done to ensure that the relationship between spiritual gurus and tourism is mutually beneficial, and not just one-sided?

References

Arora, M., & Sharma, R. L. (2021). Post-pandemic psycho-social well-being in India: Challenges and the Way Ahead. *Alina COSTIN*, 201.

Arora, M., & Sharma, R. L. (2022a). Challenges of well-being in and post-lockdown period: Exploring ayurveda, yoga and spirituality as a conduit for rejuvenation and overall wellness. *Prestige International Journal of Management & IT-Sanchayan*, *11*(1), 1–17.

Arora, M., & Sharma, R. L. (2022b). Searching for a break from the drudgery of daily din: Analysing millennials' quest for spirituality and well-being during the COVID-19 pandemic. In *Crisis management, destination recovery and sustainability* (pp. 86–96). Routledge.

Arora, M., & Sharma, R. L. (2023). Religion and strategic marketing communication: Perspectivizing key facets of consumption. In *Promotional practices and perspectives from emerging markets* (pp. 210–225). Routledge.

Arora, M., Sharma, R. L., & Kumar Walia, S. (2021). I am revisiting the inner self in times of debilitating distress: Gateways for wellness through spiritual tourism. *The international journal of religious tourism and pilgrimage*, *9*(5), 26–36.

Coleman, T. J., II, Bartlett, J. E., Holcombe, J. M., Swanson, S. B., Atkinson, A., Silver, C. F., & Hood, R. W. (2019). Absorption, mentalising, and mysticism: Sensing the presence of the divine. *Journal for the Cognitive Science of Religion*, *5*(1), 63–84.

Simone, C., & Vasudev, S. J. (2008). *Midnights with the Mystic: A Little Guide to Freedom and Bliss*. Hampton Roads Publishing.

Teasdale, W. (2001). *The mystic heart: Discovering a universal spirituality in the World's religions*. New World Library.

Chapter 11

The Effect of Tourist Guide Performance on Memorable Tourism Experiences and Revisit Intention[1]

Dilara Eylül Koç[a] and Şevki Ulema[b]

[a]Kastamonu University, Türkiye
[b]Sakarya University of Applied Sciences, Türkiye

Learning Objectives

After reading and studying this chapter, you should be able to:

- understand the definition and principles of tourist guide performance and memorable tourism experiences;
- identify the effect of tourist guides' performance on memorable tourism experiences and the impact of memorable tourism experiences on revisit intention (RVI).

Abstract

Tourist guides undertake many versatile roles as a requirement of their profession. The realisation of these roles also affects the performance of the guide. Findings obtained from empirical evidence on the effects of the tour guide's performance on memorable tourism experiences and the intention to revisit the Cappadocia region shed light on the importance of these elements on each other. Accordingly, the primary purposes of this research are to measure the effect of tourist guides' performance on memorable tourism experiences and the impact of memorable tourism experiences on revisit intention (RVI). For these purposes, the survey technique obtained data from 569 domestic and foreign tourists who participated in guided tours in the Cappadocia region. According to the results of the research, it has been observed that the

---

[1]This chapter is derived from the doctoral dissertation titled the effect of tourist guide performances on memorable tourism experiences and revisit intention.

Future Tourism Trends Volume 1, 145–170
Copyright © 2024 Dilara Eylül Koç and Şevki Ulema
Published under exclusive licence by Emerald Publishing Limited
doi:10.1108/978-1-83753-244-520241011

performance of the tourist guide influences the memorable tourism experience, and the memorable tourism experience affects RVI. In light of the results, suggestions to tourism stakeholders and researchers are listed.

Keywords: Experience tourism; tourist guide; tourism guidance; performance; re-visit intention; marketing

Introduction

It is known that the number of people participating in tourism activities is increasing daily. With the increasing number of visitors, it is seen that visitors tend to travel in a more meaningful way (Chen & Rahman, 2018). For this reason, the tourism experience for visitors also becomes essential, because all experiences produce meaning (Selstad, 2007). Tourism destinations also host tourists' experiences; tourist guides are the most influential person in providing these experiences (Lan, 2000; Weiler & Walker, 2014). The tour guide is the primary point of contact between guests and the host location. In actuality, they are the front-line staff members who play a significant role in the general opinion and satisfaction with the tour services a destination provides (Ap & Wong, 2001).

Tourist guides influence the tourist experience through their roles. Research has shown that the tourist guide's interpreter role (Ap & Wong, 2001; Black et al., 2001; Brito, 2012; Dahles, 2002; Davidson & Black, 2007; Holloway, 1981; Ham & Weiler, 2002; Rabotić, 2010; Weiler & Ham, 2000), instructor role (Ap & Wong, 2001; Davidson & Black, 2007; Reisinger & Steiner, 2006) and leadership role (Black et al., 2001; Gurung et al., 1996; Weiler & Davis, 1993) help tourists to make sense of their experiences.

Tourist guides need to fulfil their professional roles professionally to make tourists' travels unforgettable (Chandralal & Valenzuela, 2013). The tourist guide's knowledge and skills effectively ensure that tourists have memorable tourism experiences (Hurombo, 2016; Mathisen, 2012). Furthermore, tourists' positive emotional experiences are related to destination satisfaction, positively affecting future behavioural intentions (Hosany & Gilbert, 2010; Sanz-Blas & Buzova, 2016).

Although tourist guide performance remains a crucial phenomenon for memorable tourism experiences in the tourism sector, the empirical literature on the effects of tourist performance on memorable tourism experiences is still being determined. Scholars now know that some characteristics of tourist guides affecting their performances, such as interpretation, leadership and information-giver roles (Black et al., 2001; Brito, 2012; Rabotić, 2010), affect tourists' memorable tourism experiences. However, an academic understanding of the effects of tourist guide performance, personality, physical characteristics and competencies on memorable tourism experiences is far from complete.

Hence, the primary purpose of this research is to determine the effect of tourist guides' performance on memorable tourism experiences and the effect of

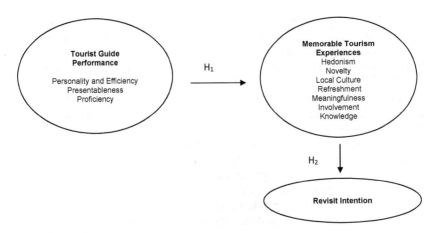

Fig. 11.1. TGP-MTE-RVI Effect Model.

memorable tourism experiences on RVI. Based on the theory of memorable tourism experience, this study is one of the first to develop and research a model that proposes the relationship between tourist guide performance and memorable tourism experience factors in Fig. 11.1.

This study makes contributions to the literature. The empirical evidence on the effects of tourist guides in this study, which fills an essential gap in the tourism management and marketing literature, is one of the first studies to demonstrate the positive impact of tourist guide performance on tourists' memorable tourism experiences. Furthermore, performance on memorable tourism experiences and the effects of these experiences on RVIs shed light on the importance of these factors on each other.

Literature Review

Tourist Guide Performance

The word 'performance' is of French origin and translates as 'performing, doing, making, fulfilment' and is also identified with the concepts of success and achievement (Akçakaya, 2012). Prakash and Chowdhary (2010) defined tourist guide performance as a concept that differs according to the qualifications and training received by the tourist guide. In light of this definition, it can be said that a tourist guide's performance depends on the guide's competencies, and the competencies gained depend on the education and training received.

Tourist guiding service is generally shaped according to the performance of the tourist guide (Huang et al., 2010). Since tourist guiding is carried out individually, tourist guides perform individually (Lugosi & Bray, 2008). Although external factors affect tourist guide performance, each guide determines his/her own success, because the performance of the tourist guide is related to his/her competencies and skills that are formed as a result of his/her training (Prakash & Chowdhary, 2010). In addition, the guide's sociability and fulfilling his/her professional roles properly affect the performance of the tourist guide (Edensor, 2000).

It is a generally accepted fact in the tourism industry that 'it is the guide who sells the next tour'. Underlying this belief is the assumption that satisfaction with the guide's performance will translate directly into the tour company's image, leading to repeat purchases and positive recommendations to potential tourists (Geva & Goldman, 1991). Tourist guide performance also contributes to the formation of tourist loyalty (Ap & Wong, 2001; Bowie & Chang, 2005).

As mentioned above, the high performance of tourist guides is significant for tourism. For this reason, it is suggested that measures such as the establishment of a professional certification and licensing system, training and codes of conduct, and the establishment of a quality assurance system (Black & Ham, 2005) can be taken to improve the performance of tourist guides. In addition, Mak et al. (2011) stated that the wages of tourist guides and their service standards and performance are directly proportional. Accordingly, giving fair wages to tourist guides in return for their services is essential for their performance, as in every profession.

Memorable Tourism Experiences

Every tourist who participates in tourism activities wants and expects a new, extraordinary and exciting experience in these activities, unlike the experience that takes place in everyday life. Kim et al. (2010) define these desired and expected experiences as the leading product tourism provides tourists.

Different definitions have been used to describe memorable tourism experiences. For example, Arsenault and Gale (2004) define it as the tourism product of tomorrow, Larsen (2007) defines it as an event that is important enough to be stored in long-term memory and is related to past travels, Chen and Rahman (2018) define it as the experiences in a touristic region that remain in memory and are recalled at another time, Kim et al. (2010, 2012) define it as a tourism experience that is remembered after the event has occurred and Howell and Guevarra (2013) define it as the experiences and evaluations that consumers obtain by remembering the pre-experience, purchase experience.

When the definitions are analysed, it can be said that there is a strong and positive link between memorable tourism experiences and memorability (Hung et al., 2016; Lee, 2015; Mossberg, 2008; Quan & Wang, 2004; Tung & Ritchie, 2011). In addition, Quinlan-Cutler and Carmichael (2010) argued that memories interact with tourist experiences and stated that positive events are remembered more clearly than adverse events.

Memory and tourist experiences should be considered as a whole. Because experiences are only valuable when stored and remembered during the recall phase (Kim, 2009). In addition, memory is a mediator of consumer behaviour that affects one's future behaviour (Zhong et al., 2017). For this reason, businesses in the tourism sector should provide their customers with memorable tourism experiences to provide better quality service.

Not all tourism experiences necessarily translate into memorable tourism experiences. Instead, memorable tourism experiences are those experiences that are selected from tourist experiences that remain in mind after the trip. Memorable tourism experiences are more important as only memorable experiences will influence tourists' future decision-making. Tourists rely on previous experiences and memories to plan future trips (Zhang et al., 2018).

No consensus exists on which components are involved in forming memorable tourism experiences. However, education, aesthetics, entertainment, escape, participation, hedonism and local culture experience dimensions play an important role in influencing tourists' memories, and thus memories become memorable experiences. However, researchers have found that tourists who describe their tourist experience as memorable recall seven dimensions more frequently, namely 'hedonism, novelty, local culture, novelty, meaningfulness, involvement, and knowledge' (Kim et al., 2012; Park & Santos, 2016).

Hedonism is derived from the Greek word 'Hedone' and means pleasure, enjoyment and the pursuit of pleasure by avoiding pain (Ünal & Bayar, 2020). Research shows that tourism products are consumed primarily for hedonic purposes, and hedonism is essential in ensuring that tourists have memorable experiences (Sthapit & Coudounaris, 2018).

Novelty, which is derived from the Latin word 'Novus (new)', has the meaning of being new as well as being striking, original and extraordinary (Cheng & Lu, 2013). Novelty is accepted as a motivation to travel through novelty seeking (Bello & Etzel, 1985; Jang & Feng, 2007). Novelty, which is effective in the decision-making phase of tourists (Petrick, 2002), is also significant for understanding tourism experiences and providing memorable experiences (Skavronskaya et al., 2020).

Local culture is also called social interaction (Göçmen, 2020). The concept of social interaction is among the antecedents of memorable tourism experiences (Fan et al., 2021). Because social factors affect the memorable tourism experience, these opportunities, which are integrated with the texture of the region and have local characteristics, enrich tourists' destination experiences by triggering memorability in the minds of tourists (Kim, 2014).

Refreshment is one of the essential elements of tourism (Kim & Ritchie, 2014), because individuals' need to relax by escaping from their daily routines motivates them to travel. Individuals are renewed by meeting their physical, social and psychological needs during travels (Akşit Aşık & Kutsynska, 2019). This feeling of renewal distracts individuals from the stress they experience daily (Coudounaris & Sthapit, 2017). For this reason, it is known that the sense of renewal is an essential motivational factor in individuals' travel decision-making processes (Ülker Demirel, 2020). Thus, the sense of renewal felt by individuals will contribute to creating a memorable tourism experience by enabling them to remember their past experiences (Kim, 2010) vividly.

Involvement is defined as the level of personal interest. It is argued that visitors are more likely to have a more memorable trip experience when participating in activities at the destination (Kim & Ritchie, 2014).

Meaningfulness is necessary for people's happiness and well-being. For this reason, people try to find meaning in their lives. People seek meaningful experiences for physical, emotional or spiritual satisfaction through tourism rather than escaping reality or seeking authenticity without meaning (Kim & Ritchie, 2014; Mahdzar, 2019). Therefore, most tourists seek unique and meaningful travel experiences to satisfy their needs and desires. It is stated that meaningful experiences have substantial effects on memory (Kim & Ritchie, 2014), and when the meaningfulness of experiences increases, they will become more memorable (Coudounaris & Sthapit, 2017).

Knowledge is information, facts or experiences (Kim et al., 2012). Aho (2001) also defines knowledge as a background, including previous tourism experiences, to choose, be informed and evaluate the available tourism experiences. It is also known that the new information tourists obtain about their destination is part of their memorable tourism experiences (Mahdzar, 2019).

The Relationship Between Tourist Guide Performance and Memorable Tourism Experiences

The relationship between the tourist guide and the tourist experience has been recognised and explored by many researchers, including De Kadt (1979), Cohen (1985), Watson et al. (1991) (Black et al., 2001). Since a tourist guide is a person who provides tourists with information about the places visited from the beginning to the end of the trip, acts as an ambassador for tourists to have a pleasant time (Güçlütürk Baran, 2019), and communicates with the group during the tour, leads the group and has an interpersonal mediation role and affects the whole tour experience by this performance (Güzel & Köroğlu, 2014).

Tourist guide performance is essential for tourists to have a unique tourism experience. Among the roles attributed to tourist guiding, the roles of ambassador, information giver (Black et al., 2001), and interpreter (Ap & Wong, 2001; Brito, 2012; Dahles, 2002; Ham & Weiler, 2002; Holloway, 1981; Rabotić, 2010), leader (Reisinger & Steiner, 2006), mediator (Weiler & Walker, 2014) and organiser (Gurung et al., 1996; Weiler & Davis, 1993) are more effective on tourist experiences.

Thus, the following hypothesis is formally submitted:

H1. Tourist guide performance positively and directly affects memorable tourism experiences.

The Relationship Between Tourist Guide Performance and Revisit Intention

Tourists' RVI is seen as one of the main determinants of the long-term financial performance of the tourism sector (Som & Badarneh, 2011). It is expressed as a tourist's willingness to make another purchase from the same business in line with their previous experiences (Çavuşoğlu & Bilginer, 2018; Hellier et al., 2003; Keskin et al., 2020).

It is possible to mention many factors that affect the RVI. One of these factors is memorable tourism experiences. If a visitor has had positive experiences in a destination that he/she has preferred, he/she will prefer the same destination in the future (Anderson & Sullivan, 1993; Fuller et al., 2007). For this reason, it is possible to say that memorable tourism experiences are among the most critical factors in determining to RVI, positive word-of-mouth advertising and future destination choices (Chen & Rahman, 2018; Gohary et al., 2020; Hoch & Deighton, 1989; Kim et al., 2010; Kim & Ritchie, 2014; Zhang et al., 2018).

Memories influence consumers' decision-making (Chen & Rahman, 2018). When a tourist intends to revisit a specific destination, he/she searches for information, and the most valuable source of information at this stage is memories (Chandralal & Valenzuela, 2013; Coudounaris & Sthapit, 2017; Hoch & Deighton, 1989; Kozak, 2001; Lehto et al., 2004; Mazursky, 1989; Wirtz et al., 2003). When deciding, tourists rely on previous experiences and memories to decide their future travels (Lehto et al., 2004). Remembering a brand, service or product positively can be decisive in consumer decision-making (De Freitas Coelho et al., 2018; Kim, 2010; Kim et al., 2012).

Therefore, the following hypothesis is proposed:

H2. Memorable tourism experiences positively and directly affect RVI.

Bearing in mind these rationales, a research model was designed to investigate the direct effect of tourist guide performance on tourists' memorable tourism experiences and memorable tourism experiences on RVI (Fig. 11.1).

Case Study

Research Methodology

Data Collection and Sampling Techniques
A quantitative research method was employed for this research. By quantifying the links between variables (the items you measure), quantitative research tries to understand how one thing (a variable) influences another in a population (Altinay & Paraskevas, 2008). This research was survey-based. One of the most common ways that researchers in hospitality and tourism gather data is through surveys (Aeknarajindawat, 2019; Yismaw, 2019). Moreover, it is one of the most often used data collection techniques since it may include a significant part of the overall population in the quantitative method (Aeknarajindawat, 2019). Since when you know exactly what to ask, need to ask many people and can ask common questions that everyone will understand and respond to, surveys are a beneficial data collection technique (Altinay & Paraskevas, 2008).

Before distributing the surveys, a pretest was done to ensure the questions were straightforward and fix any potential phrasing and grammar errors. Regarding data collection, local and foreign tourists were selected, and a sample of 569 respondents was gathered (by convenience sampling). The fieldwork took place from May 2020 to March 2021 in Cappadocia.

Variables and Measures

The study constructs were measured through a survey designed to be administered to tourists participating in guided tours. Items were adopted from previous research and discussed by tourism specialists to ensure content validity. The items that measured tourist guide performance, memorable tourism experiences and RVIwere initially written in English and were then translated into Turkish and Russian using a back-translation.

In order to evaluate the experiences of tourists during their holidays in Cappadocia, the memorable tourism experiences scale consisting of 7 dimensions and 24 items developed by Kim et al. (2012), the tourist guide performance scale consisting of 3 dimensions and 23 items developed by Sezgin and Duz (2018) and the RVI scale consisting of 4 items in the study of Huang and Hsu (2009) were used.

Results

Descriptive Statistics

Demographic Profiles of the Respondents

To make the study more understandable, additional background information, such as demographic data, is helpful before beginning the data analysis. Therefore, the samples for this study have been divided into groups based on background data gathered through a supplementary questionnaire survey. The frequency distributions of the various demographic factors are shown in Table 11.1.

Most of the respondents are female, with a rate of 59.1%. According to the age distribution of the respondents, the highest rate belongs to the 26–35 age group with 41.1%, and the lowest rate belongs to the 56 and over age group with 2.1%. Most of the respondents are single, with a rate of 61.2%. When the educational status of the respondents is analysed, it is seen that the majority of the respondents consist of undergraduate graduates, with a rate of 63.8%. When the distribution of the respondents according to the type of tourist is analysed, it is seen that the rates of foreign (46.7%) and domestic (53.3%) tourists are close to each other.

Validity and Reliability of Instruments

In order to measure the reliability of the scales used in the study, Cronbach's alpha coefficients were determined and confirmatory factor analysis (CFA) was used to analyse the validity of the scales.

Table 11.1. Profiles of Respondents.

Variable		Frequency	%
Gender	Female	336	59.1
	Male	233	40.9
	Total	569	100
Age	Below 25 years old	164	28.8
	26–35 years old	234	41.1
	36–45 years old	91	16.0
	46–55 years old	68	12.0
	Over 56 years old	12	2.1
	Total	569	100
Education level	Primary education	16	2.8
	High school	53	9.3
	Associate's degree	62	10.9
	Bachelor's degree	363	63.8
	Postgraduate education	75	13.2
	Total	569	100
Type of tourist	Local	303	53.3
	Foreign	266	46.7
	Total	569	100

Confirmatory Factor Analysis of Tourist Guide Performance (TGP)

Using AMOS 22.0 (Analysis of Moment Structures) statistical software, which is frequently preferred for structural equation modelling (SEM) analysis, CFA was performed to test the suitability of the tourist guide performance scale to be examined. The study model identifying the specified associations of the factors to the underpinning components was analysed through a CFA, which consisted of free correlations of all the components (Table 11.2).

According to the results of the analysis, the 4. (PE_4), 9. (PE_9) and 10. (PE_10) items of the personality and efficiency dimension of the scale and the 4. (PR_4) and 9. (PR_9) items of the presentableness dimension of the scale were deleted since their factor loadings were less than 0.5. After deleting, these five items were deleted, and the remaining items are shown in Fig. 11.2.

Additionally, the modification indices indicated that the model fit would be improved by drawing covariance between the error terms for item 2. (PE_2) and 3. (PE_3), between those items, the 2. (PR_2) and 7. (PR_7) items. The model, having a good fit with the latent variables, is presented in Fig. 11.2.

Table 11.2. Results of Confirmatory Factor Analysis (CFA) of the Tourist Guide Performance Scale.

Dimensions	Variable Codes	Factor Loading	Cronbach's Alfa	CR	AVE
Personality and efficiency (PE)	PE_1	0.760	0.930	0.929	0.651
	PE_2	0.823			
	PE_3	0.810			
	PE_5	0.819			
	PE_6	0.833			
	PE_7	0.807			
	PE_8	0.796			
Presentableness (PR)	PR_1	0.855	0.931	0.933	0.666
	PR _2	0.825			
	PR _3	0.765			
	PR _5	0.814			
	PR _6	0.790			
	PR _7	0.855			
	PR _8	0.805			
Proficiency (PO)	PO_1	0.710	0.839	0.844	0.575
	PO_2	0.755			
	PO_3	0.784			
	PO_4	0.783			

The factor loadings and Cronbach's alpha coefficients of the variables in the tourist guide performance scale are shown in Fig. 11.2. According to the previous information, it was stated that Cronbach's alpha coefficient should be 0.60 and above. When the values given in Fig. 11.2 are examined, it is seen that the values determined as a result of the analysis are appropriate. When the Cronbach's alpha coefficients of the scale were analysed, it was found that the reliability of two dimensions was above 0.90 and one dimension was above 0.80. These values are accepted as good reliability values. All CR values related to the scale are expected to be greater than AVE values, and the AVE value is more excellent than 0.5 (Yaşlıoğlu, 2017). All of the AVE values of the dimensions of the tourist guide performance scale are greater than 0.5, and all of them are lower than the CR values. The p-value, the statistical significance level of the relationships between the scale items and the latent variables, was significant at $p < 0.01$.

In addition to these values, the goodness of fit indices showing the fit between the data and the model should be examined. These fit indices are named χ^2, χ^2/df, RMSEA, RMR, SRMR, NFI, NNFI, CFI, GFI and AGFI. However, the values

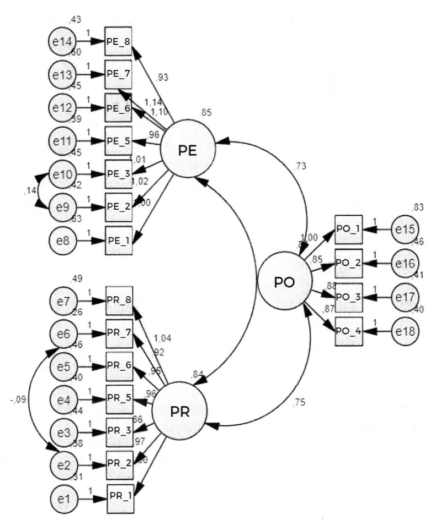

Fig. 11.2.   Dimensions and Variables of Tourist Guide Performance
Scale.

considered for model fit are χ^2/df, GFI, CFI and RMSEA values. Some studies
also consider IFI, RMR, NFI and AGFI values. However, there is no certainty
about which fit indices will be evaluated in the analyses. It varies according to the
values that the researcher wants to draw attention to (Karagöz, 2019). In line with
these statements, the fit values related to the measurement model of the tourist
guide performance scale are shown in Table 11.3. Since these fit values are within
the accepted threshold values, the measurement model is validated.

Table 11.3. Model Fit Indices of the Tourist Guide Performance Scale.

Measure	Threshold	Model Values
χ^2/df	<3 good; <5 permissible	4.526
GFI	>0.95	0.896
AGFI	>0.80	0.864
CFI	>0.95 great; >0.90 traditional; >0.80 permissible	0.944
RMSEA	<0.05 good; 0.05–0.10 moderate; >10 bad	0.079
SRMR	<0.09	0.035
RMR	≤0.05 good; 0.06–0.08 permissible	0.047
NFI	≤0.95 good; 0.94–0.90 permissible	0.930

Source: Meydan ve Şeşen (2015, p. 37), Bayram (2016, p. 78), Model Fit Indices (2023).

Confirmatory Factor Analysis of MTE

CFA to complete the validation of the memorable tourism experience scale proposed. According to the results of the analysis, the factor loadings of the items were found to be acceptable values. In addition, the *p*-value was significant at the $p < 0.01$ level.

The model was improved by drawing covariance between the error terms of 1. (NV_1) and 4. (NV_4) between those for items 2. (RF_2) and 4. (RF_4), between those for items 2. (MN_2) and 3. (MN_3). The model, having a good fit for the latent variables, is presented in Fig. 11.3.

The factor loads and Cronbach's alpha coefficients of the variables in the Memorable Tourism Experience scale are shown in Fig. 11.3.

When the values shown in Fig. 11.3 are examined, it is seen that the values determined as a result of the analysis are appropriate. When the Cronbach's alpha coefficients of the scale were analysed, it was found that the reliability of four dimensions was above 0.80, two dimensions were above 0.75 and one dimension was 0.90. These values are accepted as good reliability values. The fact that the AVE values of the dimensions of the scale are more significant than 0.5 and smaller than the CR values indicates that the scale has a good level of conformity. The *p*-value, which is the expression of the statistical significance level of the relationships between the scale items and the latent variables, was found to be significant at the $p < 0.01$ level. The fit values related to the measurement model for the memorable tourism experience scale are presented in Table 11.4. Since these fit values are within the accepted threshold values, the measurement model is validated (Table 11.5).

Confirmatory Factor Analysis of RVI

CFA was conducted to test the suitability of the RVI scale. According to the results of the analysis, the factor loadings of the items were found to be acceptable values.

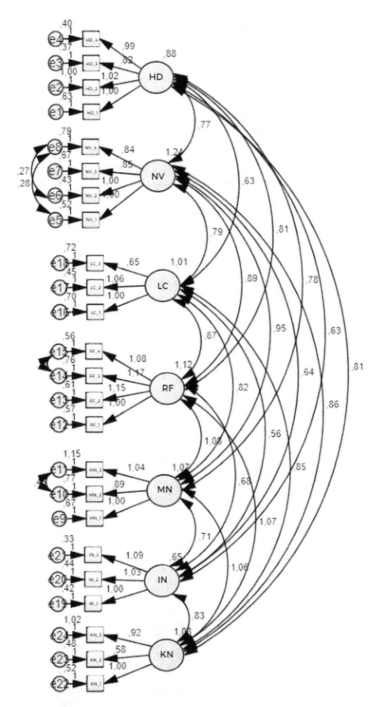

Fig. 11.3. Dimensions and Variables of Memorable Tourism Experience Scale.

In addition, the statistical significance level of the relationships between the items and latent variables was significant at $p < 0.01$.

The model was improved by drawing covariance between the 1. (RVI_1) error terms and 3. (RVI_3) items. The model, having a good fit with the latent variables, is shown in Fig. 11.4.

The factor loadings and Cronbach's alpha coefficients of the variables in the RVI scale are shown in Fig. 11.4. When the values given in Fig. 11.4 are examined, it is seen that the values determined as a result of the analysis are

Table 11.4. Results of Confirmatory Factor Analysis (CFA) of Memorable Tourism Experience Scale.

Dimensions	Variables Codes	Factor Loading	Cronbach's Alfa	CR	AVE
Hedonism (HD)	HD_1	0.763	0.841	0.851	0.589
	HD_2	0.692			
	HD_3	0.784			
	HD_4	0.827			
Novelty (NV)	NV_1	0.840	0.845	0.875	0.637
	NV_2	0.861			
	NV_3	0.756			
	NV_4	0.728			
Local Culture (LC)	LC_1	0.769	0.788	0.789	0.559
	LC_2	0.845			
	LC_3	0.611			
Refreshment (RF)	RF_1	0.814	0.90	0.896	0.684
	RF_2	0.841			
	RF_3	0.818			
	RF_4	0.835			
Meaningfulness (MN)	MN_1	0.784	0.831	0.784	0.547
	MN_2	0.724			
	MN_3	0.709			
Involvement (IN)	IN_1	0.781	0.842	0.842	0.639
	IN_2	0.782			
	IN_3	0.835			
Knowledge (KN)	KN_1	0.821	0.751	0.768	0.526
	KN_2	0.657			
	KN_3	0.688			

Table 11.5. Model Fit Indices of the Memorable Tourism Experience Scale.

Measure	Threshold	Model Values
χ^2/df	<3 good; <5 permissible	4.987
GFI	>0.95	0.855
CFI	>0.95 great; >0.90 traditional; >0.80 permissible	0.909
RMSEA	<0.05 good; 0.05–0.10 moderate; >10 bad	0.084
SRMR	<0.09	0.047
RMR	≤0.05 good; 0.06–0.08 permissible	0.077

Source: Meydan ve Şeşen (2015, s. 37), Bayram (2016, s. 78), Model Fit Indices (2023).

appropriate. The Cronbach's alpha coefficient of the scale is 0.912. The CR values showing the reliability of the measurement model are 0.908, and this value is considered a good reliability value. The fact that the AVE values of the dimensions of the RVI scale are more significant than 0.7 and less than the CR value indicates that the level of conformity is good. The relationships between the scale items and latent variables were significant at $p < 0.01$, which is the expression of the statistical significance level (Table 11.6).

The fit values related to the measurement model for the RVI scale are given in Table 11.7. Since these fit values are within the accepted threshold values, the measurement model is validated.

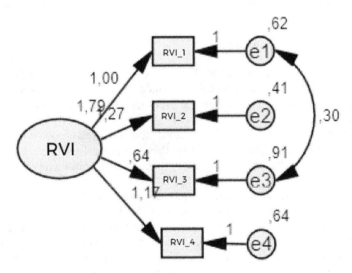

Fig. 11.4.   The Variables of the Revisit Intention Scale.

Table 11.6. Results of Confirmatory Factor Analysis (CFA) of Revisit Intention (RVI) Scale.

	Variables Codes	Factor Loading	Cronbach's Alfa	CR	AVE
RVI	RVI-1	0.861	0.912	0.908	0.714
	RVI_2	0.935			
	RVI_3	0.669			
	RVI_4	0.891			

Table 11.7. Model Fit Indices of the Revisit Intention Scale.

Measure	Threshold	Model Values
χ^2/df	<3 good; <5 permissible	3.736
GFI	>0.95	0.997
AGFI	>0.80	0.967
CFI	>0.95 great; >0.90 traditional; >0.80 permissible	0.998
RMSEA	<0.05 good; 0.05–0.10 moderate; >10 bad	0.069
SRMR	<0.09	0.006
RMR	≤0.05 good; 0.06–0.08 permissible	0.016
NFI	≤0.95 good; 0.94–0.90 permissible	0.998

Source: Meydan and Şeşen (2015, p. 37), Bayram (2016, p. 78), Model Fit Indices (2023).

Testing the Research Model

In the first stage of the two-stage SEM, CFA was performed to verify the measurement models. In the second stage, the model created for the research should be tested. The model created to test the hypotheses of the research is presented in Fig. 11.5.

Each of the one-way arrows in the model shows the relationships between the variables and represents the research hypotheses stated in Table 11.8. The paths to the hypotheses are represented by TGP, memorable tourism experience (MTE) and RVI.

Before testing the hypotheses, the model's goodness of fit statistics was evaluated to determine the fit of the model with the data obtained. In the previous information, it was stated that there is no certainty about which fit indices will be evaluated in the analyses, and that the values determined as a result of the analysis vary according to the values the researcher wants to draw attention to. In line with these statements, Table 11.9 regarding the goodness of fit values was created. According to the values shown in Table 11.9, χ^2/df is between 4 and 5; the CFI value is between 0.85, RMSEA value is between 0.06 and 0.08. The SRMR value

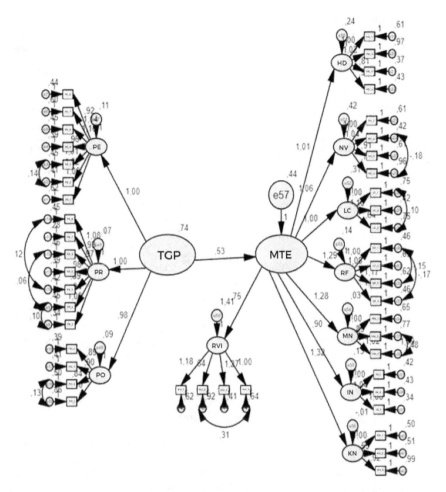

Fig. 11.5.   Path Diagram of the Research Model.

Table 11.8. Research Hypotheses.

Hypotheses	Path
H1. Tourist guide performance positively and directly affects memorable tourism experiences.	TGP → MTE
H2. Memorable tourism experiences positively and directly affect RVI.	MTE → RVI

Table 11.9. Model Fit Indices.

Measure	Threshold	Model Values
χ^2/df	<3 good; <5 permissible	4.420
CFI	>0.95 great; >0.90 traditional; >0.80 permissible	0.850
RMSEA	<0.05 good; 0.05–0.10 moderate; >10 bad	0.078
SRMR	<0.09	0.064

Source: Browne and Cudeck (1993), Garson (2006) as cited in Chinda et al. (2012, p. 100), Meydan and Şeşen (2015, p. 37); Bayram (2016, p. 78), Model Fit Indices (2023).

(Bayram, 2016), the standardised difference between the observed and estimated covariance, is 0.06. After analysing all these values, the structural model was found to have acceptable values, and the model was validated.

In order to improve the model, the 2. (PE_2) and 3. (PE_3) statements of the personality and efficiency dimension, the 1. (PR_1) and 2. (PR_2), 2. (PR_2) and 6. (PR_6), 3. (PR_3) and 8. (PR_8) statements of the presentableness dimension, the 1. (PO_1) and 2. (PO_2); 2. (NV_2) and 4. (NV_4) statements of the innovation dimension, 1. (RF_1) and 3. (RF_3) and 1. (RF_1) and 4. (RF_4), 2. (MN_2) and 3. (MN_3) of the meaningfulness dimension and 1. (RVI_1) and 3. (RVI_3) of the RVI scale was improved by drawing covariance between the error terms—the model, having a good fit with the latent variables is shown in Table 11.9.

Path Diagram for the Research Model

Within the scope of SEM analysis, two hypotheses were tested to determine the effects of tourist guide performance on memorable tourism experience and the effects of memorable tourism experience on intention to revisit. The path diagram for the findings obtained as a result of the analysis conducted for this purpose is presented in Fig. 11.6.

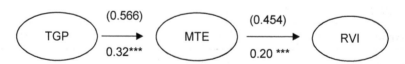

Fig. 11.6.   Path Diagram for the Research Model.

The path analysis results of the model are shown in Table 11.10.

According to the results of the path analysis for the proposed model, it was determined that the data obtained supported the structural relationship estimation expressing the *H1* hypothesis. Furthermore, it has been determined that the

Table 11.10. Path Analysis Results of the Proposed Model.

	Path	Estimated Regression Coefficients	R^2	P	Result
H1	TGP → MTE	0.566	0.32	***	Accept
H2	MTE → RVI	0.454	0.20	***	Accept

success of the tourist guide has a significant and positive effect on memorable tourism experiences. In other words, a one-unit increase in the performance of the tourist guide increases the memorable tourism experience by 0.32 units.

Thus, the performance of tourist guides positively affects tourists' memorable tourism experiences. Furthermore, the tourist guide's qualities, such as personality traits, professional competencies, etc. affect the guides' performance. Accordingly, the qualities that will affect the performance of the tourist guide enable tourists to have memorable tourism experiences. Therefore, *H1*, based on the statement 'The success of the tourist guide has an effect on memorable tourism experiences', is accepted.

According to the results of the path analysis for the proposed model, it was determined that the data obtained supported the structural relationship estimation expressing the *H2* hypothesis. Furthermore, it has been determined that memorable tourism experiences significantly and positively affect RVI. In other words, a one-unit increase in memorable tourism experiences increases the intention to revisit by 0.20 units. In this direction, memorable tourism experiences of tourists positively affect the intention to revisit. Therefore, *H2*, based on the statement 'Memorable tourism experiences affect the intention to revisit', is accepted (Table 11.11).

Table 11.11. The Results of Hypotheses.

Hypotheses	Result
H1 Tourist guide performance positively and directly affects memorable tourism experiences.	Accept
H2 Memorable tourism experiences positively and directly affect RVI.	Accept

Conclusion

Tourist guides are as vital as tourist attractions in creating memorable tourism experiences. Therefore, tourist guides significantly contribute to providing tourists with extraordinary experiences. This contribution is ensured by the tourist guides' personality traits, knowledge and skills, and the fact that they love their work and successfully fulfil the roles they have to undertake during the performance.

Arnould and Price (1993) stated that tourist guides play an essential role in providing tourists with extraordinary experiences; Chandralal and Valenzuela (2013) stated that the perceived professionalism of tourist guides is essential to make a trip memorable; Mathisen (2012) stated that tourist guides' knowledge and skills, personality traits, achievements and especially narrative skills are essential in the context of creating a tourist experience; Hurombo (2016) stated that the competencies of tourist guides are pioneers in creating memorable tourism experiences; Mossberg (2008) stated that tourist guides could transform tourists' travel from any tour into a memorable tourism experience through their professional skills that affect their achievements.

Moreover, memorable tourism experiences affect the intention to revisit. The memorable tourism experiences of tourists positively affect the RVI. The more memorable tourism experiences tourists have during their travels, the more likely they will revisit that destination. It is a known fact that the most important source of information in individuals' decision-making process for travelling is their memory (Chandralal & Valenzuela, 2013; Kozak, 2001; Lehto et al., 2004; Mazursky, 1989). Because individuals tend to choose the destination, they will visit by remembering their past experiences that have taken place in their memories before their travels. Martin (2010) argued that their memories influence tourists' intention to revisit a destination. Research has shown that memorable tourism experiences are a strong predictor of RVI and future destination choices (Chen & Rahman, 2018; Hung et al., 2016; Jefferies & Lepp, 2012; Kim et al., 2010; Kim & Ritchie, 2014; Triantafillidou & Siomkos, 2014a, 2014b; Zhang et al., 2018).

In addition, Yu et al. (2019) concluded that hedonism, local culture and involvement dimensions of memorable tourism experiences positively affect RVI. In contrast to these studies, Chandralal and Valenzuela (2013) found that novelty-seeking travellers do not intend to revisit the same destination despite having a memorable experience. However, they tend to recommend it to others due to memorable tourism experiences. Similar to this study, Kim and Ritchie (2014) examined the effect of memorable tourism experiences on behavioural intention and found that the knowledge dimension negatively affected behavioural intention, although not significantly. This result suggests that individuals who have previously learnt about the destination may want to satisfy their novelty-seeking travel motivation, an essential intrinsic motivation factor for tourists. Although individuals may have accumulated good memories in their previous tourism experiences, they may want to continue seeking new experiences by visiting a new destination or participating in a different activity they have yet to practice in their previous travels.

Discussion Questions

- How can the experiences of tourists with negative tourism experiences change with the performance of tourist guides?
- How are tourists' intentions to revisit a destination influenced by their memories?
- How does tourists' participation in various tourism activities during their destination visits affect the memorable tourism experience?

References

Aeknarajindawat, N. (2019). The factors influencing tourists' online hotel reservations in Thailand: An empirical study. *International Journal of Innovation, Creativity and Change, 10*(1), 121–136.

Aho, S. K. (2001). Towards A general theory of touristic experiences: Modeling experience process in tourism. *Tourism Review, 56*(3–4), 33–37.

Akçakaya, M. (2012). Kamu sektöründe performans yönetimi ve uygulamada karşılaşılan sorunlar. *Karadeniz Araştırmaları*, (32), 171–202.

Akşit Aşık, N., & Kutsynska, M. V. (2019). Unutulmaz Turizm Deneyimlerinin Tekrar Ziyaret Niyeti ve Tavsiye Etme Davranışına Etkisi: Ukraynalı Turistler Üzerinde Bir Araştırma. *Uluslararası Sosyal Araştırmalar Dergisi, 12*(68), 1007–1017.

Altinay, L., & Paraskevas, A. (2008). *Planning research in hospitality and tourism.* Elsevier.

Anderson, E. W., & Sullivan, M. W. (1993). The antecedents and consequences of customer satisfaction for firms. *Marketing Science, 12*(2), 125–143.

Ap, J., & Wong, K. K. F. (2001). Case study on tour guiding: Professionalism, issues and problems. *Tourism Management, 22*, 551–563.

Arnould, E. J., & Price, L. L. (1993). River Magic: Extraordinary experience and the extended service encounter. *Journal of Consumer Research, 20*(1), 24–45.

Arsenault, N., & Gale, T. (2004). *Defining Tomorrows Tourism Product: Packaging Experiences. Araştırma Raporu (Rapor No: 2004-7).* Kanada Turizm Komisyonu.

Baran Güçlütürk, G. (2019). Unutulmaz gezi deneyimleri: Turist rehberlerinden yansımalar. *Journal of Travel & Tourism Research*, (14), 1–20.

Bayram, N. (2016). *Yapısal Eşitlik Modellemesine Giriş AMOS ve Uygulamaları.* Ezgi Kitabevi.

Bello, D. C., & Etzel, M. J. (1985). The role of novelty in the pleasure travel experience. *Journal of Travel Research, 24*(1), 20–26.

Black, R., & Ham, S. (2005). Improving the quality of tour guiding: Towards a model for tour guide certification. *Journal of Ecotourism, 4*(3), 178–195.

Black, R., Ham, S., & Weiler, B. (2001). Ecotour guide training in less developed countries: Some preliminary research findings. *Journal of Sustainable Tourism, 9*(2), 147–156.

Bowie, D., & Chang, J. C. (2005). Tourist Satisfaction: A view from a mixed international guided package tour. *Journal of Vacation Marketing, 11*(4), 303–322.

Brito, M. (2012). Cultural tourists requests from their tourist guides. *The International Journal of Management Cases, 14*(1), 266–282.

Browne, M. W., & Cudeck, R. (1993). Alternative ways of assessing model fit. *Sociological Methods & Research, 21*(2), 230–258.

Çavuşoğlu, S., & Bilginer, F. G. (2018). Tüketici deneyimlerinin tekrar ziyaret etme niyetine etkisi: Bingöl ili örneği. *Türk Sosyal Bilimler Araştırmaları Dergisi, 3*(1), 72–85.

Chandralal, L., & Valenzuela, F. R. (2013). Exploring memorable tourism experiences: Antecedents and behavioural outcomes. *Journal of Economics, Business and Management, 1*(2), 177–181.

Cheng, T. M., & Lu, C. C. (2013). Destination image, novelty, hedonics, perceived value and revisiting behavioral intention for island tourism. *Asia Pacific Journal of Tourism Research, 18*(7), 766–783.

Chen, H., & Rahman, I. (2018). Cultural tourism: An analysis of engagement, cultural contact, memorable tourism experience and destination loyalty. *Tourism Management Perspectives, 26*, 153–163.

Chinda, T., Techapreechawong, S., & Teeraprasert, S. (2012, September). An investigation of relationships between employees' safety and productivity. In *Proceedings of the 3rd International Conference on Engineering, Project and Production Management (EPPM2012)*, (pp. 10–11).

Cohen, E. (1985). The tourist guide: The origins, structure and dynamics of a role. *Annals of Tourism Research, 12*(1), 5–29.

Coudounaris, D. N., & Sthapit, E. (2017). Antecedents of memorable tourism experience related to behavioral intentions. *Psychology and Marketing, 34*(12), 1084–1093.

Dahles, H. (2002). The politics of tour guiding image management in Indonesia. *Annals of Tourism Research, 29*(3), 783–800.

Davidson, P., & Black, R. (2007). Voices from the profession: Principles of successful guided cave interpretation. *Journal of Interpretation Research, 12*(2), 25–43.

De Freitas Coelho, M., de Sevilha Gosling, M., & de Almeida, A. S. A. (2018). Tourism experiences: Core processes of memorable trips. *Journal of Hospitality and Tourism Management, 37*, 11–22.

De Kadt, E. (1979). *Tourism: Passport to development?* Oxford University Press.

Edensor, T. (2000). Staging tourism: Tourists as performers. *Annals of Tourism Research, 27*(2), 322–344.

Fan, D. X., Tsaur, S. H., Lin, J. H., Chang, T. Y., & Tsa, Y. R. (2021). Tourist intercultural competence: A multidimensional measurement and its impact on tourist active participation and memorable cultural experiences. *Journal of Travel Research, 60*(1), 1–49.

Fuller, D., Wilde, S., Hanlan, J., & Mason, S. (2007). *Destination decision making in tourism regions on Australia's east coast.* Flinders business school research paper series (pp. 7–27).

Geva, A., & Goldman, A. (1991). Satisfaction measurement in guided tours. *Annals of Tourism Research, 18*(2), 177–185.

Göçmen, Ö. (2020). *Unutulmaz turizm deneyiminin destinasyon sadakatine etkisi: Bursa üzerine bir araştırma.* (Yüksek lisans tezi). Kırklareli Üniversitesi/Sosyal Bilimler Enstitüsü.

Gohary, A., Pourazizi, L., Madani, F., & Chan, E. Y. (2020). Examining Iranian tourists' memorable experiences on destination satisfaction and behavioral intentions. *Current Issues in Tourism, 23*(2), 131–136.

Gurung, G., Simmons, D., & Devlin, P. (1996). The evolving role of tourist guides: The nepali experience. In R. Butler & T. Hinch (Eds.), *Tourism and indigenous peoples* (pp. 107–128). International Thomson Business Press.

Güzel, F. Ö., & Köroğlu, Ö. (2014). Turist rehberlerinin liderlik ve aracılık rollerinin tur deneyimine etkisi. doğa turları üzerine bir araştırma. *Gaziantep University Journal of Social Sciences, 13*(4), 939–960.

Ham, S. H., & Weiler, B. (2002). Interpretation as the centrepiece of sustainable wildlife tourism. In R. Harris, T. Griffin, & P. Williams (Eds.), *Sustainable Tourism: A Global Perspective* (pp. 35–44). Butterworth-Heinneman.

Hellier, P. K., Geursen, G. M., Carr, R. A., & Rickard, J. A. (2003). Customer repurchase intention: A general structural equation model. *European Journal of Marketing, 37*(11), 1762–1800.

Hoch, S. J., & Deighton, J. (1989). Managing What Consumers Learn from Experience. *Journal of Marketing, 53*(2), 1–20.

Holloway, J. C. (1981). The guided tour: A sociological approach. *Annals of Tourism Research, 8*(3), 377–401.

Hosany, S., & Gilbert, D. (2010). Measuring Tourists' emotional experiences toward hedonic holiday destinations. *Journal of Travel Research, 49*(4), 513–526.

Howell, R. T., & Guevarra, D. A. (2013). Buying happiness: Differential consumption experiences for material and experiential purchases. *Advances in Psychology Research, 98*, 57–69.

Huang, S., & Hsu, C. H. (2009). Effects of travel motivation, past experience, perceived constraint and attitude on revisit intention. *Journal of Travel Research, 48*(1), 29–44.

Huang, S., Hsu, C. H., & Chan, A. (2010). Tour guide performance and tourist satisfaction: A study of the package tours in shanghai. *Journal of Hospitality & Tourism Research, 34*(1), 3–33.

Hung, W. L., Lee, Y. J., & Huang, P. H. (2016). Creative experiences, memorability, and revisit intention in creative tourism. *Current Issues in Tourism, 19*(8), 763–770.

Hurombo, B. (2016). *Assessing key tour guide competencies to co-create memorable tourism experiences.* Doctoral dissertation, North-West University (South Africa), Potchefstroom Campus.

Jang, S. S., & Feng, R. (2007). Temporal destination revisit intention: The effects of novelty seeking and satisfaction. *Tourism Management, 28*(2), 580–590.

Jefferies, K., & Lepp, A. (2012). An investigation of extraordinary experiences. *Journal of Park and Recreation Administration, 30*(3), 37–51.

Karagöz, Y. (2019). *SPSS AMOS META Uygulamalı İstatistiksel Analizler.* Nobel Yayıncılık.

Keskin, E., Sezen, N., & Dağ, T. (2020). Unutulmaz turizm deneyimi, müşteri memnuniyeti, tekrar ziyaret ve tavsiye etme niyeti arasındaki ilişkiler: Kapadokya bölgesini ziyaret eden turistlere yönelik araştırma. *Journal of Recreation and Tourism Research, 7*(2), 239–264.

Kim, J. H. (2009). *Development of a scale to measure memorable tourism experiences.* Indiana University/School of Health, Physical Education, and Recreation. (Unpublished doctoral dissertation).

Kim, J. H. (2010). Determining the factors affecting the memorable nature of travel experiences. *Journal of Travel & Tourism Marketing, 27*(8), 780–796.

Kim, J. H. (2014). The antecedents of memorable tourism experiences: The development of a scale to measure the destination attributes associated with memorable experiences. *Tourism Management, 44*, 34–45.

Kim, J. H., & Ritchie, J. B. (2014). Cross-cultural validation of a memorable tourism experience scale (MTES). *Journal of Travel Research, 53*(3), 323–335.

Kim, J. H., Ritchie, J. B., & McCormick, B. (2012). Development of a scale to measure memorable tourism experiences. *Journal of Travel Research, 51*(1), 12–25.

Kim, J. H., Ritchie, J. R., & Tung, V. W. S. (2010). The effect of memorable experience on behavioral intentions in tourism: A structural equation modeling approach. *Tourism Analysis, 15*(6), 637–648.

Kozak, M. (2001). Repeaters' behavior at two distinct destinations. *Annals of Tourism Research, 28*(3), 784–807.

Lan, Y. (2000). *T*he Evaluation on the International Tour Leader Training Program in Taiwan. ROC (Master's thesis). The Graduate College, University of Wisconsin–Stout.

Larsen, S. (2007). Aspects of a psychology of the tourist experience. *Scandinavian Journal of Hospitality & Tourism, 7*(1), 7–18.

Lee, Y. J. (2015). Creating memorable experiences in a reuse heritage site. *Annals of Tourism Research, pp. 55*, 155–170.

Lehto, X. Y., O'Leary, J. T., & Morrison, A. M. (2004). The effect of prior experience on vacation behavior. *Annals of Tourism Research, 31*(4), 801–818.

Lugosi, P., & Bray, J. (2008). Tour guiding, organisational culture and learning: Lessons from an entrepreneurial company. *International Journal of Tourism Research, 10*(5), 467–479.

Mahdzar, M. (2019). Tourists' perception on memorable tourism experience towards their revisit intentions to islamic tourism destination in Shah Alam, Selangor. *Journal of Emerging Economies and Islamic Research, 7*(1), 37–44.

Mak, A. H. N., Wong, K. K. F., & Chang, R. C. Y. (2011). Critical issues affecting the service quality and professionalism of the tour guides in Hong Kong and Macau. *Tourism Management, 32*(6), 1442–1452.

Martin, D. (2010). Uncovering unconscious memories and myths for understanding international tourism behaviour. *Journal of Business Research, 63*(4), 372–383.

Mathisen, L. (2012). The exploration of the memorable tourist experience. In J. S. Chen (Ed.), *Advances in hospitality and leisure* (pp. 21–41). Emerald Publishing Limited.

Mazursky, D. (1989). Past experience and future tourism decisions. *Annals of Tourism Research, 16*(3), 333–344.

Meydan, C. H., & Şeşen, H. (2015). *Yapısal Eşitlik Modellemesi AMOS Uygulamaları*. Detay Yayıncılık.

Model Fit Indices. (2023). http://statwiki.gaskination.com/index.php/CFA#Modification_indices

Mossberg, L. (2008). Extraordinary experiences through storytelling. *Scandinavian Journal of Hospitality and Tourism, 8*(3), 195–210.

Park, S., & Santos, C. A. (2016). Exploring the tourist experience: A sequential approach. *Journal of Travel Research, 3*, 1–12.

Petrick, J. F. (2002). An examination of golf vacationers' novelty. *Annals of Tourism Research, 29*(2), 384–400.

Prakash, M., & Chowdhary, N. (2010). What are we training tour guides for? *Turizam, 14*(2), 53–65.

Quan, S., & Wang, N. (2004). Towards a structural model oı the tourist experience: An ıllustration from food experiences in tourism. *Tourism Management, 25*(3), 297–305.

Quinlan-Cutler, S., & Carmichael, B. (2010). In M. Morgan, P. Lugosi, & B. Ritchie (Eds.), *The dimensions of the tourist experience. The tourism and leisure experience: Consumer and managerial perspectives* (pp. 3–26). Channel View Publications.

Rabotić, B. (2010, March 4–5). *Tourist guides in contemporary tourism, ınternational conference on tourism and environment*. Philip Noel-Baker University, Sarajevo, Bosnia & Herzegovina, pp. 353–364.

Reisinger, Y., & Steiner, C. (2006). Reconceptualising ınterpretation: The role of tour guides in authentic tourism. *Current Issues in Tourism, 9*(6), 481–498.

Sanz-Blas, S., & Buzova, D. (2016). Guided tour ınfluence on cruise tourist experience in a port of call: An ewom and questionnaire-based approach. *International Journal of Tourism Research, 18*(6), 558–566.

Selstad, L. (2007). The social anthropology of the tourist experience. exploring the "middle role". *Scandinavian Journal of Hospitality and Tourism, 7*(1), 19–33.

Sezgin, E., & Duz, B. (2018). Testing the proposed "GuidePerf" scale for tourism: Performances of tour guides about various tour guiding diplomas. *Asia Pacific Journal of Tourism Research, 23*(2), 170–182.

Skavronskaya, L., Moyle, B., Scott, N., & Kralj, A. (2020). The psychology of novelty in memorable tourism experiences. *Current Issues in Tourism, 23*(21), 2683–2698.

Som, A. P. M., & Badarneh, M. B. (2011). Tourist satisfaction and repeat visitation; toward a new comprehensive model. *International Journal of Human and Social Sciences, 6*(1), 38–45.

Sthapit, E., & Coudounaris, D. N. (2018). Memorable tourism experiences: Antecedents and outcomes. *Scandinavian Journal of Hospitality and Tourism, 18*(1), 72–94.

Triantafillidou, A., & Siomkos, G. (2014a). Extraordinary experience-based segmentation: The case of Greek Summer Campers. *Journal of Hospitality Marketing & Management, 23*(2), 122–156.

Triantafillidou, A., & Siomkos, G. (2014b). Consumption experience outcomes: Satisfaction, nostalgia ıntensity, word-of-mouth communication and behavioural ıntentions. *Journal of Consumer Marketing, 31–6*(7), 526–540.

Tung, V. W. S., & Ritchie, J. B. (2011). Exploring the essence of memorable tourism experiences. *Annals of Tourism Research, 38*(4), 1367–1386.

Ülker Demirel, E. (2020). Yabancı turistlerin unutulmaz turizm deneyimleri üzerine netnografik bir araştırma: Gelibolu yarımadası örneği. *Trakya Üniversitesi İktisadi ve İdari Bilimler Fakültesi Dergisi, 9*(1), 67–90.

Ünal, A., & Bayar, S. B. (2020). Destinasyonlara ilişkin hatırlanabilir deneyimlerin turistlerin tekrar seyahat niyetlerine etkileri: Side Örneği. *Uluslararası Türk Dünyası Turizm Araştırmaları Dergisi, 5*(1), 1–13.

Watson, A. E., Roggenbuck, J. W., & Williams, D. R. (1991). The influence of past experience on wilderness choice. *Journal of Leisure Research, 23*(1), 21–36.

Weiler, B., & Davis, D. (1993). An Exploratory ınvestigation into the role of nature-based tour leader. *Tourism Management, 14*(2), 91–98.

Weiler, B., & Ham, S. H. (2000). *Training ecotour guides in developing countries: Lessons learned from panama's first guides course.* Working Paper, No. 06/00. https://bridges.monash.edu/articles/journal_contribution/Training_ecotour_guides_in_developing_countries_lessons_learned_from_Panama_s_first_guides_course/5072908

Weiler, B., & Walker, K. (2014). Enhancing the visitor experience: Reconceptualising the tour guide's communicative role. *Journal of Hospitality and Tourism Management, 21,* 90–99.

Wirtz, D., Kruger, J., Scollon, C. N., & Diener, E. (2003). What to Do on Spring Break? the role of predicted, online, and remembered experience in future choice. *Psychological Science, 14*(5), 520–524.

Yaşlıoğlu, M. M. (2017). Sosyal bilimlerde faktör analizi ve geçerlilik: Keşfedici ve doğrulayıcı faktör analizlerinin kullanılması. *İstanbul Üniversitesi İşletme Fakültesi Dergisi, 46,* 74–85.

Yismaw, Y. (2019). *Examining The effects of customer relationship markeing on customer retentiion: The case of star rated hotels in Bahir Dar City.* Hawassa University, College Of Business & Economics, School of Hotel & Tourism Management.

Yu, C. P., Chang, W. C., & Ramanpong, J. (2019). Assessing visitors' memorable tourism experiences (mtes) in forest recreation destination: A case study in Xitou Nature Education Area. *Forests, 10*(8), 636.

Zhang, H., Wu, Y., & Buhalis, D. (2018). A model of perceived ımage, memorable tourism experiences and revisit intention. *Journal of Destination Marketing & Management, 8,* 326–336.

Zhong, Y. Y. S., Busser, J., & Baloglu, S. (2017). A model of memorable tourism experience: The effects on satisfaction, affective commitment and storytelling. *Tourism Analysis, 22*(2), 201–217.

Part 6

Film Tourism

Chapter 12

Effects of Films on Tourism

Mehmet Halit Akın

Erciyes University, Türkiye

Learning Objectives

After reading and studying this chapter, you should be able to:

- understand the relationship between alternative tourism, cultural tourism and film tourism;
- understand the concept of film tourism;
- understand whether films affect destination preferences.

Abstract

Depending on the technological, economic and sociological developments seen in the global world, the needs of potential tourists differ, and alternative tourism activities are seen in the tourism sector, which has different dimensions. Film tourism is one of the alternative tourism activities that has become prominent in recent years, especially with the opportunities it offers to reach more audiences with the development of technology. The desire of potential tourists to see different components such as filming locations, actors and local facts of the films they watch turns into a need over time. This situation directs potential tourists' decision-making and purchasing processes for their destination preferences. This chapter aims to create a body of knowledge that will have a widespread effect on the relevant body of knowledge based on current data on alternative and film tourism. In addition, it aims to examine films' effects on destination preferences based on secondary data sources. This chapter, which is designed as conceptual research with descriptive analyses and document analysis, which is one of the qualitative research methods, is vital in terms of revealing general patterns based on new trends in film tourism, which is seen as an export element and has a significant effect on destination preference.

Future Tourism Trends Volume 1, 173–184
Copyright © 2024 Mehmet Halit Akın
Published under exclusive licence by Emerald Publishing Limited
doi:10.1108/978-1-83753-244-520241012

Keywords: Alternative tourism; cultural tourism; film tourism; destination preference; conceptual evaluation; effects of films on destination preference

Introduction

In addition to the change in the habits of society with globalisation, the development of transportation and communication technologies offers various conveniences in the processes related to touristic consumption (Akın, 2021), diversifying the needs of tourists and, accordingly, their demands. This situation has revealed that the concept and types of alternative tourism, which focus on niche markets, are considered a substitute for mass tourism and one of the development stages of tourism (Gursoy et al., 2010, 2019). Alternative tourism, which has emerged mainly against the environmental effects of mass tourism and is seen as an essential tool for local development (Isaac & Eid, 2019), is an approach that includes tourism activities created by integrating different touristic goods and services against traditional tourism activities (Hacıoğlu & Avcıkurt, 2008). As can be understood from the definition, the determinant of the concept of alternative tourism is the different touristic goods and services offered.

Today, with the increasing popularity of alternative tourism, its scope in terms of touristic goods and services is also increasing (Deaden & Harron, 1994). Furthermore, with the effect of globalisation, the fact that films can be reached from many different points of the world regardless of their origin (Akdu & Akın, 2016) has increased the popularity of film tourism within the scope of alternative tourism in recent years. Film tourism is defined as touristic visits to shooting locations that create attraction, especially in films that feature touristic goods and services as well as destinations (Hudson & Ritchie, 2006). It is generally known that films that are not made to promote a destination or create attraction (Jacobs, 2013) increase the touristic demand for the relevant destination by influencing tourists' destination preferences (Josiam et al., 2014). Therefore, in addition to the spread of the sustainability approach, the tourism activity towards the destinations where the films are shot and the differing tourist preferences have revealed film tourism as an alternative tourism type.

It is known that destinations have been trying to create an attraction with alternative tourism activities in recent years. Films are watched by different people in different countries and significantly affect individuals' destination preferences. Therefore, films are seen as an essential source of income related to their field and the tourism sector. This situation enables films to be seen as an export element, especially in recent years. Therefore, scientific studies based on new trends are essential, so that film tourism practices can be carried out in a planned manner within the sustainability approach to protect resources and ensure local development. This research is aimed to present a comprehensive and up-to-date body of knowledge about film tourism in a conceptual framework based on the existing body of knowledge. In addition, it aims to examine films' effect on destination preference based on secondary data sources. Although film tourism is a well-known subject in the body of knowledge related to studies in recent years, the fact that a general pattern will be presented based on current information and new trends reveals the importance of this research. On the other hand, with the general image to be presented, this research is expected to have a widespread effect on the relevant body of knowledge.

Film Tourism

Depending on the tourism cluster, touristic activities are formed by various attractions, businesses and institutions, as well as natural and artificial resources related to tourism concentrated in a specific geography (Fundeanu, 2015). Alternative tourism is defined as tourism types that include new touristic products created to meet the demands of people (Akoğlan Kozak & Türktarhan, 2012). It offers various types of tourism through differentiation for tourists with different needs and desires and the power to spend more significant amounts (Hall, 1994), expressing the importance of meeting the different demands of alternative tourism. Therefore, it can be said that differentiated products for tourists are presented based on the natural and artificial resources of the destination.

Cultural and historical resources are one of the primary resources that provide opportunities for alternative tourism diversity of destinations (Fundeanu, 2015). Cultural resources, considered essential capital of tourism development in a specific geography (Rahayuningsih et al., 2016), are aesthetic, intellectual, emotional, psychological, etc. It forms the basis for the alternative tourism type formed by individuals searching for new experiences based on factors (Stebbins, 1996).

The recognition of films as an essential actor of culture and the presentation of cultural heritage values, in addition to the geographical and social characteristics of the destination (Yılmaz & Yolal, 2008), cause film tourism to be evaluated within the scope of cultural tourism (Çakar Çelik, 2019). Film tourism is defined as the tourist visits that occur due to the presentation of a destination or attraction on television, video or cinema and feed on the increase in international travel and the development of the entertainment industry (Hudson & Ritchie, 2006). Therefore, films that are not made primarily for the purpose of creating touristic mobility, they contributes to the creation of a significant level of touristic activity due to the inclusion of the scenario and actors as well as the attractions of the destination where it was shot.

Film tourism, also called film-induced tourism, basically emerges from individuals' curiosity and desire to visit film-induced destinations, goods, services and other attractions of the destination (Beeton, 2006). Therefore, the film's motivation brings some opportunities in terms of destination preference and development. In other words, it is seen that, like the benefits offered by product diversification within the scope of alternative tourism (Nare et al., 2017), films also offer some opportunities with the positive tendencies they create in desti-nation preferences. Therefore, films bring serious opportunities for more effective marketing, increasing awareness of destinations, extending tourist stay and increasing spending (Hudson & Ritchie, 2006). On the other hand, although it is not directly related to the promotion and marketing of destinations, it is known that films provide opportunities such as obtaining long-term welfare in society with the short-term income provided by the films (Rewtrakunphaiboon, 2009), product innovation, branding and providing a positive image and protecting the local culture by owning (Connell, 2012).

The necessity of directing the decision-making and purchasing process regarding the experiences that will meet the different expectations of the tourists and the needs of the service providers to carry out marketing activities faster and with less cost (Akdu & Akın, 2016) reveals the importance of film tourism in terms of destinations. Therefore, it is essential to evaluate the effects of the films on destination preference and to present the original outputs regarding the planning. In this direction, besides the conceptual framework, the effects of the films on destination preference were examined in detail based on secondary data sources. This chapter, designed as conceptual research with descriptive analyses and document analysis from qualitative research methods, is essential in revealing general trends and patterns based on current and new data. On the other hand, by revealing general trends and patterns, an important body of knowledge base, including guiding information, will be created. In order to achieve the goals that will have a widespread effect, this chapter is designed with a focus on the research question, 'Do films have a significant effect on destination preferences?'

Case Study

In this chapter, document analysis, one of the qualitative research methods, was adopted to create a conceptual framework based on secondary data. Document review is a technique based on creating knowledge by utilising existing materials related to the research topic (Scott & Morrison, 2005). As a method widely used in social sciences, a body of knowledge review was conducted to determine the effect of films on destination preferences with document review, and the findings and outputs of the identified research were evaluated.

Effects of Films on Destination Preference: A Conceptual Evaluation

Films are essential for forming touristic destinations (Heavens, 1995). In other words, the destinations where the films are shot create attraction in terms of some values presented in the films, attract the tourists and thus offer the opportunity to form a touristic destination with the tourist flow. Accordingly, the tendency towards recognising tourist destinations with the effect of films is increasing daily

(Li & Liu, 2020). Therefore, this situation is expressed in the relevant body of knowledge as the effect of films on destination preferences (Erdem et al., 2016; Khai & Hang, 2019; Özbek & Güllü, 2021; Spears et al., 2013; Taşet al., 2017; Zhumadilova, 2016).

As mentioned above, some values presented in films, especially cultural values, attract tourists and affect their destination preferences. In other words, the presentation of the destination components in the films directs the tendencies of the tourists regarding destination preference. This situation is also reflected in the research on the subject, and the values kept in the foreground in the films about destination preferences are also included. These values generally include the landscape and geographical structure (Özbek & Güllü, 2021), the authenticity of the place (destination, residential area, shooting location) (Şahinalp et al., 2017), local music (Im & Chon, 2008), ethnic restaurants (Khai & Hang, 2019) and cultural and literary works (Busby & Klug, 2001).

On the other hand, it is seen that the themes such as documentaries (Erdem et al., 2016; Zhumadilova, 2016), TV series (Kim et al., 2007; Saltık et al., 2010), cinematic nostalgia (Kim et al., 2019), music groups (Liou, 2010), as well as films have an effect on destination preferences. Within this chapter's scope, the research findings and outputs in the relevant body of knowledge were discussed to determine the effect of the values above presented in the films on destination preferences. In addition to the films, research on the themes above is also included.

Some studies show how films affect destination preferences based on the image they create. For example, Josiam et al. (2014) evaluated the perceptions and orientations of Indian audiences of Bollywood films regarding European destinations. Accordingly, it has been determined that including various attractions related to European destinations in Bollywood films has a significant effect on the perceptions of Indians regarding the destination image, and this effect directs the tendencies of Bollywood audiences in their destination preferences. Similarly, another study determined that Korean films and Hallyu culture have positive effects on viewers in different destinations and create a positive image perception towards Korea. In addition, it has been revealed that values such as actors, actors' interests and empathy and places create film-induced touristic mobility (Kim et al., 2007).

On the other hand, Busby and Klug (2001), in their research on the tourists coming to Notting Hill, revealed that the tourists coming to the region have a positive image perception about the destination before they come; they know the places in the films, and accordingly, they travel. Furthermore, in the study by Şahbaz and Kılıçlar (2009), it was seen that films have a significant effect on the image of the destination, which covers the practice area of the research, and on the tourists' decision to visit the relevant destination. Therefore, studies have shown that films have an important effect on image perception and positive image perception on destination preference.

The relevant body of knowledge is directly included in the research on the destination preferences of the films. For example, Wen et al. (2018) conducted a study to investigate the effect of films on the preference of Chinese tourists for international travel destinations, and it was seen that Chinese people have a high tendency to international travel. This tendency is directed to the destinations where the films are shot based on the travel motivation created by the films. In addition, Güzel and Aktaş (2016) conducted interviews to determine the effect of Turkish films released in Greece. Accordingly, it has been determined that Turkish films released in Greece positively affect Turkey's image and strengthen the desire to travel to Turkey. On the other hand, it has been seen that values such as natural beauty, historical places and local clothes presented in the films positively affect Turkey. Similarly, Beeton (2006), in his research to evaluate socio-economic effects such as alienation and economic effects in the relevant destination caused by tourism mobility based on films, revealed an important film-induced flow towards the region where a film was shot.

Related studies have revealed that values such as nature, space and food positively affect the destination image and preferability. In addition, it has been revealed that one of the most fundamental issues is the story and characters of the films (Kim, 2012). In this context, it is seen that the image perception towards destinations and the tendency towards demand depend on different themes apart from the films and the many different values and contents presented in the films. Some studies on the subject reveal concrete outputs related to this situation. For example, Im and Chon (2008) conducted a study to determine the effect of the music in the films on the destination preferences of tourists and the existence of the values that affect tourist decisions. As a result, the phenomenon of film-induced tourism was supported.

In the related body of knowledge, there are studies on different themes apart from films (Erdem et al., 2016; Kim et al., 2007, 2019; Liou, 2010; Saltık et al., 2010; Zhumadilova, 2016). In other words, there are studies to investigate the effect of different programmes based on visual aids, such as films, on the destination preferences of tourists. For example, in the research by Zhumadilova (2016) on travel-related documentaries and TV programmes that introduce the components of the destination and are used by businesses as a promotional and marketing tool, it has been revealed that depending on demographic variables, the contents of the relevant documentaries and programmes of potential tourists have a guiding effect, so the image perception of the destination and also touristic service preferences are affected. Liou (2010), who argues that celebrities in films or television should be considered as a driving factor for the tourism sector, made research on Taiwanese youth visiting Japan in order to reveal the effect of celebrities with large fan bases, such as singers, film stars and athletes on their destination preference. Accordingly, it has been determined that young people's demands for Japan are encouraged depending on dynamic factors such as celebrities' words, lifestyles, gestures and activities.

Research Box

As a tourism researcher, you noticed that while chatting with various groups, individuals were influenced by the film they watched, and accordingly, they visited the place where the film was shot. On the other hand, you understood that the tendency of these individuals to visit the relevant destination is influential in their interest in differentiated products and services because they seek diversity. Therefore, seeing that there are factors that affect the behaviour of individuals and that films have an important position among these factors, you have decided that it is necessary to research within the following research questions:

(1) What is the meaning of film tourism?
(2) In which position are the films among the differing demands and needs?
(3) How does film tourism affect tourists' destination preferences?

Conclusion

In particular, depending on the development of technology, the practices used by tourism businesses in terms of variables such as management, marketing and communication show diversity and change. This change also brings the diversity of tourism, which is also expressed as alternative tourism and emerges depending on different needs and desires. The white screen, seen as one of the most important mass media tools in the social structure, has become one of the most important tools that tourism businesses use both as a marketing tool and as a variable of attraction, depending on these changes and developments in recent years. In this context, this chapter aimed to examine the effect of films, which include many values such as space, living spaces, clothes and food, on destination preferences within the scope of existing studies in the relevant body of knowledge.

In addition to the effect of direct films on destination preference, studies in the relevant body of knowledge were examined in terms of variables such as creating the perception of destination image, taking the values presented in the films as a basis and presenting destinations in different themes other than films. The general finding in the studies with different research methods and analysis techniques in different universes and sample groups is that films significantly affect the destination preferences of potential tourists. This finding also answers the research question, 'Do films significantly affect destination preferences?' In view of the fact that different values of music, subject, content and place in the films have different effects on the participants, many different factors can affect some of the participants such as the music of the film, some of the story and some of the actors. Therefore, considering the importance of films in creating interest in the destination, they are significant in developing strategies for creating and positioning the destination brand by being interpreted correctly by the destination management organisations (Millán et al., 2016).

The fact that films positively and seriously affect the tendency to prefer and visit a destination, and that there is a significant difference between those who watch films and those who do not, in terms of their preferences and visits (Rewtrakunphaiboon, 2017), indicates that the importance of better understanding the expectations of potential tourists within the values mentioned above and themes emerges. Therefore, to create effective planning, it is important to include the subjects that will attract the attention of potential tourists before, during and after the trip (Shi & Erdélyi, 2022). At this point, it will be an important marketing tool for destinations to make films not designed as a variable of travel, considering different aspects to create touristic attraction. In addition, the fact that the effect of films on the popularity of destinations reaches not only a limited environment but also a much wider area with the effect of cumulative causation (Strielkowski, 2017) increases this importance even more.

The perception that a destination is only a film-induced destination can lead to a negative perception of the destination (O'Connor et al., 2010). However, in the development of film-induced destinations, it is necessary to make plans considering the many opportunities offered by films, such as the adoption of the sustainability approach to the destination, the revival of the local culture and the creation of the variable of attraction (Sahoo & Lenka, 2010). Considering this situation in the research examined, planning and practices that will create value for stakeholders and marketers have been emphasised. For example, Park et al. (2018) even created a design directive for collecting, arranging and presenting broadcast content in the virtual reality environment to create more effective planning.

One principal value that makes potential tourists want to experience and visit is nostalgia (Kim, 2012). Therefore, businesses that want to benefit from nostalgia and increase the destination's attractiveness by offering individuals the opportunity to experience nostalgic feelings indirectly or directly can draw more attention by using simple and creative ideas (Kim et al., 2019). Furthermore, keeping nostalgia alive, providing emotional integrity and presenting nostalgic souvenirs (Kim, 2012) with hidden stories in content and characters will increase film-induced tourism mobility to potential tourists (Liou, 2010) whose tendencies towards films have increased in order to follow the traces of nostalgia. In this context, including the nostalgic values of the films, one of today's most important communication tools within planning can provide an essential competitive advantage for destinations.

Another important finding within the scope of research is the indirect satisfaction that potential tourists can experience indirectly through films before actually visiting the destination (Kim & Kim, 2020). This is especially important for the tourism sector, which has a structure that cannot be experienced before, and therefore, for destinations as a main component. However, on the other hand, it is known that the fact that potential tourists get to know the destination through a film can increase destination preference and visit intention (Rewtrakunphaiboon, 2017). In addition, the experience of destinations by watching films beforehand positively affects the image perception of the relevant destination and the actual destination experience (Kim & Assaker, 2014).

Therefore, films are seen as one of the most important communication tools of destinations in today's technology world in terms of being experienced beforehand and giving confidence to tourists.

Touristic travels are generally a form of behaviour to meet individuals' different needs, making evaluating behavioural aspects especially important in film-induced touristic activities (Busby & Klug, 2001). In the studies in the related body of knowledge, the effect of films on the behavioural aspects of tourists on their destination preferences has been discussed. When evaluated as a whole, it is seen that films are an important tool in creating a positive image perception of destinations. Furthermore, it is seen that the combination of positive image perception and needs in potential tourists creates the desire to visit the relevant destination. In the related body of knowledge, this situation is evaluated as the effect of films on destination preferences. In particular, films created based on the values and themes mentioned earlier offer important opportunities for destinations in today's technology world to bring the distances provided by the internet and social media closer and reach more audiences. The previously inexperienced nature of destinations further increases this importance. Therefore, films are an important marketing tool in today's technology world, and their potential has a significant effect on the preferences of tourists.

Within this chapter's scope, in which films' effects on destinations as an essential tool in modern marketing are evaluated, it is possible to present some suggestions for destination practitioners. First, promotional policies of destinations can be determined, and incentives and plans can be prepared to bring destinations to the forefront in films integrated with promotional policies. Second, films with globally exciting content can be shot to promote the destination, guide potential tourists' future behavioural tendencies, increase global awareness and provide local economic development. Third, social media–based real-time marketing practices can increase films' positive image and attractiveness. Fourth, agreements and incentives can be made with national and international film-makers regarding displaying natural, historical and cultural values in films, even briefly. At this point, it is important to present the relevant values as they are. Third, establishing units based on destination and central administrations to create film-induced tourism mobility will ensure that the planning is carried out effectively. Fourth, it is necessary to consider carrying capacity, sustainability and future generations in all planning and actions, taking into account the issues that may occur with the increase in film-induced tourism mobility. Finally, it is recommended that destination practitioners show the necessary actions based on the sustainability approach regarding the use of films as a modern marketing tool.

Discussion Questions

- What is the meaning of film tourism?
- In which position are the films among the differing demands and needs?
- How does film tourism affect tourists' destination preferences?

References

Akdu, U., & Akın, M. H. (2016). Film ve dizilerin destinasyon tercihine etkileri. *The Journal of International Social Research, 9*(45), 1042–1052.

Akın, M. H. (2021). Sağlık turizmi alanyazinin bibliyometrik analizi (2015–2020). *Manas Sosyal Araştırmalar Dergisi, 10*(3), 2026–2036.

Akoğlan Kozak, M., & Türktarhan, G. (2012). Gönüllü turizmine kavramsal bir bakış. *Turar Turizm ve Araştırma Dergisi, 1*(2), 4–14.

Beeton, S. (2006). Understanding film-induced tourism. *Tourism Analysis, 11*(3), 181–188.

Busby, G., & Klug, J. (2001). Movie-induced tourism: The challenge of measurement and other issues. *Journal of Vacation Marketing, 7*(4), 316–332.

Çakar Çelik, Ö. Ç. (2019). Film turizmi ve Sığacık'a (İzmir) etkileri. *Adıyaman Üniversitesi Sosyal Bilimler Enstitüsü Dergisi, 31*, 432–460.

Connell, J. (2012). Film tourism – Evolution, progress and prospects. *Tourism Management, 33*(5), 1007–1029.

Deaden, P., & Harron, S. (1994). Alternative tourism and adaptive change. *Annals of Tourism Research, 21*(1), 81–102.

Erdem, B., Türkmendağ, T., & Akyürek, S. (2016). The effects of travel documentaries featured on television on holiday preferences of the tourists: A research on domestic tourists in Muğla. *Akademik Bakış Dergisi*, (54), 108–133.

Fundeanu, D. D. (2015). Innovative regional cluster, model of tourism development. *Procedia Economics and Finance, 23*, 744–749.

Gursoy, D., Chi, C. G., & Dyer, P. (2010). Locals' attitudes toward mass and alternative tourism: The case of the sunshine coast, Australia. *Journal of Travel Research, 49*(3), 381–394.

Gursoy, D., Ouyang, Z., Nunkoo, R., & Wei, W. (2019). Residents' impact perceptions of and attitudes towards tourism development: A meta-analysis. *Journal of Hospitality Marketing & Management, 28*(3), 306–333.

Güzel, S. Ö., & Aktaş, G. (2016). Türk televizyon dizilerinin destinasyon imajına ve seyahat etme eğilimine etkisi: Atina örneği. *Anatolia: turizm araştırmaları dergisi, 27*(1), 111–124.

Hacıoğlu, N., & Avcıkurt, C. (2008). *Turistik ürün çeşitlendirmesi.* Nobel Yayınları.

Hall, C. M. (1994). *Tourism and politics: Policy, power and place.* Wiley & Sons.

Heavens, A. J. (1995). Where movies are made, tourists will flock. *Houston Chronicle, 7.*

Hudson, S., & Ritchie, J. B. (2006). Promoting destinations via film tourism: An empirical identification of supporting marketing initiatives. *Journal of Travel Research, 44*(4), 387–396.

Im, H. H., & Chon, K. (2008). An exploratory study of movie-induced tourism: A case of the movie the sound of music and its locations in Salzburg, Austria. *Journal of Travel & Tourism Marketing, 24*(2–3), 229–238.

Isaac, R. K., & Eid, T. A. (2019). Tourists' destination image: An exploratory study of alternative tourism in Palestine. *Current Issues in Tourism, 22*(12), 1499–1522.

Jacobs, L. (2013). *Influences of films on tourism behaviour.* Multinational and Tourist Groups, Hes so//Valaıs, Wallıs.

Josiam, B. M., Spears, D., Dutta, K., Pookulangara, S. A., & Kinley, T. L. (2014). "Namastey London": Bollywood movies and their impact on how Indians perceive European destinations. *Hospitality Review, 31*(4).

Khai, N. T. N., & Hang, T. T. T. (2019). Hallyu and the impact on young consumers' preference for Korean restaurants in Vietnam. In *Proceedings of the 1st International Conference on Economics, Business and Tourism* (pp. 1–22). Vietnam: Ho Chi Minh City.

Kim, S. (2012). The impact of TV drama attributes on touristic experiences at film tourism destinations. *Tourism Analysis, 17*(5), 573–585.

Kim, S. S., Agrusa, J., Lee, H., & Chon, K. (2007). Effects of Korean television dramas on the flow of Japanese tourists. *Tourism Management, 28*(5), 1340–1353.

Kim, S., & Assaker, G. (2014). An empirical examination of the antecedents of film tourism experience: A structural model approach. *Journal of Travel & Tourism Marketing, 31*(2), 251–268.

Kim, B. K., & Kim, K. O. (2020). Relationship between viewing motivation, presence, viewing satisfaction, and attitude toward tourism destinations based on TV travel reality variety programs. *Sustainability, 12*(11), 4614.

Kim, S., Kim, S., & King, B. (2019). Nostalgia film tourism and its potential for destination development. *Journal of Travel & Tourism Marketing, 36*(2), 236–252.

Li, C. H., & Liu, C. C. (2020). The effects of empathy and persuasion of storytelling via tourism micro-movies on travel willingness. *Asia Pacific Journal of Tourism Research, 25*(4), 382–392.

Liou, D. Y. (2010). Beyond Tokyo Rainbow Bridge: Destination images portrayed in Japanese drama affect Taiwanese tourists' perception. *Journal of Vacation Marketing, 16*(1), 5–15.

Millán, Á., García, J. A., & Díaz, E. (2016). Film-induced tourism: A latent class segmentation based on satisfaction and future intentions. *Revista de Turismo y Patrimonio Cultural, 14*(4), 875–888.

Nare, A. T., Musikavanhu, G. M., & Chiutsi, S. (2017). Tourism diversification in Botswana-a stakeholder perspective. *African Journal of Hospitality, Tourism and Leisure, 6*(3), 1–14.

O'Connor, N., Flanagan, S., & Gilbert, D. (2010). The use of film in re-imaging a tourism destination: A case study of Yorkshire, UK. *Journal of Vacation Marketing, 16*(1), 61–74.

Özbek, M., & Güllü, K. (2021). Destinasyon Tercihinde Film ve Dizi İzlemenin Önemi: Kapadokya'da Film Turizmi Örneği. *Erciyes Akademi, 35*(Özel sayı), 855–873.

Park, H., Kim, J., Bang, S., & Woo, W. (2018, October). The effect of applying film-induced tourism to virtual reality tours of cultural heritage sites. In *2018 3rd Digital Heritage International Congress (DigitalHERITAGE) was held jointly with the 2018 24th International Conference on Virtual Systems & Multimedia (VSMM 2018)* (pp. 1–4). IEEE.

Rahayuningsih, T., Muntasib, E. H., & Prasetyo, L. B. (2016). Nature-based tourism resources assessment using geographic information system (GIS): A case study in Bogor. *Procedia Environmental Sciences, 33*, 365–375.

Rewtrakunphaiboon, W. (2009). Film-induced tourism: Inventing a vacation to a location. *BU Academic Review, 8*(1), 33–42.

Rewtrakunphaiboon, W. (2017). Effects of frequency of viewing Korean film on preference for Korea and intention to visit Korea. *Journal of Thai Hospitality and Tourism, 12*(1), 83–96.

Şahbaz, R. P., & Kılıçlar, A. (2009). Filmlerin ve televizyon dizilerinin destinasyon imajına etkileri. *İşletme Araştırmaları Dergisi, 1*(1), 31–52.

Şahinalp, M. S., Çiftçi, B., & Günal, V. (2017). Dizi turizmi bağlamında Karagül televizyon dizisi'nin Eski Halfeti'iyi ziyaret eden turistlerin ziyaret kararları üzerindeki etkisi. *Kesit Akademi Dergisi*, (9), 271–284.

Sahoo, S. S., & Lenka, S. K. (2010). Destination marketing through film tourism: A study on Western Orissa. *Atna Journal of Tourism Studies, 5*(1), 25–39.

Saltık, A. I., Coşar, Y., & Kozak, M. (2010). Televizyon dizilerinin destinasyon pazarlaması açısından olası sonuçları. *Anatolia: Turizm Araştırmaları Dergisi, 21*(1), 41–50.

Scott, D., & Morrison, M. (2005). *Key ideas in educational research*. Continuum.

Shi, J., & Erdélyi, É. (2022). Film tourism planning based on Chinese generation Z tourists' preference for Budapest. *Turisztikai és Vidékfejlesztési Tanulmányok, 7*(2), 114–134.

Spears, D. L., Josiam, B. M., Kinley, T., & Pookulangara, S. (2013). Tourists see tourist do: The influence of Hollywood movies and television on tourism motivation and activity behaviour. *Hospitality Review, 30*(1), 4.

Stebbins, R. A. (1996). Cultural tourism as serious leisure. *Annals of Tourism Research, 23*(4), 948–950.

Strielkowski, W. (2017). Promoting tourism destination through film-induced tourism: The case of Japan. *MARKET/TRŽIŠTE, 29*(2), 193–203.

Taş, S., Başkan, K., & Kamber Taş, S. S. (2017). Turistik destinasyon tercihlerinde filmlerin ve tv dizilerinin etkisi: Doğu Karadeniz Bölgesi örneği. *The Journal of International Social Research, 10*(54), 1134–1145.

Wen, H., Josiam, B. M., Spears, D. L., & Yang, Y. (2018). Influence of movies and television on Chinese tourists perception toward international tourism destinations. *Tourism Management Perspectives, 28*, 211–219.

Yılmaz, H., & Yolal, M. (2008). Film turizmi: Destinasyonların pazarlanmasında filmlerin rolü. *Anadolu Üniversitesi Sosyal Bilimler Dergisi, 8*(1), 175–792.

Zhumadilova, A. (2016). The impact of TV shows and video blogs on tourists' destination choice. *Tourism Today, 16*, 148–166.

Chapter 13

Standby, Action and Cut! How Bollywood Films Encourage Tourism All Around the World

Azman Norhidayah and Albattat Ahmad

Management and Science University, Malaysia

Learning Objectives

After reading and studying this chapter, you should be able to:

- understand the context of film and tourism;
- understand the definition of film;
- discover why the film is so important;
- identify five distinctive features of Bollywood films;
- understand how Bollywood films act as promotional tools to tourism destinations around the world.

Abstract

According to Yubin et al. (2023), films serve as a medium for conveying visual representations of various elements such as landscapes, buildings, landmarks and monuments, which provide a contextual backdrop for the narrative. According to Vila et al. (2021), the number of global tourists visiting film locations exceeds 80 million. In addition, according to Yubin et al. (2023), the promotion of tourism is facilitated through the utilisation of films, which serve to create novel representations, counteract negative perceptions and enhance the portrayal of underdeveloped destinations. A significant number of individuals engage in the practise of visiting movie sets with the intention of re-experiencing the emotional impact of the film. The devaluation of film marketing has been observed. This method represents a highly indirect approach to enticing tourists. This chapter examines the comprehension of

---

Future Tourism Trends Volume 1, 185–203
Copyright © 2024 Azman Norhidayah and Albattat Ahmad
Published under exclusive licence by Emerald Publishing Limited
doi:10.1108/978-1-83753-244-520241013

travellers' motivations and the perception of film-exposed locations in Bollywood films (Salnick, 2023). Film tourism provides a tailored and personalised experience for individuals. The difficulty in measuring this concept arises from factors such as the emotional responsiveness, personality traits, background and interpretive abilities of the viewers in relation to media images. According to Castro et al. (2023), the inclusion of a destination on a screen can serve as a means to enhance the diversity of a site's tourist offerings or mitigate the effects of seasonality by providing opportunities for experiential activities, showcasing notable landmarks or serving as a filming location. Film destinations have the potential to gain popularity and benefit from advertising and the perception of spectators.

Keywords: Tourism; film tourism; Bollywood; alternative tourism; niche tourism; new tourism trends

Context of Film and Tourism

Tourism is considered the largest industry in the world, but many factors also influence it. For example, according to United Nations World Tourism Organization (UNWTO) (2018), the number of international tourist arrivals worldwide reached its (current) highest increase during the global economic crisis of 2009. Furthermore, the UNWTO continues by stating that in 2017, more than 70% of total forecasted international arrivals were registered, which exceeded already the annual forecasted percentage from 2010 to 2020. Hence, the growth of tourist arrivals directly affects a particular country since they need to have enough resources and space to welcome all types of tourists. Similarly, the film industry begins by 'raising awareness of places' (Liu et al., 2023), captivating the attention of the viewer and encouraging the individual to visit a destination. In addition, Wullur et al. (2023) mention that movies, after family and friends and the internet, are the second most influenceable factor when choosing to travel to a particular country (Wullur et al., 2023). However, occasionally, the idyllic image of a destination portrayed in movies gives the viewer an impression of the cultural and social beliefs of the country, creating a distorted perception of the destination that tourists identify with and wish to explore or rediscover (Florido-Benítez, 2023; Liu et al., 2023; Wullur et al., 2023; Zeng et al., 2023).

How we consume popular media today can influence our travel behaviour: what activities we do, at which restaurant we decide to eat, in what hotel we stay in and how we interact with others. In the past, literature, music and poetry were essential to spreading the media (Zeng et al., 2023). However, before the development of film and television, only certain groups could access written works. Wullur et al. (2023) mention that during post-industrial times, film and tourism began to be related, both conceptually and historically. An example that proves this new correlation can be seen in one of the first Lumière brothers' films, which illustrated a moving train.: From this film, two symbols of modernity and technology were represented by 'offering the possibility of witnessing never-before-seen sites and sights to mass publics of the late 19th century' (Florido-Benítez, 2023; Liu et al., 2023; Wullur et al., 2023; Zeng et al., 2023). Tulsi (2023) also argues that during the 20th century, the film became one of the most utilised media communications systems, affecting the tourism industry and consequently involving moving images with travel.

Introduction

The origins of cinema date back to the 1890s, when, with the aid of technology, images could be projected on a screen using a cinématographe to create a sense of movement represented through optical illusions. The first displayed film came from the Lumière Brothers in 1895 in Paris, presented as a documentary about people and places, and was originally without sound. First, black-and-white movies were produced through tinting, toning and stencilling. Later, by 1906, colour was added to the moving images with a British Kinemacolor, which was publicly presented in 1909. Finally, the first films began to be simultaneously produced as the first automobiles.

Furthermore, the origins of mass tourism have been associated with, or even initiated by, the start of the mass production of long-distance transport. Also, both tourism and cinema are 'predicated on movement', referring to the travelling spectator in the first position and the moving image in the second. Therefore, the meaning behind the relationship between film and movement gives a clear idea that films will significantly influence the tourism industry. The film not only drives motivation to visit a place but also creates or builds an image based on other current images, thus motivating an individual to perform further research about the destination while playing a role in 'potential tourist image building and decision-making'. Although the first films lacked a structural storyline and, instead, only captured movement, film-makers developed a 'film language' – or a set of grammar rules on how to tell stories on film. Moreover, in 1914, various national film industries were established, mainly developing in Europe, Russia and Scandinavia, and being as crucial as in America. Thus, films 'became longer, and storytelling, or narrative, became the dominant form' (Florido-Benítez, 2023; Liu et al., 2023; Wullur et al., 2023; Zeng et al., 2023).

Throughout the 1930s and 1940s, cinema became one of the primary forms of popular entertainment, where people attended movies twice weekly. For instance, in Britain in 1946, the number of spectators going to the cinema was among the highest, with over 31 million weekly visits. Simultaneously, countries such as India and the United States have been consistently growing in the production and distribution of feature films yearly. However, in India, the number of digital feature films is slightly over, with more than 1,800 films released in 2018 across the country, whereas in the United States, just over 500 films were produced that same year.

Why Film Is so Important?

Most film enthusiasts like movies but may need help defining why films are vital to society. There are several reasons why films are a vital art form, yet film enthusiasts may find it challenging to define them in depth. 'Watching movies on the weekend is enjoyable' does not quite cut it. They understand that movies are more than simply a weekend diversion. They identify with the universe they have constructed in their brains and emotions.

Regarding popular culture, cinema is now regarded as one of America's most famous art forms, and arguably it is most significant contribution to global culture. It is not easy to conceive what our lives would be like without motion pictures – those flickering images displayed on a screen that have become iconic representations of our inner and outer realities, communicating ideas and emotions from one person or culture to another across time and distance. Throughout the last century, the creation of motion movies has become a substantial business in the United States and other main production hubs. Thousands of people are employed in production, screening, distribution and other associated operations. Indirectly, they generate hundreds, if not thousands, of employment by generating new markets for basics such as popcorn kernels or celluloid raw material required to produce film reels... and much more! Films also provide economic possibilities via tourism (see Hollywood Boulevard) that assist hotels, restaurateurs, store owners, etc. Here are the reasons why the film is essential:

- Amusements and Pleasure:
  For others, it is just a question of amusement and enjoyment. Most folks go to the movies to have fun. They want to be transferred to another universe for two hours, so that they may forget about the stress of their jobs and other concerns. This is one of the reasons why cinema is such an essential art form – regardless of the genre, it provides people with a small quantity of escape from reality. A film can engage an audience in ways that television and other media cannot. No other media can simultaneously engage the senses in the same manner as cinema does. The sights and sounds and the sense of being in a darkened movie theatre with dozens (or even hundreds) of equally captivated viewers provide an immersive experience, unlike watching television or playing video games alone at home.
- Authentication and Identification:
  For others, it is the ability to relate with the characters in the films they watch or a curiosity about the art that makes high-quality films possible. Humans adore movies, and with good cause. The film is the only art form that connects us emotionally with the characters. We perceive them as individuals grappling with genuine difficulties and confronting genuine obstacles. We discover our anxieties, ambitions, dreams and aspirations through them. Thus, cinema may affect public opinion on social problems and alter how we view and sometimes even feel about ourselves.

- Today, Even More, Effective:
Films have permanently altered the world but have never been as influential as they are now. The motion picture camera and projector were created around the end of the 19th century. In the 1890s, the earliest motion pictures, known as 'silent films', debuted in cinemas. Shortly afterwards, movies and television dominated American popular culture. Cinema has often altered the course of history, but it has never been as crucial as it is now. Films have always been a powerful medium for reflecting our reality. Through comedies and tragedies, tales of love, hope, victory and sorrow, films reveal who we are via the characters' lives on screen – not just the ones we relate with, but all of them, represented by performers who immerse us in their world.

  The finest films motivate us to reflect on ourselves and how we might improve our lives and society; they teach us how to better understand one another via compassion and empathy and challenge us to think critically about how we got here and where we are heading. Movies have always been an effective means to influence the world because they are mirrors that provide viewers from all walks of life with a glimpse of their own lives – or at least dramatised versions of them. This makes them attractive for spectators at home (or in the theatre) and those who make these cinematic masterpieces possible behind the scenes at every stage of this life journey.

- Instruments of Social Change:
When war films represent the actual world with harsh reality as opposed to romanticised images of warriors going into battle beneath waving flags, they may be used as vehicles for societal change. The film is a powerful medium that may be utilised for social change. When war films represent the actual world with raw reality, as opposed to stylised images of warriors going into battle beneath waving flags, they may dramatically impact how viewers understand problems of war and peace. For instance, *Saving Private Ryan* presented World War II's atrocities with horrible special effects; the opening sequence centred on the gruesome murders of many characters; many people could not watch it! In contrast, classic films often depicted patriotic views towards the conflict. In *Sands of Iwo Jima*, for instance, John Wayne portrays an American soldier who wishes to protect his nation from its adversaries. When realistic images of battle are shown on screen, viewers may be less likely to embrace military conflict as a solution to issues. This is a fantastic illustration of how films influence society!

- Broaden Horizons:
Films may give viewers a different perspective on society than they are used to, extending their minds and encouraging them to consider issues in fresh ways. They may give a unique perspective on the lives of individuals in various civilisations, offering insight into the lives and cultures of people from other countries. Cinema may teach us about communities that are very unlike our own. Films may also assist in altering people's perspectives on specific subjects. For instance, films like *An Inconvenient Truth* have been used to educate and motivate audiences about climate change.

- Art Form and Device:
A film is an art form and a vehicle for social change in this manner. It may amuse, enlighten and examine pressing societal concerns. Films may cause us

to pay attention, learn about a new culture, get a fresh viewpoint or open our eyes to an alien world. We watch movies because they are enjoyable and provoke fresh ways of thinking about situations. They do more than reflect our society; they alter it!

• Reflections of Society:
Films are vital to society because they reflect culture, alter culture and stimulate economic expansion. In several ways, movies mirror society. Consider how the messages of your favourite films have impacted you. So, cinema reflects culture. A film that appeals to forgiveness, for instance, would connect with those who forgive but not with those who do not. In addition to affecting the views, attitudes and actions of those who see them, films also alter civilisation. For instance, a documentary on child abuse may inspire you to take action against child abuse in your neighbourhood by volunteering or giving money. This is how films affect cultural transformation. The film industry contributes to economic expansion by employing tens of thousands of people from all walks of life and producing billions of dollars in annual income that is returned to the economy via taxes and another spending on products and services linked to film production (e.g. construction workers building a set).

Film and Tourism

Film and tourism can be entered under the name of cultural tourism. It refers to the increased popularity of locales due to their film portrayal. Film tourism refers to all types of travel to locations that allow people to connect with the world of film in some way. It is also divided into three kinds: *Tourism for Film Promotion, tourism for travel films, and tourism for film-induced* (Kim & Park, 2023; Sun et al., 2023). Travel is triggered by visually inspecting a film, dramatically influencing the tourist's decision. People become film tourists for a variety of reasons, for example, the desire to visit film and television parks and studios, visiting areas that are directly related to and connected to a particular film, a cinematic journey that allows individuals to descend into the film location and uses the natural views as a value of identification. Films and tourism destinations are frequently included as an efficient advertising technique to obtain economic benefits. It is achieving a significant position through its promotional and advertising offers. The percentage of revenue through tourism is significant. This revenue depends on the quality of the film and its position among the audience, and its importance promptly works to enhance tourism services in tourist destinations.

All the places in the movie have natural features that make them look good, like beautiful scenery and quiet surroundings. How a tourist destination is shown in a movie can change people's expectations and ideas about the place. It can also make people feel sentimental about the place. Also, film locations are often called 'real regions of simulation'. Tourists are fascinated by the mystery created by how fiction and reality interact, for example, Fort Aguada of Goa. This iconic fort in North Goa has appeared in several blockbuster films, including *Dhoom, Golmaal, Dil Chahta Hai, Rangeela* and others. The fort is renowned for its picturesque setting with the sea on three sides and tranquil beaches. The consumption of scenery shown on film, an exceptionally effective marketing weapon viewed as a legitimate, unbiased information source, shapes, enhances and changes such visuals (Castro et al., 2023; Sun et al., 2023). Distinguished destinations are more likely to receive extensive media coverage, which leads to the formation of specific destination pictures in the minds of visitors (Bolan & Williams, 2008). Images in still specific images of a location in the minds of potential visitors give them a taste of the site before they arrive (Kim & Park, 2023; Sun et al., 2023).

Why Do We Advertise With Film?

Film advertising is becoming a more popular kind of marketing. Often, large corporations make these short adverts and then distribute them to various theatres to be shown to audiences before and after the significant film they watch. All marketing tactics have benefits and downsides: here are the contribution, advantages and disadvantages of film advertising.

What does cinematic tourism contribute?

- Bridging the gap between industry professionals and government/authorities.
- Support cinematic tourism via conference presentations and industry discussions.
- Consultation on destination marketing.
- Film-related tourist goods development and implementation.
- Film site trips should be promoted.
- Doing market research with movie-induced visitors.

The Benefits of Film Advertising

- Advertisers recognise that, especially before a film begins, the audience is often active rather than passive. When the audience's minds are concentrated, and in the appropriate position to explore new ideas or listen to alternative points of view, this is an ideal time for commercials to be delivered to them. This implies that advertisements are more likely to appeal to audience members immediately, and they are more likely to absorb the contents being presented.
- It is a terrific approach to assist other forms of advertising. Film advertising, combined with other promotion types, such as social media commercials and billboards, is an excellent approach to raising awareness of the film while also functioning as a supporting mechanism.
- One of the primary benefits of film advertising is its cheap cost. Therefore, when considering the return on investment, it is cost-effective.
- Film advertising has a much more significant effect than other types of advertising. In contrast to social media campaigns, where the commercials do not take centre stage and are not the primary emphasis, film advertisements

have a long-lasting effect since the screen is the centre of the audience's attention.

Film Advertising Disadvantages

- Coverage is often entirely restricted. When marketers pick where to show advertisements, they make a deliberate choice regarding the placement of that commercial, and the local public benefits more from cinema advertising. Any advertiser's promotional campaign will only be visible to individuals who have visited a nearby cinema, reducing your chances of viewing various advertisements.
- Small businesses will suffer financially if they use this strategy. Distribution and film production expenses are highly costly, and you need a vast market to produce advertising films to fund.
- They have a shorter lifespan than other digital marketing media. This is because the advertisements do not have much time to run, so only a few individuals can see them before they vanish.
- Cinema advertisements may be both dull and aggravating. In general, people see commercials as a nuisance that gets in the way of viewing a film they have paid to see. Moreover, audiences known to go to the cinema often may need more time to see the exact commercial several times and turn it off when it comes to advertisements in general.

Bollywood Film

Bollywood is the name given to the movie industry in Mumbai (formerly known as Bombay), India, and the production of films takes place in the national language, Hindi. Bollywood's growth in recent times has been prolific. In 2004 alone, Bollywood released 244 films all over India, the highest number compared to movies made in other regional languages in India (Mohanty, 2022; Nanjangud & Reijnders, 2022; Nakayama, 2021). During the last decade, Bollywood has become the most popular brand internationally among Indian films. The consistent production of a mix of big-budget and low-budget movies has made Bollywood a highly commercially successful venture for its investors. In addition, the increasing amount of time, effort and money put into marketing the movies has boosted the brand with many blockbusters every year. In 2005, Bollywood surpassed Hollywood for the most significant number of feature films released, with 1,041 films as against Hollywood's 535 films (Mohanty, 2022; Nanjangud & Reijnders, 2022). It is estimated that in 2005, Bollywood sold 3.6 billion tickets worldwide (Kumar, 2022), compared to 2.6 billion tickets sold by Hollywood (Mohanty, 2022; Nanjangud & Reijnders, 2022), officially becoming the world's largest producer of films.

Why Are Bollywood Films Important to India?

Bollywood films are essential to India because they provide a platform for cultural expression and showcase the country's diversity. They also contribute significantly to the economy and create job opportunities for many people in the entertainment industry. Below is the reason why the Bollywood film is essential to India.

(1) Bollywood cinema links familiar people.

It has been noted that the vast development of filmmaking in Bollywood has profoundly influenced and impacted humans. Connecting ordinary people through cinemas and delivering good messages is very effective, particularly in India, because audiences get involved and follow the style, dialogue and messages. Cinemas are among the best and most effective ways to spread awareness to a large audience. Nowadays, film-makers have been wise enough to capture many Indian audiences by displaying the realistic lifestyle of the typical person. An ordinary guy's story for a familiar person. While such realistic films have a little direct impact on the travel and tourism industry, certain moments catch the attention of tourists, motivating them to visit India later. The skyline of Mumbai as shown in the film *A Wednesday*, where actor Naseeruddin Shah was carrying out his mission and the traditional atmosphere and shindoor khela during the Durga Puja festival in Kolkata in the film *Kahaani*, are some excellent examples of how certain scenes in a realistic film indirectly influence Indian tourism.

(2) Bollywood films display city light.

Many Bollywood movies, including *Fashion, Life in a Metro, Lunch Box, Shor in the City, Chak De India, Khosla Ka Ghosla, Vicky Donor, Raincoat, Kahaani* and *Gunday*, easily depict daily city life. The story of *Delhi Belly* is centred on various Delhi locales, and the nightlife of Mumbai was vividly depicted in the film *Jaane Tu... Ya Jaane Na*. The Bengali film *Life on Park Street* accurately captures day-to-day life in one of Kolkata's most multicultural neighbourhoods, Dharavi, which is based on one of the largest slums in the world, and Dhobi Ghat... are several features of city colours that affect traveller's feelings inadvertently. Countless scenes of upmarket Indian locales are depicted in various Indian movies. However, despite the city clamour, the tram tracks and hand-pulled rickshaws in Kolkata, the quaint alleys of Old Delhi and Mumbai Fish Harbour continue to impact the country's travel and tourism industry thanks to the bright city lights.

(3) Bollywood films introduce unexplored destinations.

Moviemakers seek unique locations to capture in their films that have never been seen or seen by anyone. As a result, individuals experience new areas, and many of those sites become popular tourist destinations. On the other hand, the Tanot Mata Temple in the Thar Desert was initially revealed in J.P. Dutta's *Border*. It is approximately 150 kilometres from Jaisalmer city and close to the Longewala battle site of the Indo-Pakistani War of 1971. It is said that many bombs fell onto this holy land of the temple during the war, but none of them exploded. This is another excellent example of how Indian cinema influences India's Travel and Tourism sector.

Coorg is quickly becoming one of the most popular weekend destinations in Bangalore. Nonetheless, it remained one of India's untouched places until the mid-1990s. The Kannada film industry has been essential in promoting Coorg as an ecotourism destination in India by producing various regional movies. Several Bollywood films, including *Ravaan* and *Saat Khoon Maaf*, were filmed in Coorg. Today, Coorg is noted for its rich spice and coffee plantations and tourist spots like Tala Cauveri, Bagamandala, Madikeri Fort, Nagarhole National Park, Nisargadhama Forest, Bylakuppe and several waterfalls.

The Malayalam film industry was effective in promoting some undiscovered Kerala places. Wayanad, the green paradise, became a favourite location for regional film-makers. Ramu Karyatt's *Nellu* was the first film filmed substantially in Wayanad. It was followed by *Panchami* in 1976, *Indradhanussu* in 1979, *Varikkuzhi* in 1982, *Nandanam* in 2002, *Anyar* in 2003 and *Pazhassi Raja* in 2009. Other prominent Tamil, Telugu, Malayalam and Hindi film filming sites include Kerala's backwaters. The song 'Jiya Jale' from *Dil Se* was filmed at Thekkady's Athirapilly Waterfalls and Periyar Wildlife Sanctuary. *Bhagyadevatha*, *Vinaythangi Varavaya* and *Kuselan* were all filmed in Alleppey's backwaters. *Nishabd* is a Bollywood film filmed amid Munnar's revitalising greenery. In their films, some regional film-makers exploited the terracotta temples of Bishnupur and the rural lifestyle of West Bengal's Purulia and Bankura regions. This area has hosted several Bengali, Bhojpuri and Oriya film shoots. *Lootera*, a Bollywood film filmed in Purulia, is one such example. Satyajit Ray's *Gupi Gayan Bagha Bayan*, *Hirak Rajar Deshe* and *Gupi Bagha Phire Elo* are the most famous movies in Indian Cinema history that have been shot mainly in Purulia and Bankura regions.

(4)   Bollywood films promoting Indian heritage.

There are almost 1000 Indian films that provide a charming image of Indian history.

The Khajuraho Temple complex was represented brilliantly in *Kamasutra – A Story of Love*. The famous song from Dev Anand's blockbuster *Johny Mera Naam* was filmed in the early 1970s among the ruins of Nalanda University and the beautiful green hillocks of Rajgir. The Vijay Vilas Palace in Mandvi, Gujarat, was used as Aishwarya Rai's home in the film *Hum Dil De Chuke Sanam*. The blockbuster film also included numerous additional sequences that drew the interest of tourists, such as the Bada Bagh in Jaisalmer, where Aishwarya Rai and Salman Khan fantasise about their marriage, and the Orchard Palace in Gondal, Gujarat, where Ajay Devgn pulls Aishwarya Rai.

The Golden Triangle towns of Delhi, Agra and Jaipur became the second home of Indian film. Some of the notable Bollywood films that have been filmed at some of Delhi's important historical sites include *Rang De Basanti, Delhi Belly, Delhi 6, Vicky Donor, No One Killed Jessica, Khosla Ka Ghosla, Band Baja Barat, Yeh Saali Zindagi, Love Sex aur Dhoka* and *Rockstar*. The prominent attractions were India Gate, Red Fort, Jama Mosque, Qutub

Minar and Humayun's Tomb. The song 'Bol Na Halke Halke' from *Jhoom Barabar Jhoom* has been wonderfully filmed at Delhi's critical historical monuments and the Taj Mahal. The song 'Dhunki' is filmed against the stunning background of the Agra Fort and Taj Mahal once again. Fatehpur Sikri, an hour's drive from Agra and a UNESCO World Heritage Site, was utilised as the setting for various sequences in Subhash Ghai's *Pardes*, particularly for the song 'Do Dil'. Jaipur has also captured the attention of the film industry. The song 'Bholi Bhali Ladki' from the film *Sabse Bada Khiladi* was filmed at Jaipur's Birla Temple. whilst a large portion of the film *Umrao Jaan* was shot in Jaipur's City Palace. In 2009, the Amber Fort was used to film Salman Khan's *Veer*, while Shiv Vilas was used to film Ashutosh Gowarikar's *What's Your Raashee?*

The Lake Palace in Udaipur, now one of India's top hotels, paved the path for an Indian film. *Yaadein* and *Yeh Jawani Hai Deewani* were filmed here. Udaipur's historic city has also been featured in various Bollywood films, including *Ram Leela, Guide, Gaddaar, Hum Hain Rahi Pyar Ke, Khuda Gawah* and others. In addition, the Gateway of India and Victoria Terminus in Mumbai have become hallmarks of Indian cinema whenever film-makers consider filming in Mumbai. Similarly, the Victoria Memorial Hall in Kolkata is a popular destination for regional and Hindi film-makers.

(5) Bollywood film promoting hill stations in India.

Likewise, an unending number of films were filmed in some of India's most prominent hill locations. Gulmarg and Srinagar in Kashmir, Manali, Dalhousie, Shimla in Himachal Pradesh, Nainital in Uttarakhand, Darjeeling in West Bengal, Ooty in Tamil Nadu and Wayanad and Munnar in Kerala are the prominent destinations:

- Shammi Kapoor's memorable love affair with Kashmir is a true testament to Indian tourism. Songs like 'Yahoo,' in which he slides down the snow-capped mountains, or 'Yeh chaand sa roshan chehra,' in which he tries to woo Sharmila Tagore while riding shikaras on the famous Dal Lake... as well as many other songs from films like *Tumse Achha Kaun Hai, Andaz, Kashmir Ki Kali or Junglee* – were shot in the picturesque Kashmir Valley.

- *Highway*, a recent Bollywood movie, is another example of how Himachal Pradesh tourism has been affected by advertising the distant Sangla and Spiti Valley. Again, the Leh-Manali Highway is brilliantly described in the song 'Yeh Ishq Haaye' from *Jab We Met*. Parts of the film were also shot at Manali and Shimla, two of Himachal Pradesh's most prominent hill stations known for their natural beauty. This film also features the historic architecture of Naggar Castle in the Kullu area. Some prominent Indian films filmed in Himachal Pradesh include *Heena, Roja, Taal, Krrish, Lootera, Desamuduru and Simla Special.*

- Nainital first came to the attention of Indian film in 1971, when Rajesh Khanna and Asha Parekh were seen boating on the Naini Lake for the song 'Jis Gali Mein Tera Ghar'. Naini Lake is a prominent tourist attraction in Nainital, and a boat ride on the lake is one of the most popular things to do in Nainital.

- Darjeeling, another prominent hill station in India, is a frequent shooting location for Indian film-makers. Darjeeling was used extensively in filming popular Bollywood films such as *Aradhana, Mausam, Barfi and Via Darjeeling.*
- Mani Ratnam's Telugu film *Geethanjali* significantly brought Ooty, one of the major hill stations in South India, to audiences' attention as a honeymoon destination. *Summer in Bethlehem*, a Malayalam film, was shot against the background of Ooty's forest, hills and farms, while Salman Khan, Sanjay Dutt and Madhuri Dixit's *Saajan* were shot mainly in the greenscape of Ooty. Some of the most beautiful scenes in the film *Hum* were shot in British Raj–era bungalows and lodges.

(6) Bollywood cinema promotes adventure activities in India.

Recently, film-makers have decided to spice up their films by including adventure activities such as trekking, skiing, mountaineering, camping and motorbiking, as well as beach activities such as parasailing, scuba diving and motorboating. Some Bollywood flicks like *Yeh Jawani Hai Deewani, Lakshya, Jab Tak Hai Jaan, Hindustan ki Kasam, Pyar Tune Kya Kia* and *Rangeela* promoted a number of adventure activities in India. The film *Kaal* is an example of Indian cinema dedicated to wildlife safaris in India. The film was shot extensively in Corbett National Park, one of India's major national parks and home to several endangered species.

(7) A Bollywood film detailing the diverse Indian culture.

Four films dilate on the dark side of Indian culture. These films are not for the faint-hearted and explore themes such as corruption, violence and social inequality in a raw and unflinching manner. They offer a unique perspective on the complexities of Indian society and its underbelly:

- *Rudali* muses on the life of a female weeper who openly expresses pain on behalf of family members who are not allowed to show emotion owing to their social rank. Then there is Sushil Rajpal's *Antardwand*, based on Pakaruah shaadi or Jabaria shaadi, a phenomenon common in western Bihar and eastern Uttar Pradesh where the bride's family abducts eligible bachelors and later forced married in order to avoid high dowry costs. The Marathi film *Jogawa* depicts caste, religion and identity.
- Finally, Aparna Sen's Bengali film *Sati* depicts the social funeral practice of some Indian communities. Glimpses of the film *Sati* may also be seen in *Mangal Pandey: The Rising*. (Please remember that Sati is no longer practised in India.) *Papilio Buddha*, directed by Jayan K. Cherian, exposes the true face of Indian casteism. The film focuses on atrocities against Dalits, women and the environment.
- *Dilwale Dulhaniya Le Jayenge, Monsoon Wedding, Vivah and Band Baaja Baraat* instil in viewers the phrase 'big fat Indian wedding'. Another draw for overseas visitors is the traditional Indian wedding style. Movies depicting key Indian holidays such as Durga Puja, Holi, Ganesh

Chaturthi, Eid and Diwali, on the other hand, are significant contributions to Indian tourism. For example, the Durga Puja Festival inspired Satyajit Ray's *Joi Baba Felunath* and Nayak and Rituporno Ghosh's *Hirer Angti, Utsav* and *Antarmahal*.

- Some Bollywood films, such as *Sholay, Holi, Darr, Baghban and Silsila*, highlight the Holi festival, one of India's major festivals. Songs such as 'Raang Barse,' 'Holi Ke Din' and 'Ang se' are excellent examples of how Indian cinema influences Indian tourism. Songs include 'Sadda Dil Vi Tu' from *Any Body Can Dance*, 'Deva Shree Ganesha' from *Agnepath*, 'Morya Re' from *Don: The Chase Begins* and 'Sindoor Lal Chadayo' from *Vaastav* also emphasise the Ganesh Chaturthi festival in India.

Five Distinctive Features of Bollywood Films

(1) Bollywood films are lengthy!

If you opt to see a Bollywood film, be prepared to be taken to another dimension for at least three hours. Practically all Bollywood films need pauses approximately halfway through to keep people involved with the plot. You could be thinking, '3 hours? Why?' The explanation is straight-forward: emotional interest in the tale. Indian film-makers feel that a lengthier film would engage people in the plot and allow them to better empathise with the characters. Not only that, but Indians are used to pro-longed entertainment. Our weddings may run up to seven days, and our festivals can continue anywhere from seven to 15 days. With so much entertainment available, it is reasonable to expect movies to retain our attention for the whole day.

(2) Bollywood films are explosively colourful.

Bollywood films are noted for their outrageous costumes, makeup and bright hues, particularly in women. Ladies in Bollywood films are dressed flawlessly in traditional saris, heavy jewellery and enormous quantities of makeup. Indians like colour and brightness in everything, and we are not afraid to show it. Subtlety is non-existent in Bollywood, which we are OK with.

(3) Bollywood films feature repeating plots.

Many Bollywood films have one thing in common: their narrative line. One of our tried-and-true stories has the protagonist (typically a guy) falling in love with a lady from a wealthy aristocratic family. The protagonist and his lady love struggle against all obstacles to marry, and after much dancing, fighting and sobbing, they are ultimately united. Isn't it wonderful? This sort of narrative line has been utilised several times, and it is charming to witness it in various shapes and settings since it demonstrates that love conquers everything. We are passionate folks who like having the drama dialled up.

(4) Bollywood films have a lot of music and dance.

Bollywood films would be complete with music and dancing. Consider pancakes without maple syrup, an ice cream sundae devoid of whipped cream and a maraschino cherry. Indian film-makers utilise music and dance to spice up their films and to help spectators remember them. Specific compositions are so memorable that they have rekindled interest in the 1970s and 1980s films. Search 'Dola Re' or 'Pinga' to discover how passionate some of the dancing performances are.

(5)   Bollywood films always have a joyful ending.
'And they all lived happily ever after' is what Bollywood films demonstrate to the fullest. Virtually, every Bollywood film concludes with the protagonist and his lady love marrying, two fighting families reconciling or the antagonist getting punished for his wrongdoings. The closure is a signature aspect of many Bollywood films because we prefer our tales to have a definitive ending.

Case Study

How Bollywood Films Act as Promotional Tools to Tourism Destinations Around the World

Bollywood has played a significant role in promoting tourism in India. The films showcase the country's diverse culture and scenic beauty, attracting domestic and international tourists to visit these destinations. The popularity of Bollywood has also led to the development of film tourism, where fans can visit shooting locations and experience the glamour of the film industry. In this section, we will discuss some tourist destinations worldwide that have received massive exposure because of Bollywood films.

Bollywood Films in the United Kingdom

Suppose there is romance on screen, which generally occurs via a song and dance sequence in a gorgeous setting. In this case, Bollywood film-makers frequently seek locations akin to the Swiss Alps, the rolling hills of the Lake District in the United Kingdom or the tulip fields of Holland. Yash Chopra, a well-known Bollywood filmmaker, originated this practice. 'Chopra recognised the sense of excitement, escapism, adventure and aspiration that an exotic location could bring to a film, particularly one with romance at its heart, and so exotic backdrops quickly became his trademark', *The Guardian* published in 2012 via its online portal www.theguadian.com. Nevertheless, the fear of terrorism made it impossible to reach these locations for filming in the late 1980s, so Yash Chopra pioneered the idea of shooting abroad as a solution. Yash Chopra was crucial in presenting Britain as an exciting and elegant holiday destination (Sundar, 2023). In 1991, he directed the legendary film *Lamhe*, which was filmed in London's Lake District. A decade later, Chopra returned to Britain to capture steamers that run between Pooley Bridge and Glen Ridding rejoicing in the national park's spinning lakes, steep fells and small winding roads for the film *Mujhse Dosti Karogi*, which he produced. In 1995, Yash Chopra produced the film *Dilwale Dulhaniya Le Jayenge*, directed by his son (reiterating the role of trust in the

Bollywood industry). He featured not only some of London's well-known tourist spots but also British Indians (non-resident Indians). He went on to become the longest running blockbuster in Indian cinema history.

Even Chopra's last film, *Jab Tak Hai Jaan*, had a song sequence filmed in and around London's top tourist spots, displaying the city's richness and magnificence. Another well-known Bollywood film-maker, Karan Johar, filmed his first two films primarily in the United Kingdom. The title track for his 1998 film *Kuch Kuch Hota Hai* was shot in Scotland in Ross Priory, Glencoe and Lake Lomond. Another song from his second album, *Kabhi Kushi Kabhie Gham*, released in 2001, solely depicts sites such as Cambridge, King's College, Cardiff's Millennium Stadium, Blenheim Palace and the British Museum's Great Court. The United Kingdom's national tourism agency, VisitBritain, which is in charge of marketing Britain's locations overseas, launched a global campaign called 'Britain You are Invited' with Karan Johar as a goodwill ambassador and even published a Bollywood Movie Map highlighting many of the Bollywood productions on its website (http://www.visitbritain.com/en/Bollywood-Britain) to entice Indian fans to visit the locations featured in their favourite movies.

Bollywood in Switzerland

The tourist sector in Switzerland is eager to attract Bollywood productions because it has discovered that a worldwide blockbuster favourably portraying its country is more successful than any other advertising campaign for national branding. Federico Sommaruga, the director of emerging markets and special projects at Swiss Tourism, stated on their official website, swissinfo.ch, that Bollywood has the greatest impact on tourism and that there is a significant correlation between the number of tourists visiting Switzerland and Bollywood movies shot there (2012) (Swissinfo.ch).

Another significant statistic, according to Switzerland tourism, is that the number of annual overnight stays of Indian tourists increased from 71,000 to 393,000 between 1993 and 2010 and that an average Indian spends SFr300 or $325 per day in comparison to the average tourist spend of SFr174, boosting the local economy. Over 200 Bollywood films have been filmed in Switzerland for the last 20 years. Bern's gorgeous mountain meadows and centre are popular locations for shooting love sequences and dance routines. Switzerland has begun to give free public places for film production. Private railway companies are also film-friendly, allowing Bollywood to film inside trains (2012) (Swissinfo.ch).

Chopra has filmed so extensively in Switzerland that he was awarded the Swiss Ambassador's Prize in 2010 for promoting 'Brand Switzerland' via his films. In 2011, he was also honoured with the title of Ambassador of Interlaken. His association with Switzerland lasted until his last film, *Jab Tak Hai Jaan*, for which he shot the closing song. As a welcome gesture, the Swiss tourist authority lavishly supported Yash Chopra in making his films – in 2013 (*The Tribune*). Following the success of Switzerland's tourism industry due to Bollywood filmmaking, Zurich-based film location in Switzerland seeks to provide services in collaboration with local authorities, thereby simplifying administrative proced-ures, location scouts and gaining access to technicians, actors and coproduction partners. Foreign production businesses may acquire customised packages for each film project and have their disbursed VAT returned. According to Miller (2006), the Swiss government has been granting free scouting visits to Bollywood moviemakers since 2006, which include round trip flights between Switzerland and India, hotel accommodations for a week and chauffeured transportation for site hunting (Ganti, 2013).

Bollywood in Israel

Bollywood films are gaining popularity in Israel, mainly since certain Indian blockbusters were filmed there. Mr Alon Ushpiz, Israel's ambassador, said that the Israeli government wants Indian film-makers, notably Bollywood film-makers, to shoot in Israel's breathtaking and magnificent locations more significantly. He has also pushed a specific site that has been one of the most popular options for Telugu film-makers from Hyderabad, South India: the Dead Sea, the lowest point on Earth's surface and the world's deepest hyper-saline lake. Mr Ushpiz has also said that Indian films made in Israel help to promote his country as a tourist destination. Mr Ushpiz is quoted as stating on the website of the Israeli Embassy in India (Miller 2006): 'Indians in Tel Aviv are doing excellent work to encourage Indian tourism to Israel. We would be delighted if more Bollywood and Telugu directors made films in Israel'. A growing number of Israelis, especially the nearly 50,000 Indian Jews who have moved to Israel and expatriates, are becoming fans of Bollywood films and music. In truth, the film *Yeh Jawaani Hai Deewani* (with Hebrew subtitles) starring Ranbir Kapoor and Deepika Padukone has had a theatrical distribution in Israel. Earlier, the film *Devdas*, directed by Sanjay Leela Bhansali, was released in 2002. Moreover, Israeli teenagers have access to popular Indian TV series such as *Indian Idol* and *Nach Baliye*, which has piqued their interest and raised their understanding of Indian cinema, music and dance.

Bollywood in Spain

The film *Zindagi Na Milegi Dobara* in 2011 was a famous example of a recent tourist boom attributable to Bollywood. The film is about three friends on vacation in Spain, labelled a three-hour infomercial for Spanish tourism. This film is believed to have boosted visitor arrivals to Spain by more than 32%, particu-larly during the first half of 2011 and in specific sites where the film was filmed. Its success in Spain has prompted nations such as Oman, Egypt, Korea, Fiji and Cyprus to investigate the possibilities. In reality, the Fiji Islands has promised that film-makers who shoot in their nation would get a 50% subsidy. Bollywood has also gained popularity in the United States, Australia, Sweden, the Czech Republic and Hungary, to mention a few. As detailed in the preceding situations, similar occurrences have been seen in various nations.

> **Research Box**
>
> Film tourism, as have been discussed as film-induced tourism, is a specialised or niche form of tourism in which visitors investigate locations and destinations that have gained popularity because of their appearance in films. Film productions can be an effective means of promoting a country's tourism offerings, both domestically and internationally; they can help to highlight a country's natural and cultural assets; inform, inspire and influence travel decisions; and promote and expand local visitor economies. Numerous locations around the globe rely on films tourism as their primary source of income. Unfortunately, improperly managed tourism can also be a source of problems. Based of previous research conducted from 2019 to 2023;
>
> (1) Please conduct a systematic review to describe the benefits and drawbacks of tourism in the contemporary world.
> (2) Based on your finding, do you believe that the advantages of tourism outweigh its disadvantages?

Conclusion

In 1971, the Indian film legend Satyajit Ray said the following about Hindi films:

> The ingredients of the average Hindi film are well known; colour (Eastman preferred); songs (six or seven?); in voices, one knows and trusts; dance – solo and ensemble – the more frenzied, the better; lousy girl, good girl, bad guy, good guy, romance (but no kisses); tears, guffaws, fights, chases, melodrama; characters who exist in a social vacuum; dwellings which do not exist outside the studio floor; locations in Kullu, Manali, Ooty, Kashmir, London, Paris, Hong Kong, Tokyo....who needs to be told?
> (Ray, in Willemen 1982, p. 25)

Ray's description of popular Indian movies, especially Bollywood, has been used to describe them for decades. Though simple, the description has been more or less accurate, but it is essential to remember why the movies have gotten this reputation. The Bollywood film is a famous movie style worldwide that always tries to compete with Hollywood. Even though the American film industry is better known and makes more money, Indian cinema has been growing steadily and has recently changed in a way that is getting more attention. Bollywood is a cultural business that shows how society and politics are changing. It had always tried to show what was happening, whether during the angry 1970s or the 1980s when unemployment and social disorder were common in India.

Today, the Bollywood film shows how India has become more globalised in every aspect of its life. Film scholars will always be interested in the film industry and connected to other countries in such a changing state. In addition, this chapter also highlights how Bollywood film helps introduce not only India but other worldwide locations, which contribute to the mass promotional activity. Film tourism is a substantial business in how films have influenced tourist numbers. However, film tourism requires the cooperation of several stakeholders, including film commissions, screen agencies, tourist agencies, local enterprises and the government. Films give access to larger audiences and the opportunity to target particular populations. They may be used as a free marketing tool and are less aggressive than typical tourist marketing efforts. Storylines arouse emotions, which may make even unorthodox settings, such as wet or chilly locales, rural areas or regions with no other attractions outside the film's landscapes and plot, intriguing to visit. Developing touristic marketing in collaboration with a film production may aid in differentiating a location from 'Any Country' by making it more appealing to visit and attracting film tourism pilgrims. After the seed of film tourism has been sown via cooperative efforts with film studios, new attractions may be developed, and existing ones can be enhanced.

Discussion Questions

- What are the advantages of using films as one of the marketing tools in tourism industries?
- Based on your opinion, how relevant is the use of films as one of the marketing tools to promoted destination image?
- Discuss the disadvantages of films as promotional tools in tourism industries.

References

Bolan, P., & Williams, L. (2008). The role of image in service promotion: Focusing on the influence of film on consumer choice within tourism. *International Journal of Consumer Studies*, *32*(4), 382–390.

Castro, D., Kim, S., & Assaker, G. (2023). An empirical examination of the antecedents of Residents' support for future film tourism development. *Tourism Management Perspectives*, *45*, 101067.

Florido-Benítez, L. (2023). Film-induced tourism is the impact of animation, cartoons, superheroes, and fantasy movies. *Tourism Review*.

Ganti, T. (2013). Corporatization and the Hindi film industry. In K. Moti Gokulsing & W. Dissanayake (Eds.). *Routledge handbook of Indian cinemas* (pp. 337–350). Routledge.

Kim, S., & Park, E. (2023). An integrated model of social impacts and resident's perceptions: From a film tourism destination. *Journal of Hospitality & Tourism Research*, *47*(2), 395–421.

Kumar, S. (2022). Movie-induced tourism for Bollywood: Event study-based analysis. *Event Management*, *26*(6), 1367–1379.

Liu, Z., Huang, X., & Xu, A. (2023). Green innovation for the ecological footprints of tourism in China. Fresh evidence from the ARDL approach. *Economic Research-Ekonomska Istraživanja, 36*(2), 2172600.

Miller, H. A. (2006). *Tonto and Tonto speak: An indigenous based film theory.* Doctoral dissertation, Montana State University-Bozeman, College of Letters & Science.

Mohanty, P. (2022). Bollywood tourism. In *Encyclopedia of tourism management and marketing* (pp. 332–334). Edward Elgar Publishing.

Nakayama, C. (2021). Film-induced tourism studies on Asia: A systematic literature review. *Tourism Review International, 25*(1), 63–78.

Nanjangud, A., & Reijnders, S. (2022). Cinematic itineraries and identities: Studying Bollywood tourism among the Hindustanis in the Netherlands. *European Journal of Cultural Studies, 25*(2), 659–678.

Salnick, K. (2023). *Creating student-centered schools: Discovering best practices in experiential, progressive public-school design and exploring the effectiveness of media and community events in creating grassroots change.* Doctoral dissertation, Northeastern University.

Sun, H., Zhang, Y., & Chen, D. (2023). Research on the development of island tourism market for college students-a case study of Dongji Island. In *SHS Web of Conferences* (Vol. 154, p. 01002). EDP Sciences.

Sundar, P. (2023). *Listening with a feminist ear: Soundwork in Bombay cinema.* University of Michigan Press.

Tulsi, G. K. (2023). Demystifying the 'Legendary': Re-visiting Amrita Pritam through Her Interface with Popular Indian Media (1947–2005). In *Amrita Pritam* (pp. 219–231). Routledge India.

Vila, N. A., Brea, J. A. F., & de Carlos, P. (2021). Film tourism in Spain: Destination awareness and visit motivation as determinants to visit places seen in TV series. *European Research on Management and Business Economics, 27*(1), 100135.

Wullur, F., Worang, F. G., & Tumewu, F. J. (2023). The influence of Korean popular culture towards the intention to visit South Korea (Survey on Student's in Sam Ratulangi University Manado). *Jurnal EMBA: Jurnal Riset Ekonomi, Manajemen, Bisnis dan Akuntansi, 11*(1), 65–76.

Yubin, H., Defeng, M., Zicong, Q., Manhong, T., Lyu, W., & Yang, W. (2023). Compare and contrast the impact of COVID-19 on small to large country. In *Tourism analytics before and after COVID-19: Case Studies from Asia and Europe* (pp. 65–86). Springer Nature Singapore.

Zeng, Y., Xu, Z., Chen, L., & Huang, Y. (2023). The influence of lens language and linguistic landscape on movie-induced tourism with empathy. *Frontiers in Psychology, 14*, 230.

Part 7

Impact of COVID-19 on Tourism Trends

Chapter 14

Exploring the Journey of Tourism Through the Dark Age of COVID-19 and the Changed Travel Intentions of Tourists During the Post-Pandemic Period

Radhika P.C.[a] *and Johney Johnson*[b]

[a]Sacred Heart College, Kerala, India
[b]Mahatma Gandhi University, Kerala, India

Learning Objectives

After reading and studying this chapter, you should be able to:

- understand how the COVID-19 pandemic has impacted the global tourism industry and the Indian tourism industry in particular;
- understand the revival strategies adopted by the industry to overcome the pandemic with particular reference to Kerala tourism;
- identify the changes in the travel intentions of tourists after the pandemic, their travel preferences and their attitude towards travel.

Abstract

Tourism is considered one of the globe's most prominent sectors, generating considerable forex revenues and employment generation, contributing to world peace and solidarity among many nations. However, it is negatively influenced by different factors like the spread of diseases, terrorist attacks, outbreaks of war, etc. The COVID-19 pandemic triggered unforeseen upheavals, resulting in demand and supply uncertainties in nearly every area of the economy (El-Erian, 2020). Thus, it is relevant to study the impact of the pandemic on the tourism industry. This chapter explains the journey of tourism during the COVID-19 pandemic by portraying the status of global tourism, how it impacted the Indian economy and its revival strategies, with

---

Future Tourism Trends Volume 1, 207–223
Copyright © 2024 Radhika P.C. and Johney Johnson
Published under exclusive licence by Emerald Publishing Limited
doi:10.1108/978-1-83753-244-520241014

special mention to Kerala tourism. The pandemic also resulted in a considerable change in the travel intentions of tourists, their travel preferences and their attitude towards travel. Hence, this chapter also presents the changed travel intentions of tourists that will help the industry players modify their products per the tourist's expectations. Finally, this chapter presents how the tourism industry recovered from the pandemic from both the supplier and demand perspectives, which will be helpful for all tourism stakeholders.

Keywords: Post-COVID travel intentions; travel bubble; virtual tourism; bio-bubble model; Kerevan Kerala; service innovation in travel

Introduction

Tourism is one of the most critical sectors in the world economy, contributing significantly to foreign exchange earnings and employment generation. Tourism involves the movement of people to different parts of the world and interactions with people, and it always acts as a vehicle for relaxation. The social importance of tourism contributes to preserving world harmony and cooperation (McCabe & Qiao, 2020). The tourism industry has evolved through the years to reach its current position, contributing 10.3% of the world's gross domestic product (GDP) and 6.8% of total exports (WTTC, 2020). However, various factors – including the spread of diseases, terrorist attacks, war outbreaks, etc. have harmed it. The COVID-19 pandemic triggers unforeseen upheavals, resulting in demand and supply uncertainties in nearly every area of the economy (El-Erian, 2020). The travel and tourism industry is among the most severely devastated sectors of the economy due to the pandemic (Shretta, 2020), which resulted in a rising level of unemployment (Malra, 2021). With widespread travel restrictions, border closures and concerns about the spread of the virus, the demand for travel and tourism has plummeted. Many businesses in the industry, such as airlines, hotels and restaurants, have suffered significant financial losses, and many have been forced to lay off workers or shut down entirely. The impact of the pandemic on the travel and tourism industry has been felt worldwide. However, it has been especially devastating in countries that rely heavily on tourism for their economies. These countries have seen a significant decline in tourist arrivals, which has a ripple effect on many other industries that depend on tourism, such as transportation, accommodation, retail and entertainment. Also, the pandemic crises have had detrimental consequences on the economy and tourist business for a long time.

The estimated adverse consequences substantially exceed those of previous pandemic crises (Škare et al., 2021). COVID-19 negatively impacted several tourist stakeholders on a social, psychological, economic and cultural level, and it will take longer to be back to normal (Abbas et al., 2021). On the other hand, the epidemic has given academics and researchers in tourism an 'abundant' new context in which to conduct investigations using applicable research methodologies. This chapter will discuss the impact of COVID-19 on the global tourism industry, how the pandemic affected Indian tourism, the revival strategies adopted by the industry with particular reference to Kerala tourism and the changed travel intentions of tourists. The last section presents the conclusion and discussion questions. To find out the effect of COVID-19 on tourism, a systematic study was done with the help of journal articles, newspaper articles and publications from the United Nations World Tourism Organization (UNWTO), World Travel and Tourism Council (WTTC), International Civil Aviation Organization (ICAO), the Indian Ministry of Tourism and the Kerala State Government. To examine the travel intentions of tourists, a survey was conducted among 450 tourists conveniently selected from tourism destinations in Kerala.

The Impact of COVID-19 on Tourism: A Global Perspective

Travel and tourism are one of the major economic activities that account for 10.4% of global GDP and include one in every 10 jobs worldwide, as per the report of WTTC (2019). As it is a multifaceted industry that is affected by seasonality and sensitive to external variables, measuring the influence of a single element on the industry is challenging. Demand for tourism is impacted by several factors, like global socio-economic conditions, terrorism, global war situations, environmental factors, oil costs and the spread of epidemics (Hadi et al., 2020, 2022; Hailemariam & Ivanovski, 2021; Škare et al., 2021). The tourism industry has been affected globally by the outbreak of several diseases in the last 53 years, namely Ebola (1976), Hendra (1994), H5N1 bird flu (1997), Nipah (1998), SARS (2002), H1N1 (2009), MERS (2012), H7N9 bird flu (2013) and COVID-19 (2019) (Škare et al., 2021). The effects of these illnesses vary greatly, but among the most devastating were those brought on by viral epidemic diseases like SARS (2002), H1N1 (2009) and the most current coronavirus pandemic. The year 2019 witnessed overall positive growth in tourism (WTTC, 2019). However, the overall foreign tourist arrivals in 2019 showed a 2% decline compared to 2018, primarily because of the uncertainty surrounding Brexit, the economic slowdown, the collapse of the world's largest travel agency, 'The Thomas Cook' and the collapse of several low-cost airlines in Europe (UNWTO, 2020). After consistently growing in the first two quarters of 2019, the industry was severely affected by the spread of COVID-19, which began in December 2019. The travel and tourism industry, including travel agencies, tour operators, hotels, restaurants and family entertainment centres, has been severely impacted (Verma & Gustafsson, 2020). The WTTC, in March 2020, stated that the pandemic would put 50 million jobs in the global travel and tourism sector at risk. Among the different regions, Asia will be the most affected continent (WEF, 2020). This prediction was proved right, with a total 70% decline in international tourism in 2020 (UNWTO, 2020a). There was an 82% decrease in tourist arrivals in Asia and the Pacific, a 73% decline in the Middle East, a 69% decline in Africa and a 68% decline in Europe and America from January to October 2020 (UNWTO, 2020b). Foreign tourist arrivals decreased by 83% (January–March 2021) compared to the same period in the previous year due to continued stringent travel regulations and poor consumer confidence (UNWTO, 2020c). Lockdown and border restrictions brought about by COVID-19 have directly impacted employment and increased the risk of food insecurity for thousands of people (Ibn-Mohammed et al., 2021). In 2020, the GDP contribution of the tourism industry declined by 50.4%, which recovered to 21.7% in 2021. Still, the pace of recovery was slowed down by the spread of the Omicron variant in the second half of 2021, which forced governments to reinstate restrictions on international travel (WTTC, 2022). In 2019, the travel and tourism industry was at the top, creating 1 in 10 jobs globally and 333 million jobs worldwide. However, there was a decline of 18.6%, with 62 million job losses in 2020, despite the conducive government measures and support. This was recovered in 2021, showing an increase of 6.7% by creating 289.5 million jobs compared to 271.3 million jobs in 2020. Thus, the industry created 1 in 11 jobs across the economies in 2021 (WTTC, 2022). The WTTC (WTTC, 2020) also presents a long-term forecast (2022–2032) that, as there is improvement in the confidence level of travellers, the industry's contribution to the global economy is expected to grow at an average annual rate of 5.8%, and is expected to create 126 million additional jobs in the future by 2032.

Impact of COVID-19 on the Aviation and Accommodation Industry

The drop in demand for air travel worldwide due to bans and restrictions has made aviation the direst situation ever. The outbreaks have resurfaced in several places, and harsher travel restrictions have made it difficult to recuperate (CCSA, 2021). In addition, the restrictions, which included border closures, quarantine requirements and mandatory testing, have made it difficult for airlines to operate. As a result, many have been forced to cancel routes or suspend operations altogether. Table 14.1 presents the impact of COVID-19 on scheduled passenger traffic and shows that, compared with 2019, the airlines reduced 50% of seats in 2020, 40% in 2021 and 26% in 2022.

Regarding the reduction of passengers, the airlines improved from a negative 60% in 2020 to a negative 29% in 2022. The gross passenger operating revenue also improved, from approximately USD 372 billion in losses in 2020 to approximately USD 175 billion in losses in 2022. The COVID-19 pandemic has profoundly impacted the aviation industry, and it may take years to recover fully.

The hotel sector has been significantly impacted by the COVID-19 outbreak, with a drastic drop in occupancy rates as travellers cancel their visits and stay home due to the restrictions and lockdowns implemented globally. During the pandemic's peak, nearly nine in 10 hotels had to lay off or furlough workers, and the industry lost 7.5 million jobs (AHLA, 2020). When this epidemic became widespread, several hotels immediately implemented defence or survival strategies

Table 14.1. The COVID-19 Impact on World Scheduled Passenger Traffic.

	Comparison to the Year 2019 Levels				
	2020 (Actual Results)	**2021 (Preliminary Estimates)**	**2022 (Estimated Results)**	**International Passenger Traffic**	**Domestic Passenger Traffic**
Overall reduction of seats	50% of seats	40% of seats	25%–26% of seats	33%–34% of seats	19%–20% of seats
Overall reduction in passengers	2,703 million passengers (−60%)	2,201 million passengers (−49%)	1,278 to 1,281 million passengers (−28% to −29%)	658 to 660 million passengers (−35% to −36%)	620 to 621 million passengers (−23% to −24%)
Gross passenger operating revenues	Approx. USD 372 billion loss	Approx. USD 324 billion loss	Approx. USD 174 to 175 billion loss	Approx. USD 123 to 124 billion loss	Approx. USD 51 to 51 billion loss

Source: Bureau, A. T. (2023). Effects of novel coronavirus (COVID-19) on civil aviation: Economic impact analysis. International Civil Aviation Organization (ICAO), Montréal, Canada, pp. 6&9.

with cost-cutting techniques (Le & Phi, 2021). With service automation and income diversification, the pandemic has accelerated 'business innovation' in the hotel industry. The adoption of innovative automated service operations, like contactless check-in/check-out, digital menus, online service ordering, mobile concierge applications and bright room control, has increased recently (Jiang & Wen, 2020). The adoption of digitalisation technology helped reduce physical interactions and provide personalised services. Compared with small and medium-sized hotels, large hotel chains are better equipped to cope with these crises efficiently (Le & Phi, 2021). The COVID-19 pandemic has significantly affected the tourism industry, with many tourism-related businesses struggling to survive. However, with the rollout of vaccines, and the easing of travel restrictions in many countries, there is hope for a gradual recovery of the tourism industry.

Impact of COVID-19 on Indian Tourism

India, a country rich in natural and cultural resources, was placed 23rd and contributed 1.23% of the international tourist arrivals in 2019 (Indian Tourism Statistics, 2020). In the Asia Pacific region, India was ranked sixth regarding tourist arrivals and tourism receipts. Also, in 2019, India registered positive growth of 3.5% in foreign tourist arrival (FTA), 25.3% in domestic tourist visits and 5.1% in foreign exchange earnings (FEE). Realising the significance of tourism, the Ministry of Tourism is focusing on strengthening and facilitating tourism by improving the country's tourism infrastructure, easing the visa requirements, ensuring quality standards, projecting the nation as a 365-day travel destination, promoting sustainable tourism, etc. (MOT Ministry of Tourism Annual Report, 2023). The first instance of the COVID-19 pandemic was reported on 30 January 2020, by three medical students who returned from Wuhan, the pandemic's epicentre (Narasimhan, 2020), subsequently, to contain the spread of the pandemic, a total lockdown was imposed in India for 45 days from 25 March 2020, onward. These restrictions continued to limit the spread of the pandemic in the country, resulting in a drastic decline (−74.9%) of FTA in 2020. As per the study conducted by the National Council of Applied Economic Research, the spread of COVID-19 has had a significant impact on the tourism sector (Jaipuria et al., 2020) which resulted in 14.5 million job losses in the first quarter, followed by 5.2 million jobs in the second quarter, and another 1.8 million jobs in the third quarter of 2021 (Mathur Swati, 2021, July 20). The first and second waves of COVID have devastated the different sectors of the tourism industry, resulting in job losses, complete closures, diversification of businesses and altering the functioning of stakeholders in tourism (Pandey et al., 2021). The Ministry of Home Affairs had limited India's e-Tourist Visa Programme to stop the spread of the pandemic; however, when nations worldwide recovered from the pandemic, these limitations were loosened. To restart inbound tourism, the government announced 500,000 free visas for international tourists (until 31 March 2022), and as of December 2022, e-Tourist Visas are available to citizens of 165 different countries. As a result of the survival measures adopted, the FTAs during 2022 were 6.19 million (provisional), with a growth of 305.4%, and the FEE recorded 106.77% growth over 2021.

The New Beginning – Steps Taken

The tourism industry had previous experiences dealing with uncertain situations and crises. It also has a high capacity for rediscovery and regeneration (Sujood et al., 2022). The industry stakeholders and the government adopted several survival measures for recovery post-pandemic, illustrated below.

Virtual Tourism

Virtual tourism has much promise to help the tourist sector recover during and after the epidemic. During COVID-19, there was only 'virtual' access to tourism due to travel restrictions; virtual tourism is anticipated to have significant potential to help the tourism sector recover. Virtual tourism significantly impacts how people choose travel destinations for in-person visits, increases people's desire to travel and the application of virtual reality (VR) can be used as an effective marketing tool (Lu et al., 2021; Marasco et al., 2018). The UNWTO, in association with Google Arts & Culture, provided virtual travel experiences to hundreds of museums and cultural locations to assist anybody in selecting their ideal virtual vacation. Google Arts & Culture, in collaboration with CyArk, has introduced Google Search for 37 cultural heritage sites from around the globe in augmented reality (AR). Utilising 360° view apps or online video, the tourist can experience a 360° view of the major tourist destinations and museums (Lu et al., 2021), move virtually and change view perspectives. Thus, virtual and augmented reality tools were widely used to provide actual travel experiences to people at the beginning of the pandemic, encouraging them to 'stay home today so that they can travel tomorrow'.

Travel and Transport Bubble

This was introduced in 2020 to restart tourism, also called travel bridges/corona corridors. Within that, countries agreed to open their borders to each other to smoothen travel between them, but the borders will be closed to all other countries (TIO, 2020). Examples include the travel bubble between Australia and New Zealand and 'The Baltic travel bubble', which is the agreement between Estonia, Latvia and Lithuania. Transport bubbles, or air travel arrangements, are temporary air travel arrangements between two countries. These arrangements are made to restart commercial passenger services during the pandemic when regular international flights are suspended. For example, India's Ministry of Civil Aviation has made such agreements with 37 countries. However, the air bubble arrangements ended with the resumption of commercial passenger flights on 27 March 2022.

Vaccination Certificate – The New Travel Ticket and Destination Tracker Application

After nine months of the pandemic, the first vaccine to prevent this viral disease was approved by the UK government, and it was Pfizer and BioNTech's COVID-19 vaccine BNT162b2 (Nawrat Allie, 2 December 2020). The vaccination certificate soon became necessary for domestic and international travel. The vaccination certificate is a document issued after taking the vaccine, with a QR code, date of vaccination, batch number and vaccine name that serves as the new ticket to travel. Along with the vaccination certificate, the traveller must adhere to each country's or region's travel rules and find it difficult to obtain information about these regulations. UNWTO has simplified this by partnering with the International Air Transport Association (IATA) to build a destination tracker application in October 2020. The UNWTO-IATA Destination Tracker is an online tool freely available through UNWTO and IATA websites. It provides information on travel requirements, quarantine requirements, COVID protocol requirements at the destination, updates on COVID-19 in terms of infection and positivity rates, vaccination status, etc.

Adoption of Technological Innovation

The pandemic has made people more health and hygiene conscious, resulting in innovations in services like self check-ins and check-outs by using electronic devices, automatic security checking mechanisms, usage of robots in restaurants, etc. The hotels are now using 'no touch' technologies like gesture controls, bio-metrics, automation, etc., to provide contactless and personalised services by maintaining social distancing and helping to reduce physical interactions (Le & Phi, 2021). Also, the pandemic boosted digital transaction usage by ensuring contactless services.

Indian Tourism Initiatives

In response to the pandemic, the Ministry of Tourism established a COVID-19 cell to assist foreign tourists per the advisories and directives issued by the Ministries of Health and Family Welfare. The Ministry of Tourism created the website 'Stranded in India' (Fig. 14.1) to assist and support international visitors stuck in India due to airline cancellations or a lockdown. Tourists got information on the State/Union Territories' (UTs') Tourism Departments and Regional Offices of the Ministry of Tourism.

As per the directions of the Ministry of Finance on 28 June 2021, Loan Guarantee Scheme for COVID Affected Tourism Sector (LGSCATSS) was established through 18 Scheduled Commercial Banks (SCBs) by the Ministry of Tourism to aid the struggling tourism industry (valid up to 31-03-2023). A loan of up to Rs. 10 lacks will be made available to each tour operator, travel agent and tourist transport operator recognised by the Ministry of Tourism. A loan of up to Rs. 1 lakh will also be made available to each regional tourist guide and Incredible India tourist guide recognised by the Ministry of Tourism/State government or UT Administration. The Ministry of Tourism developed operational guidelines for various tourism service providers of the industry to facilitate a seamless and safe return of operations to prepare for a post-COVID-19 recovery. They were established by the periodic general guidelines issued by the Ministry of Health and with state governments and tourism and hospitality partners. To restart inbound tourism, the government announced 500,000 free visas for international tourists (until 31 March 2022), and as of December 2022, e-Tourist Visas are available to citizens of 165 different countries.

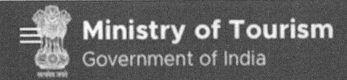

AA   Not Secure — strandedinindia.com   ↻

Ministry of Tourism
Government of India

COVID-19 Helpline Number : +91-11-
23978046 or 1075

#STRANDEDININDIA
For foreign travellers
stranded anywhere in India

The world is facing an unprecedented
situation today. The Ministry of Tourism is with
you in these difficult times. We are truly
committed towards the safety of one and all. If
you are a foreign traveller stranded anywhere
in India due to the COVID-19 pandemic, we
can help you get in touch with the concerned

Fig. 14.1.   Stranded in India. *Source:* https://pib.gov.in/
PressReleasePage.aspx?PRID=1685762.

Case Study

Kerala Tourism Initiatives

Kerala, a state located in the south-western region of India, is known for its scenic beauty, backwaters, beaches, hill stations and wildlife sanctuaries, attracting millions of tourists annually. The year 2019 was a strong year for tourism in Kerala, with an 8.52% growth in FTA and a 17.81% growth in domestic tourist arrivals compared to 2018. However, the spread of the pandemic resulted in a massive setback for the tourism industry of Kerala. Subsequently, the state government responded to the pandemic with a few novel initiatives. It opened all destinations to tourists who had taken at least the first dose of the COVID-19 vaccine after the second lockdown on 10 August 2021. To welcome and ensure protection, the tourism department rolled out a 'bio-bubble model' that offers a safe environment for travellers who will be served by vaccinated service providers such as airport ground employees, taxi drivers, tour operators, hotel, resort and homestay personnel, houseboat workers, etc. As the pandemic posed challenges for receiving guests at restaurants, the government introduced the drive-in restaurant concept, one of the creative ideas that transformed traditional restaurant dining. This was first initiated by the Kerala Tourism Development Corporation (KTDC) by launching in-car dining services in KTDC restaurants across the State on 30 June 2021 (Menon Anasuya. 6 July 2021). The government announced a COVID loss assistance scheme called 'Chief Minister's Tourism Loan Assistance Scheme (CMTLAS)' to help all tourism industry stakeholders badly hit by the pandemic under different schemes, as discussed. The government supported the industry's entrepreneurs through the 'Tourism Working Capital Support Scheme (TWCSS)'. Employees in various sectors of the industry can apply for short-term personal loans through the 'Tourism Employment Support Scheme (TESS)', and a 'Revolving Fund' has also been established to offer interest-free loans up to Rs 10,000 without any collateral security. A separate financial assistance programme for the maintenance and repairs of houseboats was also announced for the owners under 'Tourism Houseboats Support Scheme (THSS)'. For tourist guides, one-time financial assistance was given under the 'Tourism Guides Support Scheme (TGSS)' (Economic survey report, 2020).

Keravan Kerala, Kerala Tourism

In response to visitor requests and preferences in the post-pandemic age, the Kerala government unveiled a comprehensive, stakeholder-friendly caravan tourism policy, offering travellers a safe, personalised and in-touch nature travel experience. By offering incentives for purchasing caravans, establishing caravan parks and outlining the processes and procedures for its management and approval mechanisms, it aims to lay out the broad framework for growing and promoting caravan tourism in Kerala, primarily in the private sector. In addition, the KTDC currently provides Keravan Kerala packages to all of Kerala's locations. This cutting-edge product was launched to offer amenities for safe, secure and hygienic travel and lodging while appreciating the wonders of nature (Fig. 14.2).

Fig. 14.2.   Keravan Kerala. *Source:* https://www.keralatourism.org/
keravan-kerala/about.

Impact of COVID on Nepal Tourism and Its Revival Measures

Tourism in Nepal is a significant industry and an essential source of revenue for
the country. Nepal is known for its stunning natural beauty, diverse culture and
adventure activities such as trekking, mountaineering and rafting, which attract
thousands of tourists every year. As per the 2019 Nepal tourism statistics, around
1.2 million foreign visitors came to Nepal in 2019, showing a 2% rise over the
1,173,072 tourists who travelled to Nepal in 2018. The total revenue for the
tourism industry in 2019 was Nrs. 811,257,46 (about 724,337 US dollars) which
was about 16% more than in 2018 (Department of Tourism Nepal, 2020). But the
spread of COVID adversely affected Nepal's economy. The epidemic, which has
multiple negative consequences for the economic and social systems, has negatively impacted all segments of Nepal's tourism economy. The ambitious 'Visit
Nepal Year 2020' campaign, which sought to attract 2 million tourists to Nepal,
had to be suspended due to the severity of the coronavirus and its effects on public
health (Ulak, 2020). Travel restrictions across the globe caused a preliminary loss
of 14.37% to the Nepalese economy. The number of visitors that Nepal welcomed
in 2020 was 230,085 as opposed to 1,197,191 in 2019, a decrease of more than
80% (Ulak, 2020). The tourism and hospitality industries were the ones that had
been most severely impacted, among many other sectors. The Nepalese government has launched a number of initiatives to boost the tourism sector, which has
been negatively affected by the COVID-19 pandemic. One of these initiatives is a
proposal to designate the years 2023–2033 as the 'Visit Nepal Decade'. During the
announcement of the Tourism Rehabilitation Action Plan, the Minister of culture, tourism and civil aviation, Mr Jeevan Ram Shrestha, said that the government of Nepal is breaking tradition by proclaiming every year as 'Visit Nepal
Year', to undertake a prolonged campaign to encourage tourism, a significant
source of foreign cash and job creation for the nation. Nepal will begin

promotional campaigns in China, India and Bangladesh as part of the new action plan; the first two countries are Nepal's main sources of tourists during typical years (AIRNews, 2022). Also, there is a strategy to market Nepal as a venue for conferences, exhibitions, meetings and spiritual tourism by providing packages for yoga, wellness and spa. The government is also considering retirement visas and medical services for senior foreigners who choose to stay longer in Nepal. Nepal is preparing to offer more Himalayan peaks since mountaineering is a significant component of its tourism industry. More peaks between 5,800 and 8,000 metres above sea level will be made accessible for mountaineering under the action plan. Authorities claim that 414 peaks in Nepal have already opened that are higher than 5,700 metres. Other initiatives like collaboration and coordination with international airlines, a global positioning system (GPS) tracking system to make trekking and mountaineering safer, multilingual helpline support centres for tourists and many other facilities for foreigners who come to Nepal for movie shootings are all included in the action plan (ET Travel World, The Economic Times, 2022).

Changed Travel Intentions of Tourists

People's lives and habits have altered as a result of COVID-19, and economies have suffered dramatically as a result. Changes in travel habits will have a long-term effect on the industry and have to be adequately monitored by the service providers to plan accordingly. Studies show that after the spread of COVID-19, tourists care more about cleanliness and vaccinations, prefer environmentally friendly destinations, travel more within their own country and prefer private vehicles to public transportation (Chansuk et al., 2022). Most scholars have used Ajzen's theory of planned behaviour (TPB) (Ajzen, 1991) to predict the future travel intentions of tourists (Chansuk et al., 2022; Hanafiah et al., 2021). Hence, the future travel intention was explained using the constructs' 'travel attitudes', 'subjective norms' and 'perceived behaviour control'. As a result of the pandemic, studies show that travellers are now concerned about the hygiene factor and health risks associated with travel; these two constructs are also included to understand tourist travel intentions. A survey was conducted among 450 domestic tourists from the selected districts of Kerala, namely Ernakulam, Thiruvanathapuram, that have recorded the highest tourist arrivals in the years 2021 and 2022. A descriptive analysis was done to analyse the changed travel intentions of tourists. The mean value was calculated for the constructs, and the highest mean value of 4.1244 was for the 'hygiene concern', which shows that the tourists are concerned about the hygiene factor after the pandemic. The value for 'the perceived health risk' is 3.7067, showing that tourists are concerned about the spread of diseases. However, the mean value of 'travel attitudes' (3.9878) and their 'future travel intention' (3.639) are also high, showing that even though they are concerned about hygiene and health risk, they have a positive attitude towards travel, and once the pandemic is over, they will participate in travel. The mean value of 'subjective norms' is 3.551, and for 'perceived behaviour control' is 3.574.

Eighty-six percent (387) of the tourists had only participated in domestic tourism after the spread of the pandemic; they preferred sustainable tourism forms like eco or responsible tourism, cleanliness in service delivery and also less crowded places. The urge to explore has existed in people's minds from time immemorial and will continue to motivate them to participate in travel.

Research Box

Virtual Travel Vs Actual Travel

The kids had spent a lot of time planning their summer vacation travel, but suddenly the COVID-19 pandemic ruined them all. They missed all the beautiful scenery and the activities planned and had to be at home for a long period of time. Attending online classes, playing video games, chatting on social media, etc. made them really bored. At that time, I suggested the possibilities of virtual tourism, which provided a platform to explore their dream destinations with a click away. They started exploring the world using 360 degree videos with the possibility of VR tools and again started planning for their trips once the pandemic was over. I felt happy that they loved exploring the world, but I was still confused with a lot of questions, like, to what extent are virtual tourism experiences substituting for traditional travel and tourism experiences? With the COVID-19 pandemic restricting physical travel, virtual tourism has gained momentum, and its popularity has been on the rise. However, it is unclear whether virtual tourism can completely replace the actual travel industry, or if it is just a temporary alternative to physical travel. With the advancement of technologies, like developments in virtual as well as AR, it has become possible to explore the world by simply sitting at home. I think virtual tourism experiences can be integrated with traditional travel and tourism experiences to create a more comprehensive and immersive experience for travellers. Is it really possible? How do different age groups and cultures perceive virtual tourism experiences, and what implications does this have for the future of the travel and tourism industry? If people started using virtual travel over actual travel, what are the economic implications of virtual tourism for the travel and tourism industry, and how do they compare to physical travel and tourism experiences in terms of revenue generation and job creation? My mind is overflowing with questions, and this has to be researched by taking an adequate sample from those who experienced virtual travel during the pandemic. To answer these research questions, a mixed-methods approach has to be used, which includes both qualitative and quantitative research methods. A survey has to be conducted to collect data from individuals who have experienced both virtual tourism and actual travel. Additionally, in-depth interviews will be conducted with industry experts and stakeholders to gain insights on the impact of virtual tourism on the actual travel industry.

Conclusion

This chapter thus explains how the COVID-19 pandemic had affected the global tourism industry and also the Indian tourism industry. The stringent measures taken to control the spread of the virus resulted in a significant decline in tourism activity. However, vaccination programmes, and other revival measures, have resulted in the easing of travel restrictions, and now the industry is showing a positive trend. This chapter also discussed the worldwide revival steps, focusing on Indian and Kerala tourism. Technology has also played a significant role in reviving tourism post-pandemic. Virtual tourism and domestic tourism have helped keep people interested in travelling, and now tourists are putting cleanliness, health and safety measures at the top of their list of priorities. Travellers are now selecting less crowded places and are interested in eco-friendly and socially responsible travel options. Tourism service providers and the government must consider these changed travel preferences when planning future tourism activities. The tourism industry will get back on its feet after this dark age of COVID-19 because it knows how to handle uncertain situations. Overall, the recovery will likely be a gradual process requiring ongoing collaboration and innovation to navigate the uncertainties of the post-pandemic world.

Discussion Questions

- How far has the COVID-19 pandemic changed the global tourism industry and its components?
- What are the measures taken to revive the tourism industry after the pandemic?
- What are the changed travel intentions of tourists in the post-pandemic period?

References

Abbas, J., Mubeen, R., Iorember, P. T., Raza, S., & Mamirkulova, G. (2021). Exploring the impact of COVID-19 on tourism: Transformational potential and implications for a sustainable recovery of the travel and leisure industry. *Current Research in Behavioral Sciences*, 2, 100033. https://doi.org/10.1016/j.crbeha.2021.100033

AHLA. (2020, August 31). State of the hotel industry analysis: Covid-19 six months later. https://www.ahla.com/news. https://www.ahla.com/sites/default/files/State%20of%20the%20Industry.pdf

AIRNews. (2022, July 25). Nepalese govt announces numerous measures to revive tourism industry battered by COVID-19 pandemic. https://Newsonair.com/. https://newsonair.com/2022/07/25/nepalese-govt-announces-numerous-measures-to-revive-tourism-industry-battered-by-covid-19-pandemic/

Ajzen, I. (1991). The theory of planned behavior. *Organizational Behavior and Human Decision Processes*, 50(2), 179–211. https://doi.org/10.1016/0749-5978(91)90020-t

CCSA. (2021). How COVID-19 is changing the world: A statistical perspective Volume III. https://unstats.un.org/UNSDWebsite. United Nations, Department of Economics and Social Affairs. https://unstats.un.org/unsd/ccsa/documents/covid19-report-ccsa_vol3.pdf

Chansuk, C., Arreeras, T., Chiangboon, C., Phonmakham, K., Chotikool, N., Buddee, R., Pumjampa, S., Yanasoi, T., & Arreeras, S. (2022). Using factor analyses to understand the post-pandemic travel behavior in domestic tourism through a questionnaire survey. *Transportation Research Interdisciplinary Perspectives*, *16*, 100691. https://doi.org/10.1016/j.trip.2022.100691

Department of Tourism Nepal. (2020). Nepal Tourism Statistics 2019. https://www.tourismdepartment.gov.np//files/statistics/42.pdf

El-Erian. (2020, March 17). *The coming coronavirus recession and the uncharted territory beyond*. https://www.foreignaffairs.com/world/coming-coronavirus-recession

ET Travel World, The Economic Times. (2022, July 25). *Nepal announces measures to revive its tourism industry* https://Travel.Economictimes.Indiatimes.com/. https://travel.economictimes.indiatimes.com/news/destination/international/nepal-announces-measures-to-revive-its-tourism-industry/93102705

Hadi, D. M., Katircioglu, S., & Adaoglu, C. (2020). The vulnerability of tourism firms' stocks to the terrorist incidents. *Current Issues in Tourism*, *23*(9), 1138–1152. https://doi.org/10.1080/13683500.2019.1592124

Hadi, D. M., Naeem, M. A., & Karim, S. (2022). The exposure of the US tourism subsector stocks to global volatility and uncertainty factors. *Current Issues in Tourism*, *26*(4), 603–616. https://doi.org/10.1080/13683500.2022.2031916

Hailemariam, A., & Ivanovski, K. (2021). The impact of geopolitical risk on tourism. *Current Issues in Tourism*, *24*(22), 3134–3140. https://doi.org/10.1080/13683500.2021.1876644

Hanafiah, M. H., Md Zain, N. A., Azinuddin, M., & Mior Shariffuddin, N. S. (2021). I'm afraid to travel! Investigating the effect of perceived health risk on Malaysian travellers' post-pandemic perception and future travel intention. *Journal of Tourism Futures*. https://doi.org/10.1108/jtf-10-2021-0235

Ibn-Mohammed, T., Mustapha, K., Godsell, J., Adamu, Z., Babatunde, K., Akintade, D., Acquaye, A., Fujii, H., Ndiaye, M., Yamoah, F., & Koh, S. (2021). A critical analysis of the impacts of COVID-19 on the global economy and ecosystems and opportunities for circular economy strategies. *Resources, Conservation and Recycling*, *164*, 105169. https://doi.org/10.1016/j.resconrec.2020.105169

Indian Tourism statistics. (2020). *Indian tourism statistics 2020*. Ministry of Tourism India. https://tourism.gov.in/market-research-and-statistics. Accessed on February 6, 2023.

Jaipuria, S., Parida, R., & Ray, P. (2020). The impact of COVID-19 on tourism sector in India. *Tourism Recreation Research*, *46*(2), 245–260. https://doi.org/10.1080/02508281.2020.1846971

Jiang, Y., & Wen, J. (2020, June 25). Effects of COVID-19 on hotel marketing and management: A perspective article. *International Journal of Contemporary Hospitality Management*, *32*(8), 2563–2573. https://doi.org/10.1108/ijchm-03-2020-0237

Le, D., & Phi, G. (2021). Strategic responses of the hotel sector to COVID-19: Toward a refined pandemic crisis management framework. *International Journal of Hospitality Management*, *94*, 102808. https://doi.org/10.1016/j.ijhm.2020.102808

Lu, J., Xiao, X., Xu, Z., Wang, C., Zhang, M., & Zhou, Y. (2021). The potential of virtual tourism in the recovery of tourism industry during the COVID-19 pandemic. *Current Issues in Tourism, 25*(3), 441–457. https://doi.org/10.1080/13683500.2021.1959526

Malra, D. (2021). Impact of COVID-19 on tourism industry. *Journal of Interdisciplinary Cycle Research, 13*(1), 700–709. ISSN NO: 0022-1945.

Marasco, A., Buonincontri, P., van Niekerk, M., Orlowski, M., & Okumus, F. (2018). Exploring the role of next-generation virtual technologies in destination marketing. *Journal of Destination Marketing & Management, 9*, 138–148. https://doi.org/10.1016/j.jdmm.2017.12.002

Mathur, S. (2021). *Covid impact of tourism: 14.5 million jobs lost in 2020s Q1 alone.* https://timesofindia.indiatimes.com/. https://timesofindia.indiatimes.com/business/india-business/covid-impact-of-tourism-14-5-million-jobs-lost-in-2020s-q1-alone/articleshow/84573975.cms. Accessed on December 5, 2022.

McCabe, S., & Qiao, G. (2020). A review of research into social tourism: Launching the Annals of Tourism Research Curated Collection on Social Tourism. *Annals of Tourism Research, 85*, 103103. https://doi.org/10.1016/j.annals.2020.103103

Ministry of Civil Aviation. (n.d.). *Ministry of Civil Aviation.* Government of India. https://www.civilaviation.gov.in/en/about-air-transport-bubbles

MOT. (2023). Ministry of Tourism Annual Report 2022–2023. https://tourism.gov.in. Ministry of Tourism. https://tourism.gov.in/sites/default/files/2023-02/MOT%20Annual%20Report_2022-23_English.pdf

Narasimhan, T. E. (2020, January 30). India's first coronavirus case: Kerala student in Wuhan tested positive. https://www.business-standard.com/. https://web.archive.org/web/20200311040438/https://www.business-standard.com/article/current-affairs/india-s-first-coronavirus-case-kerala-student-in-wuhan-tested-positive-120013001782_1.html

Nawrat. (2020, December 2). UK authorises world's first Covid-19 vaccine, Pfizer/BioNTech's BNT162b2. https://www.pharmaceutical-technology.com/. https://www.pharmaceutical-technology.com/features/pfizer-covid-19-vaccine-approved-uk/

Pandey, K., Mahadevan, K., & Joshi, S. (2021). Indian Tourism Industry and COVID-19: A sustainable recovery framework in a post-pandemic era. *Vision: The Journal of Business Perspective,* https://doi.org/10.1177/09722629211043298

Shretta. (2020, April 7). *The economic impact of COVID-19. Centre for Tropical Medicine and Global Health.* Nuffield Department of Medicine, University of Oxford. https://www.tropicalmedicine.ox.ac.uk. https://www.tropicalmedicine.ox.ac.uk/news/the-economic-impact-of-covid-19

Škare, M., Soriano, D. R., & Porada-Rochoń, M. (2021). Impact of COVID-19 on the travel and tourism industry. *Technological Forecasting and Social Change, 163*, 120469. https://doi.org/10.1016/j.techfore.2020.120469

Sujood, Hamid, S., & Bano, N. (2022). Coronavirus: Choking global and Indian tourism economy and leaving industry on the ventilator. *Journal of Hospitality and Tourism Insights.* https://doi.org/10.1108/jhti-09-2021-0237

TIO. (2020, August 19). *Understanding the term "Air bubble" and its importance in the time of Coronavirus.* https://timesofindia.indiatimes.com/. https://timesofindia.indiatimes.com/travel/travel-news/understanding-the-term-air-bubble-and-its-importance-in-the-time-of-coronavirus/articleshow/77631541.cms

Verma, S., & Gustafsson, A. (2020, September). Investigating the emerging COVID-19 research trends in the field of business and management: A bibliometric analysis approach. *Journal of Business Research, 118*, 253–261. https://doi.org/10.1016/j. jbusres.2020.06.057

Ulak. (2020). COVID-19 Pandemic and its Impact on Tourism Industry in Nepal Nimesh Ulak. *Journal of Tourism & Adventure, 3*(1), 50–75. https://www.nepjol. info/index.php/jota/article/view/31356/24792

UNWTO. (2020a, December). World Tourism Barometer. https://unwto.org. https:// tourismanalytics.com/uploads/1/2/0/4/120443739/unwto_barometer_december_ 2020.pdf

UNWTO. (2020b, January). World Tourism Barometer. https://www.unwto.org. https://webunwto.s3.eu-west-1.amazonaws.com/s3fs-public/2020-01/UNWTO_ Barom20_01_January_excerpt_0.pdf

UNWTO. (2020c, September 25). *Travel digitally with Google on world tourism day.* https://unwto.org. https://www.unwto.org/news/travel-digitally-with-google-on-world-tourism-day

WEF. (2020, March 17). This is how coronavirus could affect the travel and tourism industry. https://www.weforum.org/. World Economic Forum. https://www. weforum.org/agenda/2020/03/world-travel-coronavirus-covid19-jobs-pandemic-tourism-aviation/

WTTC. (2019). Travel & Tourism, City Travel & Tourism Impact 2019. https://wttc. org/. World Travel and Tourism Council. https://wttc.org/Portals/0/Documents/ Reports/2019/City%20Travel%20and%20Tourism%20Impact%20Graphics% 20Report%20Dec%202019.pdf?ver=2021-02-25-201320-033

WTTC. (2020, June). *Global economic impact & trends 2020.* https://wttc.org/Portals/0/ Documents/Reports/2020/Global%20Economic%20Impact%20Trends%202020. pdf?ver=2021-02-25-183118-360. Accessed on December, 2022.

WTTC. (2022, August). Travel and Tourism Economic Impact 2022-Global Trends. https://wttc.org/. World Travel and Tourism Council. https://wttc.org/Portals/0/ Documents/Reports/2022/EIR2022-Global%20Trends.pdf

Chapter 15

Rethinking the Localisation of Leisure Space During the COVID-19 Pandemic From the Sustainable Perspective

Ahmet Elnur[a], Çağdaş Aydın[b] and Ceren Aydın[c]

[a]Ahmet Elnur Suleyman Demirel University, Türkiye
[b]Kastamonu University, Türkiye
[c]Independent Researcher, Türkiye

Learning Objectives

After reading and studying this chapter, you should be able to:

- evaluate the sustainability of leisure practices and the importance of considering social, economic and environmental factors when developing alternatives for leisure sustainability;
- discuss the different forms of leisure time evaluation that have emerged during the COVID-19 pandemic, including workation and staycation, and analyse their potential benefits and drawbacks;
- recognise the importance of continuously evaluating leisure time in the context of development-oriented functionality and ensuring leisure sustainability to promote physical activity, stress reduction, connection with nature and enhance individuals' quality of life and well-being.

Abstract

The importance and value of the leisure phenomenon are becoming more prominent daily as it becomes a determining indicator of both qualities of life and social welfare. The COVID-19 pandemic, which has caused severe disruptions in the lifestyles of individuals, has also made it inevitable to face the emergence of sociocultural conditions in which traditional daily life routines have disappeared and the reorganisation of the leisure space. In line with the conditions mentioned earlier, the characteristics of the 'new' and the 'old'

Future Tourism Trends Volume 1, 225–238
doi:10.1108/978-1-83753-244-520241015

have started to come together in the daily lives and leisure spaces of individuals in constant conflict. Under these conditions, individuals who spent their leisure time travelling from one place to another before the pandemic had to choose different leisure options. Therefore, the leisure space, which is an integral part of the social life of today's individual, has evolved into an unthinkable position independently of the COVID-19 pandemic effects. From this point of view, this study aims to examine the transformation of the leisure space due to the COVID-19 pandemic within the framework of previous studies on this subject and to discuss it in the context of sustainability. For this purpose, firstly, a general framework is drawn on the historical development of the leisure concept, and then its relationship with the COVID-19 pandemic is evaluated. In the last part of the study, the new forms of leisure that have emerged due to the process, as mentioned earlier, are discussed over the critical issues in ensuring the sustainability of leisure practices.

Keywords: Sustainability of leisure; workation; COVID-19 pandemic; localisation of leisure; new forms of leisure; staycation

Introduction

Leisure time, an essential aspect of modern life and a determining indicator of the quality of life and social welfare, has been affected by various social, cultural, religious, economic and technological changes and transformations. While in Ancient Greece and Rome, it was seen as a means of self-development and self-realisation, in the Middle Ages, it was seen as a waste of time. As a result of industrialisation, leisure time became associated with entertainment and consumption. The concept of leisure has been shaped over time by numerous factors, including capitalism and global developments such as technological advances and health-based crises. The COVID-19 pandemic has further impacted leisure activities, forcing individuals to adapt to new circumstances. Studies have shown that less preferred activities before the pandemic are now famous, and many have been moved to digital platforms. Nonetheless, individuals have discovered ways to refresh, enjoy themselves, and care for their mental, emotional and physical well-being while engaging in leisure activities.

The pandemic has led to new possibilities and limitations in social life, requiring individuals to develop new forms of leisure that promote mental health, reduce stress and build positive relationships. The pandemic has also accelerated the digitalisation of various spheres of social life, including leisure. Therefore, leisure activities must have short- and long-term spatial continuity to ensure social, economic and environmental sustainability of well-being. In this context, virtual leisure activities such as online concerts, festivals and museum tours provide sustainable alternatives to face-to-face activities, minimising environmental impacts while enhancing leisure sustainability. Furthermore, by adopting a spatially sustainable character of leisure time, individuals can expand the possibilities and benefits of leisure activities through digital innovation. The challenges and opportunities arising from transforming leisure spaces during the COVID-19 pandemic are discussed in this chapter, emphasising the need for innovative solutions that promote sustainable and equitable access to leisure spaces.

Historical Development of the Concept of Leisure

The concepts of work and leisure time have different meanings depending on the cultural structure of the era, and these two periods shape an individual's life. The concept of leisure time, also known as free time, has had conflicting meanings throughout history (Bahadır, 2016). The development of the concept of free time is examined in terms of pre-industrial and post-industrial periods (Bull et al., 2003). It is seen that the concept of free time emerged during the period when people transitioned from a nomadic lifestyle to a settled one. Free time was defined as time outside of agricultural activities during this period.

The ancient Greek period holds an important place in the historical process of the concept of free time. In this period, also known as the Classical Age (Gönen, 2005), free time was granted to aristocrats (Bull et al., 2003). The approach of ancient Greek philosophers such as Socrates, Plato and Aristotle to the concept of free time laid the philosophical foundations of free time. Free time was understood as a personal and social development method in this period. Free time was seen as a cultural arena where art, sports, music, political discussions and philosophical conversations were held (Hunnicutt, 2006, pp. 58–59). Plato's Academy, the Epicurean school founded by Epicurus, and Pyrrho's Scepticism school are examples of how free time was evaluated. In these schools, efforts were made to make sense of life and the world. According to Plato, working excessively is foolishness. Excessive work anxiety, working more than necessary and ambitions such as becoming rich or famous are behaviours and desires that limit freedom (Bahadır, 2016; Hunnicutt, 2006).

On the other hand, according to Plato, excessive laziness and idleness should not be included in the concept of free time. Instead, individuals should spend their free time with music, sports and philosophy (Hunnicutt, 2006, p. 64). According to Aristotle, free time is a time that makes individuals happy, encourages them to think, and is a time for self-realisation (Cevizci, 2001, pp. 222–223).

Leisure time in Ancient Rome was considered a means of recovery, rejuvenation and rest before returning to work. Leisure activities were not seen as a class privilege and began to be organised publicly. Leisure time, considered a complement to work life, was used for political purposes during this period. The Roman emperors saw leisure time as a political tool to entertain and appease the people (Bull et al., 2003). During this period, 200 days of the year were designated official holidays, and individuals from lower classes were encouraged to participate in leisure activities (Torkildsen, 1992, p. 19).

In the Middle Ages, the Catholic Church viewed leisure as laziness and a waste of time. During this period, leisure activities were pushed to the background, and work and religious worship were emphasised as the purpose of life. In the Middle Ages, the church separated activities that met a person's daily needs into *vita activa* and activities that involved the mind, soul and worship of God into *vita contemplativa*, redefining work and leisure time (Hunnicutt, 2006, pp. 66–67). People engaging in different activities during their free time were considered sinful during this period (Torkildsen, 1992, p. 20). In 1517, the Protestant denomination opposed the Catholic Church, and Protestant work ethics emerged. Like the Catholic Church, Protestant work ethics also characterised leisure activities as laziness (Dattilo, 1999). This period, called the Puritan work ethic, did not last very long (Bull et al., 2003, p. 4), and leisure activities began to find their place with the Renaissance. In the early 17th century, opening parks and recreational areas and publishing books on art and sports can be given as examples.

After the industrial era, the concept of leisure time changed in different periods. The Industrial Revolution caused working hours to decrease and leisure time to increase. It was seen that the concept of leisure time became a time of consumption rather than personal development. In other words, it turned into a materialistic phenomenon (Juniu, 2000, pp. 70–71). With the developing technology during this period, productivity in production increased, but demand did not increase to match this increase in production. In order to balance this situation, high wages were given to workers, and consumption was encouraged (Gorz, 2007). Leisure time was when goods and services could be sold (Hunnicutt, 2006). The increase in population and leisure time in cities paved the way for creating park areas where individuals could work outside and organise events such as fairs, concerts and theatre plays (Harvey, 2003, p. 207).

The concept of leisure time in the 1900s and the 21st century show similarities, where leisure time is evaluated as a time for consumption. Individuals desire goods and services to differentiate themselves from others and occupy their leisure time by consuming them (Aytaç, 2006). According to this understanding, work makes leisure time purchasable (Bahadır, 2016). Nowadays, the scope of creativity, self-realisation and development in cultural and social aspects through leisure time is limited to consumption-oriented activities such as shopping. On the other hand, accessibility to activities such as cinema, sports, concerts and art courses is a positive outcome of the consumption and capitalist system. Along with the development of technology, activities and participation in leisure time have undergone significant changes, such as e-sports, e-shopping and remotely conducted personal development courses (Bryce, 2001).

Due to social, cultural, religious, economic and technological changes and developments, leisure time has carried different meanings throughout history. In ancient Greece and Rome, leisure time was production-oriented and characterised as finding, developing and realising oneself. In the Middle Ages, leisure time was considered a waste of time. It became a time for entertainment, consumption and spending, with the relief of the complexity of work life through industrialisation. Nowadays, the concept of leisure time, influenced by capitalism, is affected by numerous factors. The leisure time activities that individuals choose to participate in are shaped by the sociocultural and economic conditions of both the individual and the society in which they live, as well as global developments such as technological advances and pandemics, independent of society.

Leisure Time and COVID-19 Pandemic

Leisure time comes from the Latin word *licere*, meaning to be allowed or free (Cordes & Ibrahim, 1999, p. 5). Throughout history, leisure time has been interpreted differently depending on the era's characteristics. Although there is no single definition of the concept of leisure time, it is known to be approached in different ways. These approaches include *leisure time as time, leisure time as an activity, leisure time as a state of mind, leisure time as a holistic concept, leisure time as a way of life* (Torkildsen, 1992, pp. 25–30), *leisure time as an expenditure* (Argan, 2007, p. 14) and *leisure time as personality* (Aydin, 2016, p. 33; Mannell & Kleiber, 1997).

Leisure time remains after activities that individuals must engage in to work and sustain their lives. Leisure time as an activity refers to activities in which individuals actively and creatively participate (Horner & Swarbrooke, 2012, p. 22). The concept of leisure time, defined as the time when individuals free themselves from mental obligations, is included in leisure time as a state-of-mind approach (Torkildsen, 1992, p. 28). The holistic approach suggests that leisure time varies according to culture and represents relaxation, entertainment and personal development. Leisure time as a way of life is defined as having a valuable life and freedom of thought (Goodale & Godbey, 1988). The concept of leisure time, which allows individuals to consume more goods and services, represents an expenditure-focused approach (Odabaşı, 1999). The concept of leisure time, defined as the time when individuals can find themselves and express their personality and self fully, is approached as personality (Mannell & Kleiber, 1997). Based on these approaches, we can define leisure time as the time individuals spend on activities they want to participate in to maintain and improve their physical and mental well-being (Ardahan, 2016, p. 8). It is known that individuals prefer activities that relax, refresh and satisfy them while evaluating their leisure time (Sevinç & Özel, 2018). Participating in leisure activities reduces stressful life's effects and provides resilience against mental illnesses such as depression (Nishi et al., 2010; Richardson, 2002). Therefore, leisure time activities increase life satisfaction in the long term (Menec & Chipperfield, 1997). However, since the essence of leisure time activities is human, and humans cannot act independently of the events around them, this concept's dynamic structure is formed. While adapting to changing environmental and living conditions, humans must also adapt their social life to changing conditions. Undoubtedly, one of the unexpected sociological events of the 21st century that has affected all humans is the COVID-19 pandemic (Özel & Can, 2021). This pandemic has reshaped individuals' daily life routines and social lives.

The new coronavirus disease, called COVID-19, first appeared in December 2019 in Wuhan Province, China. Researchers identified the virus on 13 January 2020, and on 11 March 2020, the World Health Organization declared it a pandemic worldwide (Ministry of Health of the Republic of Türkiye, 2020, 2023). Many countries implemented precautions to slow down the spread of the pandemic by reducing social contact. Travel restrictions were imposed between countries, and those who had to travel were isolated for a while. Schools and workplaces closed in many countries, and distance education and work continued. Restrictions were also imposed on social life, and cinemas, entertainment venues, shopping malls, events and sports competitions were cancelled. All national and international measures/restrictions have been taken to prevent the spread of the virus, wholly changed individuals' daily lives (Ünlü, 2021). Individuals who had to spend more time at home during the pandemic tried to adapt their daily routines to this process. The decrease in face-to-face communication, temporary closure of enclosed spaces (shopping malls, cafes, restaurants, cinemas, sports centres) and measures such as curfews directly affected individuals' social lives. It is stated that sectors requiring close contact between individuals, such as the entertainment and food sectors, were affected by this period (Bartik et al., 2020).

Similarly, the tourism sector, which requires close contact, has shrunk during this process (Nicola et al., 2020). Therefore, individuals' leisure time habits and activity preferences before the pandemic had to transform during the pandemic. Face-to-face communications were moved to digital platforms, and platforms (Sucu, 2020) where individuals could socialise in the digital environment gained importance. For example, online live concerts were organised. Individuals could listen to their favourite artists' online concerts from their homes without paying any fees. With the feature of sending messages during the concert, individuals could communicate quickly and easily with each other and the artists (Kaya-Deniz, 2020). Thanks to online activities, individuals started to spend more time on digital platforms (Beaunoyer et al., 2020). Sports and educational activities held outside the home were adapted to the digital platform, and digital content was prepared for individuals to continue their sports activities at home (Ettekal & Agans, 2020).

Individuals forced to spend more time at home with their families have turned to indoor activities such as watching series and movies on digital platforms, making video calls, attending online courses, painting and gardening. Among intellectual activities, reading books has been the most preferred activity (Özel & Can, 2021). Board games, brain teasers and puzzles, such as computer games, have also been preferred as leisure activities at home (Aktaş & Bostancı, 2021; Marsden et al., 2020). Along with indoor activities, spending more time in the kitchen and trying new recipes has become a popular leisure activity. The desire of individuals to share the new recipes they have tried with their social circle has also increased sharing on social platforms (Thelwall & Thelwall, 2020).

Due to the lower transmission risk in open areas compared to enclosed spaces, individuals have also turned to outdoor and indoor activities at home. Spending time in parks, hiking, camping and having picnics has become an escape for individuals. Especially camping areas provide an advantage over other tourist areas with opportunities such as accommodation and spending time in open areas where social distance can be maintained (Craig et al., 2021). Recreational activities, such as camping tourism in coastal areas, have also been preferred by individuals (Kane et al., 2021). On the other hand, city parks have become a space for movement and an option for sports activities, especially for elderly individuals.

It can be inferred from studies that activities that were less preferred before the pandemic are now more popular among individuals, and some activities have been moved to digital platforms and adapted to the transformation (Ünlü, 2021). Although individuals' leisure preferences are shaped according to cultural characteristics, society's perception of leisure, and the opportunities available, they are also shaped in the face of unexpected situations, such as a global pandemic. Individuals have had to adapt their leisure activity choices to cope with the situation they are experiencing. Even in the face of the pressure of the global pandemic that affects the whole world, individuals have created time for themselves, aiming to renew, have fun and stay mentally, emotionally and physically healthy during that time.

Case Study: New Forms of Leisure During the COVID-19 Pandemic

The COVID-19 pandemic has brought new possibilities and limitations to people's social lives, as it forced them to look at different aspects of life through the continuous and rapid change of time and space conditions. The mandatory measures such as isolation and quarantine during the COVID-19 pandemic, which led to the disruption of various dynamics of social life and the stagnation of everyday life, also had an encouraging effect on the development of new forms of leisure which are beneficial for improving mental health, reducing stress and building positive relationships (Morse et al., 2021, p. 17). On the other hand, the obligation to comply with the restrictions to reduce the spread of the virus has led to a change in the needs and priorities of individuals regarding leisure time, as well as the differentiation of daily life practices (Ünlü, 2021, p. 2). In other words, the reconstruction of the leisure space has become necessary due to the pandemic measures that directly affect the everyday life of people across the globe. At this point, it is essential to note that the pandemic has catalysed significant changes, especially in the digitalisation of various spheres of social life, such as leisure.

As stated above, the restrictive measures applied to social life to control the effects of the pandemic have necessitated the reshaping of everyday life dynamics and the spatial transformation of the leisure space in general. Harvey (1989, p. 214) argues that symbolic arrangements of space and time provide a framework for our experiences, as 'we learn who or what we are in society through this framework'. In this context, the rapid transformation of arrangements of space and time under the influence of the COVID-19 pandemic has started to force us to rethink the concept of leisure within the framework of the 'new normal'. For individuals who have to be in the same place all the time, the emergence of significant problems in adapting to this process, especially in socialising, has become apparent as a significant disadvantage in experiencing leisure time (Özel & Can, 2021, p. 89). Under these conditions, the sustainability of individuals' social lives has become problematic due to new directives and procedures that were constantly renewed and limit daily mobilities. Considering the therapeutic aspect of leisure, which is intended to reduce the negative emotions caused by the stress factors of working life, the necessity of evaluating 'new' forms of leisure begins to be felt more clearly.

The COVID-19 pandemic has caused many of the existing leisure spaces unusable, making it impossible for people to enjoy their leisure time in traditional leisure environments. Furthermore, the pandemic has undoubtedly provided a significant impetus for developing information technologies and laid the groundwork for the vital positioning of technology-mediated everyday practices. Access to technological opportunities has gained an absolute position at the point of reshaping the forms of leisure time evaluation due to the spatial constraints encountered in this period. The concept of electronic leisure, which came to the fore during the pandemic period with its specific characteristics, differs from the concept of physical leisure, especially since it offers individuals the opportunity to experience virtual reality (Güncan, 2021, p. 170). As it became essential to adapt to new realities in the arrangements for cultural leisure, which forms an essential part of individuals' daily life activities, the services offered in this field have been rapidly reorganised under online environments. The traditional forms of cultural leisure (theatre, cinema, museum, concert hall) have proven to be inaccessible or not very accessible (with less occupancy of the halls and restrictive measures for spectators). However, these conditions revealed the catalyst functionality for new original and innovative online projects (Merkoulova & Merkoulova, 2021, p. 145). Leisure activities carried out in digital environments shaped in line with the possibilities offered by new information and communication technologies have become indispensable in eliminating the problems experienced by individuals in terms of physical access to cultural leisure resources. Within the framework of the lockdown measures, online leisure activities, which have a priority due to accessibility, have gradually started to occupy more and more space in the everyday lives of individuals.

In a constantly changing leisure environment under the conditions of digitalisation, the ability of individuals to continuously evaluate their non-working time in the context of development-oriented functionality constitutes an essential indicator of ensuring leisure sustainability. The sustainability of leisure activities prioritises personal health and well-being and promotes physical activity, stress reduction and connection with nature. Effective utilisation of leisure time plays a vital role in ensuring individual participation, a sense of belonging, improving social relations and enhancing a person's quality of life and well-being (Iso-Ahola & Park, 1996, p. 169). From this perspective, leisure activities must have both short- and long-term spatial continuity to ensure the social, economic and environmental sustainability of well-being. In pandemic conditions where leisure spaces are inevitably localised, virtual museum tours, music events such as online concerts, festivals and other virtual leisure activities, which stand out as a sustainable alternative to face-to-face activities, can provide leisure-related benefits while minimising environmental impacts. In this case, revealing alternatives for leisure sustainability by considering social, economic and environmental factors make it possible for individuals to adopt a spatially sustainable character of leisure time. As a result of implementing the alternatives envisaged by this direction, the new context of leisure activities expands the possibilities of enhancing the leisure sustainability of individuals through digital innovation.

The fact that individuals' leisure activities are faced with mandatory restrictions during the pandemic also led to the emergence of alternative forms of leisure time evaluation such as 'workation' and 'staycation'. The term 'workation' is formed by the combination of the words 'work' and 'vacation' and refers to the activity in which individuals prefer to blend both work and leisure while prioritising shorter distance leisure activities and the opportunity to work from any location (Voll et al., 2022, p. 5). Workation is carried out to change the daily scenery in which routine work takes place away from home in another unfamiliar environment. Workstations have the potential to combine leisure purposes with work-related activities and become permanently integrated into the lifestyle of self-employed people. However, it is still being determined whether the same benefits and recreational effects apply to everyone (Bassyiouny & Wilkesmann, 2023, p. 8). Workation has become a viable option for many people who can work from anywhere with an internet connection, especially with the increase of remote work during the pandemic.

The term 'staycation' is formed by the combination of the words 'stay' and 'vacation' and refers to a type of vacation that people enjoy at home or somewhere close to the home that they can quickly return to (Irfan & Lahlou, 2022, p. 148). Lin et al. (2021, p. 2) describe the concept of staycation as a form of domestic tourism mainly shaped by travel to places within driving distance from home or short distances. Staycation contributes both temporally and financially to the local community, attracting attention as a holiday option that benefits other members of the community. At the same time, eliminating the necessity of long-distance travel ensures that leisure time is spent in a stable environment and that environmental habits are preserved. In addition, staycation, which is a more accessible and instant type of vacation, enables the minimisation of costs and the maximisation of vacation time since shorter distances are travelled (Rosu, 2020, pp. 34–35). Studies on the concept of staycation, which has experienced a significant increase in number after the COVID-19 outbreak, mainly focus on the benefits obtained from this experience. In this respect, Anton Clavé (2022, p. 22) points out that staycation can come to the fore in the new global extraordinary conditions that may emerge in the post-COVID-19 period. This potential is further enhanced by encouraging local economic growth, reducing the carbon footprint and enabling individuals to explore their local environment and engage in activities they might not otherwise consider. These forms of leisure can provide various benefits for individuals and society, such as enhancing health, happiness, learning and solidarity. However, they may also entail some risks or limitations, such as addiction, isolation, inequality or exploitation. Therefore, it is important to balance one's leisure time activities and to be mindful of their impacts on oneself and others.

Research Box

The COVID-19 pandemic has catalysed significant changes, especially in the digitalisation of various spheres of social life, such as leisure. However, it is essential to evaluate the new forms of leisure activities from a sustainable perspective to ensure that they have both short- and long-term spatial continuity and promote personal health and well-being, physical activity, stress reduction and connection with nature. In particular, it seems important to provide insight into the new forms of leisure that have emerged during the pandemic and their sustainability in terms of social, economic and environmental factors. For this purpose, you can conduct the study by using a qualitative research design to explore the research questions given below:

(1) How have these new forms of leisure activities affected individuals' mental health and well-being during the pandemic?
(2) What are the social, economic and environmental impacts of the new forms of leisure activities?
(3) How can the new forms of leisure activities be made more sustainable and environmentally friendly?
(4) How can the new forms of leisure activities be made accessible to all individuals regardless of their socio-economic status?

You can collect the data through semi-structured interviews with individuals who have experienced the new forms of leisure during the pandemic. The participant group would be selected using a purposive sampling method, ensuring diversity in terms of age, gender and socio-economic status. You can analyse the data using thematic analysis, which will allow for the identification of patterns and themes in the data.

Conclusion

The COVID-19 pandemic has transformed individuals' leisure time activities, forcing them to adapt their choices to cope with the situation. Restrictions implemented to control the spread of the virus have led people to socialise and spend their leisure time in new ways. Face-to-face communication has been replaced by digital platforms, with individuals spending more time online. This has driven the development of digital leisure activities, essential in overcoming the physical access limitations to cultural leisure resources. As a result of the digitalisation of various areas of social life, such as leisure time, access to technological opportunities has gained an absolute position in reshaping the forms of leisure time due to the spatial constraints encountered in this period.

Sustainable leisure activities prioritise personal health and well-being and promote physical activity, stress reduction and connection with nature. Effective use of leisure time is crucial for individual participation, a sense of belonging, improved social relations and enhanced quality of life and well-being. The concept of electronic leisure, which allows individuals to experience virtual reality, has become indispensable in reshaping leisure time evaluation due to spatial constraints during the pandemic. Alternative forms of leisure time evaluation such as 'workation' and 'staycation' prioritise local economic growth, reduce carbon footprint and enable individuals to explore their local environment and engage in new activities. These forms of leisure also benefit mental health, reducing stress and building positive relationships. By considering social, economic and environmental factors, individuals can adopt a spatially sustainable character of leisure time.

In conclusion, the COVID-19 pandemic has driven significant changes, especially in the digitalisation of social life, necessitating a reshaping of everyday life dynamics and the spatial transformation of leisure space. The development of digital leisure activities has become indispensable in eliminating the problems experienced by individuals in terms of physical access to cultural leisure resources. Furthermore, the sustainability of leisure activities promotes personal health and well-being, enhancing individuals' quality of life and well-being. At this point, alternative forms of leisure evaluation, such as 'workation' and 'staycation', have emerged, providing a sustainable alternative to face-to-face activities. By evaluating new forms of leisure, individuals can adopt a spatially sustainable character of leisure time, enhancing their leisure sustainability through digital innovation.

Discussion Questions

- How has the COVID-19 pandemic affected the leisure space, and what new forms of leisure have emerged?
- What is the importance of sustainability in leisure practices, and how can digital innovation contribute to leisure sustainability?
- How does the concept of workation and staycation provide alternative leisure time evaluation, and what are their advantages and disadvantages?

References

Aktaş, B., & Bostancı, N. (2021). Covid-19 pandemisinde üniversite öğrencilerindeki oyun bağımlılığı düzeyleri ve pandeminin dijital oyun oynama durumlarına etkisi. *Bağımlılık Dergisi, 22*(2), 129–138.

Anton Clavé, S. (2022). Theme parks, staycation practices, and COVID-19: Opportunities and uncertainties. *Journal of Themed Experience and Attractions Studies, 2*(1), 21–25.

Ardahan, F. (2016). Ciddi boş zaman faaliyeti olarak gönüllülük: AKUT Örneği. *Mediterranean Journal of Humanities, 6*(1), 47–61.

Argan, M. (2007). *Eğlence pazarlaması*. Detay Yayıncılık.

Aydin, C. (2016). *A ve B kişilik tiplerinin boş zaman davranışlarının kıyaslanması*. Master's thesis. Anadolu Üniversitesi.

Aytaç, Ö. (2006). Boş zamanın değişen yüzü: Yaşam deneyimleri ve kimlik inşası. *Sosyoloji Dergisi*, (15), 57–91.

Bahadır, M. (2016). Antikçağ'dan günümüze boş zaman üzerine bir değerlendirme. *Erzurum Teknik Üniversitesi Sosyal Bilimler Enstitüsü Dergisi*, *1*(2), 103–116.

Bartik, A. W., Bertrand, M., Cullen, Z. B., Glaeser, E. L., Luca, M., & Stanton, C. T. (2020). *How are small businesses adjusting to COVID-19? Early evidence from a survey* (No. w26989). National Bureau of Economic Research.

Bassyiouny, M., & Wilkesmann, M. (2023). Going on workation–Is tourism research ready to take off? Exploring an emerging phenomenon of hybrid tourism. *Tourism Management Perspectives*, *46*, 101096.

Beaunoyer, E., Dupéré, S., & Guitton, M. J. (2020). COVID-19 and digital inequalities: Reciprocal impacts and mitigation strategies. *Computers in Human Behavior*, *111*, 106424.

Bryce, J. (2001). The technological transformation of leisure. *Social Science Computer Review*, *19*(1), 7–16.

Bull, C., Hoose, J., & Weed, M. (2003). *An introduction to leisure studies*. Pearson Education.

Cevizci, A. (2001). *İlk Çağ Felsefe Tarihi*. Asa Yayınevi.

Cordes, K. A., & Ibrahim, H. M. (1999). *Applications in recreation and leisure: For today and the future* (2nd edn.). McGraw-Hill Book Company Europe.

Craig, C. A., Ma, S., & Karabas, I. (2021). COVID-19, camping and construal level theory. *Current Issues in Tourism*, *24*(20), 2855–2859.

Dattilo, J. (1999). *Leisure education program planning: A systematic approach* (2nd edn.). Venture Publishing Inc.

Ettekal, A. V., & Agans, J. P. (2020). Positive youth through leisure: Confronting the COVID-19 pandemic. *Journal of Youth Development*, *15*(2), 1–20.

Gönen, M. (2005). Felsefe, politika ve aydın ikilemi. *Üniversite ve Toplum*, *5*(3), 4–9.

Goodale, T., & Godbey, G. (1988). *The evolution of leisure: Historical and philosophical perspectives*. Venture Publishing, Inc.

Gorz, A. (2007). *İktisadi aklın eleştirisi* [I. Ergüden, Trans.]. Ayrıntı Yayınları. (Original work published 1988).

Güncan, Ö. (2021). Elektronik boş zaman uygulamaları "sanal rekreasyon" mudur yoksa "dijital rekreasyon" mu? *Sosyal, Beşeri ve İdari Bilimler Dergisi*, *4*(2), 163–181.

Harvey, D. (1989). *The condition of postmodernity: An enquiry into the origins of cultural change*. Routledge.

Harvey, D. (2003). *Paris is the capital of modernity*. Psychology Press.

Horner, S., & Swarbrooke, J. (2012). *Leisure marketing*. Routledge.

Hunnicutt, B. K. (2006). The history of Western leisure. In C. Rojek, S. M. Shaw, & A. J. Veal (Eds.), *A handbook of leisure studies* (pp. 55–75). Palgrave Macmillan.

Irfan, R., & Lahlou, H. (2022). Vacation into staycation: A connotative analysis. In M. Ebrahimi & U. Aydemir (Eds.), *A global pandemic: The ripple effect of COVID-19* (pp. 147–160). Universiti Malaysia Sabah Press.

Iso-Ahola, S. E., & Park, C. J. (1996). Leisure-related social support and self-determination as buffers of stress-illness relationship. *Journal of Leisure Research*, *28*(3), 169–187.

Juniu, S. (2000). Downshifting: Regaining the essence of leisure. *Journal of Leisure Research*, *32*(1), 69–73.

Kane, B., Zajchowski, C. A., Allen, T. R., McLeod, G., & Allen, N. H. (2021). Is it safer at the beach? Spatial and temporal analyses of beachgoer behaviours during the COVID-19 pandemic. *Ocean & Coastal Management*, *205*, 105533.

Kaya-Deniz, A. (2020). COVID-19 salgını sürecinde dijitalleşen eğlence anlayışı: Çevrimiçi konserler. *SSAD: Stratejik ve Sosyal Araştırmalar Dergisi*, *4*(2), 191–206.

Lin, Z. C., Wong, I. A., Kou, I. E., & Zhen, X. C. (2021). Inducing well-being through staycation programs in the midst of the COVID-19 crisis. *Tourism Management Perspectives*, *40*, 100907.

Mannell, R. C., & Kleiber, D. A. (1997). *A social psychology of leisure*. Venture Publishing Inc.

Marsden, J., Darke, S., Hall, W., Hickman, M., Holmes, J., Humphreys, K., & West, R. (2020). Mitigating and learning from the impact of COVID-19 infection on addictive disorders. *Addiction*, *115*(6), 1007.

Menec, V. H., & Chipperfield, J. G. (1997). Remaining active in later life: The role of locus of control in seniors' leisure activity participation, health, and life satisfaction. *Journal of Aging and Health*, *9*(1), 105–125.

Merkoulova, I., & Merkoulova, M. (2021). Le monde entier est un théâtre: Sémiotique de la culture à l'époque de la crise sanitaire. In I. Merkoulova (Ed.), Новая нормальность, новые формы жизни: семиотика в эПоху кризисов (pp. 144–146). GAUGN.

Ministry of Health of the Republic of Türkiye. (2020). *COVID-19 Nedir?* https://covid19.saglik.gov.tr/TR-66300/covid-19-nedir-.html

Ministry of Health of the Republic of Türkiye. (2023). Pandemic. https://covid19.saglik.gov.tr/TR-66494/pandemi.html

Morse, K. F., Fine, P. A., & Friedlander, K. J. (2021). Creativity and leisure during COVID-19: Examining the relationship between leisure activities, motivations, and psychological well-being. *Frontiers in Psychology*, *12*, 609967.

Nicola, M., Alsafi, Z., & Sohrabi, C. (2020). The socio-economic implications of the Coronavirus pandemic (COVID-19): A review. *International Journal of Surgery*, *78*, 185–193.

Nishi, D., Uehara, R., Kondo, M., & Matsuoka, Y. (2010). Reliability and validity of the Japanese version of the Resilience Scale and its short version. *BioMedical Central Research Notes*, *3*, 310.

Odabaşı, Y. (1999). Tüketim kültürü: Yetinen toplumun tüketen topluma dönüşümü. *Sistem Yayıncılık*.

Özel, Ç. H., & Can, İ. I. (2021). COVID-19 pandemisi sürecinde boş zaman aktivitelerinin dönüşümü. *Turar Turizm ve Araştırma Dergisi*, *10*(2), 63–98.

Richardson, G. E. (2002). The metatheory of resilience and resiliency. *Journal of Clinical Psychology*, *58*(3), 307–321.

Rosu, A. (2020). *Making sense of distance. Mobility in staycation as a case of proximity tourism*. Master's thesis. Lund University.

Sevinç, F., & Özel, Ç. H. (2018). Boş zaman aktivitesi olarak dalış ve yaşam doyumu ile ilişkisi. *Dokuz Eylül Üniversitesi Sosyal Bilimler Enstitüsü Dergisi*, *20*(3), 397–415.

Sucu, İ. (2020). Yeni dünya düzeninde dönüşümün iletişim ve medyadaki ilk adımları: COVID-19 sonun başlangıcında yeni bir dijital çağ. *Journal of Human and Social Sciences*, *3*(2), 556–566.

Thelwall, M., & Thelwall, S. (2020). COVID-19 tweeting in English: Gender differences. *El Profesional de la Información, 9*(3), e290301.

Torkildsen, G. (1992). *Leisure and recreation management.* E & FN Spon.

Ünlü, D. G. (2021). COVID-19 pandemisi dönemindeki ev içi boş zaman aktivitelerinin dijital yansıması. *Türkiye İletişim Araştırmaları Dergisi,* (38), 1–18.

Voll, K., Gauger, F., & Pfnür, A. (2022). Work from anywhere: Traditional workation, coworkation and workation retreats: A conceptual review. *World Leisure Journal,* 1–25.

Part 8

Impact of War Tourism

Chapter 16

How Does the Russia–Ukraine War Pave the Way to Diaspora Tourism in Ukraine?

Mehmet Yavuz Çetinkaya[a], *Yurdanur Yumuk*[b]
and Halyna Kushniruk[c]

[a]Pamukkale University, Türkiye
[b]Karabük University, Türkiye
[c]Ivan Franko National University of Lviv, Ukraine

Learning Objectives

After reading and studying this chapter, you should be able to:

- understand the meaning of diaspora and how it manifests as a type of tourism;
- be familiar with the definition and characteristics of diaspora tourism;
- be aware of the impact of the Russia–Ukraine war on Ukrainian tourism;
- know how the Russia–Ukraine war paves the way for diaspora tourism in Ukraine.

Abstract

Diaspora tourism primarily refers to various population groups, including migrants, foreign workers, political refugees, ethnic and religious minorities and overseas communities living away from their ancestral homeland for various reasons. Throughout history, people have been forced to leave their original homeland due to various factors ranging from economic crises to natural and human-made tragedies, including war. The 24 February 2022 unjustified and unproved Russia's war of aggression against Ukraine, which started on the heels of the two-year COVID-19 pandemic, has resulted in massive and terrible consequences for many domains of political, economic and social life. The Russian invasion of Ukraine has generated the largest historical migration flows at a scale unforeseen in Europe since World War II.

Future Tourism Trends Volume 1, 241–256
doi:10.1108/978-1-83753-244-520241016

Since Russia invaded Ukraine, at least 12 million people have been displaced from their homes, according to the United Nations. The unprecedented influx of the Ukrainian people raises concerns about future developments, issues and challenges associated with Ukrainians' presence in other countries, particularly neighbouring ones. Therefore, this chapter analyses the possibility of diaspora tourism for Ukrainians shortly by utilising a critical approach when the situation stabilises in Ukraine. To begin with, this chapter first explains diaspora tourism with its definition and characteristics. Furthermore, it reviews the literature on the Russia–Ukraine war and its impact on Ukrainian tourism. In conclusion, it discusses the new Ukrainian diaspora wave soon.

Keywords: Diaspora; diaspora tourism; Russia–Ukraine war; impact of war on tourism; Russia; Ukraine

Introduction

International tourism began to develop on a massive scale in the twentieth century and gained the fastest growth rates, mainly in countries where appropriate economic and organisational conditions were created. At the same time, favourable factors led to the leadership of specific regions and countries in global tourism, and conversely, undesirable factors reduced the tourist flow. In addition to internal factors (market conditions, market segmentation, advertising, human resources, seasonality, etc.), tourism development is also influenced by external factors (geopolitical, economic, socio-demographic, scientific and technical), among which we should pay attention to geopolitical factors (political upheavals, terrorist attacks, military conflicts) which affect the dynamics and distribution of tourist flows (Barvinok, 2022a). An example of such a damaging process is the Russia–Ukraine war which affected the development of tourism in Ukraine and stopped it.

From 2000 to 2014, Ukraine has been steadily increasing its tourism activities while not fully utilising its tourism and recreational potential, and the number of tourist flows has been increasing annually (Quirini-Popławski et al., 2022). However, geopolitical factors – the beginning of the Russia–Ukraine war in 2014 (Romanova, 2018), the COVID-19 pandemic in 2020 (Rutynskyi & Kushniruk, 2020), and since 2022 the outbreak of a full-scale war and hostilities – have hindered this development, leading to a decrease and, in some regions, the disappearance of tourist flows (Bashchak, 2022). Since 24 February 2022, Russia's armed aggression in Ukraine has been ongoing, resulting in substantial human losses and significant damage to infrastructure and economic sectors, including tourism. The war devastated the tourism industry, disrupted financial, energy and food markets, and caused rampant inflation. As a result, tourism in central, eastern and southern Ukraine has completely stopped. Instead of developing domestic tourism in Ukraine, millions of people have migrated, and massive departures of Ukrainian citizens abroad are unrelated to tourism (Motsa et al., 2022).

After the war, Ukraine has a big chance to restore its tourism potential by attracting foreign investment and opening new destinations, cultural monuments and cities because foreigners' interest in Ukraine has grown significantly compared to the pre-war period (Barvinok, 2022b; Fastovets, 2022a). Given that many Ukrainians have gone abroad due to the war, opportunities and prospects for developing diaspora tourism are being paved today. Those living in other countries will be motivated to travel to where they were born and where their families come from. Ukrainians will be eager to visit their heroic cities to experience history and culture after the war. Developing diaspora tourism can be crucial for recovering Ukraine's hospitality industry. Emigrants or their descendants can also spread the word about the attractions in Ukraine, being sources of valuable word-of-mouth advertising. Moreover, diaspora tourism is not necessarily seasonal and provides opportunities for employment and infrastructure use during off-peak periods.

Thus, diaspora tourism can be a sign of an undervalued tourism market. That is why there is a need to study the impact of the Russia–Ukraine war on domestic and international tourist flows in Ukraine, in greater depth to highlight, paving the way for forming a new wave of diaspora tourism as a result of enormous migration flows due to the war.

Understanding Diaspora Tourism – Its Definition and Characteristics

In today's modern world, a significant number of people tend to remember and experience nostalgia for specific locations or sites from their past, whether they are hometown, alma mater or childhood house (Oxfeld & Long, 2004). As a result, many people are often inspired to travel because they would like to come back and, thus, reconnect with their past (Pearce, 2012). There are several sorts of tourism which are associated with the phenomena of people with migrant ancestry travelling to their homeland, including *Ethnic Tourism* (King, 1994), *Personal Heritage Tourism* (Timothy, 1997), *Ethnic Reunion* (Stephenson, 2002), *Ancestral Tourism* (Fowler, 2003), *Legacy Tourism* (McCain & Ray, 2003), *Pilgrimage Tourism* (Schramm, 2004), *Roots Tourism* (Basu, 2004), *Genealogy Tourism* (Meethan, 2004), *Diaspora Tourism* (Holsey, 2004) and *Visiting Friends and Relatives Tourism* (Uriely, 2010). Diaspora tourism, which refers to those with immigrant ancestry travelling to their motherland and has expanded into a broader expression to define generated, consumed and experienced tourist activities by diaspora (Coles & Timothy, 2004), is one such example.

Diaspora, openly described, is 'the dispersal of a people from its original homeland' (Butler, 2001, p. 189). The geographical dispersion of people who belong to the same community (Bordes-Benayoun, 2002) and a forced displacement (Sheffer, 2003) from a native country with strong ethnic group identity and consciousness (Vertovec, 2004), the word 'diaspora' was initially related to the Jewish people's forced exile from Israel land to settle outside their traditional homeland. However, the term was associated with other migrant groups that uphold strong collective identities and self-defined or labelled themselves as diaspora in time (Huang et al., 2018). Many different population groups are typically referred to as diaspora, including political refugees, migrants, foreign labourers, religious and ethnic minorities, overseas communities and others living outside their homeland for various reasons (Shuval, 2000). Several generations later, these population groups always retain cultural and psychological attachments to their original locations (Stephenson, 2002).

Cohen (1997) labelled diaspora groups into five categories depending on the reason for leaving the homeland: (i) victim/refugee diaspora, including Jews and Africans (ii) imperial/colonial diaspora, including Ancient Greek, Spanish, British and Portuguese (iii) labour/service diaspora, including indentured Indians, Japanese and Chinese (iv) trade/business/professional diaspora, including Lebanese, Japanese, Chinese and Indians (v) cultural/hybrid/postmodern diaspora, including Caribbean people, Indians and Chinese (Huang et al., 2018). Diaspora groups, sharing a common heritage, are people dispersed worldwide. However, they were brought together as a community by their actual or imagined common ties, such as ethnicity, religion, culture, language, national identity and race (Coles & Timothy, 2004). They are usually very proud of their origins, actively engaged in both their home and host country, well-educated and qualified and contribute considerably to the territorial and economic intelligence of the country of origin (Paul & Michel, 2013). Furthermore, as tourists, customers and investors, the diaspora contributes to the tourism industry (Seraphin, 2020). The diaspora groups, while returning home as tourists, are eager to support the local economy and help the community's income by preferring locally produced foods and beverages, staying in hotels and dining in restaurants owned and run by local people, and purchasing cultural artefacts as well as visiting their hometown and reuniting with friends and families (Wah, 2013).

Diaspora tourism, defined as tourism, which diasporic population groups create, consume and experience (Coles & Timothy, 2004), has become an increasingly important phenomenon due to the dramatically increasing number of international migrants and their heroic wish to maintain closer ties to their ancestral hometown (Li & Chan, 2017). It stands for the people who were previously compelled to leave their homeland for various reasons, including conflicts, wars, natural disasters and economic crises throughout history and started to visit their homeland (Tanrisever, 2016). Diaspora tourism, embraced by expressions such: as *Roots Tourism, Diasporic, Genealogical, Ancestry* or *Nostalgic*, is underlined by its two significant aspects: identity and tourism. Diaspora tourists are inspired to travel to regions where they think they have roots and from where they believe their family members are thought to have originated (Corsale & Vuytsyk, 2016). Further, they visit their ancestral homeland to reconnect with their heritage (Li et al., 2020). They are more likely to feel a more substantial commitment to the visited destination than other international tourists, as their home or ancestral homeland allows them to experience the destination differently. They are typically more in favour of supporting heritage conservation and the local economy (Huang et al., 2016).

Diaspora tourism, often referred to as *Roots or Ethnic Tourism* (Morgan et al., 2003), connects migrants with the civic processes in their original country (Ostrowski, 1991), provides spiritual renewal to migrants (Pierre, 2009), maintains a collective identity (Morgan et al., 2003). Furthermore, by connecting the past and the present, diaspora tourism acts as a responsible counterpoint to prevalent types of tourism that might retain cross-cultural misunderstandings (Raymond & Hall, 2008). It also promotes authentic heritage preservation in destination settings, which aligns with the UN Sustainable Development Goals (Addo, 2011). It also provides various employment opportunities to destinations during off-peak seasons since it is less seasonal than international tourism (Perez-Lopez, 2007).

Diaspora tourism has been the subject of interest for studies to understand better how it strengthens migrants' attachment to place (Li & McKercher, 2016), ties to diasporic/ancestral culture and identity (Mathijsen, 2019), create various sorts of social capital (Elo & Minto-Coy, 2018) and improves self-esteem, life satisfaction and well-being (Li & Chan, 2020). Therefore, investigating diaspora tourism's motivations, impacts, experiences and consequences has received more attention from scholars and practitioners for 20 years (Li & Chan, 2017). Today, many tourists are inspired to participate in diaspora tourism for various motivations. These are (1) seeking homeland connection/nostalgia, (2) seeking one's roots, (3) seeking emotions, (4) discovery or homeland experience, (5) seeking pride, (6) seeking family reunion and (7) escape (Otoo et al., 2021).

Diaspora tourism comprises many complex dispersal categories, making it nearly impossible to determine their numbers and borders (Sheffer, 2006). According to the Organization for Economic Cooperation and Development (OECD), the global migrant diaspora population topped 232 million in 2003, up from 77 million in the 1960s (OECD, 2015). Over the last 10 years, more than 4 million people have moved permanently to other countries annually, with the total number of international migrants reaching 244 million in 2015. The estimated diaspora population happened to be 272 million people in 2019, by the Department of Economic and Social Affairs, Population Division in the United Nations (United Nations, 2019). Diaspora tourism offers enormous worldwide potential for destinations due to its rapid rise, expansion and prevalence across many national economies (Yankholmes & McKercher, 2015). In addition, diasporic population groups have more opportunities to travel to their country of origin since international tourism becomes more convenient and economical (Kasinitz et al., 2008), and diaspora tourism is expected to grow as travel options become more affordable (Iorio & Corsale, 2013).

Impact of Russia–Ukraine War on Tourism in Ukraine

Military conflicts can globally change the structure of tourist flows, lead the tourism industry to decline, cause loss of recreational potential and destruction of entire cities and historically attractive monuments, reduce the level of safety and protection of tourists, migration, deterioration of the country's tourist attractiveness, etc. Tourist flows express the level of tourism development in a country or region, and the tourist is the central unit of measurement of tourism activity. The increase in inbound tourism flows by 2013 demonstrated Ukraine's tourist attractiveness to tourists from other countries (Lozynskyy & Kushniruk, 2020). From 2000 to 2013, receiving about 25 million international tourists a year,

Ukraine entered the list of top 10 leading tourist destinations worldwide and became an influential recipient of international visitors.

However, the volume of international tourist flows depends on several global security factors that may threaten tourism activities, including geopolitical instability in the country (Barvinok, 2022a). Fundamental changes in the structure and volume of international tourist flows to Ukraine occurred in 2014, caused by the Russia–Ukraine war outbreak and the resulting financial and geopolitical crisis. Since 2014, Ukraine has experienced a significant decline in inbound tourist flows, which has had a negative impact on the country's socio-economic development indicators in general. In 2014, the number of inbound tourists halved compared to the previous year (Fig. 16.1). The flow of tourists from the aggressor country has also decreased. While in 2013, Russia accounted for 41.6% of inbound tourist arrivals, in 2014, this figure dropped to 18.6% (State Statistics Service of Ukraine, 2021). During 2009–2013, the number of outbound tourist arrivals steadily increased; in 2014, the number of outbound tourists decreased by 5.9%.

A record-low number of foreign tourists visited Ukraine in 2015. This decline in the development of the Ukrainian tourism industry should be attributed solely to the deterioration of Ukraine's image in the world, including tourism, due to the sense of insecurity caused by the armed conflict in Donbas, the annexation of Crimea, and mass protests in Kyiv (Romanova, 2018). Thus, in 2016, according to the World Economic Forum, Ukraine was ranked among the top 10 most dangerous countries for travelling in the world. In 2016–2018, the number of inbound tourists increased steadily: 7.3% in 2016, 6.8% in 2017 and 0.7% in 2018. The situation with outbound tourist flows improved, increasing compared to

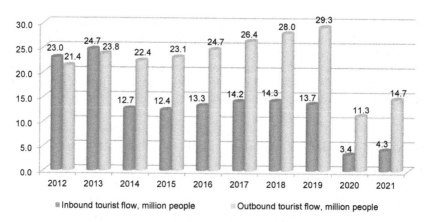

Fig. 16.1.   Tourist Flows in Ukraine, 2012–2021. *Source:* Compiled by the authors based on data from the State Statistics Service of Ukraine, 2021; Tourist Barometer of Ukraine, 2020; State Border Guard Service of Ukraine, 2021.

previous years: by 6.9% in 2016, 6.9% in 2017, 6.1% in 2018 and by 4.6% in 2019. The number of outbound tourists reached and exceeded the mark recorded before the start of the Russia–Ukraine war, reaching a record number of almost 30 million people in 2019. The number of domestic tourists in Ukraine has also changed significantly since the beginning of the Russia–Ukraine war. Since 2014, the number of domestic tourists has sharply decreased by 54.06% and remained at this level until 2020, which is mainly due to the annexation of Crimea, as many Ukrainians chose the Southern coast of Crimea for summer vacations.

In 2020 and 2021, the structure and number of tourist flows to Ukraine were significantly affected by the global crisis caused by the spread of the COVID-19 pandemic. Therefore, it becomes impossible to trace and analyse the impact of the Russia–Ukraine war during this period. According to the World Tourism Organization and the State Border Guard Service of Ukraine, Ukraine welcomed 13.7 million foreign visitors in 2019. In 2020, the number of foreigners visiting the country decreased by four times, amounting to 3.4 million. In 2020, the number of outbound tourists decreased by 61%. However, domestic tourists increased by 45.8%, driven by quarantine restrictions due to the spread of COVID-19 and border closures, so tourists rested and travelled in Ukraine.

The second half of 2021 marked the beginning of a partial recovery in Ukraine's tourism industry after the crisis caused by quarantine restrictions and border closures in 2020. A significant influx of tourists from other countries, including Saudi Arabia, also contributed to the recovery from this crisis. Statistical indicators of 2021 showed positive prospects for the growth of tourist flows and the gradual recovery of the tourism market (Fastovets, 2022b). In 2021, the number of foreigners who visited Ukraine increased by 26.5% to almost 4.3 million, and the number of Ukrainian citizens who crossed the state border increased by 30.1%.

Russia's full-scale invasion of Ukraine on 24 February 2022 threatened tourism in Ukraine and the international travel sector, which has just begun to recover from the losses caused by the COVID-19 pandemic. In fact, since 24 February, the inbound tourist flow has been lost by 100%, business tourism has been frozen, and domestic tourism has turned into a movement of internally displaced persons. This is a massive blow to Ukraine's tourism industry, as it has decreased the number of tourists for an indefinite period. Restoring many cultural and architectural monuments, nature reserves, infrastructure and transportation routes that have suffered enormous damage will require much time and significant investment. The scale of losses and destruction in 2022 due to the war cannot be accurately calculated, as part of the territory is under occupation, and hostilities continue in the border areas. The war has hurt Ukraine's tourist attractiveness, which is now nearly zero. Foreign tourists are unable and unwilling to visit Ukraine due to regular massive artillery shelling, rocket and bomb attacks, significant destruction of infrastructure, increased insecurity, military operations, closure of airspace for civil aviation and disruption of logistics in Ukraine. Thus, the Russia–Ukraine war has led to a noticeable decrease in international tourist flows (Nosyriev et al., 2022). Most foreigners who arrived in Ukraine in 2022 were journalists, diplomats, volunteers, civic activists, relatives and friends of Ukrainians. As for outbound tourism, the situation is somewhat different: most Ukrainians are interested in travelling abroad for evacuation purposes, not for vacation or leisure (Roik & Nedzvetska, 2022). Economic and financial factors affected outbound tourism and tourist demand, the devaluation of the hryvnia, transportation opportunities (only land transport is available), restrictions on travel abroad for men liable for military service and moral aspects (Bashchak, 2022).

According to the United Nations High Commissioner for Refugees (UNHCR) Ukraine, as of 18 April 2023, the number of refugees from Ukraine registered for temporary protection in Europe amounted to 8,174,189 persons. 5,044,039 refugees participate in national temporary protection and support programmes (UNHCR Ukraine, 2023). As of 16 April 2023, the most significant number of refugees with temporary protection status was in Poland – 1 million 583.6 thousand, and in Germany – 922.7 thousand Ukrainians. The Czech Republic is the third largest host country for Ukrainians, with 504.1 thousand registered for temporary protection. The United Kingdom is in fourth place with 201.0 thousand persons, Spain is in fifth place with 173.8 thousand and Italy closes the top six with 173.2 thousand persons. Ukrainians are also registered for temporary protection in Bulgaria, France, Romania, Slovakia and other countries (State Border Guard Service of Ukraine, 2022; UNHCR Ukraine, 2023). In total, 20,421,761 persons, primarily women and children, crossed the border from Ukraine to neighbouring countries between 24 February 2022 and 11 April 2023. Approximately 11,889,878 persons returned to Ukraine (excluding data from Russia and Belarus) (UNHCR Ukraine, 2023). These figures reflect cross-border movements (not individuals). However, movements back to Ukraine can be pendular and do not necessarily indicate sustainable returns as the situation across Ukraine remains highly volatile and unpredictable.

Domestic tourism is also experiencing a severe crisis due to the migration of people from dangerous regions to safer ones instead of visiting other parts of Ukraine for tourism purposes. A significant part of the population has moved from places of permanent residence in dangerous areas but has not registered as internally displaced persons. Various tourist complexes, hotels, hostels and catering establishments are used to provide accommodation for internally displaced persons. Therefore, tourism business management focuses on volunteering and turning tourism hubs into humanitarian or volunteer headquarters.

In 2022, due to the war, state budget revenues from the tourism industry decreased by almost 31% compared to 2021. Thus, the total number of taxpayers engaged in tourism activities decreased by an average of 17%. Hotels paid the most taxes – almost UAH 898 million. At the same time, there was a 46% increase in tax paid by boarding houses and hostels used as temporary shelters for refugees. There was also a decline in tax revenues from tour operators – by 35%, and from travel agencies – by 27%. In 2022, the tourist fees amounted to UAH 178 million 948 thousand, 24% less than in 2021 (UAH 235 million 461 thousand).

The decline was recorded in 14 regions of Ukraine. These are primarily territories that are temporarily occupied due to the war. For example, tourist fees decreased by 95% in the Kherson region, 90% in the Mykolaiv region, 83% in the Donetsk region and 80% in the Luhansk region. The capital replenished its budget by UAH 31 million 474 thousand for tourist fees, which is twice less compared to 2021. In 2022, the Lviv region was the leader in tourist fee payment – UAH 41 million 430 thousand, which is 79% more than in 2021 (State Agency for Tourism Development of Ukraine, 2022). Nevertheless, the tourism industry continues to function even during a full-scale war. It is important to note that the tours held in the country's west include bomb shelters along the route for protection in case of air raids, which is very important today, as the war is still ongoing.

Tourist flows will be able to resume after the complete cessation of hostilities, which is related to security factors that play an essential role in the organisation of tourism. Ukraine will need to re-establish its image as an attractive tourist destination, so the government will need to take several effective measures to overcome the consequences of the post-war period for the tourism sector, which would lead to the restoration of tourist flows. Thus, Russia's full-scale war against Ukraine has had an extremely negative impact on the development of the tourism industry in Ukraine. However, considering the experience of countries that have been tested by war, Ukraine should have new opportunities for developing both domestic and international tourism. An important place should be given to 'memory tourism' (to honour the memory of those who died during the military invasion), 'war tourism' (to highlight the scale of the war and destruction on the territory of the country), 'national-patriotic tourism' (to protect future genera-tions from the mistakes of the past) and 'diaspora tourism' (to provide an opportunity to visit the places where Ukrainians were born, those who left the country due to the war).

A New Wave in Post-War Ukraine: Ukrainian Diaspora

Ukraine, a European country broke its ties with the Soviet Union in 1991 and became an independent state (Dancs, 2009), has a long history of multicultur-alism, with various nations and ethnic groups inhabiting its territory for centuries (Corsale & Vuytsyk, 2016). With borders with seven countries and a strategic geopolitical position between the West and Russia (Sass, 2020), Ukraine's emigration history has been long and complicated, resulting in significant and diverse groups of people living in other countries (Smith & Jackson, 1999). Divisions among socialists and nationalists, Catholic and Orthodox churches, new wave immigrants, and long-settled members of the society have all strained the Ukrainian diaspora at some point (Satzewich, 2002).

At the end of the 19th century, Ukraine underwent a massive emigration process, resulting from numerous socio-economic challenges that impacted the region (Corsale & Vuytsyk, 2015). There were four primary waves of ethnic Ukrainian emigration from Ukraine (Hodovanska, 2011; Zubyk, 2013). The first wave was economical and continued until World War I starting in the early 1870s; the second one stemmed from both economic and political circumstances and happened between two world wars (1918–1939); and the third was primarily political and began during World War II and lasted until the immediate post-war period. A fourth wave, marked primarily by labour emigration, began following Ukraine's independence in 1991. Forced population mixing within the Soviet Union resulted in massive Ukrainian communities living in former Soviet countries, including Russia, Kazakhstan, Uzbekistan, Kyrgyzstan and Latvia. The first three waves of Ukrainian emigration mainly went to Canada and the United States, with smaller flows going to South America, primarily Brazil, Argentina and Paraguay, Western Europe and Australia, while the most recent one is going to Western Europe (Kacharaba, 1995, 2003).

Following Russia's unlawful and unproven military invasion of Ukraine on 24 February 2022, Ukraine underwent unprecedented historic migratory movements. Between 24 February 2022 and 7 March 2023, 19,293,161 persons, predominantly women and children, crossed the Ukrainian border into neighbouring countries (UNHCR Ukraine, 2023). This rapid influx of Ukrainian refugees after Russia's massive aggression could catalyse Ukraine's fifth diaspora wave.

Case Study

St. Patrick's Day, also known as St. Paddy's Day in Ireland, is a national religious holiday and the largest celebratory event in the Irish cultural calendar, traditionally in honour of the St. Patrick of Ireland. Starting first as an official Christian feast in the early 17th century to commemorate St. Patrick, regarded as the Apostle of Ireland, St. Patrick's Day has now become a day of significance worldwide and is celebrated on 17 March annually around the world by the Irish diaspora communities dressing up in green with massive parades, parties and plenty of great food and beverages. St. Patrick's Day, an essential component of Irish cultural identity and a symbol of the country's rich history, heritage and traditions, is an excellent example of how a cultural event can become a significant part of a country's tourism industry. The Irish government recognised St. Patrick's Day's potential as a tourist attraction and started promoting it as a significant event to attract tourists. As a vital part of diaspora tourism, St. Patrick's Day attracts a significant number of tourists worldwide, generating substantial revenue for the host country. The Irish diaspora communities, destroyed by war, famine and centuries of economic deterioration since 1800, have spread throughout the world, with significant communities in the United States, Canada, Australia and many European countries. These diaspora communities consider St. Patrick's Day an opportunity to connect with their roots, heritage and identity. They celebrate St. Patrick's Day with parades, festivals and other cultural events, which have become significant tourist attractions (Ergil, 2022; Scully, 2012).

Research Box

This study conceptually explored the future travel mobility of the Ukrainian diaspora, which emerged with the outbreak of the Russia–Ukraine war, within the scope of diaspora tourism in a cause-effect relationship. However, the most significant limitation of the study is that no empirical research was carried out to determine Ukrainian diaspora tourists' travel behaviour. For this reason, more research on the travel motivations of Ukrainian diaspora tourists should be done utilising both qualitative and quantitative research methods in the future. On the other hand, investigating intergenerational differences in travel motivations may provide an in-depth understanding of the subject. Similarly, researching the relationship between life satisfaction and well-being levels of Ukrainian tourists participating in diaspora tourism might provide a different perspective on the well-being concept, which has been extensively studied in the tourism literature recently. Finally, the role of diaspora tourism in the Ukrainian economy, its impact on heritage and culture preservation, its relationship with the global economy and its potential for promoting cross-cultural understanding and cooperation should be further researched.

Conclusion

Diaspora tourism, a unique way to explore one's identity and history, is a form of travel that involves visiting the homeland of one's ancestors or relatives and the history and culture of the country or region visited. This sort of tourism which allows people to have a deeper understanding of their family's background and to connect with their ancestral heritage in a personal and meaningful way is becoming increasingly popular among people willing to learn more about their cultural and ethnic roots and connect with their cultural heritage.

The ongoing war between Russia and Ukraine, which began formally in 2022, had far-reaching impacts on the tourism industry, particularly within the Ukrainian diaspora community, one of the biggest ones in the world with an estimated population of 20 million. In addition, many Ukrainians living abroad were significantly affected by the conflict, and some members participated in efforts to support Ukraine's independence and sovereignty.

In the aftermath of the war with Russia, there might be an opportunity for Ukrainian diaspora tourism to flourish as people from all around the world seek to connect with their roots and ancestral homeland and explore Ukraine's rich cultural heritage. Diaspora tourism has the potential to be a significant driver for Ukraine's economic recovery (Corsale & Vuytsyk, 2015) and cultural exchange, as well as offering a wide variety of attractions that showcase the country's rich history, vibrant culture and stunning natural beauty. Furthermore, Ukrainian diaspora tourists can promote Ukraine's cultural heritage and play an important role as first movers in creating new opportunities in the worldwide market. Emigrants and their descendants can also help spread the word about Ukraine's attractions, providing valuable word-of-mouth advertising (Corsale & Vuytsyk, 2015). This may result in attracting non-diaspora customers to Ukraine. On the other hand, Ukrainian diaspora communities may help to boost the country's struggling tourism industry and demonstrate that Ukraine is a safe and welcoming destination for tourists by organising solidarity tours and showing support for the country.

Many cultural sites and artefacts were damaged or destroyed during the war, and efforts were underway to restore and conserve them. By visiting these sites and supporting conservation efforts, diaspora members can help to preserve Ukraine's rich cultural legacy for future generations. Additionally, Ukrainian diaspora tourists can help the country's economic development by supporting local businesses, enterprises and organisations. By staying at locally owned hotels, eating at local restaurants and shopping at local markets, tourists can help create jobs and support the local economy.

In conclusion, Ukrainian diaspora tourism has the potential to be a significant force for economic growth, cultural interaction, peacebuilding, heritage preservation and personal enrichment in Ukraine. With continued investment and development, Ukrainian tourism can continue to grow and thrive, creating opportunities for diaspora members and visitors worldwide. Furthermore, by exploring the country's rich history and living culture, supporting local businesses and organisations, engaging in cultural exchange and promoting understanding and reconciliation of diaspora members can contribute to strengthening relationships between their ancestral homeland and adopted country and contribute to a brighter future for Ukraine and its people.

Discussion Questions

- What are the leading travel motivations of the Ukrainian diaspora?
- Which strategies can be implemented to improve the quality and sustainability of Ukrainian diaspora tourism experiences?
- What are the potential consequences of the Russia–Ukraine war on the global tourism and travel industry?
- Will Turkey continue to be a popular destination for Ukrainians after the war?

References

Addo, E. (2011). Diversification of the tourist landscape on Ghana's Atlantic Coast: Fort, castle, and beach hotel/resort operations in the tourism industry. *Journal of Tourism Consumption & Practice, 3*(1), 1–26.

Barvinok, N. (2022a). The impact of global security factors on the development of international tourism in Ukraine. *Veda a perspektivy, 4*(11), 139–151.

Barvinok, N. (2022b). Prospects for the development of military tourism on the territory of Ukraine after the end of the Russian-Ukrainian War. *The Actual Problems of Regional Economy Development, 18*(2), 206–217.

Bashchak, M. (2022). Influence of geopolitical instability on the development of tourism. *Tourism and Hospitality Industry in Central and Eastern Europe, 5,* 5–12.

Basu, P. (2004). Route metaphors of "roots-tourism" in the Scottish Highland diaspora. In S. Coleman & J. Eade (Eds.), *Reframing pilgrimage: Cultures in motion* (pp. 150–174). Routledge.

Bordes-Benayoun, C. (2002). Les diasporas, dispersion spatiale, expérience sociale. *Revue de Sciences Sociales au Sud, 22*(2), 23–36.

Butler, K. D. (2001). Defining diaspora, refining a discourse. *Diaspora: A Journal of Transnational Studies, 10*(2), 189–219.

Cohen, R. (1997). *Global diasporas: An introduction.* University of Washington Press.

Coles, T., & Timothy, D. J. (2004). "My field is the world": Conceptualising diasporas, travel, and tourism. In T. Coles & D. J. Timothy (Eds.), *Tourism, diasporas, and space* (pp. 1–29). Routledge.

Corsale, A., & Vuytsyk, O. (2015). Diasporic tourism in Western Ukraine: Perspectives and challenges. *Visnyk of the Lviv University. Series Geography,* (49), 165–179.

Corsale, A., & Vuytsyk, O. (2016). Long-distance attachments and implications for tourism development: The case of the Western Ukrainian diaspora. *Tourism Planning & Development, 13*(1), 88–110.

Dancs, L. (2009). Ukrajna társadalmi-gazdasági helyzete [Ukraine's Social and Economic Situation]. In Baranyi, B. (Ed.), *Kárpátalja [Transcarpathia]. MTA Regionális Kutatások Központja* (pp. 25–64). Dialóg Campus Kiadó.

Elo, M., & Minto-Coy, I. (2018). *Diaspora Networks in International Business.* Springer.

Ergil, L. Y. (2022). *Celebrating St. Paddy's Day and the Turkish-Irish Connection.* Daily Sabah. https://www.dailysabah.com/life/religion/celebrating-st-paddys-day-and-the-turkish-irish-connection. Accessed on March 25, 2023.

Fastovets, O. (2022a). Post-war tourism: Experience for Ukraine. *Economy and Society,* (40).

Fastovets, O. (2022b). Tourism in Ukraine during military actions. *Development of Management and Entrepreneurship Methods on Transport, 3*(80), 87–97.

Fowler, S. (2003). *Ancestral tourism* (pp. D31–D36). Insights.

Hodovanska, O. (2011). *The Newest Ukrainian Diaspora: Labour migrants in Italy, Spain and Portugal* [Новітня українська діаспора: трудові мігранти в Італії, Іспанії та Португалії]. Lviv: National Academy of Sciences of Ukraine.

Holsey, B. (2004). Transatlantic dreaming: Slavery, tourism and diasporic encounters. In F. Markowitz & A. H. Stefansson (Eds.), *Homecomings* (pp. 166–182). Lexington Books.

Huang, W. J., Hung, K., & Chen, C. C. (2018). Attachment to the home country or home town? Examining diaspora tourism across migrant generations. *Tourism Management, 68*(1), 52–65.

Huang, W. J., Ramshaw, G. P., & Norman, W. C. (2016). Homecoming or tourism? Diaspora tourism experience of second-generation immigrants. *Tourism Geographies, 18*(1), 59–79.

Iorio, M., & Corsale, A. (2013). Diaspora and tourism: Transylvanian Saxons visiting the homeland. *Tourism Geographies, 15*(2), 198–232.

Kacharaba, S. (1995). *Ukrainian emigration. Emigration movement from Eastern Galicia and Northern Bukovyna in 1890–1914* [Українська еміґрація. Еміґраційний рух зі Східної Галичини та Шівнічної Буковини в 1890–1914]. Ivan Franko National University of Lviv.

Kacharaba, S. (2003). *Emigration from Western Ukraine, 1919–1939* [Еміґрація з західної України, 1919–1939]. Ivan Franko National University of Lviv.

Kasinitz, P., Mollenkopf, J. H., Waters, M. C., & Holdaway, J. (2008). *Inheriting the city: The children of immigrants come of age.* Harvard University Press.

King, B. (1994). What is ethnic tourism? An Australian perspective. *Tourism Management, 15*(3), 173–176.

Li, T. E., & Chan, E. T. H. (2017). Diaspora tourism and well-being: A eudaimonic view. *Annals of Tourism Research, 63,* 205–206.

Li, T. E., & Chan, E. T. H. (2020). Diaspora tourism and well-being over life courses. *Annals of Tourism Research, 82,* 1–12.

Li, T. E., & McKercher, B. (2016). Developing a typology of diaspora tourists: Return travel by Chinese immigrants in North America. *Tourism Management, 56,* 106–113.

Li, T. E., McKercher, B., & Chan, E. T. H. (2020). Towards a conceptual framework for diaspora tourism. *Current Issues in Tourism, 23*(17), 2109–2126.

Lozynskyy, R., & Kushniruk, H. (2020). Dynamics and geographical structure of inbound tourism in political transit countries: The case of Ukraine. *Journal of Geology, Geography and Geoecology, 29*(2), 335–350.

Mathijsen, A. (2019). Home, sweet home? Understanding diasporic medical tourism behaviour. Exploratory research of Polish immigrants in Belgium. *Tourism Management, 72,* 373–385.

McCain, G., & Ray, N. M. (2003). Legacy tourism: The search for personal meaning in heritage travel. *Tourism Management, 24*(6), 713–717.

Meethan, K. (2004). "To stand in the shoes of my ancestors": Tourism and genealogy. In T. Coles & D. J. Timothy (Eds.), *Tourism, diasporas and space* (pp. 139–150). Routledge.

Morgan, N., Pritchard, A., & Pride, R. (2003). Marketing to the Welsh diaspora: The appeal to hiraeth and homecoming. *Journal of Vacation Marketing, 9*(1), 69–80.

Motsa, A., Shevchuk, S., & Sereda, N. (2022). Prospects of the post-war recovery of tourism in Ukraine. *Economy and Society,* (41).

National Tourism Organization of Ukraine. (2020). Tourist barometer of Ukraine. https://www.ntoukraine.org/nsts_analytics_ua.html

Nosyriev, O., Dedilova, T., & Tokar, I. (2022). The tourism and hospitality industry development in the Ukrainian economic strategy of post-conflict reconstruction. *Socioeconomic Problems and the State, 26*(1), 55–68.

Organisation for Economic Cooperation and Development. (2015). *Connecting with emigrants: A global profile of diasporas 2015.* OECD Publishing. https://doi.org/10.1787/9789264239845-en

Ostrowski, S. (1991). Ethnic tourism-focus on Poland. *Tourism Management, 12*(2), 125–130.

Otoo, F. E., Kim, S. S., & King, B. (2021). African diaspora tourism-how motivations shape experiences. *Journal of Destination Marketing & Management, 20,* 100565.

Oxfeld, E., & Long, L. D. (2004). Introduction: An ethnography of return. In L. D. Long & E. Oxfeld (Eds.), *Coming home? Refugees, migrants, and those who stayed behind* (pp. 1–15). University of Pennsylvania Press.

Paul, B., & Michel, T. (2013). Comment juguler les limitations financières des universités haïtiennes? *Haïti Perspectives, 2*(1), 57–63.

Pearce, P. L. (2012). The experience of visiting home and familiar places. *Annals of Tourism Research, 39*(2), 1024–1047.

Perez-Lopez, J. F. (2007). The diaspora as a commercial network for Cuban reconstruction. In *Cuba in transition* (p. 17).

Pierre, J. (2009). Beyond heritage tourism: Race and the politics of African-diasporic interactions. *Social Text, 27*(1), 59–81.

Quirini-Popławski, Ł., Tomczewska-Popowycz, N., Dorocki, S., Kushniruk, H., & Rutynskyi, M. (2022). Three decades of tourism development in independent Ukraine. From the collapse of the USSR to the conflict in the Donbas. In H. Janta, K. Andriotis, & D. Stylidis (Eds.), *Tourism planning and development in Eastern Europe* (pp. 117–132). CABI Regional Tourism Series. CABI International.

Raymond, E. M., & Hall, C. M. (2008). The development of cross-cultural (mis) understanding through volunteer tourism. *Journal of Sustainable Tourism, 16*(5), 530–543.

Roik, O., & Nedzvetska, O. (2022). Ways of development of the tourist sphere of Ukraine in the war period. *Scientific Bulletin of KSU.Series «Economic Sciences »,* (46), 11–15.

Romanova, A. (2018). Management of tourism industry development amidst armed conflicts. *Modern Economics*, (9), 93–104.

Rutynskyi, M., & Kushniruk, H. (2020). The impact of quarantine due to the COVID-19 pandemic on the tourism industry in Lviv (Ukraine). *Problems and Perspectives in Management, 18*(2), 194–205.

Sass, E. (2020). The impact of the eastern Ukrainian armed conflict on tourism in Ukraine. *Geo Journal of Tourism and Geosites, 30*, 880–888.

Satzewich, V. (2002). *The Ukrainian Diaspora*. Routledge.

Schramm, K. (2004). Coming home to the motherland: Pilgrimage tourism in Ghana. In S. Coleman & J. Eade (Eds.), *Reframing Pilgrimage: Cultures in motion* (pp. 133–149). Routledge.

Scully, M. (2012). Whose day is it anyway? St. Patrick's Day as a contested performance of national and diasporic Irishness. *Studies in Ethnicity and Nationalism, 12*(1), 118–135.

Seraphin, H. (2020). Childhood experience and (de) diasporisation: Potential impacts on the tourism industry. *Journal of Tourism, Heritage and Service Marketing, 6*(3), 14 24.

Sheffer, G. (2003). *Diaspora politics: At home abroad*. Cambridge University Press.

Sheffer, G. (2006). Transnationalism and ethnonational diasporism. *Diaspora: A Journal of Transnational Studies, 15*(1), 121–145.

Shuval, J. T. (2000). Diaspora migration: Definitional ambiguities and a theoretical paradigm. *International Migration, 38*(5), 41–56.

Smith, G., & Jackson, P. (1999). Narrating the nation: The 'imagined community' of Ukrainians in Bradford. *Journal of Historical Geography, 25*(3), 367–387.

State Agency for Tourism Development of Ukraine. (2022). *Official website*. https://tourism.gov.ua

State Border Guard Service of Ukraine. (2022). *Official website*. https://dpsu.gov.ua. Accessed on March 5, 2023.

State Statistics Service of Ukraine. (2021). *Official website*. http://www. ukrstat.gov. ua. Accessed on March 5, 2023.

Stephenson, M. L. (2002). Travelling to the ancestral homelands: The aspirations and experiences of a U.K. Caribbean community. *Current Issues in Tourism*, *5*(5), 378–425.

Tanrisever, C. (2016). Diaspora tourism: A case study from Turkey-Azarbaijan. *Turar Tourism and Research Journal*, *5*(2), 56–64.

Timothy, D. J. (1997). Tourism and the personal heritage experience. *Annals of Tourism Research*, *24*(3), 751–754.

Timothy, D. J., & Coles, T. (2004). Tourism and diasporas: Current issues and future opportunities. In T. Coles & D. J. Timothy (Eds.), *Tourism, diasporas and space* (pp. 291–297). Routledge.

UNHCR Ukraine. (2023). *Official website*. https://data.unhcr.org/en/situactions/ Ukraine

United Nations. (2019). Department of Economic and Social Affairs, population division. In *International Migration 2019*. Report (ST/ESA/SER.A/438). https://www.un. org/en/development/desa/population/migration/publications/migrationreport/docs/ InternationalMigration2019_Report.pdf

Uriely, N. (2010). "Home" and "away" in VFR tourism. *Annals of Tourism Research*, *37*(3), 854–857.

Vertovec, S. (2004). Religion and diaspora. In P. Antes, A. W. Geertz, & R. R. Warne (Eds.), *New approaches to the study of religion* (pp. 275–304). Walter de Gruyter GmbH & Co.

Wah, T. (2013). *Engaging the Haitian Diaspora* (p. 9). Cairo Review.

Yankholmes, A., & McKercher, B. (2015). Rethinking slavery heritage tourism. *Journal of Heritage Tourism*, *10*(3), 233–247.

Zubyk, A. (2013). *Diasporic tourism as an innovative type of tourism* [Діасцорний туризм як інноваційний вид туризму] (Vol. 59, pp. 195–199). Ivan Franko National University.

Chapter 17

The Effects of War on Tourism: Battlefields

Hande Akyurt Kurnaz[a] *and Ayşen Acun Köksalanlar*[b]

[a]Bolu Abant Izzet Baysal University, Türkiye
[b]Bursa Uludag University, Türkiye

Learning Objectives

After reading and studying this chapter, you should be able to:

- know about dark tourism;
- learn basic information about battlefields;
- discuss the impact of battlefields on tourism.

Abstract

In this chapter, we plan to describe the effects of war on tourism. Battlefield tourism was discussed within the effects of War on tourism. It is aimed to analyse the wars in world history and the consequences of these wars. War is a modern security problem with long-term severe consequences engraved on society. Wars, on any ground, always impact people's memories and activities (Smith, 1998). Wars leave their mark on society and are among the never forgotten events in history (Aliağaoğlu, 2008). Some of these events end with victory, while others end sadly. Wars affect tourism both positively and negatively. This chapter is essential to identify the contribution of tourism in battlefields, a different type of tourism, to the countries. In the context of battlefield tourism, this chapter will present a framework. It attempts to explain battlefield tourism through case studies. Document review and case study methods will be used. It is assumed that this chapter will bring the battlefields to tourism.

Keywords: War; the effects of war; war tourism; dark tourism; battlefields; battlefield tourism

---

Future Tourism Trends Volume 1, 257–267
Copyright © 2024 Hande Akyurt Kurnaz and Aysen Acun Köksalanlar
Published under exclusive licence by Emerald Publishing Limited
doi:10.1108/978-1-83753-244-520241017

Introduction

As consumer expectations of tourism change and world views gradually evolve, new searches and attractions emerge (Hacıoğlu & Avcıkurt, 2008). Special interest tourism, conducted with relatively few participants or individually, has its place and importance in the alternative tourism market. The tourist activities carried out in special interest tourism reflect the specifics of the destination (Akoğlan Kozak & Bahçe, 2009). Events such as grief, fear and death touch people, and tourism activities occur in the locations where these events occur. These tourism activities are defined as dark tourism and enhance the attractiveness of destinations from various aspects. Warfare tourism is a form of dark tourism, and battlefields are among the places that can be visited as part of dark tourism. Turkey, due to its several aspects, has experienced many wars. The act of visiting dark places is not a new concept. Some notable examples of places that can be included while discussing dark tourism are Waterloo, Vietnam, Turkey and Northern Ireland (Smith & Glen Croy, 2005). Even if the causes of War differ, they are often embedded in people's memories and influence tourist activities (Smith, 1998).

What Are Wars and Types?

In international relations, War is defined as resorting to violence through armed force between at least two organised parties to achieve results when diplomacy fails to resolve conflicts. More precisely, War is a conflict or collision involving massive physical force between countries, blocs or large groups within a country that is the main actors in the international system or large groups capable of using force within a country. Historically, the relations between states regarding using force continue through the state of War and peace and their actions. The concept of War, with its multidisciplinary structure and the new dimensions it has acquired throughout history, has an ever-increasing complexity. As a result of the gradual expansion of warfare and its qualitative deepening, terminology related to War has emerged. There are some characteristics of the concept of War: (1) War is the state of using force. (2) War involves a hostile attitude and/or action. (3) War causes a legal status. (4) The actor of War is the state. Within the framework of these characteristics, War is defined as 'a hostile intention and/or action involving the use of force, carried out by states or state groups using all or some elements of national power and considered by the parties as war' (Varlık, 2013).

In light of this definition, wars are classified along two main dimensions: size and 'scope and character'. According to their size, wars are divided into 'war of position//local war', 'limited war', 'regional war' and 'general wars'. In terms of their scope and character, wars are divided into two main subgroups: 'the reasons that characterise the final cause of the war' and 'the forces, weapons, and means of warfare employed and the change in the course of the war'. In terms of the first sub-category, 'the reasons that characterise the final cause of the war', wars can be listed as: (1) Border wars/land wars, (2) Revolutionary wars/wars of ideology, (3) Wars of independence, (4) Hegemony wars, (5) Wars of religion, (6) Wars of succession, (7) Civil wars, (8) Economy-based wars and (9) Law-based wars. The second sub-category, 'the forces, weapons and means of warfare employed and the change in the course of the war', includes (1) Regular/conventional wars, (2) Unconventional warfare, (3) Coalition and alliance wars, (4) Nuclear War, (5) Total War, (6) Asymmetrical wars and (7) Hybrid wars (Varlık, 2013). As the characteristics have changed over time, so have the types of warfare.

Today, the impact of changes, such as the fact that conflicts do not only arise from state monopoly, the short-term development of instruments of power, especially technology, on War and the concept of War are pretty significant (Öztürk, 2021).

The wars that began with the Peace of Westphalia of 1648, in which modern armies with modern weapons appeared, are called first-generation warfare. In this generation of wars, the workforce is the main tactical element instead of intense firepower, and a distinction is made between combatants and non-combatants. Second-generation warfare is total wars with heavy firepower that cover large areas. Third-generation warfare occurred with Blitzkrieg, based on the power of speed and manoeuvrability and was used by the Germans in World War II. During this period, elements of air power were brought into the equation, along with high technology. Fourth-generation warfare is network-centric warfare in which all political, economic, social and military networks are shared. Wars of this generation are warfares that aim to defeat large economies and military powers that extend over a long period and involve all sectors of social life. An example of this generation of wars is the Cold War, in which the parties pursued a policy of deterrence and balance, and sophisticated military technologies were used as diplomatic tools to prevent hot conflict. While various phenomena such as the September 11 attacks, the Ukraine war, ethnic conflict, rebellion and counterinsurgency, terrorism and counterterrorism have changed the nature of War, new types of War have emerged in the context of the actors, course and means of War. The parties are usually not states in the new generation wars, now called hybrid wars (Çelikpala, 2021).

Battlefield Tourism

Throughout history, societies have faced wars directly or indirectly. While these wars brought about the end of some societies, they enabled some societies to continue their lives by becoming more assertive. Wars are unnatural disasters irrationally resulting from the conflict of individuals or states (Prideaux, 2007). Turkish Language Association Dictionary (2005) defines the term 'war' as 'the armed struggle of states through the severance of their diplomatic relations'. This armed struggle can also take the form of a psychological, economic or political struggle. Undoubtedly, wars have left their mark on society in various ways. Over time, battlefields have become regions that attract people's attention. This is because factors such as death, massacre and War strongly influence people. This interaction leads tourism to move towards destinations with war sites.

Using the battlefields, tourists return to that time by walking through the areas where people were killed. Wars leave traces in the geographical space, and sometimes these traces are later rebuilt. Thanks to ongoing tourism research, battlefield tourism was introduced as a new phenomenon related to the growing interest in battlefields (Prideaux, 2007).

Wars have affected society in different ways. Tourism activities have also taken a new direction due to the impact of wars (Aliağaoğlu, 2008). Another form of dark tourism, in which tourist activities incorporate themes of death, fear, massacre and War, is battlefield tourism. Battlefields are essential not only for those conducting tourist activities but also for representing the era in question. The military attractions on the battlefields have led to the emergence of battlefield tourism (Aliağaoğlu, 2008).

Battlefields are crucial for tourism mobility and trigger deep emotional feelings in tourists. While wars were a source of pride for some societies, they had sad consequences for others (Prideaux, 2007). For example, the dropping of the atomic bomb by the United States on Hiroshima was a source of pride for the United States but a sad memory for Hiroshima. These examples can be increased. The effects of battlefields can also be experienced within the borders of other countries (Prideaux, 2007). For example, tourists from Australia and New Zealand visit the historic Çanakkale-Gallipoli Peninsula Historical National Park annually to hold memorial services for the Anzacs who fought in the Battle of Gallipoli.

With the development of tourism and the increase of wars and military conflicts since the beginning of the 19th century, battlefield tourism has developed (Baldwin & Sharpley, 2009). Although battlefield tourism is a part of war tourism, it falls under the concept of mourning tourism. There are numerous studies on battlefield tourism. For example, international literature includes studies of World War I and World War II battlefields and the motivations of tourists from Australia and New Zealand for Gallipoli and the Battle of Waterloo (Dunkley et al., 2007).

Many people travel to experience their vacation differently for a variety of motives, including family history, military appeal or curiosity. Leopold and Panakere claim that the specific reasons for battlefield tourism interest in learning and active role-playing (Panakera, 2007). Prideaux summarises the motivations for visiting battlefields differently. These motivations can be summarised as remembering comrades, reliving memories of loved ones who died in battle, challenging victory or being defeated (Prideaux, 2007). Walter (1993) argues that visiting a battlefield might be likened to a pilgrimage, although such experiences could be more energising religiously. Both experiences help with spiritual growth and healing on an emotional and psychological level (Shackley, 2001). Battlefields are locations where physical topography is changed by conflict, travel, commemoration and tourism into symbolic regions (Akbulut & Ekin, 2018).

Based upon a 2006 UK survey of battlefield tourism among 1000 people, 28% of participants had visited a battlefield, 45% said that they were interested in military history, 32% of the people were interested in family history and 46% of people interested in military history had visited a battlefield grave or war memorial (Baldwin & Sharpley, 2009). However, there was a difference in the experience of visiting battlefields. Veterans, leisure visitors, educational tourists, Armed Forces members (soldiers) and peace visitors are considered battlefield visitors (Baldwin & Sharpley, 2009).

Wars arouse national feelings in people; monuments and national parks have been erected to recall these feelings repeatedly. In this case, the kind of tourism that takes place on battlefields is called battlefield tourism (Aliağaoğlu, 2008). There are many national and international examples of battlefield tourism. For example, the Gallipoli Campaign, the Turkish War of Independence, the Battle of Sarikamish, the fronts where the Turkish War of Independence took place, the centres where the events that triggered the American Civil War, the Korean War, World War I and World War II took place and the regions that were exposed to the effects of these wars can be counted among the regions where battlefield tourism can be realised.

When visiting the battlefields, paying attention to many details is necessary. These details can be listed as follows:

- Mind your language.
- Dress appropriately for the battlefield.
- Show sensitivity.
- Be respectful.
- Remember that you may be walking on someone's grave.

Case Study

The Gallipoli Campaign

The Gallipoli Campaign is one of the greatest battles in human history. The naval and land battles between the Ottoman Empire and the Allied Powers of World War I on the Gallipoli Peninsula between 1915 and 1916 are referred to in the literature as the Gallipoli Campaign (2). Although the Turkish army was victorious at the War's end, it was devastated by the pain of losing hundreds of thousands of soldiers, and the War left deep scars on the Turks. The losses in the Gallipoli Campaign are also of great significance. The heavy loss of the Gallipoli Campaign was breathtakingly significant. Apart from various weapons, vehicles, equipment and ships, the enemy's losses amounted to 252 thousand people (British 205,000, French 47,000, while the loss of the Turks was 251,309) (Bircan, 1997). Anyone who visits the Gallipoli Peninsula Historical National Park, where the War was engraved on the landscape, feels this pain. These feelings also determine dark tourism and battlefield tourism, which is a part of it (Aliağaoğlu, 2008).

The Bosnian War

This occupation movement forced nearly a million Bosnian citizens to migrate. The Serbian armies committed massacres and destruction in their occupied areas, destroying mosques and historical monuments with Islamic traces. Negotiations and mediation efforts conducted at various times to resolve the Bosnia and Herzegovina issue also failed to produce results. By 1994, the War in Bosnia–Herzegovina had claimed more than 250,000 lives, and the number of people forced to migrate exceeded 1 million. In April 1994, a Bosnian-Croat federation was established in Bosnia and Herzegovina, and the struggle for peace began to erase the traces of War (10). The War in Bosnia and Herzegovina is one of the worst events of the post-modern era. The most important reason is that the media watched and broadcast the War live. Sarajevo, in particular, was the centrepiece and the most dramatic point of the War in Bosnia and Herzegovina (Bora, 1999).

Waterloo

This battle is the last battle of Napoleon. The French army fought against the British and Prussian armies, and Napoleon was defeated. However, Napoleon, one of the most influential leaders in the history of the world, was again exiled and remained there until his death (3).

The Battle of Sarikamish

The Battle of Sarikamish, which went down in the history of the War as a disastrous field battle, is an actual example in Turkish history because it was a war that took place in winter conditions and also because it holds essential and striking lessons in terms of its results (4).

Vietnam

This War, also known as the Indochina War, occurred between the United States and the United States-backed South Vietnam and North Vietnam, China and the Soviet Union. It began in 1965 and lasted until about 1975. After the Korean War, it took second place in the Cold War. Vietnam emerged victorious from the War despite losing 1.5 million citizens and a third of its territory to poisoning. On the other hand, the Americans left 58,000 dead in the region and many soldiers who returned to their country from Vietnam after the War committed suicide (1).

The Cold War

The international political and military tensions between the two powerful states, the Western bloc led by the United States and the Eastern bloc countries led by the Soviet Union, which lasted from 1947 to 1991, were called the Cold War (5).

The American Civil War

It was a controversial civil war between the South and the North of the United States between 1861 and 1865. This Civil War significantly affected the economy, as the North defended its slavery, and the South opposed this humanitarian situation (6).

The Fronts of the Turkish War of Independence

The Turkish War of Independence was a multi-front war created to protect the country's unity and establish a fully independent new Turkish state that maintained national sovereignty (7).

Pearl Harbor

On 7 December 1941, the Imperial Japanese Navy attacked the US Army Pacific Fleet and military bases at Pearl Harbor. In this attack, 2,400 American citizens died, and 1,178 people were injured. A total of 12 ships were sunk, nine were damaged and 164 aircraft were destroyed. On the Japanese side, 64 people died, five ships sank and 29 aircraft were destroyed. On 8 December 1941, the United States declared War on Japan (8).

The World War II

World War II is a war that defines the world's political map and is one of the most important wars that mark history. During this War, the balance of superpowers in the world was shaken. Adolf Hitler, who found himself in a position to commit the Holocaust, drew an incredible mass of people behind him. In this economic crisis, he resorted not only to the Holocaust but also to arms, landing soldiers in the Rhine area, violating the Treaty of Versailles signed as a result of World War I. Then he invaded Poland and started World War II. Nazi Germany occupied every place where it launched an operation and annexed it to German territory. The defeated German army in Russia returned to Berlin, and Nazi rule in the world ended with Soviet Russia's invasion of Berlin in 1945, ending World War II. At the end of the War:

- The United States and Soviet Russia have become the world's two superpowers.
- The world was divided into three blocs: the US bloc, the Soviet-Russian bloc and the third bloc formed by those who did not join these blocs, and these blocs started the Cold War.

- Due to the heavy attrition of the colonial states, the colonial period began to end.
- Many colonised countries such as India, Pakistan, Libya, Algeria and Tunisia gained independence, with the Turkish War of Independence as an example (3).

Regardless of the reason, many wars have occurred in world history, affecting countries to varying degrees. Therefore, the kind of tourism that is called battlefield tourism focuses on all attractions resulting from the mentioned wars.
Selçuk Eren, 2014-Sabah Newspaper

Battlefield Tourism for the Rich

Battlefield tourism has been a rising trend in recent years. Some go to battlefields to see War, others to experience the excitement.

Those who seek adventure, those who like action movies, those who want to collect stories to tell, those who dream of participating in close combats, those who want to be embedded journalists, those whose heart beats to help, those who want to die and even those who are after aliens... For those who experience these feelings, a new tourism fashion has begun. Thousands of people around the world are now spending their vacations on battlefields. This trend, called battlefield tourism, consists of three different phases.

Phase 1: In this phase, trips are organised to countries where thousands of people died in the past but where peace reigns today. Bosnia and Herzegovina and Vietnam are the most popular countries.

Phase 2: Those who do not want to digress into cultural war travels and do not go on an adventure tend to belong to this category. Phase 2 travels to countries with social unrest or security problems. Mexico, where more than 70,000 people have died in the conflicts between drug traffickers and security forces since 2006, is in this category. Battlefield tourists pay thousands to get to neighbourhoods known for drug cartels and bodies hanging from bridges. Ukraine is also the most popular Phase 2 country, and tourists have been known to be shown the demonstration areas for $80 per day in the country, where anti-government demonstrations have been taking place since late 2013.

'Baghdad For 40 Thousand Dollars'

Phase 3: This category is considered the pinnacle of battlefield tourism. People travel to countries where an active conflict or security is most threatened. According to battlefield tourism companies, the select countries are Afghanistan, Iraq, Somalia and Sudan. However, the most popular country is Syria, where the United Nations has lost count of even the dead. Phase 3 travel is costly because of the high-security risk. For example, the US-based company Warzone Tours takes tourists to Baghdad, the capital of Iraq, for $40,000. Other tour operators take those who want to see the Somali pirates on the ground to the Gulf of Aden for tens of thousands of dollars (9).

Research Box

Although there are various studies on the travel motivations of battlefield tourists, it is found that more comparative studies are needed. Therefore, comparative studies can be conducted.

Studies on the protection of battlefields and their transmission to future generations can be conducted as part of various projects.

It is recommended that researchers conduct studies on the importance of peace in battlefield tourism, its impact on the cinema industry, its impact on locals, economic demand analysis and applications for battlefield tourism (Çatır, 2017).

Studies can be conducted on the process of creating package tours to battlefields.

It is possible to conduct various studies on tour guides who promote battlefields.

Conclusion

The basis of tourism demand, which has grown steadily since the 1950s, is based on satisfying people's need for recreation. The increase in income level, the shortening of the period in which the services offered in the tourism sector can be used, accompanied by the development of technology, and the covering of distances in shorter periods have increased the interest in leisure tourism. Over time, tourists who discovered leisure tourism have set off on other quests, laying the foundation for the emergence of different types of tourism. Tourists have transformed their understanding of holidays into short-term, different pleasures in different places (Akoğlan Kozak & Bahçe, 2009), and market differences have emerged in terms of the attractiveness of destinations. Today, there are more and more types of special interest tourism, and destinations that have lost their market share are revived with different types of tourism.

Experiencing one's history and participating in history are essential factors in an individual's journey. In every society, some events are painful and sad to remember. Although the concept of visiting places where sad events took place is quite old, it appeared in literature only in the 1990s. Places where commemorations are held every year after the martyrdom of Hussein in Karbala, Sinop Prison, August 17, death camps, Dolmabahçe and battlefields are the best examples of this concept (Akoğlan Kozak & Bahçe, 2009).

Dark tourism is a new concept in destination marketing. The concept of visiting incredibly dark places has emerged unconsciously over the years. Dark tourism, described in the literature by Lennon and Foley about disasters, grief, pain, sadness and sorrow, is a very productive type of tourism in terms of Turkey's resources. Throughout history, many wars, for whatever reason, have been experienced or were unavoidable. One of the best ways to bring the remnants of the wars to the new generations is to protect the battlefields. Protecting various military attractions that are part of the elements of War will ensure that the results of wars are not forgotten (Aliağaoğlu, 2008). Although wars differ in terms of the reasons for their occurrence, there is a common resistance and defence in societies that are forced to go to War. The tourist attraction potential of destinations where wars are exhibited as a tourist product is increasing. This is because people have begun to see the other side of tourism.

Discussion Questions

- Can you give information about the battlefields as a form of dark tourism?
- What should be done to develop the battlefields for tourism? What should be taken into consideration?
- What are the positive and negative aspects of battlefield tourism?

References

Akbulut, O., & Ekin, Y. (2018). Battlefield tourism as cultural heritage tourism: A geographical information system analysis of war monuments in Turkey. *Hitit University Journal of Social Sciences Institute, 11*(1), 395–420.

Akoğlan Kozak, M., & Bahçe, S. (2009). *Special interest tourism.* Detay Publishing.

Aliağaoğlu, A. (2008). A typical place to battlefield tourism: Gallipoli Peninsula Historical National Park. *Milli Folklor, 20*(78), 88–104.

Baldwin, F., & Sharpley, R. (2009). Battlefield tourism: Bringing organised violence back to life. In R. Sharpley & R. S. Philip (Eds.), *In the darker side of travel: The theory and practice of dark tourism.* Channel View Publications.

Bircan, O. (1997). *Atatürk's life with documents and photos (Belge ve Fotoğraflarla Atatürk'ün Hayatı).* Meb. Yayınları.

Bora, T. (1999). *The hunting ground of the new world order-regions-problems/Bosnia and Herzegovina (Yeni Dünya Düzeni'nin Av Sahası-Bölgeler-Sorunlar/Bosna Hersek).* Birikim Yayınları.

Çatır, O. (2017). Battlefield tourism: A literature review. *Journal of Turkish Tourism Research, 1*(1), 21–31.

Çelikpala, M. (2021). *War.* Tubitak Encyclopedia.

Dunkley, R. A., Morgan, N., & Westwood, S. (2007). A shot in the dark? Developing a new conceptual framework for thanatourism. *Asian Journal of Tourism and Hospitality, 1*(1), 54–63.

Hacıoğlu, N., & Avcıkurt, C. (2008). *Touristic product diversification (Turistik Ürün Çeşitlendirmesi).* Nobel Yayın Dağıtım.

Öztürk, B. H. (2021). Re-classification of the Concepts of War in the Context of Changing Character of War. *SAVSAD Savunma ve Savaş Araştırmaları Dergisi The Journal of Defence and War Studies, 31*(2), 225–262.

Panakera, C. (2007). World War II and tourism development in the Solomon Islands. In C. Ryan (Ed.), *Battlefield tourism: History, place, and interpretation* (pp. 125–141). Elsevier.

Prideaux, B. (2007). Echoes of war: Battlefield tourism. In C. Ryan (Ed.), *Battlefield tourism: History, place and interpretation* (pp. 17–29). Elsevier Limited.

Shackley, M. (2001). Potential futures for Robben Island: Shrine, museum or theme park? *International Journal of Heritage Studies, 7*(4), 355–363.

Smith, L. V. (1998). War and tourism, An American ethnography. *Annals of Tourism Research, 25*(1), 202–227.

Smith, N., & Glen Croy, W. (2005). *Presentation of dark tourism:* Te Wairoa, The Buried Village. In C. Ryan, S. Page, & M. Aicken (Eds.), *Taking tourism to the limits: Issues, concepts and managerial perspectives* (pp. 199–213). Elsevier Limited.

Turkish Language Association. (2005). *Turkish Dictionary*. Ankara: 4. Akşam Sanat Okulu Matbaası.

Varlık, B. A. (2013). Identifying war: A terminological approach. *Avrasya Terim Dergisi, 1*(2), 114–129.

Walter, T. (1993). Modern death: Taboo or not Taboo? *Sociology, 25,* 293–310.

http://www.traveller.com.au/vietnam-back-to-the-battlefields-grzhfs

http://www.gelibolu.info/canakkale_savaslari.php

https://www.tarihiolaylar.com

http://www.sarikamis.gov.tr

https://www.savaslar.gen.tr/soguk-savas.html

https://www.savaslar.gen.tr/amerikan-ic-savasi.html

http://muharipgaziler.org.tr/kurtulus-savasi/

https://tr.euronews.com/2016/12/26/pearl-harbor-saldirisi-nedir-pearl-harbor-da-neler-yasandi

https://www.sabah.com.tr/pazar/2014/02/09/zenginler-icin-savas-turizmi

http://enfal.at/bosnahersek.htm

Part 9

Toy Tourism

Chapter 18

'Toyrism' in India – Present and Future

Adit Jha and Praveen Choudhry

Vivekananda Global University, India

Learning Objectives

After reading and studying this chapter, you should be able to:

- understand the concept of toyrism;
- exhibit the contribution of toys to the economic growth of the country;
- understand various government schemes for the development of toy tourism in India.

Abstract

Chapters explore the concept of toy tourism (Toyrism) with the objective of the study of the Indian toy industry and the impact of toys on the tourism economy of the country. The first part of this chapter deals with introducing Indian toys and their growth aspect. Study conducted to identify different determinants of the toyrism, as per the previous studies, culture, co-creational values and experiential values has strong association with toyrism. Culture has strong associations with toys which reflect regional culture, elaborate culture through toy storytelling such as puppet shows in Rajasthan, internationally Barbie dolls replicate American culture. Co-creational values have considered toys as innovative characteristics, and experiential values of toys related to created experiential aspects of toys, which tourist can explain and the concept is well taken by the Walt Disney with their creation of Disneyland Toy Story. The next part of this chapter discusses some of the government schemes to create toys for all travellers to develop indigenous, innovative toys with development of clusters. The last part of this chapter included the conclusion and way forward to research.

Future Tourism Trends Volume 1, 271–281
Published under exclusive licence by Emerald Publishing Limited
doi:10.1108/978-1-83753-244-520241018

Keywords: Toy tourism in India; factors of toy tourism; importance of toyrism; determinants of toy tourism; play fullness with toys; cultural toys; development of toyrism through government policies

Introduction

Toys today are not just things to play with but also used as learning tools, showcasing tradition, spirituality, history, culture and character identities. The best toys are those which children can play together and can improve the creative skills of children. Today toys are of many types in the market, such as plastic toys, soft toys, electric toys, robots, wooden toys, handcrafted toys, educational toys, etc. The history of toys in India is as long as the country. It is almost 5,000 years old from the age of Mohenjo-Daro and Harappa. Indian toys are well known for depicting their rich traditions over the last many years (Toy Story Promotion of Indigenous Toys of India, 2020). Toys have been defined as 'something for a child to play with' (Definition of toy, 2022) the toy, an object for children to play with (Oxford's learner's dictionary). India has a living tradition of making indigenous toys that uses materials in their best way and works on simple science theories. A basic example of these types of toys can be seen in various *Mela* toys, which contain simple science principles and the best materials to play with (Khanna, 1987).

> Many toys and games popular all over the world has ancient Indian origin like chaturanga is the predecessor of modern chess, and pachisi is predecessor of modern day ludo.
>
> (Mohit Bhasin, 2021)

All the states of India carry their legacy of toy making and exhibiting their couture and tradition. As an Indian state, Uttarakhand is famous for miniature versions of handheld drums, wooden toy making; folk toys of Punjab; Kathputli art Fig. 18.2 (Kathputli Rajasthani theatre art) from Rajasthan; Kondpalli Toys and Etikoppaka toys from Andhra Pradesh; Channapatna Toys Fig. 18.1 (Channapatna Toys – The story of Karnataka's most famous wooden arte-facts); Thanjavur dancing dolls from Tamil Nadu; etc. The next phase of this research discussed emerging trends in the Indian toy industry, export–import of Indian toys, safety rules and regulations for toys, the impact of the Chinese toy industry on India and innovations in Indian toys. These states have a significant part of their travel revenue from these local and specialised toy things.

Defining Toyrism

The term 'Toyrism' refers to toy tourism; at its core, toy tourism reflects the physical presence of toys with their owner during travel, narrative stories through toys, and attracting tourism through the toy's physical appearances.

Fig. 18.1.   Channapatna Toys. *Source:* Channapatna toys – The story of Karnataka's most famous wooden artefacts.

Fig. 18.2.   Rajasthani Kathputli Kraft. *Source:* Kathputli Rajasthani theatre art.

Toy tourism occurs when toys travel either as travel companions of their owner or single handedly as is organized services provided by toy travel agencies.

(Heljakka, 2013; Katriina Heljakka, 2020)

Scholars in toy and tourism, the combination of both refers to toyrism and is defined as

> Toyrism refers to a non-human tourism conducted with character toys, also have the virtual and mobile tourism conducted by tourists from various types of character toys, such as dolls, soft toys, action figure.
>
> (Katriina Heljakka, 2021)

Toy tourism in India depicts a different narration together; in a country like India. Every place has its legacy, culture and characters defined in regional areas. Regional character toys create curiosity among tourists to know more about the region. Apart from the association with toy travellers, Indian toys are significant from a tourism perspective and tourism attractions. Indian toys have a story-telling capability through various stories of Ramayana and Mahabharata; patriotism, characterisation and all these together made the Indian toy industry more tourist attraction in all toy clusters (Toy Story Promotion of Indigenous Toys of India, 2020).

Toy Clusters and Impact on Development of Tourism

Every state of India has its own culture and tourist attractions. Some of the states are well known for their toy clusters and toys. Recently the government has concentrated on developing local culture under the slogan of vocal for local and Aatmanirbhar Bharat (Malhotra, 2021). Toys in the market have local and cultural identities; at the time of a tourist visit, any toy shop owner talks about the legacy behind the toy. Channapatna Toys from Karnataka has its recognition as a tourist and unique attraction. Table 18.1 gives a brief about the states and their toy crafts.

Table 18.1. Indian States and Their Toys.

S.No.	State	Toyrism Attraction
1.	Chandigarh	Wooden Boards, Wooden Jali, God Statute
2.	Haryana	Babushka dolls, lacquer dolls, string puppets, clay Indian toys, leather toys
3.	Tamil Nadu	Thanjavur Thalaiyatti Baommai, Choppu Saman
4.	Himachal Pradesh	Wooden Toys
5.	Uttarakhand	Wooden Toy Making
6.	West-Bengal	Toys, Terracotta Toys, Wooden Toys, Batik print Cloth Toys, Bamboo Musk

Table 18.1. *(Continued)*

S.No.	State	Toyrism Attraction
7.	Jammu and Kashmir	Walnut wood craving
8.	Kerala	Kathakali dance dolls, animal-shaped toys, woodcraft
9.	Rajasthan	Kathputli Art, Wooden Toys
10.	Karnataka	Channapatna Toys
11.	Telangana	Nirmal Toys
12.	Madhya Pradesh	Adivasi Gudia, Betel nut's toys
13.	Maharashtra	Wooden toys of Sawantwadi Toys

Source: Toy Story promotion of indigenous toys in India, Ministry of Tourism.

There are many toy tourism attractions when the market has the potential to attract tourists through their toy availability, and footfall increases due to the same. Tourists are interested in toys because of their children and use them as an alternative to home décor, the identity of culture and geographical indication. The main tourist attractions in Rajasthan are handcrafted wooden toys from Udaipur and handmade puppets from Jaipur.

Research Box

Defining Research Question Related to Toys and Refining the Research Question

One of my friends completed his studies from the National Institute of Design, and he was fascinated to working with toys and craft related aspects. He was fascinated to see the processes of toy making and study of various aspects of toys. During one of our meetings, he has shared that he wants to pursue toys as his research topic but a little bit confused how he can choose toy-related concept for the research. After someday, the government announced to open new toy clusters in various states of India and invited new entrepreneurs to work on innovative toy start-ups. I have discussed this with my friend, and he found the opportunity to enter in the toy research. In the process of identifying the topic for research, he has started reading relevant literature on toy industry, various concepts related to the industry, government schemes and latest developments in toy sector. After analysing the literature, he found that

(Continued)

(*Continued*)

researches on toys are still in its nascent stage. While reviewing the literature, he found some interesting facts about the Indian toy industry, that Indian toy industry has a market of $ 1 billion USD in 2021, and likely to grow by $ 2 billion USD by 2024–2025, while the exports are less than 1%, 70% of toy market is unorganised. Literature also revealed that most of the research practitioners have worked on children's association with toys, impact of toys in children development, use of toys as a tool of education, export and import of toys, tourism aspect of toys, cultural aspects of toys, etc. After knowing the deep status of the domain, he identified the following research topics:

- Analysing toy concept with respect to children's psychology;
- Analysing novel toy concepts, entrepreneurial opportunities with respect to the toys;
- Toy tourism aspect, present and future;
- Impact of government policy on the income of artisans.

Thus, a good review of literature can lead to an extremely insightful research question; further, the success of the research relates to identify correct sample, research design and that to analyse data.

Toyrism Determinants

The concept of toyrism evolved around some essential determinants which have been described by various researchers value dimensions, playful artefacts, value co-creation (Katriina Heljakka, 2021), cultural dimensions, character dimensions (Katriina Heljakka, 2020) and building heritage (Khanna, 1987). Apart from these main determinants, the Indian toy tourism is also concerned with associations of patriotism (see Table 18.2).

Table 18.2. Toyrism Determinants.

S.No.	Determinant	Author
1.	Value Co-Creation; Playful artefacts	Katriina Heljakka (2021), Alves and Rodrigues (2022), and Walmsley (2013)
2.	Cultural Dimensions, Heritage Experience	Katriina Heljakka (2020), Mohit Bhasin (2021), and Sudarshan khanna (1987)
3.	Toy Experiences, Arts and Craft Experiences	Suja John

Source: Authors' compilation.

Value Co-creation

Co-creation is defined as a 'collaborative Journey' that producers embark on with audiences in an attempt to create something new together (Govier, 2009). Co-creation refers to creating value by adding innovation in existing products, creating value through experience (Trevail, 2012). Co-creation is one of the important aspects of toy tourism; all over the world, toys have represented as the one which attract tourist through crating innovative experiences during their travel (Walmsle, 2022). Creating toys as co-creational activities also included the social aspect which varies to interpersonal and intergroup behaviour. Walt Disney has created another level of co-creation with favourite Disney character toys, toy story characters, to create enthusiasm in travellers. Tourists from all over the world come to see the parade of toy story characters (Alves & Rodrigues, 2022).

Cultural Dimension and Heritage Experience

Toy tourism has great implications as understanding the cultural aspects all over the world. Toys origin itself narrates a folk story about the region, people, their journeys, patriotism, history, heritage, etc. International toy player Mattel has set a cultural benchmark in the American market in 1959 by introducing Barbie doll as an identity of a modern, self-dependent, bold and beautiful girl and to explore brands all over the world. Indian culture and heritage is well depicted by its folk toys, regional toys and fair toys which represented the cultural essence of the region. The tourists during the regional fairs mostly purchase these types of toys with the capacity of storytelling, for example stories of Mahabharata through toys, small artefact to play and to decorate interiors of Indian households. Like the Barbie doll, in India dolls are one of the famous playthings. Tourists with their children look for the places where they can enjoy with their children. In India, there are lots of museums, but Shankar's Dolls Museum at New Delhi, the Dolls Museum at Jaipur have different types of doll collection. The collection of 6,000 dolls representing 85 countries and their culture attracts tourist to see various international dolls in their costumes.

Toy Experiences, Arts and Craft Experiences

Toy making is not only considered as play but also seen as art works created by artisans. These artisans use various types of woods, cloths, rubbers, etc. to create their art works. These art works attract tourists from all over the world and indicate geographical specialties (Table 18.3) such as:

Table 18.3. Toy Experiences, Arts and Craft From Various Regions of India.

S.No.	Craft Work/ Toy	Representation	Toy Experience
		National Art Work	
1.	Kathputli Art	Local culture of Rajasthan, used to narrate various types of stories and increase tourist activities in local region.	Kathputli art works provide the experience of royal looks in the form of Kathputli. Kathputli is not only used as a plaything by children but also represented home décor item, also give an opportunity to storytelling.
2.	Rajasthan's woodcraft	Rajasthan wooden toys	Rajasthan wooden toys showcase culture of Rajasthan, toys related to Rajput warriors as a leader, storytelling through miniature toys of various palaces of Rajasthan which attracts tourists to understand culture and history of the state.
3.	Channapatna Toys	Karnataka Art Work	Toys identifying regional culture by using wood and making Channapatna toys craft famous in world.
4.	Coir-Dried Coconut Toys	Kerala Toy Cluster	Making toys out of dry coconut and coir. Tourist all over the world found these toys interesting and use it as a decorative piece of toy.
5.	Varanasi Toys	Spiritual wooden toys	Tourist from all over the world come to Varanasi for a spiritual connects, which also reflected in the local toys, art and craft.

Source: Author's own compilation.

Government Schemes for the Development of Toy Tourism in India

Recently, Prime Minister Narendra Modi called Indian youth and artisans to team up to make the Indian toy industry self-reliable under the slogan of vocal for local under Aatmanirbhar Bharat. Domestic toy market opportunity is approximately USD 2 bn by 2025, and global exports are targeted to be 2% by 2024, which is currently less than 1%. For improvement of the toy industry, Indian government has launched some schemes like:

- India's first virtual toy fair attracts many B2B people and tourists to explore new and latest toys in the market.
- The Toycathon is organised by the Ministry of Education through Institution's Innovation Council on 10 different themes to develop new ideas and start-ups linked with the Indian knowledge system.
- The government launched the National Action Plan for toys to strengthen the growth of Indian toys.
- Increasing the import duties on toys to encourage the Indian toy industry. The hikes are given from 20% to 40%.
- Development of 19 new toy clusters; Karnataka government has taken Koppal as a toy manufacturing cluster; similarly, the Rajasthan government has dedicated an industrial area near Khushkheda, near Bhiwadi Rajasthan, etc.

(Mohit Bhasin, 2021)

Case Study

Channapatna Toys

Channapatna is a village at a distance of 60 kms from Bangalore, Karnataka state. Channapatna has its own identity with its soft wooden toys; World Trade Organization (WTO) also identifies Channapatna toys as a geographical indication. These toys were started in the era of Tipu Sultan; the primary wood used to make this type of toy was Aale Mara and now sandalwood, rosewood, teal and rubber. The uniqueness of Channapatna toys is their design which is round from all sides with no edges, suits children and is environment friendly. Channapatna has a home for more than 5000 skilled artisans. Everything was going fine before the pandemic, later on the pandemic hit artisans badly, and hundreds of toy manufacturing units were closed. The artisans have got fewer benefits from the governments, and some private help were given during the COVID-19 pandemic (Tripathi, 2020).

Barbie Doll Representation of American Culture and Indian Dilemma

Barbie, as a brand of Mattel, originated in Germany and was taken as a concern by Ruth Handler. The origin of Barbie is said to be a German doll 'Lilli' in 1950.

Ruth Handler thought to take 'Lilli' in American market place with the new look of Lilli according to the American market, consumer psychology, and better representation of modern, bold, beautiful American women. In 1959 Barbie debuted in American Toy Fair, after the launch Barbie got great success in the United States and other countries. They created the first Indian Barbie in 1982, and debuted in Asia in 1986 by acquiring toy manufacturers in Japan, Bandai toys, in Hong Kong ARCO industries. In manufacturing of Barbie, hundreds of designers worked, 105 million yards of fabric were used to create 1 billion Barbie dolls. Mattel launched Barbie in every country through licencing of their own models without considering culture of the host country; they adapted the ethnocentric approach in entering the international market, which substantially caused the failure in Indian market. Apart from the cultural diversity, license raj, strict foreign direct investment rules were some core reasons which caused Mattel to fail in India initially (Nemani, 2011).

Conclusion

Toy tourism is growing in India as the toys convey their regional scopes, heritage and culture. Rajasthan, famous for its history and culture, attracts tourists for the same. The capital of Rajasthan is famous for its 'Kathputli Art or Puppet Art' toys. These toys depict the regional aspect, culture and heritage of Rajasthan. The market of Kathputli toys itself has the capacity of storytelling or tell stories of kings–queens, Rajput heritage and culture. Toys are in the form of playthings and are marketed to tourists. Every state of India has its own toy story, toy culture and folk stories that describe the region well. The Heaven of country, Jammu and Kashmir has its own toys decor pieces like small wooden shikara's to attract tourism; on the other hand, southern states of patriotism and the same have been delivered through the toys to tourists. The Government has launched new schemes for toy development which will also increase toyrism in the country.

Discussion Questions

- Why can having the strict marketing approach from all over the world be harmful for the success of a company?
- Barbie was well accepted all over the world, but why did she fail in the Indian market?

References

Alves, A. P. C. C., & Rodrigues, F. (2022). Brand identity co-creation dilemma. *Brazilian Journal of Marketing, 21*(5), 1845–1902.

Deffinition of toy. (2022). www.merriam-webster.com. https://www.merriam-webster. com/dictionary/toy

Govier, L. (2009). *Leaders in co-creation: Why and how museums could develop their cocreative.* http://www2.le.ac.uk/departments/museumstudies/rcmg/projects/leaders-in-cocreation/

Heljakka, K. (2013). *Principals of Adult Play (fulness) in contemporary toy cultures from wow to fllow to glow.* Doctoral Dissartations. Alto University.

Katriina Heljakka, P. L. (2020). *Toy tourism from travel bugs to characters with wanderlust.* Taylor and Francis.

Katriina Heljakka, J. R. (2021). Puzzling out "Toyrism": Conceptualizing value co-creation in toy tourism. *Tourism Management Perspective, 38,* 100791.

Khanna, S. (1987). Indian toys & toy makers our design heritage. *Indian Express.*

Malhotra, K. (2021). *Indian toy industry: A step towards self-reliance.* www.tpci.in/indiabusinesstrade/blogs: www.tpci.in/indiabusinesstrade/blogs/indian-toy-industry-a-step-towards-self-reliance/

Mohit Bhasin, V. J. (2021). *State of Play India's Toy Story – Unboxsing fun and beyond.* KPMG.

Nemani, P. (2011). Globalization versus normative policy: A case study on the failure of the Barbie doll in the Indian Market. *Asian-Pacific Law & Policy Journal, 13,* 96.

Toy story promotion of indigenous toys of India. (2020) Ministry of Tourism, Government of India.

Trevail, F. A. (2012). *Brand together: How co-creation generates.* Kogan Page.

Tripathi, S. (2020). *Toy-making artisans of Karnataka's Channapatna struggle to stay afloat without government help in lockdown.* Art & Culture News.

Walmsle, B. (2022). Co-creating theatre: Authentic engagement or inter-legitimation? *White Rose Research, 22*(2), 108–118.

Part 10

Wellness Tourism After Pandemic

Chapter 19

Wellness Tourism After The Pandemic

Gonca Aytaş[a], Fatma Doğanay Ergen[b] and Engin Aytekin[a]

[a]Afyon Kocatepe University, Türkiye
[b]Isparta University of Applied Sciences, Türkiye

Learning Objectives

After reading and studying this chapter, you should be able to:

- understand the position of wellness tourism, especially health tourism, in the tourism industry;
- learn the perspectives of tourists on wellness tourism during and after the pandemic;
- give an overview of health tourism and wellness tourism in the post-pandemic period in the tourism industry.

Abstract

Human life has been unfavourably impacted by COVID-19, which has impacted the entire planet. Contrastingly, it is now crucial to discern the significance of health in human life and pay more attention to protecting health. Owing to COVID-19's influence on lifestyle, it is evident that the pandemic contributes to the development of health tourism and that wellness tourism, which was in the pre-pandemic growth trend, is favoured more often. Therefore, it is indisputable that stakeholders in the health and tourism industries view the rising demand for health-focused holidays as a potential. However, on the opposite hand, it is meaningful to broaden the number of products made available within the context of wellness tourism, to pinpoint areas that are conducive to health-related activities, to generate the infrastructure and superstructure required in these areas and to step up marketing initiatives in order to make the most of this opportunity. To address these concerns, it is deemed crucial that the parties involved in the tourism and health sectors coordinate their efforts.

Future Tourism Trends Volume 1, 285–298
doi:10.1108/978-1-83753-244-520241019

Keywords: Wellness tourism; epidemic; health tourism; after pandemic; COVID-19; SPA

Introduction

Health tourism brings people a revitalising experience to enhance and preserve their physical and mental health while away from home; instead of focusing on physical considerations, psychological aspects (cognitive, emotional and behavioural) are affiliated with health (Sivanandamoorthy, 2021, p. 163). Nearly all regions, including Europe, America, Asia, Australia and New Zealand, include some forms of health tourism (medical services, medical surgery clinics, medical health facilities or spas) (Widarini et al., 2020, p. 407). However, due to the substantial alterations in people's lifestyles following the pandemic, health tourism has grown more widespread than before the pandemic (Choudhary & Qadir, 2022, p. 139). Therefore, it is noticeable that wellness tourism, a subset of health tourism defined as travel to take advantage of thermal springs, entertainment, beauty and health services, is climbing (Han & An, 2022, p. 3). According to the studies evaluating the perspective of tourists on health tourism and especially wellness tourism after COVID-19, tourists end up choosing health tourism in the post-COVID-19 era, they are willing to spend more time travelling to improve their health, and they are willing to pay more for health services or related activities while travelling. However, it is speculated that how tourists perceive wellness tourism before and after COVID-19's emergence is dissimilar. However, it is still discernible that tourists now favour wellness tourism after COVID-19 for reasons such as removing stress/relaxing, protecting the well-being and improving mental health (Datta, 2022; Han & An, 2022; americanexpress.com, 2021; GWI, 2020). On the other end, it is evident that research on wellness tourism after COVID-19 is scarce, and it is anticipated that studies in this area would advance the field's literature and the industry. 'Health tourism' and 'health wellness/SPA tourism', a subset of tourism, have been defined in this context. Following an evaluation of the pandemic's effects on wellness tourism both during and after COVID-19, suggestions believed to advance this field were presented.

Health Tourism

People may frequently travel to countries other than their own on a planned basis to seek treatment or use healthcare services (Ünüvar, 2020, p. 68). Another interpretation of health tourism asserts that it encompasses all travel-related activities to enhance and preserve health or resolve a health issue (Özsarı & Karatana, 2013, p. 137).

According to the research conducted by UNWTO/ETC in 2016, health tourism includes certain types of tourism which have as a primary motivation the contribution to physical, mental and spiritual health through medical and wellness-based activities, which increase the capacity of individuals to meet their own needs and perform better as individuals in their environment and society (UNWTO/ETC, 2017, p. 12; 2018, p. 9).

The association between tourism and health has been revealed, with affirmative and negative implications. On the brighter side, this connection pertains to the tourists' travel and medical treatment. However, so far, the relationships around visitor health are a drawback and can seriously harm the industry. The SARS sickness case in the Far East nations in 2002 serves as an illustration of tourist health. According to estimates of the World Travel and Tourism Council (WTTC) (2003), after SARS broke out in China, Hong Kong, Vietnam and Singapore, which were most severely affected, approximately 3 million people lost their jobs in the tourism industry, resulting in losses of over $20 billion (Kuo et al., 2008; Özsarı & Karatana, 2013, p. 137).

Nonetheless, the repercussions of the COVID-19 outbreak, which first surfaced in 2019 and spread throughout the world in 2020, on the tourism industry were investigated in the study carried out by WTTC (2023). The study findings indicated that 62 million individuals lost their jobs, and the number of employees, which was 333 million in 2019, reduced by 18.6% to 271 million in 2020. Still, it was noted that domestic tourist spending would fall by 47.4% in 2020 while overseas visitor spending would fall by 69.7%.

Health tourism activities are reviewed from the perspective of sub-categories such as medical tourism, thermal tourism, spa and wellness tourism according to the aim and scope of travels. In addition, geriatric tourism, which includes the third age group participating in health tourism activities, and barrier-free/accessible tourism activities intended to encourage disabled people to participate in tourism activities actively are also incorporated into the definition of health tourism (Zorlu, 2018, p. 8).

Geriatric and disability tourists represent the sources of demand, whereas thermal, wellness, SPA and medical tourism constitute the sources of supply. Mutual engagement is a consistent pattern among these many forms of tourism, which comprise health tourism subfields. However, unlike other tourists, those who engage in senior, third-age or geriatric tourism may have a more significant desire for therapeutic services such as thermal cure applications, medical tourism and rehabilitation services due to some old-age health complications. In addition, due to the time flexibility of the elderly and third-year tourists, their spare time and purchasing power, they increase their opportunities to benefit more from thermal tourism and wellness and SPA services to protect their health (Temizkan, 2020, p. 282).

Mueller and Lanz (1998) differentiated between the two forms of health tourism into 'cure/rehabilitation' and 'health measures/protection'. Wellness and specialised health protection are the categories under which health protection is categorised (Polat, 2020, p. 99).

Wellness/SPA Tourism

Many changes have been brought about by the shift from Patagonesis to Salutogenesis in the understanding of health. Working to live replaces living to work as preserving and boosting health become increasingly crucial. Having a happy life is becoming the norm. Since well-being is sighted as the opposite of disease, the idea of health steadily loses ground to it (Ergüven, 2015a, p. 137).

A unique definition of health is contained in the wellness concept. This wellness explanation parallels the definition of health formulated in the Ottawa Declaration of the World Health Organization. Wellness can be summed up as enhancing physical, spiritual and mental health through maintaining equilibrium. It is commonly acknowledged that the term 'wellness' is an artificial word that was first used in the United States and was created by fusing the words 'well-being' and 'fitness'. According to Dr Halbert Luis Dunn's wellness philosophy, each person is responsible for enhancing and safeguarding their health. Furthermore, it has been asserted that the term 'wellness' was first used as 'wealnesse' or 'good health' not in the 20th century but three centuries ago on average (1654). Moreover, in modern society, wellness has become a phrase that is only utilised positively and as the antidote to stress (Polat, 2020, p. 84; Toktaş, 2015, p. 158).

The concept of wellness has become associated with relaxation, well-being and rest. The concept of SPA with the origin of thermal therapy has caused passive practices (massages, body care, baths, etc.) to come to the fore. As a result, the ideas of SPA and wellness have started to coexist and have expanded to conventional and historical spa enterprises. While traditional spa treatments such as baths, mud massage and showers remained the same, beauty, aesthetics and body and skin care were added, and the second group became more dominant. SPA treatments have evolved from treating illnesses to focusing on beauty, care and preventive medicine (Toktaş, 2015, p. 158).

Wellness has a healthy body, mind and spirit. Individual responsibility, physical fitness, healthy diet, relaxation, mental activity, education, interpersonal relationships and environmental awareness are the components that impact wellness. The four components that make up the tourist supply are wellness, a healthy diet, mental stimulation/education, rest and physical fitness (Polat, 2020, p. 88). Reading books, going on nature hikes, actively participating in fitness classes, engaging in spiritual purification practices like yoga and meditation, eating healthily, detoxing, getting massages at spas and taking care of one's body are just a few of the many and varied activities that fall under the umbrella of personal development within the wellness activity (Zorlu, 2018, p. 29). However, concerts, reading days, exhibitions and handicrafts that encourage people's creativity, painting, keeping flowers in pots can encourage mental activities and can be included in the wellness spectrum (Polat, 2020, p. 91).

When people visit and stay somewhere to protect or improve their health, this is characterised as wellness tourism (Polat, 2020, p. 95). Another understanding of wellness tourism involves improving and balancing all aspects of daily life, including physical, mental, emotional, professional, intellectual and spiritual aspects (UNWTO, 2018, p. 10).

While wellness is related to health as a form of tourism offering in Germany (such as a wellness holiday or wellness hotel), it is characterised as a phenomenon in the United States that promotes health directs daily life, and embraces working life (Ergüven, 2015b, p. 39).

The wellness industry's largest segment comprises, by far, wellness holidays. In contrast to regular rest vacations, wellness holidays feature programmes that improve one's health and well-being. Wellness holidays are increasingly prevalent at locations that demand an average of three hours to reach by private transport. The multiplicity of wellness services facilitates the ability to meet a variety of demands (Ergüven, 2015a, pp. 131, 135). The main driving force behind wellness tourists is the desire to partake in proactive, preventative and lifestyle-improving activities like exercise, healthy eating, relaxation, pampering and remedial therapy (UNWTO, 2018, p. 10).

It is conceivable to categorise visitors into two groups based on the investigation of wellness visitors. Passive wellness visitors are those who desire to take pleasure in their vacation. These people place more excellent value on participating in various wellness and beauty programmes than engaging in active exercise and taking advantage of good eating options. Conversely, 'active wellness tourists' favour acting proactively and health-consciously and doing something for their health as their primary goal. Finally, research led to the term 'advanced wellness tourists', who know the need to encourage a healthy lifestyle and seek wellness packages (Polat, 2020, p. 96).

All individuals who aspire to feel positive and prioritise health are intended as the target audience. Those between the ages of 25 and 65 with high levels of education and income make up most of the guests. This information enables the classification of wellness visitors into two groups. The first category involves people who work and deal with daily stress, and the second includes seniors. This group of guests intends to spend ageing pleasantly, so they are interested in their body and mental health (Ergüven, 2015a, p. 135).

While comparing the past few years, it can be realised that average wellness customers have mostly stayed the same. According to the study, women who were, on average, 39 years old made 64% of the reservations. They admitted to travelling with at least one other person, 54.25% of them said they liked to achieve it with their partners and 25.78% said they intended to do so with friends. Female wellness clients reported making reservations for two primary reasons: 62% to try something new and 80% to relax. In addition, 53.98% of the women reported taking a wellness vacation at least once annually, and at least one-third expressed that they took multiple wellness vacations. The female respondents claimed they explored the hotel's facilities, mainly what they would get for their money and what kind of services would be included in the fixed fee. Nonetheless, 68.15% of women and 47.81% of men said they value an excellent price–service ratio (Polat, 2020, p. 131).

Impacts of the COVID-19 Pandemic on Tourism

In 2020, the COVID-19 pandemic surfaced first in November 2019 and began to spread globally. The framework of modern human life has undergone enormous alteration due to COVID-19, which has impacted numerous industries. The tourism industry was one of the areas most affected by COVID-19. As a result of the rapid spread of COVID-19 around the world, travel restrictions have been introduced and quarantine policies have been implemented. These restrictions and policies have affected tourism. In addition, mass transportation services were abruptly and simultaneously discontinued due to the state's extraordinarily severe and widespread social and physical distance requirements. With the sharp decline in international visitor numbers and reservation cancellations and cutbacks, the burden on the tourism industry has become increasingly apparent (Widarini et al., 2020, p. 402).

It is well-documented that before COVID-19, the global health tourism industry was very advanced. The growing trend of wellness tourism, a subset of health tourism that focuses on improving one's quality of life to balance one's body, mind and spirit, has also been recognised as a critical strategy for drawing travellers. Humans can live in peace and health thanks to this sector of the economy. As a result, this sector continues to garner considerable interest from tourism stakeholders (Koerniawaty & Sudjana, 2022, p. 10082; Sivanandamoorthy, 2021, p. 160). COVID-19, on the other hand, has significantly impacted the tourism industry globally while highlighting how crucial it is for people to safeguard their health and well-being (Choudhary & Qadir, 2022, p. 134). In this process, the demand for persons who have undergone and recovered from the COVID-19 process to regain their health has caused health and wellness tourism to become one of the significant and most rapidly growing sectors of national economies (Oborin, 2022, p. 3). It has additionally been thought of as a way to help individuals avoid boredom and help them adjust to the altered normal. Health tourism has several essential ingredients for secure and comfortable travels and practical instructional benefits for the body (Widarini et al., 2020, p. 402). Due to its tangible and intangible resources, health might present various opportunities in today's tourism industry. The pandemic has increased people's attention to managing their health and accorded it greater importance. As a result, health stakeholders can take advantage of this opportunity to create new healthcare products in response to the rising desire for holidays that emphasise good health (Choudhary & Qadir, 2022, p. 138).

For this reason, this process has been regarded as a beacon of hope for tourism operators in the health sector amid the stagnation of the tourism sector (Widarini et al., 2020, p. 402). Further, the COVID-19 pandemic-related international crisis makes wellness tourism, particularly health tourism, a potent generator of regional growth in the context of international economic competitiveness (Oborin, 2022, p. 1). So, despite this process and the challenges brought on by the epidemic, health and wellness tourism kept improving its position. This circumstance has impacted both local and international tourism markets, which has impacted the growth of nations and regions and the overall economic structure. According to research on how tourism affects the world economy, it can help build local infrastructure, increase employment opportunities and boost the service sector. Moreover, notwithstanding previous crises, tourism has demonstrated a remarkable ability to innovate, adapt quickly to shifting market demands and rebound from external shocks (Oborin, 2022, p. 7).

Wellness Tourism After The Pandemic

Health and wellness tourism is one of the tourist industries most impacted by the COVID-19 pandemic (Oborin, 2022). Wellness tourism grew 8% annually from 2017 to 2019, reaching 720 billion dollars. Later, in 2020, the market took a big hit, shrinking 39.5% to $436 billion. While travellers worldwide carried out 936 million domestic and international wellness tours in 2019, this figure decreased to over 600 million in 2020 (GWI, 2022).

Once the wellness economy is analysed by region before and after the pandemic, Table 19.1 illustrates that Asia-Pacific was one of the fastest growing wellness markets from 2017 to 2019 (8.1% growth) while also being the region that shrank the least (-6.4%) during the pandemic. North America, as opposed to that, had the most robust rate of wellness growth from 2017 to 2019 (8.4%) while being one of the region's most negatively impacted by the pandemic (-13.4%).

After the quarantine and isolation period experienced during the COVID-19 process, it is distinguished that tourists prefer to travel to non-crowded or even unusual places. At the same time, their interest in secondary destinations and exploring nature has increased. However, it is noteworthy that during this period, tourists became more dependent on sustainability, affecting their travel preferences. Contrariwise, about the situation regarding health tourism, the curfews introduced in this process shed a brighter light on healthy life and general health issues, leading tourists to seek more healthy life experiences (WTTC, 2022, p. 24). For instance, revenues for the fitness subsector (gyms, studios and classrooms) decreased by 37% in 2020. In contrast, fitness technology expanded by 29.1% in 2020 as millions of people spent money on digital platforms related to exercise (GWI, 2022). Healthy diet, nutrition and weight loss are more examples. The wellness industry, which witnessed positive growth (3.6% growth) during the pandemic, has generated a surge in interest in home cooking, healthy eating and supplements and foods that promote the immune system. As a result, the industry expanded from $858 billion in 2017 to $912 billion in 2019 and $945.5 billion in 2020 (GWI, 2022).

In May and July of 2020, a study titled 'Global Think Tank Consumer Wellness Travel Trends Two phases research' was conducted by the Global Wellness Institute (GWI), with more than 2000 responses from more than 80 countries, including 42% in Australia, 22% in North America and 36% in other countries. 33% of respondents indicated that they had used or purchased any new online health app or offer since COVID-19. In comparison, 24% of participants reported participating in a new health service they had never considered before. In addition, 53% of respondents answered that they would be willing to spend extra for a holiday that satisfies their health requirements. 87% of the participants stated that they plan to take a vacation when the restrictions are lifted, and 76% stated that a health component would be included. The top 5 health expectations for post-COVID-19 travel are listed as follows: connection with nature (72%), fresh quality local food (45%), outdoor activities (42%), quality accommodation (34%), spa (30%) and sustainability/eco-focused (28%) (global-wellnessinstitute.org, 14.03.2023).

Table 19.1. Wellness Economy by Region, 2017, 2019, 2020.

Country	Wellness Economy Size US$ Billions			Average Annual Growth Rate		
	2017[a]	2019	2020	Per Capita 2020	2017–2019	2019–2020
Asia-Pacific	1,370.5	1,602.8	1,500.2	360	8.1%	−6.4%
North America	1,288.1	1,514.0	1,310.8	3,567	8.4%	−13.4%
Europe	1,168.3	1,288.6	1,141.5	1,236	5.0%	−11.4%
Latin America–Caribbean	311.7	302.1	235.4	360	−1.5%	−22.1%
Middle East–North Africa	104.7	120.9	107.7	215	7.4%	−10.9%
Sub-Saharan Africa	74.0	81.7	73.7	65	5.1%	−9.8%
World	**4,317.3**	**4,909.9**	**4,369.3**	**563**	**6.6%**	**−11.0%**

Source: Global Wellness Institute (2022).

[a]2017 figures have been revised since GWI released the previous version of the Wellness Economy Monitor.

Table 19.2. Wellness Economy Sectors, 2017, 2019, 2020.

	Wellness Economy Size			Average Annual Growth Rate	
	(US$ Billions)				
	2017[a]	2019	2020	2017–2019	2019–2020
Personal care and beauty	1,021.6	1,097.3	955.2	3.6%	−13.0%
Healthy eating, nutrition and weight loss	858.1	912.3	945.5	3.1%	3.6%
Physical activity	789.5	873.8	738.1	5.2%	−15.5%
Wellness tourism	617.0	720.4	435.7	8.1%	−39.5%
Traditional and complementary medicine	376.2	431.9	412.7	7.1%	−4.5%
Public health, prevention and personalised medicine	328.3	359.1	375.4	4.6%	4.5%
Wellness real estate	148.5	225.2	275.1	23.2.%	22.1%
Mental wellness	N/A	122.3	131.2	N/A	7.2%
Spas	93.6	110.7	68.0	8.7%	−38.6%
Workplace wellness	47.7	52.2	48.5	4.6%	−7.0%
Thermal/mineral springs	56.1	64.0	39.1	6.8%	−38.9%
Wellness economy	**4,317.3**	**4,909.9**	**4,369.3**	**6.6%**	**−11.0%**

Source: Global Wellness Institute, based on extensive primary research and secondary data sources.

[a]2017 figures have been revised since GWI released the previous version of the Wellness Economy Monitor.

Note: Figures do not sum to the total due to overlap in sectors.

Once the wellness economy sectors in Table 19.2 are examined, it can be pictured that during the pandemic period, physical activity, wellness tourism, spas and thermal/mineral springs all experienced significant declines. This is because these sectors all require a physical presence for people's experience or participation. By contrast, areas including public health/prevention/personalised medicine, wellness real estate, mental wellness, and healthy eating/nutrition/weight reduction have all grown significantly during the pandemic (GWI, 2021). Similar findings likewise support the research undertaken by the GWI. According to participants, the reasons for choosing wellness travel following COVID-19 would be to reduce stress and relax, preserve well-being, improve mental health, restore well-being and concentrate on adventure seeking and fitness (global-wellnessinstitute.org, 14.03.2023).

According to Amex Trendex (2021), a trend report from American Express covering the United States, the United Kingdom, Australia, Japan, Mexico, India and Canada, 66% of respondents accepted that the pandemic had encouraged them to spend more money on objects or experiences that help enhance their general mental health. Additionally, 76% of respondents stated that they would be willing to spend more on travel in order to improve their health, 70% articulated they planned to try a new fitness activity in order to enhance their well-being and 55% mentioned they would be willing to spend more on health-related or companion expenses while travelling. However, 81% of respondents cherish the freedom to travel more now than before the pandemic, and 88% think that travel helps them improve their mental health (americanexpress.com, 13.03.2023).

Case Studies

Huang et al. (2022) proposed a new approach to wellness tourism by which organisations could offer wellness services to their employees as part of their online-to-office (O2O) services. In the study, targeted group data from 319 participants revealed that medical professionalism, accuracy of medical reports and privacy protection influence the choice of health check provider. Together with medical services and wellness tourism providers, organisations can employ these results to offer personalised wellness tourism packages to their employees accordingly, evoking a sense of perceived organisational support (POS) among them. This proposed tripartite collaboration could offer a lifeline to all parties in this post-pandemic era.

Indonesian People Regard Health Tourism as a Solution

The study done to ascertain visitors' perceptions on health and wellness tourism, a subset of health tourism that emerged following COVID-19. The study by Koerniawaty and Sudjana (2022) noted that physical wellness, which includes more spas associated with the physical health dimension of the body, renders an optimal opportunity for the development of wellness tourism. The COVID-19 pandemic, a consequence of this, has gradually impacted Indonesians' standard of life. Environmental tourism featuring physical activity has been recognised as a viable solution as society advances increasingly concerned with protecting its members' health. In contrast, wellness tourism encounters a similar set of difficulties.

Wellness Services Affecting the Satisfaction of Wellness Tourists Visiting India

Datta's (2022) study performed in India aimed to find out the preferences and changing needs of wellness tourists after COVID-19. The study was conducted on 400 foreign tourists visiting India and revealed the preferences and changing needs of tourists on various variables of wellness tourism post-COVID-19. The study shows that out of the core wellness services, yoga, Ayurveda, spirituality, meditation have a stronger impact contributing to the satisfaction level of wellness tourists.

Research Box

The research article named 'Comparison of Perceptions of Wellness Tourism in Korea Before and After COVID-19: Results of Social Big Data Analysis' was carried out by Han & An (2022).

Purpose: This study explored strategies aimed at revitalising wellness tourism in the post-coronavirus 2019 (COVID-19) era, and investigated consumer perceptions of wellness tourism before and after the outbreak of COVID-19. Design/methodology/approach: Keywords pertaining to wellness tourism were extracted from social media platforms, such as Naver, Daum and the social network service (SNS) Facebook, as well as from the search engine Google. Text mining, frequency analysis, centrality analysis and CONCOR analysis were conducted on the extracted keywords. The study period was divided into pre- and post-COVID-19 outbreak periods (4,984 and 4,360 keywords, respectively). In total, 100 and 50 searches were analysed in the pre- and post-outbreak periods, respectively.

Findings: Prior to the outbreak, awareness of wellness tourism and programmes appear to have been high, while after the outbreak specific wellness tourism destinations, including Jeju and Gangwon, were recognised. In addition, the desire for healing of both body and mind appeared to be greater after the outbreak.

Research Limitations/Implications: In the post-COVID-19 era, local governments and policymakers will need to develop programmes to boost local wellness tourism. Advertising and promotion on online social media platforms and SNS, emphasising the positive effects of wellness tourism such as healing and meditation, could further increase the number of visitors to these destinations. Comparative research on wellness tourism in different countries will also be important as perceptions of COVID-19 may vary among various countries such as Korea, Japan and China.

Originality/Value: In the past, wellness tourism studies focused on research topics such as tourism development and tourism motivation, but this study resulted in the expansion of the research by applying the social media big data analysis method, which has recently attracted attention in the hospitality industry.

Conclusion

With the emergence of COVID-19, almost all sectors have come to a standstill, and human life has been detrimentally affected due to countries' curfews and travel restrictions. However, it is clear from this process that people's health awareness enhanced and started to accord more significant value to health-related products. In order to improve their mental health, people are willing to travel, spend more on their travels and pay more for medical services. Hence, the demand for wellness tourism, mainly health tourism, will keep rising in the coming years. Wellness tourism is anticipated to rise by 21% annually and reach $1.1 trillion by 2025, according to GWI (2022).

Wellness tourism, particularly health tourism, is one of the sectors incentivised to expand in our homeland despite Turkey's acknowledged potential in the industry due to its thermal resources and natural beauty. Parallel to the predictions that the demand for wellness tourism will grow together with the impact of COVID-19 on wellness tourism, it is argued that it will be advantageous to carry out comprehensive studies for the growth of this industry in our country. Similarly, in the study conducted by Andreu et al. (2021) for the Spanish Salou destination, it is grasped that in the aftermath of the pandemic, both public and private agencies believed that health tourism could improve innovation, provide a competitive advantage and help reduce seasonality. However, still, it is suggested that in the post-COVID-19 era, tourism should be resurrected, with wellness tourism as its core. The following suggestions add to the literature and the sector in this context.

- In order to better evaluate the potential of the country in wellness tourism, it is considered essential to increase the product range offered within the scope of wellness tourism, to identify suitable regions for health-related activities, to carry out necessary infrastructure and superstructure works in these regions and to intensify marketing activities. Therefore, it is crucial that all parties involved in the health and tourism sectors, particularly municipal governments, cooperate to address these concerns.
- It is considered fundamental to assemble a staff of professionals knowledgeable about the services provided in wellness/SPA tourism and to include health professionals in this workforce. In this framework, government initiatives to support the industry would be advantageous.
- While it is observed that there are studies on distinct subjects to find out the impact of the pandemic on the tourism industry during COVID-19, it is spotted that there are limited studies on the post-COVID-19 effects. Therefore, carrying out studies to ascertain the preferences of tourists in wellness tourism after the pandemic will contribute to bridging the gap in the literature and guiding the development of the wellness tourism sector.

Discussion Questions

- How does wellness tourism, especially health tourism, differ from traditional tourism?
- How has wellness tourism been affected during the COVID-19 process?
- How will the developments in wellness tourism evolve after COVID-19?

References

American Express. (2021, September 29). *Amex Trendex: Consumers Prioritizing Wellness and Mental Health with their Time, Money and Travel Plans.* https://about.americanexpress.com/newsroom/press-releases/news-details/2021/Amex-Trendex-Consumers-Prioritizing-Wellness-and-Mental-Health-with-their-Time-Money-and-Travel-Plans-09-29-2021/default.aspx. Accessed on March 13, 2023.

Andreu, M. G. N., Font-Barnet, A., & Roca, M. E. (2021). Wellness tourism-new challenges and opportunities for tourism in Salou. *Sustainability*, *13*(8246), 1–13.

Choudhary, B., & Qadir, A. (2022). Wellness tourism in India post COVID-19 era: Opportunities and challenges. *TURIZAM*, *26*(3), 134–143.

Datta, B. (2022). Preferences and changing needs of wellness tourists: A study from Indian perspective post COVID-19. *GeoJournal of Tourism and Geosites*, *42*(2), 782–786.

Ergüven, M. H. (2015a). Wellness turizmi. In S. P. Temizkan (Ed.), *Sağlık turizmi*. Detay yayıncılık.

Ergüven, M. H. (2015b). Sağlık turizminde wellnessın önemi ve wellnessın geleceğine turizm bağlamında bir bakış. In M. Altındiş (Ed.), *Termal turizm*. Nobel akademik yayıncılık eğitim danışmanlık tic. ltd. şti.

Global Wellness Institute. (2020). Latest GWI consumer research what is the opportunity right now? Katherine Droga, Chair of the Wellness Tourism Initiative. https://globalwellnessinstitute.org/wp-content/uploads/2020/10/GWI-WTI-RESEARCH-2020.pdf. Accessed on March 14, 2023.

Global Wellness Institute. (2021). *Research report- the global wellness economy: Looking beyond Covid.* https://globalwellnessinstitute.org/press-room/press-releases/2021-gwi-research-report/. Accessed on March 15, 2023.

Global Wellness Institute. (2022). *2022 The global wellness economy: Country rankings.* https://globalwellnessinstitute.org/industry-research/2022-global-wellness-economy-country-rankings/. Accessed on March 12, 2023.

Han, J. H., & An, K. S. (2022). Comparison of perceptions of wellness tourism in Korea before and after COVID-19: Results of social extensive data analysis. *Global Business & Finance Review*, *27*(2), 1–13.

Huang, Y. T., Ru, L. T., Goh, A. P. I., Kuo, J. H., Lin, W. Y., & Qiu, S. T. (2022). Post-COVID wellness tourism: Providing personalized health check packages through online-to-offline services. *Current Issues in Tourism*, *25*(24), 3905–3912.

Koerniawaty, F. T., & Sudjana, I. M. (2022). Prospects of wellness tourism in Indonesia as tourism sector recovery effort post-COVID-19 pandemic. *Budapest International Research and Critics Institute-Journal (BIRCI-Journal)*, *5*(2), 10082–10091.

Kuo, H. I., Chen, C., Tseng, W., Ju, L., & Huang, B. (2008). Assessing impacts of Sars and Avian Flu on international tourism demand to Asia. *Tourism Management*, *29*(5), 917–928.

Mueller, H. R., & Lanz, E. (1998). Wellnesstourismus in der schweizer: Definition, abgrenzung und empirische angebotsanalyse. *Tourismus Journal, 4*.

Oborin, M. (2022). Health and wellness tourism development on global markets in a pandemic. *Anais Brasileiros de Estudos Turísticos*, *12*(Special Issue), 1–8.

Özsarı, S. H., & Karatana, Ö. (2013). Sağlik turizmi açısından Türkiye'nin durumu. *Journal Agent*, *24*(2), 136–144.

Polat, N. (2020). *Wellness Turizminde sürdürülebilirlik yönetimi.* 1. Basım. Nobel bilimsel eserler.

Sivanandamoorthy, S. (2021). Exploring the impact of COVID-19 on wellness tourism in Sri Lanka. *International Journal of SPA and Wellness, 4*(2–3), 160–172.

Temizkan, S. P. (2020). Sağlık turizmi. In R. Temizkan, D. Cankül, & F. Gökçe (Eds.), *Alternatif Turizm (Turizmin 41 türü.* 1. Baskı. Detay yayıncılık.

Toktaş, H. (2015). SPA-Wellness uygulamaları. In M. Altındiş (Ed.), *Termal turizm.* 1. Baskı. Nobel akademik yayıncılık eğitim danışmanlık tic. ltd. şti.

Ünüvar, İ. (2020). Türkiye'de sağlık turizmi ve ekonomik boyutu. In M. Tuncer (Ed.), *Farklı boyutları ile sağlık turizmi.* Detay yayıncılık.

UNWTO. (2017). *3. Implementation of the general programme of work for 2016-2017.* UNWTO Executive Council Documents. https://www.e-unwto.org/doi/pdf/10.18111/unwtoecd.2017.6.g51w645001604507

UNWTO/ETC. (2018). *World Tourism Organization and European Travel Commission Exploring Health Tourism – Executive Summary.* UNWTO. https://doi.org/10.18111/9789284420308

Widarini, P. S. I., Wijaya, M., & Naini, A. M. I. (2020). *Wellness tourism opportunities amid COVID-19 pandemic: Literature Study.* In *Sciendo 4th International Conference of Social Science and Education (ICSSED) 2020.*

WTTC. (2022). *Travel & tourism economic impact 2022.* Global trends August 2022. World Travel &Tourism Council.

WWTC. (2023). *Economic impact sector.* https://wttc.org/research/economic-impact

Zorlu, Ö. (2018). Sağlık Turizmi. In S. Çelik & B. Yalçın (Eds.), *Termal Turizm ve İşletmeciliği.* 1. Baskı. Detay Yayıncılık.

Chapter 20

Wellness Tourism After the Pandemic: Real Experience of Wellness Tourism After the Pandemic in Sri Lankan Context

RHSK de Silva[a], Puwanendram Gayathri[b], Krishantha Ganeshan[c] and Suranga DAC Silva[a]

[a]University of Colombo, Sri Lanka
[b]University of Sri Jayewardenepura, Sri Lanka
[c]98 Acres Resort and Spa, Sri Lanka

Learning Objectives

After reading and studying this chapter, you should be able to:

- discuss the trends in Sri Lanka;
- To discuss wellness tourism trends and demands this study selected a homestay, hotel sector, and wellness activity.

Abstract

The first section will be the introduction which discusses the global scenario of wellness tourism after the pandemic. The second section of this study is wellness tourism after the pandemic in Sri Lanka. This title is an overview based on the homestays which are practicing wellness tourism at the Veludvara Wellness Stay, 98 Acres Resort and Spa and Ella Yoga Hub, and it examines the tourist perspective on wellness tourism after the pandemic. The third section discusses global best practices and policy development in this regard. The fourth section of this study focuses on demand and trends that can be promoted to future wellness tourism and conclude with recommendations. This study followed a qualitative method which is carried out with interviews, observation and secondary data such as books, websites,

---

Future Tourism Trends Volume 1, 299–307
Published under exclusive licence by Emerald Publishing Limited
doi:10.1108/978-1-83753-244-520241020

research papers, articles and other published materials. The impact of this research work is focused on stakeholders in wellness tourism, such as service providers, entrepreneurs, policymakers and other relevant authorities to fulfil gaps in the wellness tourism sector. Furthermore, this will be a good overview for tourists who are willing to get the experience of wellness tourism after the pandemic and identify its future values and demands.

Keywords: Wellness tourism; health tourism; COVID-19; resort; spa; new trends

Introduction to Wellness Tourism

The term 'wellness' has historical roots. Ancient civilisations from the East (India, China) to the West (Greece, Rome) can be used to trace the origins of the essential principles of wellness as both preventive and holistic. Parallel to the development of traditional medicine in the 19th century in both Europe and the United States, numerous intellectual, religious and medical movements emerged. These movements have laid a solid foundation for health today, with their emphasis on holistic and natural techniques, self-healing and preventive treatment.

The Global Wellness Institute (GWI) defines wellness as the active pursuit of activities, choices and lifestyles that lead to a state of holistic health (Institute, 2020 Compendium Resetting the World with Wellness, 2020). These activities of wellness are multifaceted, encompassing physical, mental, emotional, social, environmental and spiritual dimensions. To engage in healthy activities, people must be empowered, proactive, purposeful and responsible.

The GWI defines wellness tourism as a travel associated with the pursuit of maintaining or enhancing one's well-being (Institute, Wellness Tourism, 2023). The idea that those who travel to destination spas, health resorts or yoga and meditation retreats are a small, affluent and elite group of leisure travellers is a widespread one. In actuality, travellers who are interested in wellness are a far bigger and more varied set of consumers with a wide range of motivations, interests and beliefs. According to the GWI, wellness travellers are of two types, they can be identified as primary wellness traveller and secondary wellness traveller. The primary wellness travellers are primarily motivated by wellness tourism and their choice for selecting a trip or destination is wellness tourism. Secondary wellness travellers are who seek to maintain their wellness while travelling during any type of trip for leisure or business. Spas, wellness retreats, thermal/mineral springs and boot camps are just a small portion of the wellness tourism industry, which is far broader in scope. To maintain their wellness lifestyle while travelling, wellness travellers (especially secondary wellness travellers) look for opportunities to do so.

Purpose of the Study

The purpose of this study is to identify and examine the situation of wellness tourism after COVID-19 with real experiences. Also, it is intended to identify with case studies in Sri Lanka and identify the global scenario. The study will provide global best practices for policy development in wellness tourism and provide demand and trends based on the case studies. Furthermore, it brings recommendations for the development of wellness tourism.

Wellness Tourism After COVID-19 in Global Scenario

Health authorities recommended unorthodox health measures like social withdrawal, avoiding physical contact with people and staying at home when the disease started to get worse. Many people experienced severe emotional and mental health hardship during the months when these policies were in place. Add to that, the sorrow of losing loved ones to the illness as well as the omnipresent fear of getting the infection. These feelings have persisted in many people for a large portion of the year, and they have highlighted the need to strike a balance between health constraints and the need to offer people proper mental healthcare.

According to a recent UK survey, compared to 23% before the pandemic, more than 33% of UK consumers say that their health and wellness are key aspects of their life. When restrictions are eliminated, roughly 78% of respondents in 48 countries said they will travel for wellness purposes, according to a separate study by the Wellness Tourism Association. The GWI predicted in February 2020 that the wellness travel market will reach $919 billion, or roughly 20% of all tourism worldwide. The institution also predicted that by 2022, the wellness tourism market will expand at a 7.5% average annual pace (Magazine, 2023).

Accor Hotels, Rosewood Hotels, Radisson Hospitality and Hyatt Hotels are just a few of the major global players in the tourism sector that have embraced new growth strategies to increase their wellness offerings and create new business models to satisfy the expanding demand for well-being. To help visitors unwind, many hotels now include spa treatments, exercise courses, yoga sessions and luxury picnics (Magazine, 2023).

North American, European and Asian nations have led the wellness tourism industry, with the United States, Germany, China, France and Japan accounting for close to 60% of the global market. The availability of traditional Chinese medicine and Ayurvedic therapies in China and India, however, has helped them climb the rankings in recent years, adding a combined 39 million wellness vacations between 2015 and 2017 (Magazine, 2023).

Wellness Tourism in Sri Lanka

It is considered that Sri Lanka is a wellness tourism destination; it is enriched with a large number of potentials which can be identified as Ayurvedic, spa, yoga, meditation and many more. This study discusses three different cases that refer to Veludvara Authentic Wellness Stay, 98 Acres Resort and Spa and Ella Yoga Hub. These three cases refer to three different areas in wellness tourism.

Case Study 1: Veludvara Authentic Wellness Stay

The operation of the wellness homestay consists of two rooms, a shared living and kitchen area and a separate room for Ayurvedic consultations for wellness, particularly sustainable healthy living through Sri Lankan traditional medicine, urban home gardening, waste management through the 3R principle, use of solar energy, a biogas plant and other nature-related activities like birdwatching, etc. with a backyard waterbody and wetland. The major goal of this is to provide a new service product to the wellness tourism sector that contributes to the environmental, economic and social facets of the Sustainable Development Goals (SDGs). The most of wellness tourism's aspects are included in this distinctive service package, which is operated as a family business while upholding Sri Lanka's destination uniqueness (Silva, 2023).

This lifestyle may include healthy eating, mind–body practices which connects with nature, interactions with locals, etc. Therefore, immune-enhancing food and beverages are added to their meals and relax their mind by offering free health consultation for prevention. Once the country opened for travellers, the accommodation had two guests, and they were diagnosed with COVID-19 infection. They selected Veludvara because it says that this place is giving free Ayurveda consultation for guests. They requested from the accommodation to treat them with traditional medicine, so the host had taken the challenge and treated them well and cured them successfully without any complications. They also stayed in Veludvara for nearly one year until the country followed the new normal (Silva, 2023). Some guests were from the quarantine centres which were run by hotels. Due to unaffordability, they selected this place because of free Ayurveda consultation. At that time, there was no proper transportation system. The host went to the quarantine centre and provided free transport to them.

Case Study 2: 98 Acres Resort and Spa

It is a genuinely one-of-a-kind Ella spa resort to come home to because all herbals and other treatment materials are manufactured from tea and other herbal plants planted on their very own 98 acre tea estate. Enjoy the breeze, unwind and take in the warmth of the spa while taking in the stunning valley views. The list of spa services is available here (*Ella spa resort: Spa at 98 Acres Resort & Spa*, 2023). During the pandemic, the situation was bad for every worker in the premises. The best market for this property is mostly from England.

During the curfew employees faced a difficult time. While providing the wellness experience during the pandemic, both host and guest had hard time while adhering to the safety protocols. They wore double mask and safety wears, which made it hard for them to work. The relaxing mind of both host and guest is much important in these kinds of services. But due to the fear of disease and other problems, the host and guest faced similar fear. They went through Ayurvedic remedies for the safeguarding of host and guest. They did not get any COVID-19 positive guest during the treatment due to the support from front office. After every treatment, they sanitised the surrounding environment and the materials.

The details of every tourist kept updated during these periods rather than earlier. Since most of the tourists were interested in Ayurvedic and wellness tourism, it was of much benefit for the hotel (Carmer et al., 2023).

Case Study 3: Ella Yoga Hub

The pandemic affected considerably the yoga activities provided by Ella yoga hub. Because wearing masks and adhering to the guidelines was much difficult when conducting meditation and other yoga activities. But, because of its tendency to be a mentally and physically recovering remedy, most of the travellers were interested to do yoga activities. When yoga is considered as a healing activity, the methods include meditation, breathing exercise, yoga and other relevant methods. But virtual experiences such as online yoga sessions are not that much effective due to the disturbances and background noises. It is better to introduce yoga based on Buddhist teaching such as *Anapanasathi, Samatha meditation, Vipassana Meditation*, walking meditation and spirituality-based sessions. Introduce *Kundalini Meditation* which was practiced by King Ravana is another trend in Yoga and wellness tourism. These things were able to attract new tourism market for Sri Lanka wellness tourism. The number of practitioners is very low in Sri Lanka and knowledge sharing is also low level even though these Yoga activities bring benefits. The considerable barrier is language even if Yoga is in much demand during COVID. Only few practitioners are there to conduct these sessions for the international market even Sri Lanka enriched with many potentials (Indika, 2023).

Global Best Practices and Policy Development for Wellness Tourism

The wellness tourism sector has advanced quickly since it first gained widespread consumer awareness a few years ago. New tactics, products, experiences and locations are being developed by businesses and governments. As businesses experiment with new collaborations and business models to offer expanded services and programming that will help passengers incorporate wellness into every element of their travels, wellness, hospitality and travel are coming together in a variety of novel ways. As per the global wellness tourism industry, the new parameters can be identified as outdoor holistic healing, personalised nutrition, urban wellness and fly healthy. These are a few trends which can be recognised recently.

Retreats that incorporate yoga and mindfulness meditation are becoming increasingly popular as a result of recent research showing that these practices are effective, tried-and-true strategies to reduce stress. In addition to offering daily yoga courses, resorts also immerse their visitors in serene environments that foster a sense of connection with the natural world. On the beach, regular yoga sessions like Yin, Vinyasa and Kundalini are frequently practiced, the sound of the waves evoking a profound sense of serenity. In contrast, Ananda in the Himalayas is built atop a hill with views of the verdant landscape below. It all comes down to accepting ancient traditions that increase your resilience while allowing nature to exercise its therapeutic impact (Watson, 2022).

Consider scheduling a five-star luxury vacation at a resort like the Marbella Club Hotel in the posh Spanish resort town of Marbella. After discussing your goals, health issues or wishes and preferences, each member of your family can focus on their nutritional consumption while you're on vacation. For one or more members of your family to have meals with others while adhering to the nutritionist's suggested plant-based, low carb or whole diet, your nutritionist can communicate with health and wellness chefs. Similarly, fitness experts can design a focused fitness programme that will guarantee you obtain the ideal balance of work and leisure. Some hotels, like the renowned The Farm at San Benito, specialise in Asian vegan food and dishes produced with locally cultivated fresh ingredients (McGroarty, 2019).

Imagine spending days in a city sightseeing and then taking a break. According to the Global Wellness Summit (GWS), this is precisely the kind of city/wellness getaway that discerning visitors desire. Urban bathhouses, free pop-up fitness sessions, water sports in the centre of busy cities like Madrid or Tokyo and other human-made beaches are all signs that more and more cities are being remade to embrace accessible wellness options. According to the GWS, the tendency extends far beyond the traditional city hotel with a lovely spa. New urban wellness resorts that are entirely devoted to holistic well-being are being opened by renowned wellness brands like Six Senses, One&Only and Aman.

Given that flying can be a stressful and harmful experience, airports and airlines are encouraging health and wellness initiatives for passengers to help them cope with extended flight periods, interrupted sleep, confined quarters and stress. Airports, airlines and wellness companies are working together in a variety of ways: Travellers can now discover yoga sessions, spas, peaceful relaxation rooms, nap pods, healthier meals, virtual reality (VR) technology and even therapy dogs in airport terminals and airline lounges all around the world. Travellers in Singapore have access to fitness centres, upscale spas, a rooftop pool, a jacuzzi, outdoor flower gardens and even the meditative practice of wood carving at Changi Airport. Rentals of inline skates, bicycles and Nordic walking poles are available in Zurich, Switzerland, to entice visitors to work out in the nearby conservation area. The Vitality, Wellbeing and Fitness Centre at Hamad Airport in Qatar offer a pool, hydrotherapy services and showers. To create guided walking circuits within airport terminals, the American Heart Association has teamed up with airports all over the country. Adding natural light, plant walls and outdoor and indoor green spaces, as well as using natural and locally produced materials are just a few of the biophilic and healthy design strategies that many airports are experimenting with (McGroarty, 2019).

According to the study, policy development of wellness tourism should be focused on the following areas. Developing the wellness sector calls for a diversified strategy. Through the discussion hosted by the GWI, the first stage has been accelerated. Keep talking to the appropriate businesses and service providers. Intensify your cooperation with academic institutions. It is possible to build wellness academies, which can be used to coordinate research projects including wellness and wellness tourism with PhD and masters students. The market for managing and offering wellness services is lacking, according to experts.

Natural medicine, using mineral waters in spas and real activities like the advantages of wellness culture require more research. To advertise the area as a wellness destination, forge stronger partnerships with governmental organisations. Inform consumers about the many services that are offered, as well as the advantages of wellness. Create awareness by participating in events like Global Wellness Day. Increase the number of qualified wellness coordinators to assist in informing clients about the value and advantages of wellness practices.

Demand and Trends for Future Wellness Tourism

The size of the worldwide wellness tourism market was estimated at USD 814.6 billion in 2022, and from 2023 to 2030, it is anticipated to increase at a compound annual growth rate (CAGR) of 12.42%. A person's physical, mental and spiritual well-being can be improved and enhanced by participation in wellness tourism activities. By participating in yoga, spa treatments, pilates, meditation and trips to hot spring resorts, tourists delight in physical, spiritual and cerebral pursuits. The practice of conversing with residents at a destination who have travelled to and experienced many cultures fosters individual well-being (Wellness tourism market size & trends analysis report, 2030 2022).

The ever-evolving needs of its clients are what drive demand for wellness spas. As consumers get more adept at using social media, anti-ageing products are growing in popularity. The market is being propelled by an increase in demand for skincare products that fight ageing. Increased consumer disposable income, particularly in emerging nations, is fuelling demand for these services. During the projection period, the wellness activities category is anticipated to experience significant expansion. This is explained by rising consumer spending on spas, body massages, yoga, Ayurveda therapy and other such services. Due to the growing need and demand for self-care during the pandemic, the in-country transportation and food and beverage segments will also experience considerable growth during the forecast period.

In the upcoming years, the primary category is anticipated to have significant expansion. Around the world, more people are integrating health, preventive care, self-fulfilment and mindfulness practices into their daily lives. Nowadays, people prefer to keep up their exercise routines and live healthy lifestyles even when they travel, which is promoting segment growth. Primary visitors from within the country spend about 178% more than the average traveller, according to GWI. On a global scale, they spend 53% more. To boost revenue, the government is concentrating on luring family tourists. This should accelerate segment growth. Asian nations like Malaysia and Thailand are popular tourist destinations with affordable service costs. In addition, category growth is being fuelled by rising expenditure on social and physical well-being, particularly as a result of concern for a healthy lifestyle.

Conclusion

The market was significantly impacted by the COVID-19 pandemic. The main causes of the market downturn were restrictions on international travel, orders for delivery to customers' homes and business closures. Many nations barred foreign travel and shut down international flights. As a result, there was a sharp decrease in the number of visitors. GWI estimates that there were 600.8 million wellness excursions worldwide in 2020, a decrease of 35.8%. Businesses closed, people lost their jobs, there were layoffs and consumer spending power decreased as a result of the abrupt global economic slowdown. People were discouraged from visiting abroad because of this and the fear of contracting an infection.

To reduce hosts' stress and give them a sense of home away from a home with wellness, offer Sri Lankan traditional medicine, food, and beverages. We also always share our thoughts with great hospitality. We should also assess their service potential within the demand and supply modes across health tourism. It's time to understand the best mode of supply of Sri Lankan traditional medicine to increase the demand for Sri Lankan authenticity. After the COVID-19 pandemic, a sizeable market for Sri Lankan traditional medicine has emerged, and this development must be acknowledged as a result of larger global processes.

One of these trends, which also provides a forecast of the inventions that will support the strengthening of the economy through high-level research and development, is the development of numerous goods based on local indigenous herbs. However, recent past events have demonstrated that the main obstacles to the growth of trade in health tourism products and services related to Sri Lankan traditional medicine include a lack of funding for care and insurance coverage, uncertainty about results when compared to modern sciences, a lack of accreditation and standards and requirements for foreign exchange, among others.

The Sri Lankan government is committed to promoting the aforementioned elements that will help the business become more resilient, such as globally recognized accreditations, staff training for this industry and the creation of internationally renowned goods and services. Additionally, the Sri Lankan tourism industry is well-positioned to continue driving sustainable economic growth thanks to its strong brand image with Sri Lankan traditional medicine, spectacular and alluring natural environment and cultural assets.

Sri Lanka has an authentic yoga tradition and culture which can be promoted for the international wellness tourism market. These products have the potential to develop based on Buddhist cultural practices and authentic yoga teaching methods with spirituality. Sri Lanka is a potential country enriched with pristine beaches, forests, monasteries and a calm environment to practice this kind of wellness activity. The readymade packages can be introduced with a variety of activities such as birdwatching, nature trekking, village tours, community-based tourism, tea-based tourism, etc. These things enable us to attract more wellness travellers to Sri Lanka.

One national holistic programme that combines conventional treatments, western medicine and wellness regimens will give consumers access to new international markets. VR, augmented reality (AR), big data and artificial intelligence (AI) can all be employed as diagnostic tools. Applications for mobile health (m Health), contactless health and wellness consultations will provide value to Sri Lankan medical travel. Through augmented intelligence, healthcare professionals can collaborate digitally from the comfort of their homes to hone their abilities and share clinical judgements enhancing services through the use of AI, which will analyse images of the body's sections and then suggest Ayurvedic therapies. An application for therapy that uses body treatments which is based on augmented reality (AR).

Discussion Questions

- What was the trend for your wellness activity before the pandemic?
- What kind of barriers you faced during the pandemic?
- What are the remedies you have made to overcome these problems?
- What kind of suggestions and recommendations are you providing for this situation?
- What are the tourist involvement and interest in wellness activity after the pandemic?

References

98 acres. (2023). *Ella spa resort: Spa at 98 Acres Resort & Spa.* resort98acres. https://www.resort98acres.com/facilities/well-being.html

Carmer, M. S., Gayathri, P., & Interviewer. (2023, May 10). *Ayurvedic and wellness tourism.*

Indika. (2023, May 18). Ella Yoga Hub. (P.Gayathri, Interviewer).

Institute, G. W. (2020). *2020 compendium resetting the world with wellness.* GLOBALWELLNESSINSTITUTE.ORG.

Institute, G. W. (2023, April 29). *Wellness tourism.* https://globalwellnessinstitute.org/what-is-wellness/what-is-wellness-tourism/

Magazine, M. T. (2023). *Wellness travel will be the focus in the post-pandemic era.* RSS. https://www.magazine.medicaltourism.com/article/wellness-travel-will-be-the-focus-in-the-post-pandemic-era

McGroarty, B. (2019, January 2). *New Gwi Research: 5 trends in wellness tourism.* Global Wellness Institute. https://globalwellnessinstitute.org/global-wellness-institute-blog/2018/12/03/new-gwi-research/

Silva, D. d. (2023, April 30). Experience during COVID 19. (P.Gayathri, Interviewer).

Watson, H. (2022, September 12). *Wellness tourism trends to watch out for.* Insights. https://insights.ehotelier.com/insights/2022/09/14/wellness-tourism-trends-to-watch-out-for/

Wellness tourism market size & trends analysis report, 2030. (2022). Wellness Tourism Market Size & Trends Analysis Report, 2030. https://www.grandviewresearch.com/industry-analysis/wellness-tourism-market

Index

Printed in the USA
CPSIA information can be obtained
at www.ICGtesting.com
JSHW011457130624
64754JS00004B/67

9 781837 532452